Confronting
the
PRESIDENTS

Confronting
the
PRESIDENTS

NO SPIN ASSESSMENTS FROM
WASHINGTON TO BIDEN

BILL O'REILLY
AND MARTIN DUGARD

ST. MARTIN'S PRESS
NEW YORK

First published in the United States by St. Martin's Press, an imprint of
St. Martin's Publishing Group

www.stmartins.com

Design by Meryl Sussman Levavi

The Library of Congress Cataloging-in-Publication Data is available
upon request.

ISBN 978-1-250-34641-4 (hardcover)
ISBN 978-1-250-34643-8 (ebook)

Our books may be purchased in bulk for promotional, educational, or business
use. Please contact your local bookseller or the Macmillan Corporate and
Premium Sales Department at 1-800-221-7945, extension 5442, or by email at
MacmillanSpecialMarkets@macmillan.com.

First Edition: 2024

1   3   5   7   9   10   8   6   4   2

To Madeline and Spencer:
The World Awaits

Contents

Confronting
the
PRESIDENTS

Prologue

Imagine being the most powerful person in the world. All your daily needs taken care of, full-time luxury, the ability to change the lives of millions of people, for better or for worse.

There have been forty-five male presidents of the United States. One woman, Hillary Clinton, came close. But who are these people, really? The answer to that seemingly simple question is the quest of this book. And the answer is complicated because so many different circumstances are involved.

There have been bad people elected to the highest office of the land as well as noble ones. It's sometimes difficult to make the judgment. But we, the authors, will decide based on the facts we have uncovered.

Some presidents were drunks. Some corrupt. A few outright racist. Almost all had hidden eccentricities that may startle you. All endured heartbreak.

And each president has affected you by the way they conducted themselves in office. Decisions made hundreds of years ago resonate today.

Thus, our history book series switches from the "killing" concept to the "confronting" arena. But the style is the same. No fussing around, right to the point. Different eras, strange occurrences, dubious behavior. These will be vividly chronicled as we assess the leaders who made the United States what it is today.

For better or, in more than a few cases, for worse.

The election of 2024 is looming as we write this book. As in 1860, we are an intensely divided nation—one that could descend into social chaos. Political bitterness is in the air.

However, the country has been through this before and emerged stronger for it. Will that happen this time? Impossible to predict.

There is no political slant to this book. Our points about the presidents are made on the back of reality. You may read things that you will not like. But those things will be true.

After the Revolutionary War, some Americans wanted George Washington to be king. There was a strong movement encouraging that. But the general himself said no. He would serve as president under a system of checks and balances devised by the Founding Fathers.

So that's what happened, despite a few citizens being somewhat skeptical about George. They included Washington's own mother, who did not much like her son, as you will soon see.

American history is fading somewhat in the nation's classrooms. This is dangerous because failing to understand your country can stimulate poor decision-making and personal failure. All of us should seek the truth. It is our mandate as a free people to do that.

We hope this book will help. We write it to illuminate the American pathway. We believe the United States is essentially noble but flawed. We also believe most of the presidents were patriots, but not all.

So, there you have it. Thanks for coming along for a lively ride. It is our privilege to "confront" the presidents and arm you with facts about your country, which remains the land of opportunity.

They say knowledge is power. Prepare to get stronger.

Chapter One

George Washington is mad at his mother.

    The former Revolutionary War hero now turned citizen farmer sits at the small wooden desk in his study. He is nearly fifty-five years old and deeply involved with the formation of the new United States of America. Washington rose before 5:00 a.m. to sort out the paperwork for his eight-thousand-acre plantation, as per usual. He is meticulous in keeping financial records. Travelers on the road north to Philadelphia and New York City often stop to pay their respects—so many that Washington compares his home to a tavern. Best to conduct personal affairs before well-meaning individuals interrupt him on this cold winter day.

Some two months from now, George Washington will ride on horseback 150 miles to Philadelphia to participate in a "Constitutional Convention" with delegates from twelve American states. The main goal is to determine the most effective way to choose a national leader. There are other issues, such as how many representatives each state will have in Congress and how to count slaves for the purposes of taxation and representation.

Washington well knows that he is under consideration to lead the country. But at this point, he has no idea *how* that will happen. However, what currently matters most is his mother's ire. She is torturing him. So, Washington dips his quill in the ink well and resumes writing.

"In the last two years I made no crops," he informs Mary Washington, nearly eighty years old, referring to his financial hardships. "In the first I was obliged to buy corn and this year have none to sell, and my wheat is so bad I cannot neither eat it myself nor sell it to others, and tobacco I make none. Those who owe me money cannot or will not pay it."*

Despite his situation, George Washington will not refuse his mother's pleas for money. He is stoic, never once speaking out against her behavior. "In consequence of your communication of your want of money," he replies to Mary's most recent financial demand, "I take the first safe conveyance to . . . send you 15 guineas, which believe me is all I have."

This is not the first squabble between mother and son over cash. It has been forty-four years since Washington's father, Augustine, died of a fever after riding horseback in a storm. His mother never remarried. In her solitude, Mary has been obsessed with money. She blames her son George because he, not Mary, inherited the bulk of his father's property. He is now considered the head of the family. As a result, Washington's mother believes she is poor and that it is George's fault. He regularly offers her personal loans, which are never repaid. Mary frequently complains to neighbors and friends that she lives in "poverty"—even though she receives substantial amounts of money from her small plantation just outside of Fredericksburg.

All of this is a major annoyance to George and his wife, Martha, who are embarrassed by Mary Washington's public complaints. She never writes a single word of praise or congratulations. After his Revolutionary War victory at Yorktown, George Washington left the battlefield and rode directly to his mother's home. She was not there. He could not wait, as pressing military duties were upon him. Unhappy, Mary Washington quickly wrote a bitter letter scolding her son for his departure—and never once mentioning his triumph that effectively defeated the British once and for all.

Also in 1781, Mary again embarrasses her oldest son by appealing to the Virginia legislature, demanding a pension. George Washington quickly writes his friend Benjamin Harrison, Virginia legislator and father and grandfather to two future American presidents, suggesting that the

---

* This letter can be found in the National Archives.

request be denied. In the letter, Washington details the true state of his mother's affairs, telling Harrison that "she has not a child that would not divide their last sixpence to relieve her from *real* distress."*

The Virginia legislature turns down Mary Washington's pension appeal. That increases her anger: "I never lived so poor in my life," she writes to her son John just before his death. "I should be almost starved."

On August 26, 1789, Mary Washington dies of breast cancer at the age of eighty. George Washington does not attend her funeral or pay for her headstone. He is otherwise occupied in New York City, having been elected president of the United States on February 4, 1789, by the Electoral College. Years later, President Andrew Jackson lays the cornerstone for a monument to the great George Washington's mother, but the project stalls for six decades. Finally, in 1894, work is completed. President Grover Cleveland unveils the monument.

George Washington is not exactly thrilled to lead the new nation. The seat of power is the office and residence Congress has rented at 1 Cherry Street in Manhattan. The crowded three-story mansion is 240 miles northeast of Mount Vernon. Washington has a private working space, as well as a public room for greeting dignitaries. Appointed with new mahogany furniture, the building is home not only to George and Martha but also to seven members of their enslaved household staff, who dress in uniforms of red and white—the Washington family colors. There is no security detail. The new president believes it vital that Americans meet him in person, so the residence is open to the public during certain days and times each week.

In addition to official visits by members of Congress, the judiciary, and foreign diplomats, Washington puts aside Tuesday afternoons so that male visitors may pay their respects. Less formally, Martha hosts a

---

* Mary Washington gave birth to six children by Augustine: George, Betty, Samuel, John, Charles, and Mildred. Five of them survived to adulthood. George outlived them all.

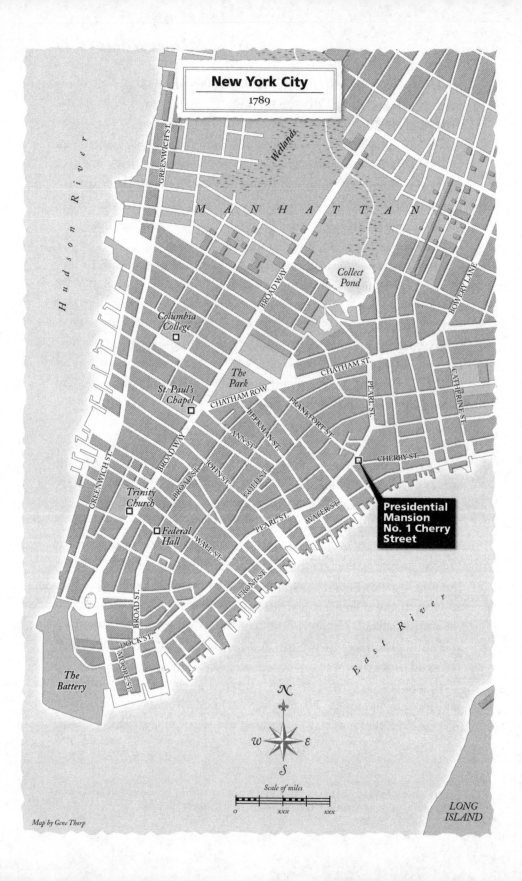

New York City

1789

Hudson River

GREENWICH ST.

Wetlands

M A N H A T T A N

Collect Pond

BROADWAY

BOWERY LANE

Columbia College

The Park

CHATHAM ST.

PEARL ST.

CATHARINE ST.

St. Paul's Chapel

CHATHAM ROW

FRANKFORT ST.

CHERRY ST.

BEEKMAN ST.

ANN ST.

BROADWAY

JOHN ST.

GOLD ST.

GREENWICH ST.

BROAD ST.

Presidential Mansion No. 1 Cherry Street

Trinity Church

WALL ST.

PEARL ST.

WATER ST.

Federal Hall

FRONT ST.

BROAD ST.

DOCK ST.

MOORE ST.

The Battery

East River

N

W E

S

Scale of miles

0   xxx   xxx

LONG ISLAND

"levee"—reception—every Friday afternoon for anyone who wishes to attend. Lemonade and ice cream are served in the summer.[*]

Martha Washington is not a New York City kind of gal. "Lady Washington," as she is often addressed, much prefers the country lifestyle of Mount Vernon. In New York, she must dress formally every day and play a prominent role in the local community—both of which she despises. Martha Washington strongly opposed George's return to public life following the Revolutionary War. But for the sake of her husband's new job, she remains with him rather than return home.

Martha is now fifty-seven years old, plump, and of fair complexion. She stands five feet tall. Although Washington is cash poor, his wife's inheritance from her first marriage brought hundreds of slaves and seventeen thousand acres of land into the marriage.

But today it is not Mount Vernon that is on George Washington's mind. On April 30, 1789, one week after moving into the presidential residence, Washington steps out the front door of the gray stone mansion and into a horse-drawn coach. The streets are packed with well-wishers who call out his name. Washington waves but otherwise remains silent. He is calm but nervous as he is driven to Federal Hall on Wall Street, where the crowds are even larger. Locals and tourists alike have come to witness the first Inauguration Day.

General Washington is cheered as he steps from the carriage. The crowd parts as he walks up the steps and strides out onto the public balcony in full view of citizens, soldiers, and foreign diplomats. Vice President John Adams is among the dozen dignitaries standing behind him. At six feet two, Washington stands several inches taller than Robert Livingston, the chancellor of the state of New York, who will administer the oath of office.

Washington faces Livingston and places his right hand on a Bible. He wears a brown coat with breeches, a matching vest, and pants and

---

[*] Washington was not elected president by popular vote but through a handful of specially chosen representatives known as the Electoral College. This body convened in their home states on February 4, 1789. New York failed to name their eight electors in time and did not cast votes. North Carolina and Rhode Island had not ratified the Constitution and were also not able to participate. So the election of 1789 was decided by only ten states. The individual with the most votes would be president. The man with the second-most votes would serve as vice president. Out of 138 votes cast, Washington received 69 and John Adams 34. Ten other men also secured votes, including famous names like John Hancock, John Jay, and George Clinton.

white stockings. His long gray hair is pulled back off his face. Washington repeats the simple thirty-five-word oath of office outlined in the Constitution, in which he promises to perform his presidential duties and defend that document. Afterward, Washington raises the Bible to his lips, kissing the holy book. Livingston cries out to the crowd, "Long live George Washington, president of the United States."

Thunderous cheers rock lower Manhattan, followed by a salvo of thirteen cannon blasts.

There will be fireworks later tonight. But for now, that's supposed to be the end of the ceremony.

Yet Washington has other plans.

He wishes to give a speech.

So, he faces the crowd and begins to read his prepared words. He has faced years of difficult situations on the battlefield and never showed signs of fear. Yet Washington's voice trembles and his hands shake as he speaks to the crowd. He stares at the paper, never lifting his eyes. Very often, the president stumbles over his words.

The speech is mostly pedestrian, expressing gratitude for the position. Washington, however, does depart from politics, speaking about the "Almighty Being." He injects a deep religious belief into his remarks.

The reason the new president stumbles over the speech is that he has only one tooth of his own. The rest of his dentures are made up of animal teeth, the bicuspids of other humans, and ivory. This makes it very difficult for him to chew hard food, let alone give a public speech. He is voracious in his pursuit of knowledge and is a great horseman. Those who know him well marvel at his feats of physical strength, such as throwing a rock across the width of the Rappahannock River and climbing the 215-foot-tall limestone crag known as the Natural Bridge in Virginia.

Yet despite his reputation for virility, one of the general's great frustrations is that he is sterile and unable to father children of his own. He makes do by serving as stepfather to Martha's two children from a previous marriage—though his preference for corporal punishment as a form of discipline clashes with his wife's more maternal approach to parenting.

★★★

George Washington gets right to work. His first task is defining what it means to be president. Problems quickly mount. America has a massive national debt from the Revolutionary War, no standing army, and a navy that has no ships.

Yet the greatest headache George Washington endures is the hand-picked group of men he has chosen to advise him. This bickering "cabinet" of four politicians includes Thomas Jefferson, Alexander Hamilton, Secretary of War Henry Knox, and Attorney General Edmund Randolph. Jefferson and Hamilton, in particular, loathe each other. At issue is whether the federal government should be a strong central power, as Hamilton believes, or if the states should wield the most strength, as in Jefferson's point of view. This debate will continue for generations to come.

For now, Alexander Hamilton will win this argument. And it is George Washington who casts the deciding vote.

Secretary of the Treasury Hamilton is the man charged with fixing America's debt problem. He is a thirty-four-year-old former military aide to Washington known for his impetuous behavior and intellectual brilliance. In January 1791, Hamilton proposes that the government begin taxing alcohol distilled within the United States. This seems like a legitimate way to raise revenue. Secretary of State Thomas Jefferson, however, fights the tax, believing it infringes on states' rights. But Congress passes the bill into law.

The group hurt most by Hamilton's tax are small farmers on the country's western frontier. Their crops of corn, rye, and wheat spoil during the long trip east to market. The only method of transport is a caravan of slow packhorses. The rugged Pennsylvania roads cross the steep Allegheny Mountains. The journey is risky, the crops constantly exposed to the elements. The farmers' solution is distilling them into whiskey and rye, allowing a profit from spirits.

Thus, the farmers refuse to pay the new levy. Even worse, tax collectors are beaten, tarred, and feathered when they attempt to do their jobs.

And so begins the first true challenge to federal authority in America. At stake is the future of the national government—and the presidency.

George Washington prefers to let the matter play out slowly. He likes to avoid confrontation and seeks consensus. He politely urges the farmers to go along with the new tax. The matter simmers for three long years. Then, in 1794, word arrives from Pennsylvania that more than five hundred "whiskey rebels" set fire to the home of a tax collector outside Pittsburgh.

George Washington can remain silent no longer.

He is now sixty-two years old. His second term in office is well underway. Washington has temporarily moved the nation's capital to Philadelphia, awaiting the completion of facilities in the new District of Columbia location.

One block from Independence Hall, the president now occupies the former headquarters of British general William Howe. The residence is three and a half stories high and made of red brick with white window frames. Washington likes the new home better than his New York City office because it is closer to Virginia.

In Philadelphia, Washington continues his habit of rising before dawn and having a breakfast of corn cakes and three cups of tea. He drinks that beverage throughout the day.

Dinner is served at 2:00 p.m.—usually soft food and Madeira wine. Later the president will snack on nuts, cheese, and bread. George Washington usually retires no later than 9:00 p.m.

In his office, President Washington is battling crisis after crisis. America has declared itself neutral in the war between England and France, yet British warships are seizing American merchant vessels. In 1793, Thomas Jefferson abruptly resigns as secretary of state in protest over Washington's refusal to aid the French cause. But even as he deals with these issues, the threat to federal power in Pennsylvania is foremost in Washington's mind.

The president sends out a call for soldiers to battle the whiskey rebels. Thirteen thousand men answer the call. The troops meet at Fort Cumberland, Maryland, more than two hundred miles west of Philadelphia. It has been over a decade since Washington commanded men on the battlefield, but he climbs aboard a white stallion, dons his old blue uniform, slides into his knee-high riding boots, and gallops forth to meet the new troops.

Washington has put on weight. He has a small paunch. The uniform is tight. A sword dangles from his hip as he reviews the men assembled in formation. Some fought with him in the Revolutionary War. Others are new. But to a man, they are armed and committed to obeying their commander in chief. Washington orders the militia to march on Pittsburgh, hotbed of the whiskey rebels. He personally leads the way.

It is over quickly. No shots are fired. Observing Washington's forces, the rebels flee in disarray. More than 150 are arrested for treason. Two of their leaders are found guilty, only to be pardoned later by Washington.

The power of a strong central government is affirmed.

President Washington's first term in office was a time of experimentation as the country got used to his leadership. But his second four years are marked by increasing press criticism and divisive infighting.[*]

Washington laments the growing power of political factions and their ability to frustrate him as he goes about his job. He has authorized the building of six modern naval warships to fend off foreign attack, but he strives to keep the nation neutral, fearing that involvement in foreign wars will destabilize the young republic. Yet this very focus on neutrality encourages England and France to view America as vulnerable and weak.

There is nothing in the Constitution limiting the amount of time a man might serve as president, but a weary George Washington chooses to step down after his second term. After eight years as vice president, a job he calls "the most insignificant that ever the imagination of man contrived," John Adams will be elected to replace him.

On March 4, 1797, George Washington leaves office. Martha wants to go home. The life of a gentleman farmer at Mount Vernon awaits.

Washington does not deliver in person what will become known as his "farewell address." His dentures have become a painful problem, noticeably reshaping the lower portion of his face and limiting how often he speaks. Instead, he allows the message to be published in newspapers across the country.[†]

It is George Washington himself who makes the best assessment of his presidency in this message. He does not focus on the things he has

---

[*] There were more than twenty newspapers in Philadelphia. Some of them criticized Washington harshly. It is widely believed that Thomas Jefferson encouraged that criticism.

[†] Alexander Hamilton and James Madison wrote Washington's farewell address.

done well but instead cautions against the areas in which he has failed. Washington writes the letter to calm the American people. Many in the United States fear the fragile new nation will collapse without his leadership. But it was always his intention to leave office when the Constitution was strong enough to stand on its own. So, despite the divisions, the growing power of the press, and increasing animosity with both England and France, George Washington gracefully steps down, leaving America stronger than when he took office.

His successor will be hard-pressed to make the same claim.*

---

* Washington died thirty-nine months later on December 14, 1799. His cause of death was very similar to that of his father. Washington was on horseback inspecting Mount Vernon when he was caught in a snowstorm. He returned home and ate dinner without changing out of his wet clothes, then became ill soon after. A throat infection was followed by death two days later.

Chapter Two

NOVEMBER 2, 1800
WASHINGTON, DC
8:00 A.M.

John Adams feels the overwhelming presence of George Washington. As America's second president celebrates his first day in the brand-new President's House, he breakfasts in the East Room. The now sixty-five-year-old Adams and his wife, Abigail, moved in yesterday, yet the mansion is far from complete. White-gray sandstone was used in constructing the outer walls, giving the new residence a stunning appearance that contrasts sharply with the more common red brick. But the roof leaks. Rooms are barely furnished. Official business is conducted on the ground floor, family quarters on the second, and the third level is an attic. There are plans for a grand staircase leading to the second floor, but it has not yet been built.

Now, Abigail Adams hangs laundry on a rope line strung from one side of the East Room to the other. This is the largest space in the building. With no fence around the "President's House," she is somewhat fearful their clothing will be stolen.*

The East Room is also President Adams's new breakfast nook.

---

* The four surviving Adams children are all adults. Abigail Adams is thirty-five and living on a farm in New York with her husband and four children. John Quincy Adams, thirty-three, is the American minister to Prussia and lives in Berlin. Charles Adams, thirty, is an attorney living in New York City. Thomas Adams, also a lawyer, is twenty-two and resides in Philadelphia.

And the only decoration is a portrait of George Washington hanging on the wall, his direct gaze looking over as Adams starts his day. Washington stands tall in the eight-foot-high painting; he is dressed in a black coat, eyes staring straight out of the canvas at his former vice president.

Adams and Washington both have blue eyes, but that is where comparisons end. At a little over five feet six, Adams is eight inches shorter. The athletic Washington was a man of action, while the portly Adams is a thinker. When the two dined together, the passionate Adams did most of the talking. Their personal habits are also quite different. For proof, Adams has to look no further than the glass of his favorite breakfast beverage resting on the table in front of him.

It is not tea.

Adams labors in the great Washington's shadow, which is only natural. They worked together for eight years and were friends for decades prior to that, going back to the forging of the Declaration of Independence. As vice president, Adams's most prominent official duty was to cast tiebreaking votes in the Senate—which he did twenty-nine times. Washington did not invite Adams to cabinet meetings or seek his advice, which irritated the prideful New Englander. But when cabinet members like Alexander Hamilton and Thomas Jefferson left the government in Washington's second term, he did begin seeking his vice president's point of view.

Now, a great silver coffee urn has been placed on the table before President Adams by his household staff. None of them are slaves, as Adams believes slavery is antithetical to America's promise of freedom.

Adams certainly enjoys his coffee, but that will have to wait until after his morning libation. Lifting the glass to his lips with relish, he downs a gill of two-year-old hard apple cider. He does this every morning before breakfast, believing its health benefits include preventing scurvy.*

John Adams has devoted his life to American democracy. It is a pursuit that has led him to serve as a diplomat in London and Paris. He signed the Declaration of Independence. But no matter where in the world he travels, hard cider is his constant daily companion. Since his days in college at Harvard, America's second president has reveled in the "refreshing and salubrious" taste of this potent potable. And that

---

* A gill is one-fourth of a pint, or four ounces. The cider Adams is drinking has an alcohol by volume (ABV) level of between 8 and 12 percent and can be an intoxicant if too much is consumed.

is not the only spirit he enjoys. While preparing to sail to France on a diplomatic mission, Adams ordered that the hold of the frigate *Boston* contain his own personal keg of rum, a barrel of Madeira, and bottles of port. During his first term in the Continental Congress, Adams even boasted to Abigail of the bottles of "Madeira, claret, and brandy" consumed by the delegates during their evening happy hour.

Over the years, Adams has cut back on his consumption of wine and fortified spirits. But the cider remains. It is now "all the liquor I can drink without inconvenience to my health," he believes.

Morning ritual complete, John Adams makes his way to the southeast corner of the mansion and his new presidential office. He is a solitary man, not comfortable in the presence of strangers. His upbringing in Braintree, Massachusetts, outside of Boston, was simple. His father, "Deacon John" Adams, was a pastor, shoemaker, farmer, and member of the local militia. John was the oldest child, and he dutifully went to church but also rebelled against attending classes at Braintree Latin School, insisting he wished to become a farmer. But at his father's command, Adams learns academic discipline. By the age of thirty, he is one of Boston's most prominent attorneys.

After successfully defending British soldiers in the Boston Massacre case, Adams rises to national fame. He becomes an ardent patriot—teaming with his second cousin Samuel Adams to publish essays against the king. Along with John Hancock, Adams defines the rebellion in New England, signing the Declaration of Independence.

Early in his law career, John Adams admits his weakness: "I can treat all with decency and civility and converse with them when it is necessary on points of business, but I am never happy in their company."

Despite his social awkwardness, Adams becomes a powerful politician in the Federalist movement.*

---

* The Federalist Party was led by George Washington and would be considered the Republican Party today. The "Democratic-Republican Party" back then was led by Thomas Jefferson and James Madison. It would be the Democratic Party today.

John Adams and his predecessor, George Washington, have one thing in common: they both loathe the press. Washington decides to leave office partly because of a "disinclination to no longer be buffeted in the public prints by a set of infamous scribblers." At the turn of the nineteenth century in America, the press is notoriously partisan and personal. The *Philadelphia Aurora* describes the second president as "old, querulous, bald, blind, crippled, toothless Adams."

The ever-devious vice president Thomas Jefferson plants a story about his boss in the New York papers, calling the president a "hoary-headed incendiary."*

The fact is that world events are giving the press even more power. There are multiple newspapers in almost every town of significance. The primary discussion is whether the United States should get involved in European wars. Diplomatic relations between America and France broke off during the Washington administration, with the French believing the US is more aligned with their mortal enemy, Great Britain. After taking office in March 1797, Adams seeks to clear up that relationship, sending a three-man team of diplomats to Paris. But the group is snubbed. They are not allowed to meet with French leadership unless they pay a huge bribe.

The American diplomats refuse. When news of these demands reaches the United States, many call for a declaration of war against France. Anti-French sentiment rises to new levels as a "quasi-war" between the two nations begins. Factions within Adams's Federalist Party demand all-out war, while Vice President Jefferson's Republican Party favors a diplomatic solution.

President Adams knows war would be ruinous to the new country, and though not pro-French, he refuses to confront Paris. The subsequent press viciousness toward Adams from both sides is relentless. Many stories are complete fiction, written by editors eager to sell newspapers through virulent attacks.

Finally, President Adams decides to act.

---

* In the election of 1796, Adams defeated Jefferson by just three electoral votes. The process then was not a vote by party but a roll call of the states. There were sixteen states, each given electoral voters based on population size. Each of the 139 electors cast two votes. The individual receiving the second-most votes would be named vice president. This marks the only time in American history that the president and vice president were from different parties.

Free speech is guaranteed in the Constitution, but Adams believes criticism of *his* policies by Jefferson and the Republicans is a *threat* to the United States. There is also a growing fear that French nationals living in America will be emboldened by the media attacks to perform acts of sabotage.

On the political front, staunch Federalist Alexander Hamilton, now a private citizen and avowed enemy of John Adams, publicly demands the president declare war on France. In response, Adams sends a messenger to Mount Vernon requesting that George Washington return to duty as commander of the army. Washington agrees. However, he immediately requests Alexander Hamilton be named second-in-command.

Adams refuses—and a stalemate ensues.

The press hatred toward President Adams gets worse.

So, during a two-week period beginning on June 18, 1798, the Federalist-controlled Congress passes four bills known as the Alien and Sedition Acts. Adams signs these "war acts" into law on July 14. The most powerful of these limits the freedom of the press, making it illegal to publish "false, scandalous, and malicious writing" against the president. The intent is clear: Republican editors will be jailed if they criticize John Adams.

Five large newspapers immediately test the new law. Their editors are quickly accused of libel. James Callender, a journalist actually paid by Thomas Jefferson to smear Adams, is arrested and put into prison.*

As the controversy over press freedom continues, John Adams is under enormous duress. Abigail fears for her husband's life. Much of the nation prefers the Federalist Party and backs the anti-press laws, but furious Republicans are threatening riots. These threats are led by Vice President Thomas Jefferson. However, they never come to fruition.

---

* James Callender served nine months in a Richmond prison and paid a $200 fine. After his release, he felt abandoned by his former friend Thomas Jefferson and switched to the Federalist cause. Callender began writing stories suggesting that Jefferson had several children by one of his slaves. In all, twenty-six scribes were imprisoned for sedition. The grandson of Benjamin Franklin, twenty-nine-year-old Benjamin Franklin Bache, editor of the *Philadelphia Aurora*, was arrested on sedition charges but died of yellow fever before his trial.

As the nation's chief executive, John Adams arises each morning at 5:00 a.m. He enjoys a five-mile walk, firmly believing that "move or die is the language of our maker in the constitution of our bodies." While serving as a diplomat in Paris, Adams was often joined on these walks by his twelve-year-old son, John Quincy. The young man will later adopt these morning rituals as president.

Breakfast is at 8:00 a.m. For the first three years of his presidency, John Adams occupies the same Philadelphia mansion where George Washington once lived. It is not until there are just five months left in his first term that he will move into the wilderness of the District of Columbia.*

President Adams works throughout the day, pausing for dinner with Abigail at 3:00 p.m. He favors boiled fish and meat, in the New England tradition. Cheese, potatoes, and bacon are staples of the meal. When John Quincy was a teenager, Adams would spend evenings helping him study, followed by a game of cards. President Adams has two dogs—Juno and Satan. He also has a horse named Cleopatra. This makes him the first president to have pets while in office. This menagerie expands shortly after Adams moves into the president's mansion when the Marquis de Lafayette gifts him with an alligator, which is kept in a bathroom in the East Wing.

The Adams family often entertains—at least when Abigail is in town. Very often, she returns to their Massachusetts farm to get away from the rigors of being First Lady. Though Abigail learned a great deal about dining with high-ranking officials during John's years abroad in London and Paris, it is through her friendship with Martha Washington that she comes to understand exactly how to please domestic guests.

Abigail is fifty-three when her husband takes office. She is the mother of five, a sharp-witted woman who maintains the same rigid

---

* The final choice for the location of the US capital was between Philadelphia and an undeveloped area straddling Maryland and Virginia. The Residence Act of July 16, 1790, selected the second site to appease southern pro-slavery states, who feared a more northerly location would encourage anti-slavery abolitionists. It would be located within an independent federal district instead of a state. The deal was brokered by Alexander Hamilton, Thomas Jefferson, and James Madison. In 1791, the city was named Washington in honor of the first president. Columbia, a feminine form of Columbus, was chosen as the name of the federal district.

early morning schedule as her spouse. It is Abigail who manages the family farm and cash flow, a necessity demanded by John's long absences during the Revolutionary War. Because of her vital role in keeping the family afloat, Abigail is openly in favor of full education for women. She is also just as politically oriented as her husband. Abigail is unafraid to share her opinions, warning President Adams about members of both political parties who might be a threat.

Among those she despises most is Alexander Hamilton. "The very devil," Abigail calls him. "Lasciviousness itself."

President Adams serves only one term in office. He will develop the American navy into a juggernaut, soon to be the equal of any in the world. He will forge peace with France. But a hallmark of those four years is the enduring hatred Adams will develop for Alexander Hamilton as well as for his own vice president, Thomas Jefferson. His rivalry with Hamilton will divide the Federalist Party, and in little more than two decades, it will cease to exist. As for Hamilton, he writes of Adams that he "is a mere old woman and unfit for a president."

On October 2, 1798, Alexander Hamilton *again* demands a "decisive rupture" with France. Adams says no. He well understands Hamilton's machinations, writing to Abigail that he is a "conceited hypocrite with debauched morals." As president, John Adams is certain Hamilton's "High Federalists" will bring down the party, allowing Republicans like Thomas Jefferson and the powerful New York lawyer Aaron Burr to steal the presidency during the next election in 1800.

Alexander Hamilton becomes even more adamant about developing a strong American military and declaring war. Yet, in 1799, Adams again refuses. Almost immediately, the Federalist Party implodes. President Adams fears a political coup will rob him of the presidency in the next election. In October, Adams and Hamilton meet face-to-face to discuss their differences. Hamilton demands the president recall an envoy about to sail for France. Adams refuses—and fate is on his side. The Convention of 1800 soon follows, ending hostilities with France.

The moment is an enormous victory for John Adams. He has brokered peace, regained the upper hand within his fractured party, and silenced Alexander Hamilton's war drumbeat.

But Hamilton will have his revenge. During the election of 1800, he draws a battle line—publicly stating he will *never* support Adams for reelection, even if that means the hated Thomas Jefferson becomes president.

Hamilton then urges that Adams's name actually be dropped from the presidential ballot of 1800 and publishes a pamphlet listing the president's deficiencies. "The American government might totter, if not fall, under [Adams's] auspices," Hamilton writes.

Yet John Adams fights on. His popularity is such that he carries every Federalist ballot in the 1800 nomination process. Hamilton is then discredited for trying to destroy the party with his libelous statements.

The vote is marred by rumor and mudslinging. Newspapers say Adams demands to be called "His Highness." Others write that Thomas Jefferson is an enemy of the Constitution. It is one of the nastiest presidential campaigns in the history of the United States.

In the end, there are four candidates. President Adams receives sixty-five electoral votes.

Thomas Jefferson receives seventy-three. But Aaron Burr wins seventy-three votes as well. Charles C. Pinckney of South Carolina receives sixty-four.

As a tiebreaker nears, Abigail Adams, knowing her husband has lost, roots for Thomas Jefferson because "neither party can tolerate Burr."

The Constitution establishes that a tie for the presidency is thrown to the House of Representatives, then decided by a vote of each state. America has expanded from her original thirteen colonies and now numbers sixteen states. A majority of nine state votes is required to be named president. On each of the first *thirty-four* ballots, Jefferson receives eight votes, Burr six. Electors from two states, Maryland and Vermont, cannot agree on a candidate and cast no vote.*

Then a lone man rises to lobby the proceedings, launching personal

---

* Because Adams did not defeat Jefferson and Burr in the original vote count, he was eliminated from the tiebreaker.

attacks and insults against Aaron Burr that decide the election in favor of Thomas Jefferson.

That man is Alexander Hamilton.

And those personal attacks will one day lead to his demise in a most brutal fashion.*

It is 4:00 a.m., Wednesday, March 4, 1801. John Adams rises an hour early to depart the President's House. Today is the inauguration of Thomas Jefferson, marking the first time in American history that power will be peacefully transferred from one political party to the other. Jefferson has *not* invited Adams to attend. There is also talk of violence between Federalists and Republicans. The president does not want to provoke bloodshed by making an appearance. Abigail has already made the journey home, leaving three weeks ago.

As previously arranged, the Alien and Sedition Acts expire on this very day. Thus, Thomas Jefferson will endure the press without legal recourse to stop the attacks.

Before dawn, John Adams enters a carriage, beginning the arduous journey to Massachusetts, where he will live out his days with Abigail. They will be married for fifty-four years.

Among Adams's greatest friendships in later life will be the man he currently loathes more than any other. The man who succeeds him as president of the United States.

Thomas Jefferson.†

---

* On July 11, 1804, Alexander Hamilton and Aaron Burr shot a duel in Weehawken, New Jersey, that resulted in Hamilton's death at age forty-nine—though the actual date of his birth is still in doubt. Burr was vice president at the time he killed Hamilton. He was charged with murder, but a trial was never held.

† On January 1, 1812, after eleven years of estrangement, John Adams wrote a letter to Thomas Jefferson seeking to renew their friendship. The two would correspond for the rest of their lives, with the last of their hundreds of letters sent from Adams to Jefferson on April 17, 1826. The two men would both pass away on the same date, July 4, 1826, with Jefferson preceding Adams in death by a few hours. He succumbed to toxemia, urea, and pneumonia. Not knowing his longtime friend had already passed, Adams's last words were "Jefferson still lives."

Chapter Three

Thomas Jefferson knows most Americans do not want him to be president.

So, he strives to convince them that he is worthy.

Today is the first presidential inauguration in Washington, DC. Jefferson rises with the sun, as per his normal routine. He likes to brag that he hasn't arisen later than dawn in fifty years. That habit does not change at his Washington boardinghouse this morning. He rises, soaks his feet in ice water (another longtime daily habit), shaves, and then breakfasts at 8:00 a.m. with the other guests here at the Conrad and McMunn establishment at the corner of New Jersey Avenue and C Street.

Meals are taken at a single communal table. Jefferson makes it a point not to request a prominent seat or receive special treatment. He prefers a large morning meal, enjoying coffee, muffins with butter, and cold ham. The new president is dressed simply for today's inauguration. George Washington wore a sword and silver buckle shoes and was driven to his swearing-in via coach. John Adams wore an elegant suit and also enjoyed a carriage ride to the proceedings. But the Capitol building is just a few blocks away. Fifty-seven-year-old Thomas Jefferson prefers to walk. He wears a plain suit to portray himself as a simple, ordinary citizen.

A crowd of police officers, local militia, and congressmen and senators form a small parade as they follow closely behind.

The weather is fine for a winter day, not too cold. Thomas Jefferson walks up the Capitol steps and enters the Senate Chamber, which is crowded with more than a thousand guests. He is freckled and tall. The oath of office is delivered by Supreme Court chief justice John Marshall. The two men are distant cousins but equally far apart politically, agreeing on nothing at all.

They will soon become bitter enemies.*

It is time for Thomas Jefferson to deliver his address.

The Senate Chamber is acoustically sound, making it possible for the new president to speak without raising his voice, despite the large crowds. Jefferson stands six feet two, his long graying hair tied back.

Suddenly, Jefferson begins his speech. But his voice is so low it is almost a whisper. "Friends and fellow citizens," he says, as the crowd strains to hear him. Almost immediately, the new president acknowledges that the job is "above my talents." Jefferson goes on to say that he will seek a source of "wisdom, of virtue, and of zeal on which to rely under all difficulties."†

The modest tone catches the Senate Chamber off guard. This is unexpected. Yet the room is still charged with animosity. There are questions about this transfer of power. John Adams spent his time before leaving office appointing Federalist judges to fill as many judicial openings as possible. These "midnight appointments" were intended to deprive the new president of power to appoint justices—and they will.

Thomas Jefferson has done a great deal for his country, spending the last twenty-five years engaged in the revolution that brought a republican government and freedom from English rule. But many Federalists

---

* John Marshall, as the first head of the Supreme Court, dedicated himself to making the Court as powerful as possible. He wanted authority over the president and Congress in constitutional interpretations. As one of the architects of the Constitution, Jefferson bitterly resented that.

† For Jefferson, the source of wisdom to which he refers was not spiritual but attained through constant study. He was a frequent user of the term *knowledge is power,* a phrase originally attributed to Francis Bacon in 1597.

loathe him, and most are certain he planted some of the negative newspaper stories about John Adams, which he did.

Some critics label Jefferson a "godless atheist." Still others consider
him a "radical" bent on tearing apart the national fabric. Martha Washington called his election to the presidency the second-worst day of her
life after the death of her husband.

But President Jefferson also has friends in this chamber, men like
James Madison of Virginia. The framer of the Constitution will become
Jefferson's secretary of state. The new president's towering height and
Madison's diminutive stature make for a sharp contrast. Yet they both
share a vision for America and are committed to pulling the country away from any fondness for British royalty. Jefferson, in particular, believes John Adams has an "unhealthy fascination" with England's
monarchy.

After pausing briefly, Jefferson lays out his bold plan for the United
States. He talks about the "Revolution of 1800," in which he will weaken
the federal government. Jefferson believes the Founding Fathers wanted
the states to have most of the control. However, the new president will
also pay off the national debt. In addition, he wants to get rid of the
standing army, fearing it is a threat to national freedom. There will be
no favored nation status in foreign policy: "Honest friendships with all
nations. Entangling alliances with none."

President Jefferson wants the people to know he is not at war with the
Federalist Party. He speaks to the citizens directly: "Every difference of
opinion is not a difference of principle." Jefferson says he will heal the
national divide. Americans are "brethren of the same principle. We are
all Republicans. We are all Federalists."

His inaugural speech finished, Jefferson returns to the Conrad and
McMunn boardinghouse, where he takes a seat near the fire at the communal table. He spends the first night of his presidency in the company
of his fellow boarders. His speech has been a triumph, effecting the
transfer of power without "confusion, villainy, and bloodshed," in the
words of one eyewitness.

On March 19, 1801, Thomas Jefferson moves into the President's
House. For the next eight years, he will forever alter the shape and size
of the United States. The permanent shift from a collection of British

colonies hugging the Atlantic seaboard to a nation spanning the width of a continent has begun.

In reality, Thomas Jefferson has always been a man of the wilderness. Raised in western Virginia by his father, Peter, who died when the future president was just fourteen, Jefferson went on to study at William and Mary College, earning a degree in law. But such is his intellect that the future president also immersed himself in ethics, religion, history, and the study of agriculture. In 1768, he began constructing Monticello ("Little Mountain" in Italian), a large plantation home in which he indulged his passion for science, design, and farming. Four years later, Jefferson married Martha Wayles Skelton, a twenty-three-year-old widow.

Their marriage was the happiest time of Jefferson's life. Even while helping write the Declaration of Independence more than two hundred miles away in Philadelphia, his thoughts were on home. But Martha died mysteriously in 1782, leaving Jefferson shattered. He never married again. History does not record what killed Martha Jefferson at the age of thirty-three, shortly after giving birth to their sixth child. Only two of the Jefferson offspring, daughters Mary and Martha, will survive to adulthood. His wife, Martha, is buried at Monticello, which Thomas Jefferson purchased through funds from his inheritance.

As a young man, Jefferson devotes his energy to redesigning and rebuilding his plantation. He rises each morning at dawn, as soon as there is enough light to see the clock of his own design at the foot of the bed. Then he makes a fire to warm himself, soaking his feet in ice water because he believes it encourages greater health. However, Jefferson does not routinely immerse the rest of his body in a bath, believing that maximum personal hygiene can be achieved solely through washing the hands and face.

When at Monticello, Jefferson prefers a large breakfast of coffee or tea, butter, and hot corn bread. His days are then spent writing letters in his study—Jefferson will pen more than twenty thousand in his lifetime. He often rides through the property, taking notes of plant size and other farming results. These are written in pencil on a notebook made of ivory. The notations are later transferred into a record book.

Dinner is in the late afternoon, a hearty meal consisting of rice soup, a beef or fowl entrée, and perhaps fried eggs. Ice cream and fruit are served if guests are present.

When Thomas Jefferson is alone, he prefers a great assortment of vegetables with a small portion of meat. Later in life, after his years in Paris, he will add wine to the menu.

Like many of the group labeled the "Founding Fathers," Thomas Jefferson has very specific political views and is intolerant of opposition. Thus, he develops feuds with influential figures like Patrick Henry, John Adams, and Alexander Hamilton. In time, those disagreements go well beyond civil behavior. Governor Henry, in particular, used to be a friend who became an avowed enemy because Henry wanted America defined as supporting an established church while also supporting religious freedom. Jefferson was once enamored of the orator. But in later years, his animosity is so great that Jefferson will write to James Madison that "we must pray for [Henry's] death."

In 1803, President Jefferson boldly purchases 828,000 square miles of land west of the Mississippi River. He pays France $15 million, or roughly four cents per acre. Ironically, for a president opposed to a strong federal government, this is an enormous abuse of executive power because there is nothing in the Constitution that allows the president to purchase lands from foreign governments—a fact that his Federalist enemies are only too happy to note.

President Jefferson also violates his personal opposition to a strong national bank. As secretary of state under George Washington, he criticized the banking system as providing too much power to the new federal government. But now he uses the national bank to advance his own personal agenda—one born of a lifelong love for maps and discovery. Jefferson believes in wide-open spaces and the right of Americans to own land free of big-city overcrowding. The "Louisiana Purchase," as this new expansion is known, offers just that. On

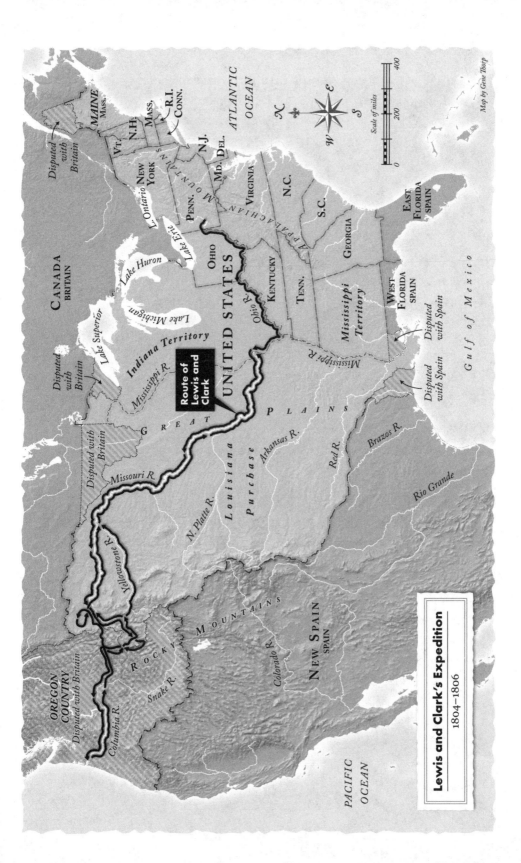

Lewis and Clark's Expedition

1804–1806

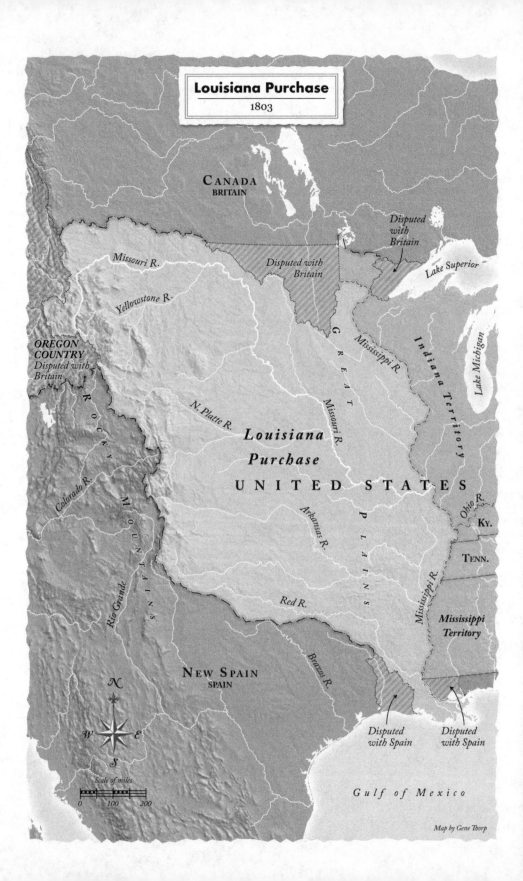

October 20, 1803, the Senate ratifies a treaty with France that seals the transaction.

There are other bold moves made by the new president: He eliminates Alexander Hamilton's unpopular whiskey tax that caused violence in Pennsylvania a decade ago. He also reduces the national debt and allows American warships to fight pirates off the coast of North Africa, thereby demonstrating the growing military might of the country.*

Yet his greatest accomplishment is the Louisiana Purchase.

At the time, little is known about this vast new possession, other than what fur trappers and traders report. There are tales of vast prairies and mountains greater than the European Alps. To learn more, President Jefferson sends his personal secretary, thirty-year-old Meriwether Lewis, along with a thirty-three-year-old former soldier named William Clark, to explore the new territory. Their subsequent journey leads the two men and forty-five others to the Pacific Ocean.

Jefferson's prescience in organizing the expedition opens up America to westward expansion. The new lands make the nation larger than any Founding Father could have imagined when forging the Constitution.

But all is not calm in the Jefferson administration. Back home in Monticello, he owns *seven hundred slaves* and opines that slavery is a necessary part of America's growth. Secretly, he has fathered children with a slave named Sally Hemings who is thirty years younger than he is. Throughout his life, Jefferson never acknowledges his six slave offspring.

There is also the issue of the Native American population. Tribes living on the newly purchased lands have made their homes there for generations. They will claim that America does not "own" this property any more than the French did. In 1893, the 150th anniversary of Thomas Jefferson's birth, the great American frontier will officially be declared closed. And although Thomas Jefferson could not know it, the journey of Lewis and Clark will set the scene for the brutal wars

---

* North African pirates charged a "tribute" to foreign ships entering their ports. Vessels unwilling to pay were raided and their crews enslaved. The amount of the tribute was increased as Jefferson took office, and he refused to pay. Instead, the president sends US warships to the Barbary Coast. These vessels bombard pirate fortresses. In 1805, the pirates surrender. They resume their activity in 1807, leading to a second war in 1815 in which the United States Navy was once again victorious.

between Indians and settlers that will take place almost constantly for ninety years.[*]

It is now 1806. The Napoleonic Wars are underway in Europe, and American merchant ships are increasingly boarded and searched by British warships. Yet, as Thomas Jefferson attempts to put an end to this larceny on the high seas, an even greater threat presents itself in the newly purchased Louisiana Territory. Aaron Burr, the former US vice president who shot and killed Alexander Hamilton, is now forming an army in New Orleans. His goal is to conquer North American lands controlled by Spain. He plans to peel away territories such as Texas and California, which are part of "New Spain," along with Mexico. This has the potential to drag the United States into the Napoleonic Wars, which are being waged by Britain, France, and Spain.

On January 22, 1807, Thomas Jefferson declares Burr to be a traitor. A warrant is issued for his arrest.

On January 17, Aaron Burr is captured north of New Orleans. He escapes but is recaptured. Burr is later acquitted of treason. While awaiting trial on other charges, he escapes to England.[†]

At the start of Jefferson's second term, he is sixty-one years old. He is no longer the young idealist directing the course of freedom and is now descending into eccentric behavior. Once a man fond of the finest clothing, he now wears slippers and a robe to work. His clothing is a mixture of styles dating back decades, a lack of decorum that infuriates one British diplomat. He makes his office in the State Dining Room, using the adjacent Red

---

[*] The authors of this book wrote extensively about the Indian wars in *Killing Crazy Horse*.

[†] Burr borrows money from his family physician and escapes by ship to London. There, he spends four years trying to gain support for his plans to lead an invasion that would sever the western region of North America from the United States. When that fails, Burr returns home and resumes his law practice. All charges against him are dropped due to time elapsed. He will live out his days in New York, dying at the age of seventy-seven from a stroke. Prior to his death, Burr's wife files for divorce. She chooses Alexander Hamilton Jr., the son of the man with whom Burr so famously fought a duel, to represent her.

Room for entertaining. The president keeps a pet mockingbird in a cage, often letting it fly around the office as he conducts business.

As his second term comes to a close, President Jefferson can look to the successful Louisiana Purchase and ending piracy along the Barbary Coast as complete successes. Also, he has taken drastic action to end the British policy of halting US ships at sea to "impress" sailors, forcing them to join the British navy. Rather than use military force to achieve this goal, the president pushed for the passage of the Embargo Act of 1807, which made it illegal for American ships to leave their home port to trade with European nations until British and French raids on American vessels ended. European economies are severely impacted by the lack of American goods flowing into their nations.

But the US economy suffers, as well. American farmers no longer have a place to sell their goods overseas. Unemployment and bankruptcies rise sharply. Within a year of the Embargo Act passing, the US economy sees a 75 percent drop. By the end of 1808, Jefferson signs legislation to repeal the act.

On balance, the American people approve of Jefferson, but tensions continue to escalate with Great Britain. A strong British presence in Canada threatens America's northern border, the Royal Navy continues to impress American sailors, and there is a growing clamor from the citizenry to expand the frontier into lands under British control. But as his time in office comes to an end, Thomas Jefferson can no longer right the wrongs. It will be up to his successor to manage these international issues as war looms.

In 1812, the war scenario becomes reality.

The time has come. Thomas Jefferson never liked city living, although he has spent decades in New York, Paris, Philadelphia, and now Washington. Yet he prefers the woods of Virginia and the tranquility of life at Monticello. So it is with delight that Jefferson attends the inauguration of his good friend James Madison on March 4, 1809.

As Madison well knows, Thomas Jefferson can't wait to get out of town.

The streets are muddy after yesterday's rain, though Jefferson is so eager to begin private life that he does not care. His coach is ready.

Thomas Jefferson boards, bound for Monticello. He will never again leave the state of Virginia.[*]

---

[*] Sally Hemings—known as "Black Sal" by Jefferson's Virginia neighbors—did not live in the slave quarters at Monticello. She slept close to Jefferson in the mansion. The relationship started when Sally was a teenager. Though Sally Hemings never lived in what would become known as the White House, she bore Thomas Jefferson three children during his presidency. She moved out of the mansion after Jefferson's death in 1826 and then lived with two of her sons in nearby Charlottesville. She died of natural causes in 1835 at the age of sixty-two. The site of her grave is unknown.

Chapter Four

The Executive Mansion is ablaze.

And no one can find James Madison.

Two years into the "War of 1812" between England and America, British troops have overrun US lines and are terrorizing the nation's capital. Forces under Major General Robert Ross burn the city down, one government building at a time. The nighttime sky is a vivid orange as flames span the horizon. Citizens of Washington have been fleeing for two days, anticipating the British arrival. So, the city is silent as the enemy army advances. Major General Ross is under orders to destroy everything he can and then retreat, rather than hold captured ground. British soldiers, in their traditional red uniforms, now roam freely, moving from the Capitol to the Executive Mansion in their quest to destroy America's capital city.

★★★

Inside the mansion—now nicknamed the "White House" by newspapers because of the lime-based whitewash applied to the exterior—First Lady Dolley Madison is insistent on *saving* Washington—the eight-foot-tall portrait of *George* hanging in the East Room. It is one of the few national treasures possessed by the young American nation, which is less than forty years old. But her task is not easy. The enormous painting is bolted to the wall, forcing the forty-six-year-old Dolley to demand that a steward and gardener hack away at the gilded frame. She is a charismatic woman known throughout Washington for her charm and social graces—the exact opposite in personality to her dour husband.

The last time Dolley saw her husband, James, he was riding out to a Maryland battlefield to watch the fighting. He has yet to return, so decisions about what is to become of the Washington portrait rest on her shoulders. Dolley's greatest fear is that it will fall into the hands of British soldiers, who will delight in destroying the image of the general who defeated their army in the Revolutionary War.

Incredibly, two passing visitors from New York, financier Jacob Barker and shipping merchant Robert G. L. De Peyster, enter the White House and ask if they might lend a hand. The First Lady entrusts them with the painting, as well as the family silver and her husband's official papers. She stuffs a copy of the Declaration of Independence into her own suitcase.*

Then, the socially proper Dolley orders that a banquet be laid out for the advancing British officers at the president's mansion. She puts food and wine on the sideboard and tables, allowing for a large gathering. Only after that does she flee the White House just hours before the British arrive.

But where is the president?

★★★

James Madison is on the run. He spent the day on the field of battle in Maryland, watching the British defeat the American position. As US troops begin their retreat, the sixty-three-year-old Madison rides his horse back to Washington. But he finds his wife already departed. So, the president saddles a new steed, packs a bag, and gallops to the Potomac ferry in search of Dolley.

The Madisons eventually find each other, as the president is informed that Dolley is staying at the home of their good friend Major Charles Carroll. They then return to Washington to find it burned to the ground. The disaster coincides with an all-time low in the president's popularity.

---

* The two New Yorkers were friends of the president and First Lady and were trapped during the British advance. They visited the White House as a courtesy on their way out of town, hoping to be of assistance.

Citizens from around the nation are demanding his impeachment for the bungled war with Great Britain.*

Amid the chaos, the portrait of George Washington is secure, hidden by the two New Yorkers in the barn of a Maryland farmer. Going forward, the Madisons will live in a brick building in Washington known as the Octagon House as the White House is rebuilt. But when the President's House reopens four years from now, the painting will once again hang in the East Room—as it does to this day.†

The presidency is the natural conclusion to James Madison Jr.'s long career in public life. Born in 1751 at Belle Grove Plantation near Port Conway, Virginia, Madison grows up the son of a tobacco farmer. A second cousin, Zachary Taylor, will later become president, as well.

Madison's father, James Sr., moves the family to a plantation he dubs Montpelier when his son is fourteen. Young Madison's height never exceeds five feet four, but his ambitions are lofty. He does not attend William and Mary College, as is common with young Virginia men, choosing instead to study at the University of New Jersey—soon to be renamed Princeton. Aaron Burr, the ill-fated future vice president, is a classmate. Rather than study law, as he had planned, Madison immerses himself in political philosophy. It is only later, upon returning to Montpelier with no career plans, that he teaches himself the law. He is a healthy individual but is often incapacitated by anxiety. On one occasion, he loses his hat while traveling. Fearful of being seen in public without a head covering, Madison hides inside for two days until a new one can be brought to him.

Despite these idiosyncrasies, James Madison seeks a spotlight. He becomes radicalized in the late 1760s, caught up in the growing rift between the thirteen American colonies and the British monarchy. He is

---

* President Madison himself signed the declaration of war against the king because Britain was blockading ports, impressing US sailors, and providing arms to Native Americans so they would fight settlers pushing westward. But American forces were not strong enough to defeat the experienced British army. Most historians believe Madison should have known that.

† On August 24, 2006, President Barack Obama welcomed a dozen descendants of Paul Jennings into the White House to view the Gilbert Stuart painting of George Washington. Jennings was the slave and valet who helped Dolley Madison pull the painting off the wall in 1814 and remove it to safety. The date of their visit coincided with the day the painting was moved into hiding.

active in Virginia politics and begins a lifelong friendship with Thomas Jefferson, the governor of Virginia at the time. As America wins its independence from England, Madison becomes immersed in the ideals of the new nation. He serves in the Continental Congress and attends the Constitutional Convention in Philadelphia, drafting many key tenets of the document. Madison's loyalty to Jefferson leads his political philosophies away from the conservative Federalist beliefs of George Washington and Alexander Hamilton.

It is Jefferson and the young James Madison who form the new Democratic-Republican Party in the 1790s. The movement advocates less federal power over individuals and the states. Madison advocates for a system of checks and balances among the executive, legislative, and judicial branches of government to ensure that no group acquires more power than any other.

In 1794, James Madison gets married. Dolley Payne Todd is an engaging twenty-six-year-old widow whose first husband died of yellow fever. The couple are introduced by the great American scoundrel, Aaron Burr. Dolley is seventeen years Madison's junior, but the two are very much compatible. Both are accomplished equestrians and love to ride together. Her outgoing nature helps him deal with the social anxiety triggered by his growing public prominence. She calls him "Jemmy," a nickname he has carried since childhood as a play on his first name.

Despite their attachment, Madison likes solitary time. He often seeks out a secluded spot to read, which he does voraciously. He is also known to sip a pint of whiskey each day to calm his nerves—an amount considered moderate at the time.

The marriage prospers, as does James Madison's relationship with Thomas Jefferson. He oversees the third president's successful 1800 election bid and serves as his secretary of state.

Due to the weakened influence of the Federalist Party after the feud between Alexander Hamilton and John Adams in 1800, James Madison is easily elected president in 1808. He is fifty-seven years old when taking office, the same age George Washington and Thomas Jefferson were. In contrast to those men, James Madison looks tired and worn. One audience member in the Senate Chamber watching the inauguration calls the new president "a withered little apple-John."

★★★

Yet withered or not, the Madison White House is full of energy. The president rises with the dawn and is dressed by his fifteen-year-old slave and valet, Paul Jennings. Madison has a simple breakfast with tea at 7:00 a.m. and then begins his workday in his upstairs office. He smokes cigars, a habit he will continue until his death. As the day winds down, Madison prefers to be in bed no later than 10:00 p.m.

Except when Dolley is throwing a party. The First Lady is tall and plump, fond of using "snuff" and then blowing her nose on a bandana followed by a linen handkerchief.* She likes to say the first coarse cloth is for "the rough work" and the more refined fabric is for the "polish." Blue eyes, fair skin, black curls. To enhance her appearance in rooms lit by oil lamps, she adds rouge to her cheeks, defying those who believe makeup is for women of ill repute. This is a far cry from the young girl raised in a strict Quaker household, forbidden to wear anything but the plainest of clothing.

The White House lost much of its social luster during the Jefferson administration. Unlike George Washington, Thomas Jefferson did not open the mansion to the public except on the Fourth of July and New Year's Day. There were daily guided tours, but without any guarantee of meeting the president.

Not so during the Madison administration. Dolley realizes that the lifeblood of Washington is politics. Most congressmen live in dreary boardinghouses. Visiting diplomats, used to doing business in Paris and London, find Washington a desolate backwater without amenities.

So, Dolley Madison begins elevating the social scene by redecorating the White House. British-born architect Benjamin Henry Latrobe adds vibrant reds and blues to the drab interior, with large oil lamps and enormous mirrors. When author Washington Irving visits in 1811, he describes "emerging from the dirt and darkness" of Washington into "the blazing splendor of Mrs. Madison's drawing room."†

Dolley Madison cultivates politicians and diplomats, famous men like Irving, and wealthy members of Washington society in her attempts

---

* Snuff is a finely ground mixture of tobacco leaf and stalk that is inhaled through the nose.

† Washington Irving wrote *The Legend of Sleepy Hollow* and other successful stories.

to build a new social order for the capital. She dresses lavishly and exhausts herself learning the names of every important official in the city. Dolley circulates during each gathering, even as her husband finds a quiet corner to discuss politics. Young local girls play guitar and piano as the socializing begins and then are encouraged to befriend bachelor members of Congress.

Dolley also resumes the practice of weekly afternoon soirees. Instead of a levee, as Martha Washington once called them, Dolley names the get-togethers "dove" parties. She is fond of serving ice cream as a dessert, her favorite flavor being oyster—though she also allows the tastes of asparagus, parmesan, and chestnut. These bustling parties are nicknamed "squeezes" due to the First Lady's penchant for filling her bright-red drawing room to capacity with guests.

In this way, the White House becomes the social center of Washington society.

Until it burns down.*

War with Britain was on the horizon long before James Madison became president. Throughout the first year of his administration, trade with Britain was prohibited. However, the British continued to seize American cargo and impress sailors to fill out crews on their undermanned vessels. A group of congressmen called "War Hawks," among them Henry Clay of Virginia and John Calhoun of South Carolina, push Madison to take a more aggressive stance. On June 17, 1812, as Madison's first term in office is coming to an end, the Senate approves a resolution already passed in the House that war be declared on Britain.

Madison signs it.

But America isn't ready for war. The young nation has little revenue and few ways to fund a conflict. Volunteers are not keen on joining the regular army, with its few trained officers. The British are a professional military force. The Royal Navy is the best in the world. Within two

---

* The Madison White House maintained between twelve and fourteen slaves. Madison brought some with him from Montpelier and then rented others from local Washington slave owners. Slaves received no income. They lived inside the White House, in quarters off the ground-floor corridor.

months, the British capture Fort Detroit, a vital fortress on the American frontier. The entire Michigan Territory falls soon after.

As American military losses mount, the economy takes a hard hit. Exports drop. British soldiers destroy cash crops like tobacco. The burning of the White House is yet another epic display of America's inability to protect itself.

Yet President Madison is saved. Commodore Oliver Perry stunningly defeats the British at the naval Battle of Lake Erie. Then, General Andrew Jackson annihilates a British force at the Battle of New Orleans. Both victories actually convince some Americans their country won the war militarily.*

On balance, James Madison's two terms in office did advance American progress. The nation is expanding due to an improved road network and Robert Fulton's steam-powered paddleboat, which will make river travel faster and more efficient.

There is also the issue of cotton. America ceased the importation of slaves from Africa on January 1, 1808, by a congressional act. President Madison, a slave owner himself, does not object to the legislation and supports a policy that would return black slaves to their African roots. However, a worldwide demand for cotton is leading plantation owners in the South to insist that the federal government allow individual states to have their own laws about slavery. This effectively divides America between pro-slavery and anti-slavery advocates. As the country expands west, the slave controversy will grow violent.

James and Dolley Madison celebrate the inauguration of the new president, James Monroe, on March 4, 1817. Monroe, a close confidant of Madison, had no trouble winning the election against Federalist Rufus King from New York.

The couple then travel back to Virginia to live out their lives on Madison's plantation. He dies on June 28, 1836, at the age of eighty-five. Dolley

---

* The War of 1812 ends with the Treaty of Ghent, signed December 24, 1814. The United States receives all lands in the Northwest Territory.

lives on for thirteen more years but encounters severe financial problems when a son from her first marriage, John Payne Todd, mismanages her estate to pay his many gambling debts. She returns to Washington in 1837 and resumes her social life but is ultimately forced to sell Montpelier, the family slaves, and many possessions to stay solvent.

Meanwhile, back in Washington, President James Monroe is facing a number of growing problems. Not only is Great Britain once again violating American law, but Native Americans are in rebellion.

Yet Monroe knows he has at least a partial solution to that problem: a warrior who doesn't like to take prisoners.

Chapter Five

President James Monroe authorizes action.

General Andrew Jackson crosses the border into Florida, leading an army of eight hundred US regular soldiers and nine hundred Georgia militia. Thousands more Tennessee volunteers are a couple days behind. Southern plantation owners have complained for years that escaped slaves are being sheltered in the Florida swamps by Seminole Indians. In addition, the tribe is raiding farms in Mississippi and Alabama. Jackson has been ordered by the president to travel from his home outside Nashville and then lead a force over the border to stop the Indian incursions. Florida is a Spanish colony, but that is not Jackson's concern.

Monroe was sworn in on March 4, less than one week ago. Since 1805, when he served a brief stint as special envoy to Spain, he has coveted Florida. The new president believes in the expansion of the United States that was greatly accelerated by the Louisiana Purchase, which he personally brokered with Emperor Napoleon Bonaparte's top diplomats. Andrew Jackson, a national hero and a man known for waging absolute war, is the perfect individual to carry out Monroe's ambitions. The president's orders are simple: "Seize Florida."

Jackson strikes quickly. Moving deep into the territory along the path of the Apalachicola River, he captures two Seminole leaders. These men are immediately hanged. General Jackson's troops travel light, carrying just eight days' rations as they press farther into Florida. One thousand head of cattle are captured after a brief skirmish outside a Seminole village, depriving the tribe of their main food source. Three hundred homes are burned by Jackson's force as the Native Americans flee.

Two British subjects are captured soon after. Alexander Arbuthnot is a seventy-year-old trader from Scotland. Robert Ambrister is a soldier of fortune. Jackson considers them hostiles, intent on making war on the United States. An impromptu court martial sentences the elderly Arbuthnot to hanging and Ambrister to a whipping. But Jackson finds that punishment too light. So, instead, he demands that Ambrister be shot.

The sentences are carried out the following morning.

Andrew Jackson and his men continue to plunder and attack, finally capturing the Spanish port at Pensacola. Jackson then sets up a US military governorship in clear violation of Spain's ownership.

This leads to a formal protest by Spain to President Monroe. The US Congress does not take any further action. Secretary of State John Quincy Adams, knowing the president's point of view, is an enthusiastic Jackson supporter. That will not last long.

In addition, much of the American public loves the aggressive general who now has become a national icon.

The turbulence in Florida ends. And the Monroe administration enters a period of time that will be known as the "Era of Good Feelings."

James Monroe is a boring guy.

But he's lived the most interesting life of any president since George Washington.

Monroe is born on April 28, 1758, in rural Virginia. His father is a prosperous planter who traces his lineage back to a grandfather who fought alongside King Charles I in the English Civil Wars. When the king was captured and executed in 1649, the elder Monroe fled to exile in Virginia.

By the time James is a teenager, both of his parents are dead of unknown causes, with mother Elizabeth preceding husband Spencer. James inherits the family plantation but leaves at age sixteen to attend the College of William and Mary. The year is 1774, and the American colonies are growing restless for independence from Great Britain. After taking part in a successful raid to loot the British armory in Williamsburg, young James drops out of school and joins the Virginia infantry. By the winter of 1776, he is a lieutenant in the Continental army serving under George Washington at the Battle of Trenton.

The midnight raid on Hessian mercenary troops fighting for the British will long be remembered for Washington's "crossing of the Delaware," sending an army over the ice-choked river on Christmas night. The eighteen-year-old Monroe charges an enemy cannon in a driving snowstorm and almost loses his life in the surprise attack. A musket ball passes through his shoulder and nicks an artery. Only the timely intervention of a battlefield physician saves Monroe.[*]

Much more happens to James Monroe on his way to the presidency. Between 1776 and his inauguration in 1817, Monroe winters at Valley Forge with George Washington, studies law with Thomas Jefferson, forms a close friendship with James Madison, serves as governor of Virginia, is elected to the United States Senate, and, finally, serves as George Washington's minister to France. He goes on to perform the role of secretary of state under James Madison. With all that on his résumé, James Monroe becomes one of the most dominant presidential candidates in history, winning the election of 1816 with 68 percent of the vote and a landslide Electoral College victory.

The new president is fifty-eight years old when he takes office. He is six feet tall, slender, with a full head of gray hair. His inauguration is the first to take place outdoors; Monroe is sworn in on a raised platform in front of the Old Brick Capitol because the original was burned by the British. Eight thousand citizens are in attendance, making his inauguration the largest so far in history.[†]

As the Virginian takes the oath, he looks out over a capital city still

---

[*] In Emanuel Leutze's iconic 1851 painting "Washington Crossing the Delaware," an image of James Monroe can be seen just behind a standing George Washington's right shoulder, clutching an American flag. Critics of this depiction point out that Washington did not stand while leading troops across the river that night, Monroe was already marching to Trenton to join the fight, and Leutze's depiction of the Delaware looks much more like the Rhine River from his home country, later to be known as Germany. For a full description of this turning point in the Revolutionary War, please read Killing England.

[†] The temporary US Capitol building operated from 1815 to 1819. During the Civil War, it would serve as a prison. That location is currently the site of the Supreme Court Building.

under reconstruction. The new president was among the last to evacuate Washington, DC, on the night the British burned it. He will not move into the newly renovated White House for six months but has already begun a radical new interior: chairs, plates, and glassware from France—a sharp contrast from the British look favored by Dolley Madison. A fifty-three-setting service of porcelain china is being commissioned bearing Monroe's initials, beginning a new presidential tradition. A designer is being sent abroad to oversee these purchases.

On the policy front, President Monroe believes it is time to see the expanding nation for himself. The summer of 1817 is spent on a fifteen-week grand tour of New England and the Midwest. Monroe's goal is to unify the nation—a task in which he proves quite successful. The new president also hopes to weaken the power of political parties, an ambition that becomes more difficult than he thought. The Federalist Party will be gone by the time James Monroe leaves office, but his own Democratic-Republican Party will be opposed by a new group known as the Whigs in 1824.

It is during this time of travel that a Boston newspaper labels the Monroe presidency the "Era of Good Feelings."

On the personal side, the president is married to the former Elizabeth Kortright, the daughter of a successful New York merchant he met while serving in the Continental Congress. She has given birth to three children, with an extraordinary gap of thirteen years between her first and second. That second child, a son named Spencer, dies at sixteen months from yellow fever. James Monroe is devastated. A third child, daughter Maria, is born soon after.

First Lady Elizabeth Monroe—a stately woman of great beauty—is not always capable of playing her public role of a president's wife. As James Monroe guides the nation, fifty-one-year-old Elizabeth battles chronic poor health. The president's oldest daughter, thirty-two-year-old Eliza, often stands in for her mother at social functions. On those occasions when Elizabeth is well enough to invite guests to the White House, the list is exclusively limited to political associates.

President Monroe rises each day at dawn. He is a known Francophile due to his years serving as minister to France but prefers Virginia cuisine for breakfast in the form of egg bread (also known as French toast), flaky lard biscuits, and a breakfast roll known as Williamsburg buns.

Like Thomas Jefferson, James Monroe learned to appreciate wine during his time in Paris. A small scandal erupts early in his administration when 1,200 bottles of burgundy and champagne from France are purchased for the White House with $30,000 earmarked by Congress as the "Furniture Fund." This will be just one of many financial conflicts Monroe has with that legislative body. Their failure to reimburse him for improvements made to the White House will lead to financial hardship for the Monroes once he leaves office.

All in all, life in the new White House is routine and orderly during the first two years of the Monroe presidency. He enjoys an enormous popularity with the American people that no president had seen since George Washington's first term.

★★★

Then comes the Panic of 1819. A decline in imports, exports, and agricultural productivity leads to the first American depression since the 1780s. Foreclosures and high unemployment have many questioning Monroe's financial policies. Large money institutions are declaring bankruptcy. The president responds by easing mortgage payments on lands purchased from the federal government. Otherwise, he does nothing, believing that the expanding economy must right itself.

That will take four years.

But it is the increasingly divisive subject of slavery that is the first real test of Monroe's ability to govern. As America expands westward, the matter of whether or not to allow enslaved human beings in new states becomes a heated issue. Missouri is denied admission to the Union in 1819 due to its pro-slavery stance. The Missouri Compromise is then brokered by Monroe. In exchange for allowing Missouri statehood, the northern anti-slavery territory of Maine is also made a state. This maintains a legislative balance between South and North. Monroe only signs the bill into law when he is satisfied it is constitutional. Ironically, though many in American politics consider Monroe the "last framer" of the Constitution, he did not vote for the document's ratification.*

The Missouri Compromise is an explosive issue that will prove a temporary solution to a long-term problem. Yet despite the Panic of 1819 and the slavery controversy, James Monroe's popularity never slips.

In 1820, he is reelected. He runs unopposed, the last time that will happen in American history.

Spain leaves Florida.

In the aftermath of what will become known as the First Seminole War, the Spanish lose their ability to govern their colony. Spain's influence in the Americas began with the arrival of Christopher Columbus more than three centuries earlier. At one time, the Spanish not only controlled Florida but also Mexico, large portions of the American West, and lands in the Caribbean and South America. But in 1819, Spain chooses to give up on Florida entirely. The territory is ceded to the United States for $5 million. This display of weakness soon fuels the seeds of revolution already sown in Mexico and many South American nations, all of whom succeed in attaining independence from Spain.

This terrifies other colonial powers in Europe.

Incredibly, just a decade after they fought one another in the Napoleonic Wars, European nations rally to the Spanish cause. Britain and France plot to intervene in North America, fearing that uprisings similar to those against Spain will soon spread to territories under their control in Canada, the Caribbean, and Oregon.

The time has come for James Monroe to make another bold move.

After consulting with Secretary of State John Quincy Adams of Massachusetts, President Monroe inserts a warning to Europe into his 1823 message to Congress, also known as the State of the Union.

The date is December 2. The Capitol is still being rebuilt, but chambers for the House and Senate have been usable since 1819. The nation now

---

* In 1788, James Monroe voted against ratifying the Constitution because it gave too much power to the federal government. He later backed the document when a Bill of Rights implementing individual freedoms was added in 1791.

numbers twenty-four states, so the audience is forty-eight senators and more than two hundred representatives. Monroe's speech is written by hand on a piece of unlined stationery and runs more than thirty pages.

Standing before the Eighteenth Congress, the president starkly warns Europe not to meddle in North America. There will be no more colonization of American lands. Any attempt to do so will be considered an act of war.

In exchange, the United States will not intervene in European affairs.

The threat of war will become known as the Monroe Doctrine, and for the next 150 years, it will guide American foreign policy.[*]

At age sixty-six, President Monroe is ready to return to Virginia. His two terms have been successful. However, Monroe has just witnessed a brutal political spectacle—the 1824 presidential campaign between John Quincy Adams and Andrew Jackson. The election is thrown into the House. Adams wins, but a shroud of bitterness descends on the United States. Monroe watches silently as charges of a "corrupt bargain" swarm over Washington.

As the son of John Adams takes power in March 1825, James and Elizabeth retire to Oak Hill, their plantation home in Western Virginia, just a few miles from Thomas Jefferson's Monticello. The former First Lady's chronic poor health worsens when she suffers severe burns after collapsing near a fireplace in 1826. She dies of her maladies on September 23, 1830.

James Monroe, now a widower, is forced to sell Oak Hill to pay his debts and eventually moves to New York City to live with his oldest daughter. There, Monroe becomes extremely ill, dying less than a year after his wife. He is seventy-three.

As with his friend Thomas Jefferson and his political opponent John Adams, the date of President James Monroe's death is July 4.

---

[*] President John F. Kennedy will cite the Monroe Doctrine during the Cuban Missile Crisis of October 1962 as a warning to the Soviet Union.

Chapter Six

John Quincy Adams is naked.

The president of the United States bathes in the Potomac nearly every morning, stripping down on the riverbank, placing his clothes upon a rock, and then wading into the cool current. He stands five feet seven and is fifty-eight years old. The president is lean and balding, with a tonsure of white hair along the sides of his head and chin. Adams has no problem whatsoever standing nude along the riverbank in full view of strangers.

In fact, some of the onlookers join him. Also, Adams's sons John and George accompany their father when they are home from Harvard. The president's personal valet, Antoine, sometimes strips down to join his boss, as well. A Dutch diplomat named Ten Cate is another occasional nude bather.

For John Quincy Adams, the ritual is not a casual thing. His consistent swims are a cornerstone of his daily schedule. "I follow this practice for exercise, for health, for cleanliness, and for pleasure—I have found it invariably conducive to health and have never experienced it the slightest inconvenience," Adams writes in his daily journal.

The only precaution Adams takes is to place his clothes high enough on shore that the tide does not sweep them away—which has almost happened on two occasions.

"I rise usually between four and five—walk two miles, bathe in the Potomac River, and walk home, which occupies two hours," he writes, then describes a morning spent having breakfast, reading, and writing, only stepping into the office shortly after noon.

But as the president ages, his personal physician cautions him to take it easy on the skinny-dipping. He loves being in the Potomac perhaps too much. "Dr. Huntt and all my friends think I am engaging in it to excess," he writes, then adds, "The art of swimming ought in my opinion to be taught as a regular branch of education."*

John Quincy Adams is lucky to be president. He actually lost the popular vote to Andrew Jackson by a wide margin. However, Jackson did not reach the 50 percent threshold in the Electoral College vote, and there were three other men in contention, including Adams. In a series of backdoor moves, Adams was able to convince Henry Clay to give him his votes. The other candidate, William Crawford of Georgia, paralyzed and nearly blind from a recent stroke, kept his small tally.

Clay, from Kentucky, was Speaker of the House and not a natural ally to Adams. However, after Adams secured Clay's support, he named him secretary of state. That action is widely known as the "corrupt bargain."

So, John Quincy Adams becomes the first son of a former president, John Adams, to also become president. He is sworn in on March 4, 1824. Like his father, Adams is intellectual and opinionated, with a broad vision for the ideals of American liberty.

He was born at the family farm in Braintree, Massachusetts, on July 11, 1767, the eldest son of John and Abigail. He spends much of his youth abroad as his father serves as a diplomat in London, Paris, and the Netherlands. He becomes fond of languages. Soon fluent in French, Dutch, German, and Russian, he has no success learning Italian. In time, a teenaged John Quincy Adams serves as his father's private secretary.

Being the son of a high-level government official grants Adams access to the nation's most influential figures at an early age. By fourteen, he travels to Russia and serves as secretary for American diplomat Francis Dana in Saint Petersburg. After returning to America and graduating

---

* These quotes are all taken from the private journal of John Quincy Adams.

from Harvard in 1787, Adams turns his back on politics to open a private law practice. But President George Washington appoints him minister to the Netherlands in 1794, despite Adams being just twenty-seven years old. From that moment until his death more than fifty years later, John Quincy Adams will serve the American people.

It is his overseas experience that allows Adams to meet Louisa Catherine Johnson, whom he will marry in 1797. The London-born Louisa is fair-skinned and ginger-haired—and every bit his equal. Louisa is fluent in French, intellectual, charismatic, and a strong believer that women should have equal say in a marriage.

John and Abigail Adams oppose the union, believing their son should not marry anyone born in England. This is an argument they lose. John Quincy and Louisa will never separate, but theirs will be a difficult life together, punctuated by long separations due to his diplomatic work.

After a series of miscarriages, Louisa finally gives birth to three boys and a girl. The daughter, also Louisa Catherine, dies of dysentery at the age of one while John Quincy Adams is serving as minister to Russia. Louisa's grief is only made worse when her husband travels alone to Ghent, Holland, to spend a year brokering the treaty ending the War of 1812.

From then on, the couple slowly begin living separate lives. Upon her husband's election to the presidency, the First Lady quickly learns that she does not enjoy life in the White House, which she considers shabby and run-down. Louisa will entertain infrequently, suffer illnesses she will describe as psychosomatic, and complain about gender inequality.

The presidency of James Monroe is the making of John Quincy Adams. As secretary of state, he oversees the acquisition of Florida, writes much of the Monroe Doctrine, and gets the British to agree to joint occupation of the Oregon Territory. Yet these successes don't make Adams an obvious choice for the presidency in 1824. That's because, by his own admission, he is not a people person.

"I am a man of reserved, cold, and austere forbidding manners," he writes in his diary. "I am certainly not intentionally repulsive in my manners and deportment, and in my public station I never made myself inaccessible to any human being. But I have no powers of fascination; none of the honey the profligate proverb says is the true fly-catcher."

So, the election becomes an ordeal for Adams. There are now twenty-four states in the Union. Eighteen allow their residents to directly vote for president. Six states still require state legislatures to make the choice of who will serve in the Electoral College.

The charismatic Andrew Jackson has no problem defeating Adams in the popular vote, but, as mentioned, he does not get enough electoral votes to win the election outright. Therefore, a deal favoring John Quincy Adams is made.

And so begins the single-term presidency of Adams. Dogged by Andrew Jackson's charges that he became president through a "corrupt bargain," the New Englander is never secure in his position. However, Adams undertakes an ambitious agenda to build new roads and canals with federal money. The nation is not at war, and the great recession is past. He will fund these grand projects through the sale of public lands. In 1828, the most ambitious of these programs begins when President Adams breaks ground on the 185-mile C&O (Chesapeake and Ohio) Canal running from Washington to Pittsburgh.

Adams's other great projects fail. He longs to form lasting national institutions mirroring the great places of learning in Europe. The president proposes a university, a new naval academy to train seafaring officers, a national observatory, and even a standard system of weights and measures. None receive congressional support.

As for foreign policy, it is nonexistent. This is odd for a former diplomat and secretary of state but Adams focuses his attention completely on solving domestic problems. "America goes not abroad," he states, "searching for monsters which to destroy."

The 1826 midterm elections doom John Quincy Adams. Andrew Jackson does not hold political office but is already a declared candidate for president in the upcoming election of 1828. The "Jacksonians"—an offshoot of the Democratic-Republicans—pick up several crucial seats in Congress, further stiffening opposition to President Adams.

The election of 1828 comes up fast. But it is no contest. Andrew Jackson rolls over John Quincy Adams, winning 178 electoral votes to 83.

Louisa, who campaigns vigorously for her husband's reelection, is relieved to be leaving the White House.

In truth, so is John Quincy Adams.

★★★

That relief is short-lived. He and Louisa return to Massachusetts, expecting to retire. But their twenty-eight-year-old son, George Washington Adams, commits suicide in 1829. The couple is stunned. Then, in 1830, John Quincy Adams is nominated and wins a seat in the House of Representatives. He will be the only man to ever serve as a congressman after being president.

Adams and Louisa return to Washington, where he will serve in Congress for seventeen years. In that time, they will suffer the death by alcoholism of another son, John Adams II. Of their four children, only Charles Frances Adams will outlive his parents.

John Quincy Adams speaks his mind freely on the House floor, in particular railing against slavery, of which he is an avowed opponent. Some southern members of Congress oversee the passage of a "gag rule" to prevent him and others from attacking slavery. Adams fights this measure for eight years before finally gaining the votes for its repeal.

In 1841, John Quincy Adams argues before the Supreme Court as part of the divisive *Amistad* case. African slaves had revolted and taken command of a Spanish slave ship of the same name. The prosecution argues that these men should be returned as property to the slave owners who commissioned the ship. Adams argues for the defense, stating that these slaves are free men, illegally captured, and destined to be sold in violation of American law. The verdict will set a precedent about the legality of enslaved people taking action to seek their own freedom. Southern states believe a victory for the defense will encourage slaves to use violent force to escape their owners.[*]

John Quincy Adams wins the case. The court rules in favor of the slaves. They are returned to their homes in Africa as free men.

★★★

---

[*] Steven Spielberg made *Amistad*, a movie about the incident, in 1997. Anthony Hopkins played the role of John Quincy Adams.

Throughout his long career, Quincy continues his nude morning swims. He keeps a daily diary for six decades, where he writes about sliding into the Potomac in the buff one morning at age seventy-eight. Seeing the famous politician enter the water, a group of young men begin calling his name. "John Quincy Adams!" they shout excitedly. Then, stripping off their clothing and placing it on nearby rocks, they jump into the river to swim with him.

Adams never leaves political life. On February 21, 1848, while participating in a heated discussion on the floor of the House concerning the Mexican-American War, Adams suffers a cerebral hemorrhage and collapses. He is carried to the Speaker's Room inside the Capitol building. A doctor is summoned, but death is imminent.*

John Quincy Adams dies in the Speaker's Room on February 23, wife Louisa at his side. His son Charles is not able to make it in time. Adams is eighty years old.

He speaks his last words in those final moments: "This is the last of earth. I am content."

On balance, John Quincy Adams did more for the country as a congressman than as president. His passion against slavery led to a growing abolitionist movement in New England. But he was never the people's choice.

It is beyond any doubt that Adams's blue-blooded heritage led him to the White House. But the country is changing dramatically as the population of America explodes. Now, "populist" candidates are replacing aristocrats.

And the most populist of all is about to step onto the big stage.

---

*   John Quincy Adams was opposed to the Mexican-American War, believing it an attempt to add more slave states to the Union. The 1846–1848 conflict added California, New Mexico, Nevada, and Utah to the United States, along with large portions of Texas, Arizona, Colorado, Kansas, Oklahoma, and Wyoming.

Chapter Seven

A ndrew Jackson is getting bad reviews.

From his enemies, of course—but not from the thousands of Americans who have thronged to Washington for his inauguration.

As the seventh president awaits the beginning of his address, he well knows America's elite despises him. Thomas Jefferson described Jackson as a "dangerous man." His predecessor, John Quincy Adams, has refused to attend today's speech, calling Jackson "a barbarian who could not write a sentence of grammar and could hardly spell his own name."

The press is brutal, as well: "Ought a convicted adulteress and her paramour be placed in the highest office of this free and Christian country?" wrote one newspaper.

Not to be outdone, former secretary of state Henry Clay, the man who sabotaged Jackson's presidential chances in 1824, describes the new president as "hypocritical, corrupt, and easily swayed by base men."

The criticism, of course, angers the short-tempered Jackson. But he knows the people love him because he is one of them. On this late winter day in Washington, Jackson stands on the East Front of the Capitol. More than twenty-one thousand spectators look back at him. Such is Jackson's popularity that half of this crowd traveled to Washington specifically for the inauguration, coming from as far away as his home state of Tennessee. The city's inns and boardinghouses do not have room for all of them, so many in the crowd sleep on tavern floors or outside. Pickpockets roam through the crowd. The streets are so choked that Andrew Jackson was forced to travel on foot from his suite at the National Hotel to the swearing-in and then enter the Capitol secretly through a basement door so as not to be mobbed.

This is the "People's Inaugural" Jackson had hoped for. The mood is exuberant, a condition heightened by the strong drink many in the crowd have been consuming since sunrise. When the general steps out into the pale sunshine between the two columns of the portico, the crowd erupts at the sight of their charismatic new president. "The peal of shouting that arose that rent the air and seemed to shake the very ground," one eyewitness recalls.

As Andrew Jackson prepares to speak, a twenty-four-gun salute heralds his appearance. The general is sixty-one years old and stands six feet one, with bright silver tufts of hair. A white scar mars his forehead. Jackson wears a black waistcoat and tie. He requires round-framed glasses to read his speech. Despite the thrill of being sworn in as president, this is also a time of mourning, for his sixty-one-year-old wife, Rachel, died just two months ago from a heart attack. A crushed Jackson blames John Quincy Adams for her death, charging that the former president and his supporters defamed Rachel during the 1828 campaign, calling her a bigamist. Adams departed the White House at 9:00 p.m. last night, spending the last hours of his presidency in a rented home in the northern portion of the city. In so doing, Adams evades a showdown with Jackson, but the new president will never forget those slights. Jackson arrived in Washington three weeks ago and since that time has intentionally snubbed President Adams—denying him all access to the transition.

Now, President Jackson is sworn in by Chief Justice John Marshall and begins his inaugural address. There is no amplification, and most in the crowd are too far away to hear him. A hush settles over the gathering, allowing the new president to speak without interruption.

"As long as our government is administered for the good of the people and is regulated by their will; as long as it secures to us the rights of person and of property, liberty of conscience and of the press, it will be worth defending," Jackson tells the crowd, his voice shrill but powerful.

There are fears that the crowd may attempt to storm the ceremony to get closer to Jackson. So, a ship's cable is stretched across the Capitol steps to block their way. Constables stand at the ready.

As soon as Jackson utters the final words of his address, spectators press forward. Jackson quickly walks through the west side of the Capitol, where an aide waits with a white horse. Jackson and his bodyguards gallop up Pennsylvania Avenue to the White House.

★★★

Then, chaos.

A public reception has been planned. Many revelers choose to skip the inauguration and go straight to the President's House. Those who cannot get through the doors climb through windows. President Jackson makes his way inside and is immediately confronted by the roar of the crowd. Glassware and presidential china are shattered by the rowdy mob. Waiters carrying great bowls of orange punch laced with bourbon are knocked to the ground, spilling gallons of liquid onto the White House carpeting. Men wearing boots stand on top of expensive upholstered chairs for a better view of Jackson. Trays of food are ravenously consumed even before servants can place them on tables. "High and low, black and white, old and young," marvels Supreme Court Justice Joseph Story, from "the highest and most polished down to the most vulgar of the nation."

The crowd presses toward President Jackson, eager to shake his hand. He finds himself against a wall with no way out. Jackson is exhausted and not feeling well. Long lines of well-wishers wait to enter. To prevent Jackson from being crushed, aides form a protective circle around him.

Chief steward Antoine Michel Giusta, a French deserter from Napoleon's army who had previously worked in the Adams White House as a valet, adroitly moves the party outside onto the lawn. But the furniture and carpets are already ruined. The damage will cost the federal government thousands of dollars.

Finally, President Andrew Jackson slips out of the White House and rides back to the National Hotel, where he can at last relax. He will skip tonight's inaugural ball because he is still in mourning.

"It was a proud day for the people," says Amos Kendall, a close adviser. "General Jackson is their own president. Plain in his dress, venerable in his appearance, unaffected and familiar in his manners. He was greeted by them with an enthusiasm which bespoke the hero of a popular triumph."

★★★

The opulence of Washington is something a young Andrew Jackson could never have imagined. Born into poverty on March 15, 1767, Jackson's father is already dead on the day of his birth. Just twenty-nine years old, Andrew Jackson Sr. is killed in a logging accident only three weeks before Andrew Jr. is born.

His mother, Elizabeth, does not remarry, preferring to rely on nearby family members to help raise her three sons. This is unusual for a woman in the Waxhaws region of the Carolinas, a backwoods frontier of poor soil and meager population. And while she offers her sons, Hugh, Robert, and young Andrew, little in the way of formal education, each inherits her tough Irish demeanor.

Soon, Andrew learns to shoot and hunt from uncles and cousins. He is quick to anger, independent, fond of fistfights, and guided by a deep sense of honor. The boy also suffers from a condition known as hyper-salivation, which causes him embarrassing episodes of drooling. This leads to more fights as he combats insults. Despite his limited education, Andrew shows a knack for cartography and is proficient enough in Latin that his mother hopes he will someday become a minister. Instead, he uses his skills to help the illiterate by reading books to them aloud. In 1776, a nine-year-old Jackson is called on to read the Declaration of Independence to the local community.

His brother Hugh dies first, succumbing to heat stroke during the Revolutionary War at the Battle of Stone Ferry. This leads thirteen-year-old Andrew and sixteen-year-old Robert to enlist in the local militia. Two years later, both are captured by the British. When Andrew refuses to polish an officer's boots, the Briton slashes him across the face with his saber. Andrew Jackson will carry the scar the rest of his life.

Soon after that, Robert dies from smallpox. Andrew also contracts the disease but lives. Elizabeth Jackson, mourning son Robert's loss, travels to Charleston, South Carolina, to treat Americans being held by the British as prisoners of war. There, she contracts cholera and dies in November 1781 at the age of forty-one.

As the Revolutionary War ends, a now orphaned Andrew Jackson immerses himself in the world of gambling: cards, cockfights, horse races. But higher aspirations soon lead him away from that lifestyle. He learns the law before he turns twenty. In 1788, Jackson moves to Nashville, Tennessee, where he is appointed public prosecutor at the age of twenty-one. By 1796, Jackson is elected to Congress as Tennessee becomes a state. One year later, the state legislature elects him to fill an open Senate seat. But Andrew Jackson is an unremarkable legislator and finds life in Philadelphia, the nation's capital at the time, boring. So, he quits the Senate in 1798, vowing to leave public life forever.

That does not happen.

Jackson returns to Nashville and is named a judge. Using that platform to increase his celebrity, he successfully runs for the elected position of major general of the Tennessee state militia, even though his only military experience consists of being a Revolutionary War courier.

That election takes place in 1802. The military title will mean little for the next ten years. But as the War of 1812 begins, "General" Andrew Jackson petitions President James Madison to fight the British by invading Canada.

But Madison has a better idea: he sends Jackson to New Orleans.

★★★

Twenty-six years earlier, upon first arriving in Nashville, Jackson boards at the home of Rachel Donelson, a widow whose husband had been one of the city's founders. He soon falls in love with her nineteen-year-old daughter, also named Rachel. But the black-haired teenaged beauty known for her "sweet oval face with smiles and dimples," in the words of one friend, is *already* married to a land speculator named Captain Lewis Robards. Then, in 1790, Robards deserts Rachel, going to Kentucky. Believing she is divorced, Rachel marries Andrew Jackson the following year. She is a Presbyterian fond of reading the Bible. The last thing she imagines is being known as an adulteress and bigamist.

However, as Andrew Jackson's celebrity in Nashville grows, it comes to light that Lewis Robards *never* divorced Rachel. She now has *two* husbands. A legal divorce is quickly arranged, and Rachel and Andrew undertake their wedding ceremony a second time in 1794. But charges of bigamy will follow Rachel for the next thirty-five years.

The Jackson marital situation erupts again in 1806, when Nashville attorney Charles Dickinson makes careless remarks about Rachel. Andrew Jackson demands that pistols settle the matter. In a duel, Jackson kills Dickinson. But he is hit in the chest by a musket ball, which misses his heart by inches. The projectile will remain lodged there for the rest of Jackson's life.

The bigamy insults, as well as their inability to have children, are sources of sadness to the Jacksons. But their years together will also be a time of great joy. Despite his hardscrabble upbringing, Andrew has developed some public polish. Rachel, brought up in the Nashville wilderness, can be coarse. She enjoys the unladylike habit of smoking a pipe. In time, Rachel will grow plump and matronly while her husband will remain thin.

The Jacksons live on four hundred acres outside Nashville. The farm is called Hermitage, a place of solitude. Andrew's many connections in the city have allowed him to branch out from law into land speculation and cotton trading. This money finances Hermitage. A whiskey distillery is constructed. Log cabins are built. In time, the plantation will feature a stately mansion, grow to more than a thousand acres, where he owns 150 slaves.*

Jackson is *not* kind to the enslaved. One woman is whipped for "putting on airs." Those caught trying to run away are placed in chains. A public reward for one escapee, a young man named Tom, includes a ten-dollar bonus for anyone inflicting one hundred lashes upon him.

In time, slave ownership will be the primary source of Andrew Jackson's wealth. When one young man dies as a result of cruel treatment, Jackson castigates the overseer, demanding "a full account of your guardianship with the loss of my property."

Hermitage is where Jackson will set out to lead the Tennessee militia in wars against the Creek Indians. His toughness will earn him the nickname "Old Hickory." Making up rules, Jackson revels in his military

---

* Hermitage is a major Tennessee tourist attraction to this day.

duties, executing treaties with Indian nations he has no power to authorize.*

It is, however, Jackson's January 8, 1815, victory at the Battle of New Orleans that makes him a national hero. Communications are so slow he does not know the war is already over. Though the fight takes place after the Treaty of Ghent ends the War of 1812, Americans accord Jackson the same adulation showered on George Washington when he defeated the British at Yorktown.†

President Andrew Jackson is elected as a man of the people. Yet he has the food and wine tastes of an aristocrat. The president rises at dawn and enjoys a breakfast of coffee, chicken hash, hot waffles, and blackberry jam. But it is the evening meal that shows the dichotomy in Jackson's food preferences. His favorite dish is something called "leather britches"—green beans cooked in bacon fat. He also enjoys fried ham, gravy, apple pie, and a country dish known as Old Hickory soup, made from nuts, hot water, and sugar. Jackson is equally fond of game such as venison and braised duck. He enjoys a tipple of bourbon before and after dinner.

The White House chef hired by Andrew Jackson is French. The president soon earns the nickname "King Andrew" by critics who mock him for gourmet cuisine served on fine china with expensive silver. The White House dining room table is in the shape of a horseshoe, a reminder of Jackson's fondness for horses. "Daniel Webster's punch," named for the American politician and Jackson supporter, loosens tongues with its potent mixture of brandy, champagne, claret, sugar, green tea, banana, pineapple, and strawberry. Oysters are a personal favorite.

In the absence of a wife, Jackson selects niece Emily Donelson to serve as First Lady. She has traveled from Nashville to live in the White House with her husband, presidential namesake Andrew Jackson Donelson, who works as an aide.

---

* Hickory is known for being one of the toughest types of wood.

† The Battle of New Orleans saw Jackson's force of 5,700 militia, regular infantry, US Marines, and French pirates attacked by 8,000 experienced British troops. Jackson's men were dug in near the Mississippi River in fortifications consisting of cotton bales and mud. The British suffered more than 2,000 casualties, Jackson's forces just 71.

At twenty-one, Emily is young for the role and not educated in the art of formal entertaining. Yet, as the daughter of Rachel's brother, Emily has a long fondness for the president and tends to him in moments of mourning. And while she gives birth to three children during the Jackson administration, she will add to the president's grief in 1836, dying of tuberculosis at the age of twenty-eight.

In addition to immediate family, President Jackson brings fourteen slaves to the White House from Hermitage—eight male and six female. Four of these—Adam, Jesse, Jim, and Emmeline—are younger than nine years old.

Thus, surrounded by vestiges of Tennessee, Andrew Jackson makes the White House a home. Toilet usage still requires a walk to an out-door privy in all sorts of weather, but running water is installed in the mansion for the first time, allowing Jackson to enjoy daily bathing in a combination "shower-bath." Partitions are set up between the family residence and White House corridors to prevent onlookers from see-ing the family. The squawk of Jackson's pet African gray parrot echoes through the corridors. Originally a gift to Rachel, he brought it with him from Tennessee. Poll, as the bird is named, has learned more than a few swear words from Jackson and is prone to letting loose, much to the surprise of White House visitors.

Late in his second term, President Jackson will gather his young nieces and nephews in the White House for a Christmas celebration. As the anniversary of Rachel's funeral, Christmas Eve is always a tough day for Jackson. Yet he takes the children for a sleigh ride through Washing-ton, delivering gifts to friends such as former First Lady Dolley Madison and Vice President Martin Van Buren. The children ask if Santa Claus might visit the White House that night. Jackson tells a story of a boy without a father who never received a single Christmas present but ad-vises the youngsters to hang their stockings before going to bed. For the first time in his life, President Jackson hangs one, too.*

Every stocking is full the next morning, including Jackson's. The pres-ident receives a corncob pipe and slippers. Later that Christmas Day, he presides over a snowball fight on the White House lawn.

---

* The boy the president was referring to was himself.

But such moments are few. From the date of his first inauguration to the time he leaves office, "King Andrew" will know one crisis after another.

★★★

First up, the Native American problem.

Andrew Jackson has years of experience dealing with the growing conflict between Indian tribes and the waves of settlers moving onto their lands. In May 1830, he seeks to solve the problem by separating white settlers and Indians completely. Tribes in Mississippi, Alabama, and Florida are stripped of lands they have owned for generations and are forcibly relocated west of the Mississippi. By the end of his two terms, Jackson will remove almost all tribes east of that river—seventy thousand individuals. The brutal relocation will become known as the Trail of Tears due to the thousands of men, women, and children who die from disease, unsanitary conditions, and exposure to the elements while making the long march to the Oklahoma Territory.

★★★

Meanwhile, the slavery controversy escalates.

In 1831, a group of slaves and black free men rebel, traveling from farm to farm in Virginia to free as many slaves as possible by force. More than fifty-five white people are killed in what will become known as Nat Turner's Rebellion, named after the thirty-year-old black preacher who plots the uprising.

The gamble will end badly for Turner, who is executed along with nineteen others who joined his cause.

But that is only the beginning. No longer satisfied to divide the nation into slave and free states, a new group known as abolitionists seeks to end slavery and emancipate slaves everywhere. This leads to violence in the South as pro-slavery advocates fight back. The controversy escalates as the territory of Texas gains independence from Mexico and then declares itself an independent republic—a step before being annexed into the United States.

But Andrew Jackson stalls on the annexation. He is secretly involved in Texas's fight for independence against Mexico, allowing guns and money to be smuggled to aid the rebellion. Jackson is also convinced that Great Britain is interested in gaining Texas as a new possession and then using the land as a base for further expansion into the Americas.

In addition, Texans are demanding the *right* to own slaves.

So, Jackson, believing annexation will split his increasingly fractured Democratic Party even further, does not allow Texas into the Union.

That is, until his last day in office, when the election of Martin Van Buren to replace him is already secured. Jackson recognizes Texas as an independent republic, although it will not be annexed until 1845.

Meanwhile, Jackson remains at odds with his former vice president, the pro-slavery John C. Calhoun. An ardent proponent of the southern way of life, Calhoun proposes "nullification," a practice that allows states to reject laws passed by the federal government. At first, this is done in response to tariffs Calhoun feels unfairly favor the North. But the vice president's obvious intent is to prevent the banning of slavery.

In a well-choreographed fit of pique, Calhoun resigns as Jackson's vice president in late 1832. The act is symbolic because Martin Van Buren has already been selected as vice president for Jackson's second term. Calhoun is quickly elected to a seat in the Senate by South Carolina. For the next four years, he will focus his energy on defeating Jacksonian policies across the board.

On March 3, 1837, Andrew Jackson's last full day as president, he states that his only regret as president is not shooting John C. Calhoun.[*]

President Jackson's two terms in office featured the following: the Trail of Tears, tariffs, slavery in Texas, the abolition of the national bank, and the admittance of Arkansas and Michigan to the Union. As president, he governed capably, with unbending will. Future presidents Abraham Lincoln, Franklin Roosevelt, and Donald Trump will publicly reference his presidency as a model for their own. In fact, when asked if Andrew Jackson could have prevented the Civil War, President Harry Truman wrote, "If Jackson had been president instead of Old Buch [James Buchanan] the war might never have happened."

---

[*] Although Andrew Jackson was a slave owner, he was violently opposed to any politician or state failing to follow the Constitution. He was staunchly pro-Union and opposed to secession.

Upon leaving office, Andrew Jackson retires to Tennessee and the Hermitage. He remains a powerful figure in American politics for the rest of his days. Eventually, he becomes a loud voice in favor of Texas joining the Union, which it did in December 1845. On June 8, 1845, at the age of seventy-eight, Jackson dies of edema, tuberculosis, and heart failure. He is surrounded by family and friends. The former president does not free his slaves upon dying.

Within two days, more than three thousand mourners travel to Hermitage for Jackson's funeral. Poll, the African gray parrot, is present as the service begins but is removed by order of the minister when he begins swearing during the Presbyterian liturgy.

The date is June 10, 1845. Andrew Jackson is laid to rest alongside his beloved Rachel.

★★★

The old adage says that "opposites attract." So it is that when President Andrew Jackson leaves the White House, his opposite in demeanor replaces him. The sycophantic Martin "Little Magician" Van Buren is elected the eighth president of the United States. The election takes place between November 3 and December 7, 1836.

He will not make anyone forget Andrew Jackson.

Chapter Eight

The Little Magician has lost his magic.

Martin Van Buren, Andrew Jackson's handpicked successor, receives the devastating news that powerful banks in New York City are in deep financial trouble. This is causing panic in the major commercial centers of Philadelphia, New Orleans, and Baltimore, in addition to New York City. Americans are making a run to tellers' windows, desperate to withdraw their funds. The economy is collapsing.

"The volcano has burst and overwhelmed New York," writes that city's former mayor, Philip Hone. "The commercial distress and financial embarrassment pervade the entire nation."

Van Buren is a youthful fifty-five years old. He recently promised to "tread generally in the footsteps of Andrew Jackson," believing that continuing his predecessor's fiscal policies is the best course for the nation.

True to his word, Van Buren has not veered from Jackson's way of governing.

The new president is most certainly leading the nation—straight into a major depression.

The United States has 850 banks. Hundreds of these will soon fail. Thousands of Americans will lose their jobs and homes. A coincidental bad wheat harvest will lead to outrageous food prices and widespread hunger.

Perhaps the worst thing is that this "Panic of 1837" was preventable.

The root cause goes back five years to President Jackson's decision to shutter America's national bank. Also, his Specie Circular of 1836 required all purchases of land to be made in gold and silver instead of paper or coin. That policy was supposed to prevent widespread inflation.[*]

In the face of the panic, Martin Van Buren still has time to make bold changes to America's financial system.

But he will do nothing.

Instead, the five-foot-six president acquires a *new* nickname: "Martin Van Ruin."

A little more than two months ago, it was a far different story. Van Buren and the physically declining Andrew Jackson ride to his inauguration in a wooden coach constructed from planks of the fabled USS *Constitution* warship—symbolism not lost on those aware that this year is the fiftieth anniversary of the US Constitution.

As the carriage parades through the streets of Washington, soldiers on horseback provide escort, followed by a marching band playing patriotic tunes. Twenty thousand people line the streets on this March morning, warmed by a "balmy vernal sun," in the words of one eyewitness.

The crowd has come to see Van Buren sworn in and hear him deliver his inaugural address. But today is also a very public farewell to Andrew Jackson. The crowd's adulation for Old Hickory clearly overshadows their affection for Van Buren. "The rising sun was eclipsed by the setting sun," writes Senator Thomas Hart Benton, referring to the waves of applause lavished on Jackson when he takes a bow from the Capitol porch.

Martin Van Buren stuns the crowd by mentioning the word *slavery* in his inaugural address. This is the first time that has ever been done. As a boy in upstate New York, the new president's family was financially

---

[*] Due to Jackson's decision to close the national bank, the United States did not issue currency at the time of the 1837 panic. Instead, each individual bank put out their own paper money. Financial institutions were not limited to how much they could produce, leading to an enormous supply. With the federal mandate that land payments be made in hard currency known as "specie" (gold and silver), paper money rapidly depreciated. When banks refused to redeem their notes for specie, as happened on May 10, 1837, commerce came to a halt.

middling but owned six slaves. Thus, Van Buren is not opposed to the practice. His speech makes this clear: "I must go into the presidential chair being a flexible and uncompromising opponent of every attempt on the part of Congress to abolish slavery in the District of Columbia against the wishes of the slaveholding states, and also with the determination to resist the slightest interference with [slavery] in the states where it exists."

This is obvious pandering to the southern states by a northerner and another clear reminder that Van Buren will not deviate from the policies of Andrew Jackson.

In closing, the new president makes another reference to Jackson, wishing "that he may yet long live to enjoy the brilliant evening of a well spent life."

Martin Van Buren is a successful politician in New York State, but on the national level he is lost without Andrew Jackson. He is not a natural leader. His reddish-brown hair will soon turn gray under the strain of governance. Van Buren has taken orders all his life. And he is good at that. But directing the fate of a growing nation is a far more difficult task.

Just after Jackson lost the 1824 election to John Quincy Adams, the savvy Van Buren steps up to console Old Hickory—telling Jackson that he could unseat Adams in 1828. He quickly ingratiates himself with the general and begins undermining the Adams administration.

Van Buren works in the Senate to form a pro-Jackson coalition. He is a believer in Jackson's interpretation of the Constitution: enhanced states' rights, a deferential federal government, and little funding from Congress for roads and other internal improvements. Van Buren even persuades a group of fellow Jackson acolytes to form a new political alliance known simply as the Democratic Party, a name taking the place of "Jacksonians."*

But Martin Van Buren's rising profile creates some scorn.

---

* The demise of the Federalists in 1824 left just one major political party, the Democratic-Republicans, who favored more power to the states. In 1824, John Quincy Adams won the presidency running as a Democratic-Republican. In 1828 and 1832, Andrew Jackson ran as a Democrat. But the group grew divided over the issue of presidential power during Jackson's second term. In the 1830s, a new party was formed, called the Whigs. It was a loose coalition of people who did not like Andrew Jackson. The Whig Party lasted into the 1850s.

"He is what the English call a dandy when he enters the Senate chambers," former congressman Davy Crockett of Tennessee says of the fastidious Van Buren. The homespun Crockett is known for his backwoods sense of humor and adventurous spirit. Crockett despises Van Buren so much that he promised friends he would move to Texas if the "dandy" is elected president—a vow he will keep.*

"In the morning," Crockett continues in his rant, "he struts and swaggers like a crow in the gutter. He is laced up in corsets such as women in town wear, and if possible, tighter than the rest of them. It would be difficult to say from his personal appearance whether he was a man or a woman."

Ironically, Martin Van Buren's upbringing is quite the opposite of a dandy. He comes from Dutch lineage, with his father a tavern owner and farmer. The future president is raised in humble but comfortable surroundings. English is his second language. His father served in the American Revolution even as Martin's birth in 1782 will make him the first president to not be alive during that conflict. This also means he was never a British subject, something no other American leader until now can state.

Van Buren's study of law begins at the age of fifteen. However, he soon learns about life as well. His instructor and mentor, Congressman Peter Silvester, takes note of Van Buren's simple coarse clothing and urges him to take more pride in his appearance—a message young Martin never forgets.

In 1803, at the age of twenty-one, Van Buren opens a law practice. Its success allows him to shift his focus to politics. By 1812, he is elected to the New York Senate. His "Albany Regency" becomes a well-known political machine—leading to his 1821 election to the United States Senate. This is when he earns the nickname "Little Magician" for his ability to craft political deals that seem impossible. His enemies prefer to call him the "Sly Fox."

In 1828, Van Buren returns home to run for governor of New York.

---

* Davy Crockett spent three terms in Congress—six years total. After that, he departs for Texas in November 1835. He is killed at the Battle of the Alamo on March 6, 1836, at the age of forty-nine.

Not only does he win, but just twelve weeks after taking office, President Andrew Jackson calls him to Washington to be his secretary of state.

In this vaunted position, so often seen as a stepping stone to the presidency, Van Buren serves as an extension of Jackson on the international stage. The bond between the two grows deeper in 1831, when Jackson requests that Van Buren serve as minister to Great Britain. The Senate confirmation vote ends in a draw, with Vice President John C. Calhoun set to cast the tiebreaking ballot.

Incredibly, Calhoun votes against Van Buren, and by extension Jackson, even though the three men are all in the same party. This is a public attempt to humiliate both Van Buren and the president. Calhoun cackles with delight that this is the end of Van Buren's career and brags to friends that his backstabbing will "kill [Van Buren] dead" politically.

But, as usual, Andrew Jackson has a plan of vengeance. Calhoun resigns as vice president, Jackson replacing him with Martin Van Buren as his running mate for a second term in 1832.

As everybody in Washington knows, Vice President Van Buren never disagrees with Andrew Jackson. Thus, a new word is formed that becomes synonymous with agreement.

Among Martin Van Buren's many nicknames is "Old Kinderhook," in reference to his town of birth. This is often shortened to OK. Coincidentally, Andrew Jackson prints this abbreviation on official documents. When he wants to approve something as all correct, he simply writes *OK*. Despite his proficiency in Latin and law, Jackson is such a poor speller that he believes *all correct* is spelled *ole kurrek*.

Thus, *OK* enters the American lexicon as a verbal affirmation and eventually becomes the most used word in the entire world.*

Like Andrew Jackson, President Van Buren lives in the White House without a spouse. His wife, Hannah, whom he marries in 1807, dies in 1819 from tuberculosis. The couple have five sons together.

---

* On March 23, 1839, "OK" will appear in the *Boston Morning Post*, the first time that term is used in print. In 1840, when Van Buren runs for a second term, his supporters will form "OK Clubs" around the country, using the slogan "OK is all correct."

Van Buren is a man not prone to self-reflection, yet he spends much time writing letters and reading in addition to his presidential duties. He is also fond of entertaining, spending large sums on wine and champagne. To help arrange White House functions, former First Lady Dolley Madison introduces her cousin Angelica Singleton to the president. An alliance is sealed when the president's son, Abraham, begins courting the vibrant young South Carolinian. Thirty-one-year-old Abraham and twenty-year-old Angelica are married in the White House on November 27, 1838. Angelica takes up residence in the mansion with her new husband, providing the White House with a live-in hostess for the first time since the death of Andrew Jackson's daughter-in-law in 1836.

But soon Angelica makes a mistake. The Panic of 1837 crushes the Van Buren presidency but not his daughter-in-law's lavish entertaining style. These ostentatious displays will badly damage Van Buren's reelection chances in 1840.

Most Americans see themselves as ordinary people. And, as the financial panic pushes citizens to their breaking point, President Van Buren's continuing extravagance is widely criticized. In fact, Whig congressman Charles Ogle ridicules Van Buren, calling him a "Democratic peacock."

The damage is done. As the campaign of 1840 emerges, Van Buren's opponent, William Henry Harrison from Ohio, is portrayed as a common man.

Martin Van Buren loses the election of 1840 in a landslide. William Henry Harrison becomes the first Whig elected president.

Image aside, Van Buren was a poor president who simply could not solve vexing problems. The nation does not emerge from the economic disaster of 1837 for six years—long after Van Buren has been voted out of office.

And Old Kinderhook is ineffectual in many other ways. He is unable to halt further warfare between the Seminole Indians and Florida settlers. The matter of Texas annexation lingers throughout his presidency as Van Buren is reluctant to deal with the complex matter.

And in the divisive *Amistad* case before the Supreme Court, he takes a rare public stand, siding with slaveholders. That further alienates him from the anti-slavery electorate.

Martin Van Buren leaves Washington and returns to his hometown in rural New York. But he runs for president again in 1848, this time representing the Free Soil Party. The Little Magician receives just 10 percent of the vote.

Martin Van Buren lives long enough to see Abraham Lincoln elected the sixteenth president of the United States. He is seventy-nine when he dies at Lindenwald, his estate in Kinderhook.

The end of Van Buren's term, 1840, is a dismal year. Many citizens are destitute and angry. So, they turn to a man of action.

Old Tippecanoe is ready for his close-up.

Chapter Nine

APRIL 3, 1841
WASHINGTON, DC
8:30 P.M.

William Henry Harrison utters his last words.

America's ninth president lies on his deathbed in the White House residence. The celebrated Indian fighter has been in office just one month. It is his ritual to start each morning with a long walk, and ten days ago he got caught out in a driving rainstorm. Harrison was not wearing a coat or hat. Two days later, the president began experiencing symptoms of pneumonia. Yet Harrison insisted on leaving the mansion yet again for another walk the following morning. He is a robust man, known to be kind and humble, raised in Virginia but living on the Ohio frontier for decades, prior to statehood, when the region was known as the Northwest Territory. The president is five feet eight, sixty-eight years old, and wears his gray-brown hair combed forward over his forehead. He is the oldest man ever elected to the White House up until that time. Harrison is also the last former British subject to take the highest office in the land.

Now, Harrison's pulse is weakening. His fingers and toes are cold and blue. He is confused. His wife of forty-six years, Anna, is not at his bedside. She remains at their farm in North Bend, Ohio. The sixty-five-year-old First Lady was too ill to make the long steamboat and railroad journey to Washington for last month's inauguration.

So, President Harrison will die alone.

His doctor, Thomas Miller, diagnoses Harrison's condition as liver congestion and pneumonia of the lower lobe of the right lung. Miller has prescribed opium, castor oil, bloodletting, and enemas, but nothing works.

Tragically, Dr. Miller is treating the *wrong* disease. President William Henry Harrison is not dying from pneumonia but something far worse—and very preventable.

Usually vigorous and healthy, Harrison's morning walks have a purpose. He journeys to the local farmer's market to inspect and buy produce for the White House dinner table. This is not only a task the general enjoys but one he insists on performing, for he has a deep fondness for fresh food. Harrison's favorite meal is known as burgoo, also called squirrel soup. He is an enthusiastic consumer of vegetables—beets, peas, cabbage, cauliflower, celery, and artichokes, all available for purchase when in season.

Like President John Adams, Harrison is also extremely fond of hard apple cider. He makes no attempt to hide this indulgence. Indeed, the president's campaign rallies were notable for the amount of liquor consumed by his supporters—and Harrison himself. He drank so much that some joked he should be named the "Hard Cider Candidate."

William Henry Harrison is taken ill before he can even form a White House routine. He is popular with ordinary Americans but has had no time to formulate policy.

So it is that Harrison's legacy will not be defined by legislation, daring foreign relations, or fiscal decisions. What he will be remembered for is his presidential campaign.

Displaying a populism and theater unlike anything George Washington ever imagined, Harrison viciously attacked his rival, President Martin Van Buren. He scorned the Little Magician as a "fop" and even accused Van Buren's running mate, Richard Johnson, of sleeping with

African American women.* Johnson is dropped from the ticket, leaving Van Buren without a vice presidential choice.

Harrison, hero of the Battle of Tippecanoe, runs on the slogan "Tippecanoe and Tyler, Too," a reference to running mate John Tyler of Virginia. His rallies sometimes feature parades three miles long with tens of thousands of supporters. Harrison's campaign panders openly to the electorate, offering food and drink to those who would vote for him. Normally a dull, stolid individual, Harrison draws enthusiastic applause when he concludes his stump speech with a series of Indian war whoops—reminding the crowd that his victory over the legendary chief Tecumseh helped define the western frontier.

William Henry Harrison's impact on presidential campaigning can also be seen in terms and words still used today. It was the first mass public campaign for the presidency.

One bunch of his Whig supporters push a large ball made of paper and tin, decorated with pro-Harrison slogans, more than a hundred miles. Other backers distribute bottles of whiskey in log cabin–shaped bottles to rally attendees. The liquor is distilled by the E. C. Booz company.

So, in a single campaign, Americans acquire *keep the ball rolling* and *booze.*

★★★

Contrary to his public image, Harrison was born into a wealthy family in 1773. His father is Benjamin Harrison, a former Virginia governor and signer of the Declaration of Independence.

Young William studies the classics and history at Hampden-Sydney College in Prince Edward County and then continues his education at the College of Philadelphia—later to be known as the University of Pennsylvania. There, he learns medicine under Dr. Benjamin Rush, another Founding Father and signer of the Declaration. But in 1791, the eighteen-year-old Harrison is forced to quit school. His father has died.

---

* Richard Johnson, a lawyer, becomes a politician based on his heroism in the War of 1812. He campaigned to end debtor's prisons, reform the army, and support the widows of fallen soldiers. In 1815, Johnson purchased a female slave named Julia Ann Chinn, who bore him two children. But Kentucky law stipulated that Johnson and Chinn could not marry. Instead, the slave served as Johnson's common-law wife until her death from cholera in 1833. Up until the end, he would not emancipate her.

His oldest brother, Carter, inherits the estate and refuses to further fund William's education.

The future president does not enjoy his medical studies, so he is not saddened by this turn of events. However, he lacks an inheritance and needs a career. Longtime family friend Henry "Light-Horse" Lee, governor of Virginia and yet another signer of the Declaration of Independence, arranges a low-level commission in the army. Harrison is ordered to serve in what is known as the Northwest Territory—what will later become Ohio and Indiana.*

It is during this time that Harrison meets Anna Tuthill Symmes, a New Yorker whose father has just traveled west and purchased land on the "north bend" of the Ohio River. The couple marry in 1795, Harrison at twenty-two, Anna nineteen. They will go on to have ten children.

Harrison resigns his commission in 1798. He establishes a reputation as one of the finest horse breeders in the Northwest Territory, which becomes his primary source of income. He goes on to represent the Ohio Territory in Congress and then serves as governor of the Indiana Territory. Among Harrison's duties is quelling Indian attacks on frontier settlements. On November 7, 1811, a coalition of tribes led by a charismatic chief named Tecumseh attacks Harrison's armed force at their camp along the Tippecanoe River. Harrison suffers the loss of 190 men but repulses the attack by more than one thousand warriors. Only later does he learn that Tecumseh himself was not present.

On October 5, 1813, during the War of 1812, Harrison and Tecumseh finally clash. The general defeats a combined British and Indian force. Tecumseh is killed during the fight. Though Harrison did not pull the trigger, this elevates William Henry Harrison to the level of national hero.†

---

* "Light-Horse Harry" Lee, so nicknamed for his ability on horseback, served as an officer under General George Washington during the Revolutionary War. Fort Lee in New Jersey, the modern terminus of the George Washington Bridge into Manhattan, is named in his honor. He is also the father of Civil War general Robert E. Lee.

† The Battle of the Thames, as this fight was known, took place in Canada. Chief Tecumseh and his 1,000 warriors were joined by 800 British troops in the clash against Harrison's attacking force of 3,760 US soldiers. The Americans were attempting to retake control of the Detroit region. Tecumseh was killed during the fighting. Harrison takes credit for the chief's death because he is the commanding general, but it is Martin Van Buren's 1840 running mate, Richard Johnson, who actually pulls the trigger. American soldiers stripped and scalped Tecumseh's body and then peeled off pieces of his skin as souvenirs. The location of the chief's remains is unknown to this day.

Harrison eventually resigns his commission and returns to the family estate at North Bend. There, Anna gives birth to their tenth child, James, who dies from cholera in 1819 at the age of four.

Meanwhile, William Henry Harrison leaves the family for large periods of time, serving in the US Congress and Senate, the Ohio state senate, and as minister to Colombia in South America. Along the way, he develops a strong belief system. He advocates pushing Native Americans off their lands to make way for settlers. As a slaveholder, he does not think Congress should exclude slaves from these new territories. He thought slavery was a matter left to the states and that the federal government should have no role in determining whether there should be slavery in the territories—or individual states. As a politician, he didn't want to alienate southern voters so he didn't condemn it. "We might look forward to a day when a North American sun might not look down on a slave," he writes.

Harrison is a humble man, nicknamed "General Mum" for his reluctance to push his opinion on others. The Reverend Timothy Flint, a local minister who visits North Bend frequently, describes him as "urbane, hospitable, kind, and utterly unpretentious."

As his children grow older, Harrison's small income and savings are stretched by the expenses of college and weddings. In addition, he takes on the significant debts of his son William upon his death in 1838. To help, friends in Ohio arrange for Harrison to serve as clerk of courts for Hamilton County, if only to provide him an income, a position he holds until elected president. Sadly, though many of William and Anna's children grow into adulthood, six will die before their father. Nine will die before Anna's death in 1864.*

In 1836, William Henry Harrison decides to run for president under the banner of the Whig Party. He has three rivals, so, predictably, the four Whigs split their party vote. Democratic candidate Martin Van Buren emerges triumphant.

---

* The last surviving child will be son John Scott Harrison (1804–1878). He is the father of Benjamin Harrison, who will serve as the twenty-third president of the United States. This makes John, himself a member of the House of Representatives, the only man to be the son and father of a president.

Four years later, William Henry Harrison is the only Whig candidate. Some critics claim he has no place in Washington, having spent much of his adult life in the wilderness. In reality, Harrison had government experience in Washington and back in Ohio and Indiana. Nonetheless, Harrison is portrayed by many as a dumb old backwoods general who would rather sit on his log cabin porch drinking hard cider than run the country. Yet Harrison's raucous campaign combines with the failed presidency of Van Buren to lead him to an easy victory. The new president wins the electoral vote 234–60.

Anna is most unhappy. She tells confidants, "I wish my husband's friends had left him where he is, happy and contented in retirement." Yet she campaigns vigorously for him, entertaining voters at their North Bend home. The death of thirty-four-year-old son Benjamin, a married medical doctor, five months before the election ends her campaigning. Now, at age sixty-five, Anna is soon to be the oldest First Lady up to that time. She plans to be in Washington by May, when the weather is warm enough for travel.

William Henry Harrison is inaugurated in a driving rain on March 4, 1841. He delivers the longest address on record, more than two hours. Attempting to assuage fears that he is too old for the job, Harrison shows his frontier toughness by not wearing a coat, hat, or gloves.

Some believe that macho posture led to his death.

They are wrong.

There is, in the Washington, DC, of 1841, a large area where human waste—"night soil," as it is known—is dumped in a field near the White House. The city has no sewer system. This excrement is collected from chamber pots and outhouses and then hauled to this field each day by government workers. The refuse becomes a breeding ground for the *Salmonella* bacteria responsible for typhus and its derivative, paratyphus. Together, these are known as endemic fever and wreak havoc on an individual's gastrointestinal tract. Mental confusion, dizziness, diarrhea, and vomiting soon follow as the body lapses into septic shock.

A small stream runs through the middle of this field of waste, forming a marsh. Incredibly, this is also the main water supply for the White House, which is seven blocks downstream. Weakened by the sickness brought on by his long walks in the cold and rain, Harrison's body is not strong enough to fight off the bacteria in his drinking water.

Dr. Miller's choice to administer enemas to President Harrison is unfortunate because these perforate the ulcers in the intestines caused by *Salmonella*. The bacteria then enter the bloodstream. This, in turn, makes the president's body septic.

And that is deadly.

President William Henry Harrison dies at 12:30 a.m. on April 4, 1841. He becomes the first president to pass away while in office, having served just thirty-two days. Church bells toll in mourning. The funeral service is held in the White House East Room before Harrison's body is transported to Ohio for burial.

Vice President John Tyler is visiting family in Williamsburg, Virginia. Two days later, he returns to Washington and is sworn in as the tenth president of the United States.

"Tyler Too" will spell trouble for the expanding United States. He is a man of divided loyalties, and the damage he will soon do will echo throughout history.

Chapter Ten

President John Tyler has no friends.

"His Accidency," as enemies refer to America's tenth president, is being expelled from his own political party. It is five months since the stubborn fifty-one-year-old Virginian took office. The problems began on day one. His decision to immediately be sworn in as chief executive rather than serve as "acting president" sets an unpopular precedent. Many, such as Whig Party leader Henry Clay, do not believe the Constitution allows for a vice president to automatically assume the highest office in the land. Clay still refers to Tyler as a "regent"—a placeholder. His handpicked choice to lead the nation is Senator Samuel Southard of New Jersey, a man he knows he can control. Southard currently serves as president pro tempore of the Senate and is first in line of succession to the presidency after Tyler. Henry Clay will stop at nothing to see that come true.*

Long before the 1840 election, there were doubts the aging William

---

* Article II of the Constitution is vague about whether or not the vice president automatically becomes president if the person in power is unfit to remain in office or dead. Tyler's precedent was followed soon after by other vice presidents after deaths and assassinations. It is not until the Twenty-Fifth Amendment, passed in 1965 and ratified in 1967, that this line of succession is codified.

Henry Harrison would live long enough to serve a full term. Tyler is asked about this repeatedly during the campaign but makes it clear he has no desire to become president should bad fortune befall Harrison. Indeed, after being sworn in as vice president on March 4, 1841, Tyler returns home to Virginia to be with his ill wife, Letitia, thinking himself unneeded in Washington.

Harrison concurs and does nothing to stop him.

After William Henry Harrison dies on April 4, 1841, things begin to move quickly. The cabinet immediately votes that Tyler will serve as "acting president" until they can determine a successor. These men take their orders from Senator Clay, who believes he alone has the power to choose America's next leader.*

At sunrise on April 5, a messenger from Washington knocks on the door of Tyler's Williamsburg, Virginia, home to pass along the grim news. Tyler tells his family over an early breakfast and then begins the 150-mile journey to Washington. He travels twenty-one hours by steamship and then train.

He arrives at 4:00 a.m. the next morning, eager to be sworn in. Tyler immediately summons Federal District Court judge William Cranch to his room at Brown's Indian Queen Hotel to deliver the oath. President Tyler then moves immediately into the White House.

As a sign of respect for William Henry Harrison, the new president doesn't fire a single member of Harrison's cabinet. This is a mistake. Very quickly, they will try to undermine him.

That very day, the cabinet informs Tyler that he must put all important presidential decisions to a vote of this advisory group, letting the majority decide policy. Tyler refuses. "I shall be pleased to avail myself to your counsel and advice," he tells the group during the first White House meeting. "But I can never consent to being dictated what I can and cannot do."

Tyler delivers a shocking handwritten message to Congress on April 9, stating he is done with the Whig Party. Tyler now espouses the ideals of

---

* The cabinet was composed of six members: the secretaries of state, treasury, war, and navy, as well as the postmaster general and attorney general. They all subjugated themselves to Clay.

a Jacksonian Democrat. So, a man who was elected vice president on the Whig ticket has jumped to the opposition.

Tyler immediately supports closing the national bank, thereby giving states more economic power. This is exactly the opposite of Whig policy.

The battle of wills continues throughout the sticky Washington summer, coming to a head on September 11, 1841. Senator Henry Clay introduces a bill seeking to resurrect the national bank. Tyler vetoes it— twice. In a display of rehearsed theatrics, cabinet members then offer their resignations. Only Secretary of State Daniel Webster chooses to remain.

Two days later, Clay orders that John Tyler be kicked *out* of the Whig Party. The president is branded a traitor. Senator Clay's declaration is sent to newspapers throughout America. Clay and the Whigs then demand that Tyler resign the presidency.

He refuses.

But Clay is not done. One year later, as John Tyler vetoes yet another bill endorsed by the Whigs, Congress begins the first proceedings to impeach a president.

But there are not enough votes to do that. So, Henry Clay is forced to settle for a simple censure attempt by the Congress.*

Much more horrifying is the secession issue. It is during the presidency of John Tyler that the United States of America actually begins to dissolve. Tyler is a virulent slaver, born into a landed Virginia family. This is precisely *why* he was chosen to be William Henry Harrison's running mate—a wealthy and polished southerner balancing out the gruff frontiersman. The Whigs believe the ticket would appeal to Americans on both sides of the slavery issue.

---

* There are no legal implications for a congressional censure, which is also known as a reprimand. Former president and now congressman John Quincy Adams and his fellow Whigs led the movement to censure Tyler in 1842, claiming "continued and unrelenting exercise of executive legislation, by the alternate gross abuse of Congressional power and bold assumptions of power not vested in him by any law." To the Whigs' dismay, Tyler's censure resolution did not gather enough votes to pass the House.

John Tyler's path to the White House begins with his birth on March 29, 1790. From childhood, raised on the family plantation named Greenway, he is taught to believe in the infallibility of the Constitution. He grows into a thin, six-foot-tall young man with a sharp nose, weak chin, blue eyes, and light-brown hair. Like many of Virginia's elite, he attends the College of William and Mary and studies law.

Tyler's political career begins at age twenty-six, when he is elected to Congress. He goes on to serve as governor of Virginia and then returns to Washington as a senator. By the time John Tyler becomes president, he is the father of nine children—ranging in age from newborn to fifteen. He has built a new Virginia plantation home called Woodburn, where he owns twenty-nine enslaved men and women—half of them under the age of ten.

Once in the White House, Tyler must confront the dual issues of slavery and the annexation of Texas, which he supports. "Tyler and Texas!" will be his 1844 reelection campaign slogan.

But there will be no reelection for John Tyler. He is not even nominated for president. The Tyler administration descends into chaos, both political and personal.

The date is September 9, 1842. Letitia Christian Tyler sits alone in her wheelchair, reading. Her room is on the second floor of the White House, where she is occasionally visited by distinguished visitors like authors Charles Dickens and Washington Irving. But mostly she is by herself, not taking any part in her husband's social calendar. She refuses to read anything other than the Bible or books of prayer.

Letitia, a name meaning "happiness," married John Tyler when both were twenty-three years old. Seven of their nine children have survived infancy. In her lifetime, the dark-haired, pale-skinned Letitia has been First Lady of Virginia, Second Lady of the United States, and now America's First Lady. She is fifty-one years old and is considered a warm and gracious person by all who know her. Depression and confusion, however, have now taken control of her life.

Shortly before her husband is elected vice president, Letitia suffers a stroke. But her health stabilizes, making it possible for her to travel from the plantation to the White House.

Now, alone in her room, Letitia Tyler has another stroke. She dies the following morning. Thus, Letitia becomes the youngest First Lady to pass away while her husband is in office. Her coffin will lie in state in the East Room before being returned to Virginia for burial. A devastated John Tyler orders the White House to be decorated in black to show mourning.

★★★

Managing the rigors of his job begins draining John Tyler. He loves having his children close to him in the White House, but that is a distraction. The president is also fond of animals, owning a greyhound and a favorite horse named The General. Tyler will soon keep a canary, Johnny Ty, who will die after the president tries to mate it with another canary—only to find out later that both birds are males.

Another distraction is that after being married for nearly thirty years, the widower Tyler is lonely. And, at age fifty-two, the president is still a relatively young man.

Months before his wife's death, President Tyler is introduced to the beautiful twenty-two-year-old New York socialite Julia Gardiner at a White House reception. He is smitten, as are many of the other men in the room. Julia soon receives marriage proposals from two congressmen and a Supreme Court justice.

The young woman returns to Washington the following February. The now-single president invites Julia to a private card game at the White House. Afterward, he playfully chases her around the tables.

Thus begins the secret romance between President Tyler and a woman thirty years his junior. He proposes two weeks after the card game. The couple weds in New York City one year later, making John Tyler the first president to get married while in office. Only after their nuptials are complete does Tyler release the news to the American public.[*]

The nation is intrigued. There is some criticism about the age difference, and many feel the president married too soon after Letitia's death. But otherwise, America is curious about the new First Lady. She soon shows herself to be an adept hostess, throwing formal balls and dinners

---

[*] Julia Gardiner was raised in East Hampton, Long Island. She is the daughter of David Gardiner, a wealthy landowner and state senator. The Gardiner family owns an island in the Long Island Sound to this day.

that return the White House to the European elegance of the John Quincy Adams years. She dresses in the finest gowns, often wearing feathers in her hair.

Public dancing has long been considered taboo, so there is a bit of puritanical fury directed at Julia when she introduces the waltz and polka at White House functions. President Tyler had been reluctant to dance in public until she coaxes him onto the floor. Composers soon write "Julia waltzes" in her honor, which prove popular with the American electorate.

Julia Tyler also enjoys drinking at public functions. This angers the growing temperance movement.

The First Lady is proud of being nontraditional. She drives a coach pulled by four well-groomed horses, keeps a pair of Irish wolfhounds as pets, and enjoys receiving guests while sitting in an armchair slightly elevated above the rest of the room. When President Tyler offers annexation to Texas in 1845, she begins wearing the pen he used to sign that legislation around her neck.*

By 1844, John Tyler's cabinet is completely composed of southern conservatives. The agenda is tariff protection for cotton and tobacco planters, states' rights, and pro-slavery protection—ideals that will drive the impending Civil War.

The following year, Tyler signs a bill making Texas the twenty-eighth state in the Union. But he makes the huge mistake of asking Secretary of State John C. Calhoun to handle the negotiations. Calhoun is a secessionist who once attempted to take South Carolina out of the Union. His ardent pro-slavery views are so powerful that abolitionists fear the addition of Texas will mean another slave state. Tensions rise. But then comes a temporary savior.

Andrew Jackson is back.

The seventy-seven-year-old retired president publicly comes out in

---

* The thoroughly loyal Julia Tyler is the architect of a new presidential anthem. She orders the Marine Band to play it when her husband walks into an official reception. To this day, "Hail to the Chief" is part of White House protocol.

favor of Tyler's admission of Texas. But Jackson has not lost his guile. He believes John Tyler is incapable of being reelected. So, behind the scenes, he urges the president to pull out of the 1844 campaign.

Tyler refuses, even though he has little support in either party.

The upshot is that a relatively unknown Tennessee politician, James K. Polk, running on the Democratic ticket, wins the presidency.

On his last day in office, John Tyler is handed his final rebuke: for the first time in American history, Congress overrides the presidential veto of a minor appropriations bill. Thoroughly humiliated, Tyler leaves Washington on March 3, 1845, returning to his estate called Sherwood Forest near Richmond, Virginia. Julia accompanies him on the 110-mile journey south. The now former First Lady is happy to be leaving the White House—she wants to start having children. Her northern roots are in the distant past. Julia is looking forward to becoming a southern belle.

John and Julia sire seven children at Sherwood Forest, where he runs the plantation. The rapid birthing means John Tyler is now the father of sixteen, the most offspring for an American president.

Things take a turn for the worse when the Civil War breaks out in 1861. The former president chooses to serve in the Confederate House of Representatives. Many label him a traitor to the United States. A few months later, on January 18, 1862, Tyler dies of a stroke while staying at the Exchange Hotel in Richmond. He is seventy-one years old. Without much ceremony, Tyler is buried at the Hollywood Cemetery in Richmond. This is also the final resting place of James Monroe.[*]

Her husband's death shocks Julia. And the war forces her to return to family in New York. Meanwhile, Union troops capture Sherwood Forest and free the family slaves, turning the mansion into a desegregated

---

[*] Hollywood Cemetery is so-named for the stately rows of holly trees. In addition to two presidents, the cemetery will become the burial site for eighteen thousand Confederate soldiers, Confederate president Jefferson Davis, and generals J. E. B. Stuart and George Pickett.

school. Julia Tyler remains in New York after the war, losing much of her fortune in the Panic of 1873. However, she eventually repurchases Sherwood Forest from the Bank of Virginia. It remains in the Tyler family to this day.

On June 10, 1889, Julia Gardiner Tyler suffers a stroke while staying at the Exchange Hotel, dying in the same place and of the same cause as her husband. They are buried together at the Hollywood Cemetery.

John Tyler will go down in history as having few admirers. His accomplishments in office were scant, despite the addition of Texas to the Union. His defection to the Confederate cause sullies the presidential legacy. Tyler entered Washington having few friends and left it with *no* friends.

So, the nation, descending into slavery-driven turbulence, badly needs a new leader. In 1845, that politician emerges.

He will be a man of destiny.

Chapter Eleven

President James K. Polk has a stomachache. As usual.

The letter he holds in his hand is brief and to the point: "Hostilities may now be considered as to have commenced," writes General Zachary Taylor, a man whom Polk despises.

Nearly two thousand miles from the president's White House office, on a hot and dusty Texas morning, Mexican troops wade the Rio Grande and cross into Texas. Armies of the two nations have been skirmishing for months. Two weeks later, US forces take the offensive and push into Mexico. Finally, it is war.

With the exception of ongoing Indian wars, the invasion is the first time since the War of 1812 that US forces are engaging another nation. President Polk incited this war, convincing Congress to vote for a Declaration of War. Now that it has begun, the United States *must* win at all costs. Nothing less than total victory is required—and the world is watching. Technological advances in papermaking have made the news more affordable to citizens of all income levels. A newspaper can be had for as little as a penny. Even Europeans are eager for updates about the American war with Mexico.

"A retreat," writes the French *Journale des Debats*, in a story reprinted in the *Times* of London, "would be translated into a defeat. The Mexicans would be persuaded that they had beaten the Americans."

No wonder the president has indigestion—a chronic condition.*

President Polk has been in office a little more than a year. He has promised to serve only one term and is working so hard that his wife, Sarah, feels he is headed to an early grave—which he is. The eleventh president is a dour man. Gray eyes. Brown hair. Small in stature. The fifty-year-old Polk prides himself on being the consummate professional when it comes to shaking hands, the scourge of all politicians, favoring an aggressive technique of grasping the fingers instead of the fist to prevent larger men from overpowering his grip.

Polk is America's second president from Tennessee. He grew up worshiping Andrew Jackson, the first. In fact, it was Jackson who introduced James Polk to the intelligent and well-read Sarah, who is six years younger than her husband.

At the center of Polk's presidential agenda is an ambitious plan to double the size of the United States. War with Mexico, should it be successful, will secure lands known as Upper California, Colorado, and New Mexico. Whether or not these territories become slave havens is unclear. President Polk owns dozens of slaves and sees no reason why the practice should not expand westward.

In his first Annual Message, delivered December 2, 1845, Polk writes that the United States should cover *all* of North America. As a wave of European immigrants arrives—particularly the Irish, fleeing a potato famine in their homeland—the nation is pushing west. The former frontiers of Ohio and Missouri are completely settled and are now jumping-off points for expansion. Americans are traveling in wagons and horseback across the continent to settle Pacific regions like the Oregon Territory, which Polk is intent on seizing from Great Britain.

A new doctrine known as Manifest Destiny guides the president's thinking. This belief holds that America should span all territories between the Atlantic and the Pacific—"sea to shining sea." A new American naval academy has opened in Maryland to complement the army school at West Point. Indeed, many young lieutenants recently graduated from

---

* James K. Polk suffered from diverticulitis, an inflammation of the digestive tract. This caused severe abdominal pain and forced him to eat a high-fiber diet, also making him prone to passing wind.

"the Point" are now fighting in Mexico. Their names will soon become synonymous with the Civil War: Ulysses S. Grant, Robert E. Lee, James Longstreet, and Stonewall Jackson.

But all that is to come. First, Polk must win the war with Mexico.[*]

The roots of the Mexican-American War can be found in Texas. Mexico City does not recognize it as American territory, and its admission to the Union has enraged Mexican officials. The United States and her southern neighbor also cannot agree on the border line separating the two countries, the Mexicans favoring a line much farther north than the Rio Grande.

The specter of war is heavily debated in the US Congress, with Representative Abraham Lincoln among those publicly doubting its necessity. In Massachusetts, a philosopher named Henry David Thoreau refuses to pay his taxes, believing the money will be used for the war. Thoreau is promptly thrown in jail.

President Polk intentionally aggravates the situation on January 13, 1846, by ordering General Zachary Taylor to lead troops into contested land. Polk orders Taylor to specifically claim the Rio Grande as part of US territory. "We have not one particle of right to be here," Colonel Ethan Allen Hitchcock writes home. "It looks like the government sent a small force on purpose to start a war, so as to have a pretext for taking California and as much of the country as it chooses."[†]

In April 1846, American troops blockade the Mexican city of Matamoros. In response, Mexico sends an army into Texas, giving Polk the pretext he has been seeking. "Mexico has passed the boundary of the United States, has invaded our territory, and has shed American blood upon the American soil," he tells Congress. "The two nations are now at war."[‡]

---

[*] On July 1, 1845, New York Jacksonian Democrat John L. O'Sullivan coins the term *Manifest Destiny* as a rebuttal to those who oppose the annexation of Texas. Sullivan also uses the phrase *sea to shining sea* to describe the extent of his vision.

[†] Hitchcock is the grandson of Revolutionary War hero Ethan Allen. He graduated from West Point in 1817. During the Civil War, he served as a major general for the Union.

[‡] The Mexican-American War lasted two years and ended with US troops occupying Mexico City. The Treaty of Guadalupe Hidalgo, signed on February 2, 1848, ended the conflict. American losses will amount to fifteen thousand killed—mostly from diseases such as cholera. Mexican losses will number at least twenty-five thousand killed, with twenty thousand missing in action, most of whom deserted.

★★★

It has been a dazzling first year in office for Polk, a man whom few thought would make it to adulthood, let alone be elected president. Perpetually ill as a child, he frustrated his rugged planter father, Samuel.

James Knox Polk was born in North Carolina in 1795, with his family moving to Columbia, Tennessee, soon after. He is a weak child, unable to perform manual labor on the plantation and showing little interest in his schoolwork.

In 1812, as young James continues to suffer from excruciating chronic pain in his lower extremities, the decision is made to seek the help of a top doctor. Samuel Polk and his son ride 250 miles on horseback from their Tennessee plantation to the office of Kentucky surgeon Ephraim McDowell. The Edinburgh-trained doctor is at the forefront of the new field of abdominal medicine. McDowell will later write that he found the teenager to be "uncouth and uneducated, a meager boy with pallid cheeks, oppressed and worn down with disease."

After a consultation, seventeen-year-old James is led into an operating theater. He is placed on a table and immobilized with thick leather straps. His pants are removed, and surgeon's assistants take firm hold of his legs. Anesthesia will not be discovered for three more decades, so James is given ample portions of brandy to dull the coming pain. The memory of this moment is so intense that Polk will never again drink spirits.

Using a sharp knife, Dr. McDowell slices open the perineum and inserts a slim, pointed tool known as a gorget through the prostate gland and into the bladder, where he successfully removes a urinary stone through a process known as a cystolithotomy.

The surgery renders James Polk sterile—and perhaps impotent—for the rest of his life. However, despite the condition, he becomes a diligent student. The future president never weighs more than 135 pounds but enjoys a reputation for tenacity. After graduating with honors from the University of North Carolina in 1818, he becomes a lawyer and moves to Nashville. There, Polk begins a lifelong friendship with Andrew Jackson. Polk is elected to Congress, where he rises to become Speaker of the House.

And yet, when James K. Polk enters the 1844 election field, he is an unknown. The two leading candidates are Whig Henry Clay and Democrat Martin Van Buren. Both oppose annexation of Texas because they fear it will bring war with Mexico—and result in agitating the divisive issue of whether slavery should expand into new territories. Polk, meanwhile, openly advocates Texas statehood, going to war with the British to annex Oregon, and acquiring California. Amazingly, Americans agree strongly with the small man from Tennessee. His longtime mentor, Jackson, firmly suggests that his fellow Democrats select Polk as their presidential candidate—which they do.

"Who is Polk?" becomes the Whig rallying cry. They soon find out. He wins both the popular vote and the Electoral College by solid margins.[*]

Prior to meeting Sarah Childress, James Polk is not much of a lady's man. His political ambitions leave little time for relationships. But by his midtwenties, thoughts of matrimony enter his mind. He seeks guidance from Andrew Jackson.

"Look no further than Miss Sarah Childress," Jackson responds, pointing out that she is "wealthy, pretty, ambitious, and intelligent."

Which she is. Nineteen-year-old Sarah is educated and opinionated. The couple are soon inseparable, and they wed six months later, on New Year's Day 1824. Sarah will long remember that they never speak a harsh word to each other. They have been a couple for twenty-one years as President Polk is sworn into office. The Polks have no children and no pets as they move into the White House.[†]

Sarah is Presbyterian, her husband Methodist, having undergone a late-in-life conversion at the age of thirty-eight. The couple worship together each Sunday, with the president attending Presbyterian services to humor his wife. It is only when she is ill or out of town that he attends the Methodist church.[‡]

As for a daily routine, James K. Polk has no hobbies, avocations, or interests beyond politics. Even his enemies marvel at the intensity of his nonstop work habits.

---

[*] The Democrat Polk secured 170 Electoral College votes to 105 for Henry Clay. The popular vote was 1,339,494 for Polk and 1,300,004 for Clay.

[†] Other than Donald Trump, James K. Polk is the only president not to have a pet or a horse.

[‡] The Presbyterian and Methodist churches are Protestant. Both believe in the sovereignty of God and faith in the New Testament. But Presbyterians believe that whether you go to heaven or hell is preordained at birth. Methodists do not believe fate is set in stone.

Yet in his four years in office, President Polk is that rare chief executive who accomplishes everything he sets out to do. The war with Mexico is a rousing victory. Most importantly, it adds one million square miles to the size of the United States.

Among those additions is California, which becomes increasingly important in 1848. There, on January 24, a man named James Marshall discovers gold at a place near Sacramento called Sutter's Mill. Almost immediately, Americans stream west in search of gold.

As he promised, James Polk leaves office on March 4, 1849, having served a single term. His achievements are enormous. Yet he is considered by many to be only the second-best president from Tennessee. Andrew Jackson will be remembered as significant, while James K. Polk is all but forgotten. Jackson's former home, Hermitage, sees millions of visitors a year. Polk's family residence in Columbia, Tennessee, receives just a few hundred.

James and Sarah Polk depart Washington on March 6, 1849, and begin a roundabout journey to see the country. He is exhausted from his years of hard work, having lost weight. He has deep circles under his eyes and lines in his face. After stopping in New Orleans, the couple travel by paddlewheel steamboat up the Mississippi River to Kentucky. There are isolated outbreaks of cholera throughout America, so upon reaching his new home at the corner of Union Avenue and Seventh Street in Nashville, the former president takes the precaution of secluding himself indoors. There, he spends his days reading and answering correspondence.

Cholera finds him anyway. The disease is spread through contaminated drinking water. Symptoms include long bouts of vomiting and diarrhea leading to severe dehydration and then death. Unfortunately, this is unknown to medical professionals in 1849, so the standard course of treatment is laxatives—a practice that only increases the dehydrated condition.

James K. Polk contracts cholera in early June and is dead within two weeks. He passes away on June 15, 1849, a little more than three months after leaving office. He is fifty-three years old.

"I love you, Sarah," are his last words. "For all eternity, I love you."

Polk's burial in a section of the Nashville City Cemetery reserved for cholera victims is the first of many internments. The following year, his remains are moved to the grounds of his home, where they stay for forty-three years. Before his reburial, Sarah insists that the coffin be opened to make sure her husband is inside.*

Four years of the taciturn Polk gives a far more flamboyant man the opening he needs to be elected president. General Zachary Taylor is the polar opposite of James Polk, and the two detest each other. The general's informal nature, some say crude, and political affiliation as a Whig greatly disturb the fastidious Democrat Polk. President Polk even replaces Taylor as leader of the American forces early in the Mexican-American War, despite several major victories. However, Polk already foresees that General Taylor's rising national celebrity will make him a formidable presidential candidate.

Three months before his death, on March 5, 1849, President Polk attends the inauguration of president-elect Taylor. It is a Monday. Ironically, army captain Robert E. Lee and Illinois congressman Abraham Lincoln work together to coordinate the festivities. Taylor's speech is short, focused on obeying the Constitution. He makes no reference to slavery—nor does he mention James K. Polk, a notable slight.

Fighting men have always captured the imagination of Americans. George Washington, Andrew Jackson, William Henry Harrison, and the Alamo defenders are known to all as the new decade approaches.

Thus, it is no surprise that a military hero is the growing nation's new leader.

"Old Rough and Ready" has arrived.

---

* James K. Polk's death was the quickest for any president after leaving office.

Chapter Twelve

JULY 4, 1850
WASHINGTON, DC
MIDDAY

The man with five days to live is watching a monumental occurrence. On an extremely hot afternoon.

President Zachary Taylor, sixty-five years old, gazes upon the unfinished Washington Monument as Senator Henry S. Foote delivers a long Independence Day speech. Thousands of citizens gather to celebrate. Ground breaking for the monument took place two years ago, a remarkable ceremony attended by the current president and four future presidents. Inside the enormous cornerstone, which now rests thirty-seven feet underground, is a portrait of George Washington, a Bible, and copies of the Declaration of Independence and the Constitution.*

The president sits on a special shaded platform, but there is no denying the extreme heat and humidity. Taylor did not sleep well last night and has already attended a patriotic musical recital this morning. He is a physically fit man who spent forty-one years in the military, so he has no qualms about enduring discomfort. Taylor even plans a walk along the Potomac after the orators finish their speeches.

The cholera epidemic that killed James K. Polk is still sweeping the country, and the citizens of Washington, DC, have been told not to eat

---

* James K. Polk, James Buchanan, Abraham Lincoln, and Andrew Johnson all attended the ground breaking.

or drink certain items that could lead to sickness. Among these are fresh fruit and milk. The link between cholera and contaminated water is still four years away from being discovered, but connections between these foods and the disease are already suspected.[*]

Yet when Zachary Taylor returns to the White House at 4:00 p.m., he is hungry and parched. Immediately, he eats several large bowls of acidic cherries doused in cold milk. The president also wolfs down green apples with several glasses of ice water.

Soon, the president is in great distress. His doctor diagnoses the cramping as gastroenteritis. Coincidentally, the heat has also affected several members of Congress in the same fashion.

Two days later, it appears that Taylor is getting better. He works from his White House office on Saturday, July 6, signing a bill into law and sending a thank-you note for a gift of salmon.

But the next day, the president is back in bed. An infection has taken hold in his digestive system, and he is racked by pain and diarrhea. His doctors prescribe opium.

It doesn't work.

Zachary Taylor is dying. Rumors about his health swirl throughout Washington. By Tuesday, July 9, he is fading.

"I am about to die. I expect the summons soon," he tells family gathered around his bed. "I have endeavored to discharge all my official duties faithfully. I regret nothing, but I am sorry I am about to leave my friends."

At 10:35 p.m., the president passes away.

First Lady Margaret Taylor refuses to allow her husband's body to be embalmed. This means a hasty burial. Within days, a hundred thousand people will line the streets of Washington for the funeral. Taylor's horse, Old Whitey, is paraded behind the caisson, the president's empty boots placed backward in the stirrups, signaling a soldier's death.

"Zachary Taylor is dead and gone to hell," says Mormon leader Brigham Young, one of the few Americans not mourning the popular president's passing. "And I am glad of it."[†]

---

[*] British doctor John Snow will make the connection in London's Soho District in 1854. His suggestion that the city turn off a water pump on Broad Street will end cholera in that area.

[†] "I dislike the willfully corrupt," Brigham Young said about Taylor. Young also believed that the president insulted the Mormon people, who were controversial in the 1840s for their religious beliefs and plural marriages.

The morning after his death, President Taylor's body is placed inside a coffin, and the lid is closed. Suddenly, Margaret demands it be reopened so she can have one more look at her husband of forty years.

The casket lid is dutifully raised, then closed again.

Whereupon Margaret repeats the request.

Two more times.

It will be 141 years before the casket is opened again so the world can know for certain whether or not Zachary Taylor has been murdered.

For all his lack of pretense, Zachary Taylor stemmed from a distinguished lineage. Born on a Virginia plantation in 1784, Taylor is descended from William Brewster, a pilgrim who came to America on the *Mayflower* and signed the Mayflower Compact. James Madison is a distant cousin, as is Robert E. Lee.

Taylor's father, Richard, a Revolutionary War veteran, is wealthy but restless. As an infant, Zachary's family moves westward to the Ohio River, settling near what is now Louisville, Kentucky. Growing up, the Indian wars are still ongoing as young Zack walks from the family log cabin to his local school. Taylor will long remember the sight of classmates being abducted and scalped by Native Americans.

The future president might have stayed on the family plantation, which grows to more than ten thousand acres. Or he might have studied law or medicine, like many other wealthy young men. But while Zachary Taylor is intelligent, he is a poor student. He also has trouble spelling. So, he chooses to join the army, personally receiving his commission from President Thomas Jefferson. While in the military, Taylor begins speculating in land and bank stock. The five-foot-eight soldier grows wealthy as a very young man, owning plantations in Louisiana and Mississippi along with an estimated two hundred slaves.

During this time, Taylor marries Margaret Smith, a wealthy young woman from Maryland whose father also fought in the Revolutionary War. The couple meet when she travels to Kentucky to visit a sister. Zachary's father gives them a farm as a wedding present. "Peggy" remains on that farm to raise their firstborn daughter, Ann, as her husband begins lengthy periods of duty in remote army outposts. But she soon leaves the comfort of home and joins him, a habit that will continue for most of Taylor's career.

Peggy is described by one admirer as a "delicate female" who succeeds in raising "worthy and most interesting children" at wilderness forts in locations as diverse as Wisconsin and Louisiana. The plainspoken brunette will be thirty-eight when she delivers the last of the couple's six children. That boy, Richard, is their only son. He will go on to serve as a general in the Confederate army during the Civil War.

This is not the Taylor family's only connection with the southern cause. Their second child, Sarah Knox Taylor, will marry Jefferson Davis, a former West Point graduate and US senator who becomes president of the Confederacy. At the time of their first meeting, Davis is serving under Zachary Taylor at Fort Crawford, Wisconsin, during the Black Hawk War in 1832. General Taylor adamantly opposes the nuptials because he doesn't want his daughters marrying military men due to the nomadic lifestyle.

Three months after the wedding, Sarah Knox Davis dies of malaria, the mosquito-borne disease she contracted while visiting her sister-in-law's plantation in Louisiana. She is just twenty-one.

★★★

Zachary Taylor's long military career sees him fight in the War of 1812, the Black Hawk War, and the conflict with the Seminole Indians. He rises to major general during the Mexican-American War. Taylor is known for his casual form of leadership, with soldiers nicknaming him "Old Rough and Ready" for his rumpled appearance and tactical brilliance. His leadership style is to not manage each detail of a fight, instead leaving his commanders to make decisions based on the flow of battle.

Taylor's time fighting for his country also makes him a staunch patriot, putting loyalty to America over his ties to slavery and the South, and he openly disagrees with southerners who believe in secession from the Union. And for those who insist that slaves should be allowed in new western territories, Taylor responds that there is no cotton or sugar grown there and thus no need for the large amount of manpower required on a plantation.

In 1840, Zachary Taylor steps back from the army, taking a full year of leave. In addition to the death of daughter Sarah, he and Peggy have lost two other daughters, Octavia and Margaret, from a "bilious fever." The strain of years in remote outposts and the death of three children are placing great strain on Peggy, who is now becoming a recluse. The hiatus is a chance to reunite and travel the country as a family.

It is during this time that Zachary Taylor begins considering a post-army career in politics. He wisely keeps his party affiliation a secret, referring to himself as an independent. This leads President Polk to select him as commander of American forces in the Mexican-American War. Other top generals, such as Winfield Scott, are openly Whig, and Polk does not want to give them the chance to leverage battlefield glory into a successful run for president.

The Mexican surrender demand arrives at 11:00 a.m. on February 22, 1847. General Taylor and his army are in central Mexico, surrounded by an enemy force under General Antonio López de Santa Anna. American troops are positioned seven miles away, near a great hacienda called Buena Vista. The message arrives by courier, reminding Taylor that he "cannot in any human probability avoid suffering a rout, and being cut to pieces with your troops," in Santa Anna's handwritten words. "I wish to save you from a catastrophe."*

Taylor is given one hour to submit.

Santa Anna has an army of twenty-one thousand men and twenty-one artillery pieces; Taylor has approximately five thousand men. The Mexican general encourages his troops, many of whom are from poor villages, by telling them they will be allowed to loot American corpses after the battle is won. Many of these same soldiers fought at the Battle of Monterrey five months ago; thus, revenge becomes a motivator for the Mexican army.

---

* General Santa Anna also commanded Mexican forces at the Alamo in 1836. He was a controversial figure in Mexico, elevated to the presidency three times but also banished from power after battlefield losses at the Alamo and in the Mexican-American War. He wore a prosthetic leg of wood, cork, and leather, having lost his left limb to a cannonball in the 1838 "Pastry War" with France. He removed the leg to enjoy lunch after the 1847 Battle of Cerro Gordo in the Mexican-American War. Soldiers from the Fourth Illinois Regiment overran his position, and he was forced to flee, leaving the artificial leg behind. It can now be seen at the Illinois State Military Museum in Springfield.

Zachary Taylor will not surrender. He quickly drafts a response, which is then edited by his chief of staff, Major William Bliss, because the original contains so many expletives. "In reply to your note of this date, summoning me to surrender my forces at your discretion, I beg leave to say that I decline," Taylor states for history.

The Mexican messenger gallops back to Santa Anna. Now, all that is left is the fight.

The American forces are outnumbered but hold the high ground. Taylor's left flank is staffed by troops from the First Mississippi Regiment, under the command of his former son-in-law, Jefferson Davis.

Taylor believes this is where the Mexican attack will take place.

He is correct. At 3:00 p.m., Santa Anna's forces skirmish the left flank in force. Though numbers are in their favor, the Mexicans are stymied by the four hundred battle-hardened Mississippians and the deep valley and rocky plateaus providing the Americans with defensive superiority.

As night falls, General Taylor orders Colonel Davis and his men to pull back to a town called Saltillo—an American supply depot. Marching in a cold rain, the Americans quickly arrive but find no Mexican threat. So, Jefferson Davis immediately marches his men straight back to the front. They soon hear the thunder of cannon and join the fight. The scene is chaotic. The American army is in full retreat, running for their lives, routed by the Mexican force. Dead bodies are everywhere.

But General Taylor's belief in letting commanders make their own battlefield decisions now pays off.

Jefferson Davis quickly aligns his troops with the Third Indiana Regiment. The Americans form a V formation to fend off the Mexican charge. The enemy on horseback carry lances and move closer. Then, the order is given for the American line to hold its fire. But many of the men are volunteers who are not well trained. Military discipline breaks down.

One rifle fires. Then another. The fury of the American volleys sends the Mexicans into flight.

The Americans pursue. The rout is on.

In the end, Santa Anna's force loses 3,400 men, Taylor's army 650.

The Battle of Buena Vista causes General Zachary Taylor's legend to grow, which disturbs President Polk. Taylor is ordered to halt so Polk can send a new general to lead the attack on Mexico City. He well knows that the general is becoming a national hero and a viable presidential candidate for 1848. So Polk replaces General Taylor on the battlefield.

Taylor is furious at his demotion, but he dutifully remains in Mexico until the war ends. In November 1847, he sails home to his Louisiana plantation, where he receives a hero's welcome. Congress awards him three Congressional Gold Medals for his battlefield success.

Soon, both the Whig and Democrat parties try to recruit Taylor as a presidential candidate. Finally, the general makes a decision: he will run on the Whig ticket.

Zachary Taylor may be finished fighting the enemy with guns. But now he is going into another treacherous battlefield: Washington.

Prior to 1848, voting for president took place over several weeks, from November into early December. But November 7 of this year is the first time the entire nation casts all their votes on the same day. Zachary Taylor has run on the unusual platform of having no platform at all. In addition to not expressing an opinion on a single issue, the general does not actively campaign. The Whigs believe Taylor's military record is enough to attract voters.

They are correct.*

General Taylor wins the popular vote over Michigan Democrat Lewis Cass and the Free Soil Party's Martin Van Buren. He also takes the electoral vote, 163 to 127, over Cass, with Van Buren receiving zero in the Electoral College.

And so begins an unusual presidency. Soon after his victory, Taylor is riding on a train when a man, not knowing who he is, tells of his disdain for the new president. Zachary Taylor plays along.

"Are you a Taylor man?" the stranger asks.

"Not much of one," responds the president. He adds that he didn't vote for Taylor because his wife was opposed.

This is true. Peggy Taylor is chronically in pain from years of sickness and depression. Her life in Washington will revolve around spending

---

* Taylor picked up the Whig banner because he believed them more patriotic and also because he had a belief in shared leadership between the three branches of government. However, once he became president, Zachary Taylor mostly governed using a strong executive branch.

time in her room, attending Sunday services at St. John's Episcopal Church, and coming downstairs for family dinners.*

In addition to a depressed wife, the new president is making enemies.

Politicians from the South, in particular, are furious that Taylor has taken a strong stand against slavery in the newly acquired western territories. The president even counsels California and New Mexico to write their own constitutions before applying for statehood, precluding Congress from adding language about the slave issue.

America now has thirty states, evenly divided between slave and free. But Taylor's actions tilt the balance. Southern states, determined to uphold the institution of slavery, talk more openly about seceding. They grow even more enraged when Taylor opposes the Compromise of 1850, which includes a fugitive slave law.

In the face of this criticism, President Taylor responds by stating he will personally hang any individual who attempts to destroy the Union.

President Taylor's sudden death is a national shock. Many Americans are refusing to believe Old Rough and Ready was killed by ice water and a bowl of cherries. Conspiracy theories abound saying pro-slavery factions found a way to murder him.

Zachary Taylor is buried in the Congressional Cemetery on July 13, 1850. Three months later, as his casket is moved to his family burial plot in Louisville, questions about Taylor's death linger.

Time passes. Zachary Taylor is all but forgotten as a president. His short time in office did not allow him to achieve anything of consequence. His foreign policy, in which he had no previous experience, was almost non-existent. Yet the question of who killed Zachary Taylor *never* goes away.

Modern times.

The mystery of Taylor's death may finally be solved. It is 1991. Historical

---

* Amazingly, President Taylor is traveling alone on the train. In those days, presidents had no security.

marker 1412 sites the location of the long-deceased leader's burial site in Louisville. Now, 141 years after his sudden passing, there is new evidence that Taylor may *not* have died from cherries. By the order of a local judge, his body is being removed from its Tennessee marble crypt so tests can be performed.

The morning air is cool but extremely humid, with a soft northwest breeze. Two hundred curious onlookers, many of them parents with young children at their sides, watch as the hermetically sealed coffin is carried to a hearse. An American flag is draped atop the black walnut casket, which still bears silver cords and blue braids from the 1850 funeral procession. It takes several men to lift the lead-lined coffin, all of whom will comment on the strong musty smell inside Taylor's burial vault.

Historian Samuel Eliot Morison once wrote that Zachary Taylor was killed by "a combination of official scandals, Washington heat, and doctors." The official cause of death was cholera. But a contemporary investigation has suggested that Taylor may have died from arsenic poisoning. This can only mean murder.

In June 1991, the hearse arrives at the Jefferson County Coroner's office. County Coroner Richard Greathouse opens the coffin with a power saw and finds what is left of the president: a skeleton, an eyebrow and scalp hair, a small amount of soft tissue on his pelvic bones, and a full set of teeth with front incisors worn down—suggesting that Taylor grinded his jaws. Samples of hair, bone, and fingernails are taken, and then the coffin is closed and immediately returned to the president's mausoleum.

Two weeks later, the test results are announced.

No conspiracy. Death by bad food and water.

★★★

The year is 1850. A second vice president is now elevated to the pinnacle of power. And like the accidental president, John Tyler, it will not work out well.

Chapter Thirteen

JULY 10, 1850

WASHINGTON, DC

MIDDAY

America is now entering dark times.

The new president stands in the House chamber for his swearing-in. He raises his right hand and places his left on a Bible. "I, Millard Fillmore, do solemnly swear . . ."

For the next ten years, the nation will decline. And it begins with America's thirteenth chief executive. The New Yorker has no idea what is going on in Washington. President Taylor has completely shut him out. In fact, Fillmore is actually unwelcome in the White House. The gossip is that Fillmore's only friend is Old Whitey—the president's knock-kneed buggy horse that strolls the White House grounds inside the new iron fence. Fillmore is known to be fond of the animal, offering him carrots and apples because he has little else to do.*

The contrast to President Taylor is striking, especially in dress. Taylor is usually rumpled, wearing ill-fitting clothing. Millard Fillmore is tall and well-dressed, a man of five feet nine who has grown larger through

---

* Old-line Whig politician Fillmore obeyed party policies without argument. His boss, Zachary Taylor, disparaged that. "I am a Whig but not an Ultra Whig," he wrote to a friend. "If elected . . . I would endeavor to act independent of party domination and should feel bound to administer the government unbound by party schemes." For this reason, Taylor did not trust Fillmore.

a significant weight gain during his four terms in Congress. He is fifty years old, his hair completely white.

Somewhat incredibly, Zachary Taylor and Millard Fillmore do not meet in person until *after* being voted into office. From the start, the two are at odds. In fact, Fillmore is the butt of jokes from Whig leaders, including Taylor.

But now the punch line is president.

Millard Fillmore declines to deliver an inaugural address.

Apparently, he has nothing to say.

Born in a log cabin on the New York frontier in 1800, President Fillmore is the second of eight children and is named for his mother, Phoebe Millard. His father, Nathaniel, leases land as a tenant farmer. Young Millard's childhood is demanding and poor; he works on the small family farm, occasionally attends one-room schools, and endures extreme poverty. At fourteen, Nathaniel Fillmore apprentices his son to a local cloth maker, but Millard chafes at the menial labor and quits. Seeking to better himself, the teenager begins to read voraciously, even as he takes work in a local textile mill. Millard is so eager to get an education that he enrolls in a small academy. He is nineteen years old. Among the other students is the redheaded Abigail Powers, who is two years older. The couple fall in love but do not marry for six years due to lack of money.*

During that time, Millard Fillmore balances work with the study of law. He turns down offers from the biggest firms in nearby Buffalo to remain a small-town attorney in East Aurora, New York, where he and Abigail build a one-and-a-half-story clapboard house. The couple soon have two children, son Millard and daughter Mary. Both will survive childhood. To make ends meet, Abigail takes work as a teacher, an act that makes her the first president's wife to work outside the home after getting married.

However, Abigail doesn't have to work for long. Millard Fillmore is an ambitious man. His law practice soon provides a substantial income. He is blue-eyed and has a stately bearing. His hair is dark and wavy as

---

* Seven presidents were born in log cabins: Andrew Jackson, James K. Polk, Millard Fillmore, Franklin Pierce, James Buchanan, Abraham Lincoln, and James A. Garfield.

a young man, pushed back off his high forehead. Fillmore is known to be articulate and possessing a good sense of humor. He does not smoke, drink, or gamble.

As Fillmore's public stature rises, the attorney is approached by a new political party about running for the New York state legislature. The short-lived Anti-Masonic Party is essentially anti–Andrew Jackson. Fillmore is easily elected and goes on to serve three terms in Albany. Then, in 1832, he is elected to the US Congress as an Anti-Mason but soon becomes a Whig. Like most American politicians, his views on slavery are the litmus test, and Millard stands squarely in the middle—believing that compromise between North and South is vital to holding the nation together.

That ambivalence places him in direct opposition to his boss, Zachary Taylor.

A major disagreement between Taylor and Fillmore is the Compromise of 1850, a legislative attempt at a balance between "slavery and anti-slavery views" rather than outright abolition. Many who opposed slavery opposed its expansion into the territories but were not abolitionists. The bill would prohibit the selling of slaves in Washington and enact a new fugitive slave law to appease the South. Most important, it allows California to enter the Union as a free state. Vice President Fillmore tells Taylor he will vote to pass the act if called upon. This infuriates the president.

The author of the compromise is Senator Henry Clay of Kentucky, Fillmore's strongest ally. On July 10, members of the late Zachary Taylor's cabinet tender their resignations to protest the slave compromise. Fillmore responds by appointing an all-Whig cabinet who share his beliefs. Within a month, the president begins pushing for passage of Clay's legislation. He also demands Congress reject the Wilmot Proviso, which would ban slavery in all lands acquired in the Mexican-American War.*

One month later, President Fillmore signs an updated Fugitive Slave Act. This allows federal officials to return *suspected* escaped slaves even if there is no proof of prior enslavement.

Essentially, this legalizes the kidnapping of black people.

---

* On August 8, 1846, Pennsylvania congressman David Wilmot introduced legislation to ban slavery in territories acquired from Mexico. This attempt passes in the House but fails in the Senate, despite several attempts over the next two years to get the bill passed.

Soon, this colossal blunder blows up. Northerners are irate, standing more firmly against slavery than ever before. Southerners, in turn, grow increasingly more adamant that the practice of enslavement must be extended to *all* new territories. The argument dooms Fillmore's aspirations for a second term.

Millard Fillmore is the last Whig president. By 1856, the party will cease to exist, undone by the Compromise of 1850. From now on, every chief executive will be affiliated with either the Republican or Democratic Party.

During his two years and 237 days in office, President Fillmore experiences national upheaval. A "women's rights" convention is held in Worcester, Massachusetts. The controversial anti-slavery novel *Uncle Tom's Cabin* is published and becomes a bestseller. And the German revolutionary Karl Marx publishes a series of articles on his communist beliefs in the *New York Tribune*.

At home in the White House, there is decay. Guests notice the nicked and tattered furniture and are surprised by springs poking out from the frayed cushions. It has been more than thirty years since the building was refurbished after being burned in the War of 1812.

On the personal front, even taking a bath in the mansion is an ordeal. Kettles of hot water are carried upstairs and poured into portable tubs. However, Millard Fillmore does make one improvement: the first flush toilets are installed in the White House.

Socially, the president entertains very little. Abigail has an ankle problem that limits her ability to stand. Friday evening receptions find the president and First Lady attending, but only for a short time.

Just three weeks after Millard Fillmore leaves the presidency, Abigail passes away from pneumonia at the Willard Hotel in Washington. She contracted the illness while standing at her husband's side during a snowstorm for the swearing-in of new president Franklin Pierce.

Tragically, their daughter, Mary, contracts cholera and dies three months later at twenty-two years old.

★★★

Millard Fillmore is one of America's forgotten presidents. His term was short, his accomplishments few. For a seasoned politician, his time in office was remarkably inept, misjudging the mood of his own party. Perhaps his greatest legacy was sending an American fleet under Commodore Matthew Perry to Japan, arriving in 1853 after Fillmore leaves office but opening up the US presence in the Pacific.

Millard Fillmore dies of a stroke on March 8, 1874. He is seventy-four years old and is laid to rest at the Forest Lawn Cemetery in Buffalo. At the time of his death, he has seen five other men serve as president. In his case, turbulent times and a timid personality worked against his administration. Fillmore was a weak chief executive who failed to grasp the growing danger America was facing from a slavery-driven insurrection.

His successor will be even worse.

Chapter Fourteen

JANUARY 6, 1853
OUTSIDE ANDOVER, MASSACHUSETTS
1:30 P.M.

Franklin Pierce needs a drink.

It all happened so fast. His train leaves Andover bound for Concord, New Hampshire. Boston and Maine Railroad. Below-zero winter afternoon. America's newly elected fourteenth president, his wife, Jane, and their eleven-year-old son, Benny, are returning home from a funeral.

President-elect Franklin Pierce has a deep voice and is nicknamed "Handsome Frank." He pronounces his last name "purse." He is wiry, five feet ten, dark-haired, personable, and known to have such an amazing memory that he never forgets a name or face. As a young man, his feats of athletic strength are celebrated, and he still enjoys vigorous work on his farm.

President-elect Pierce is scheduled to take the oath of office in two months. He is forty-eight and has been married eighteen years. Franklin and Jane are opposites in many ways. She is a deeply religious teetotaler, while he is not as pious and is known to hit the bottle hard. Jane is a Whig and Franklin a Democrat. But both are in agreement about their deep love for Benny. He is the only one of three sons still alive; Franklin Jr. and Frank Robert died from disease at ages three days and four years, respectively. Benny Pierce is intelligent and kind. His mother makes sure the child attends church every morning. Franklin is said to "idolize" his son. The child sits with his parents as the train begins the one-hour journey north.

Suddenly, the president-elect hears a loud crack as one of the train's axles breaks in two. The passenger car derails and tumbles twenty feet down a rocky embankment. Screams. Hysteria. Bodies hurled from their seats. The car "broke in pieces like a cigar box," the *New York Times* will state.

America's new president-elect climbs out of the wreckage as it rolls to a halt. He is badly bruised but otherwise unhurt. Jane is distraught but not injured. Yet Franklin Pierce cannot find his son. He frantically searches the carnage, believing Benny might have been ejected from the train. He sees several women are badly contused. One man has two broken legs. But so far, every passenger has survived.

Then disaster. Franklin Pierce finds Benny's lifeless body. It is crushed. Flying metal has struck his son in the back of the head, almost decapitating him. "The little boy's brains were dashed out," another paper, the conservative *New-York Daily Times*, will report.

The president-elect moves quickly to shield his wife from what he sees, throwing a cloak over the corpse. But he is too late. At the sight of her precious boy, Jane Pierce lets out wails of grief that continue into the night.

"Mrs. Pierce was taken away in a very high state of anguish," the *Times* will report. "Her screams were agonizing."

Six days later, a shattered Franklin Pierce writes to good friend and fellow Mexican-American War veteran Jefferson Davis, soon to be named his secretary of war: "How I shall be able to summon my manhood and gather up my energies for the duties before me it is hard for me to see."

On March 4, 1853, Franklin Pierce recites the oath of office on a bitter cold and wet Friday. Standing on the East Portico of the Capitol, he places his right hand on a law book instead of swearing on a Bible. Thus, he is the first president to be *affirmed* instead of taking an oath. Pierce does so because he believes God is punishing him for past sins by killing Benny, and he is unworthy of taking a biblical oath. The new president then becomes the first chief executive to recite his inaugural address, in this case a thirty-three-minute speech, from memory. "I believe," he states, making his pro-slavery views known, "that involuntary servitude . . . is recognized by the Constitution."

Still in mourning, Jane Pierce is not in attendance.

"You have summoned me in my weakness," President Pierce tells America. "You must sustain me by *your* strength."

Franklin Pierce is in decline as he takes office. The death of Benny continues to weigh heavily. And Pierce's long history of bad habits is catching up with him. Chronically depressed long before the death of his children, Pierce often drinks to excess. The president usually goes to bed at 11:00 p.m., whereupon his alcohol intake leads to a night of snoring and poor sleep until 5:30 a.m. This causes him to nap at midday. He is impulsive. Franklin Pierce has a chronic cough along with fever and chills brought on by the malaria he contracted while serving in the Mexican-American War.

Now, as he and Jane settle into the White House, the new president must somehow prevent another war.

Born in 1804, Franklin Pierce is the son of New Hampshire governor Benjamin Pierce. He is a descendant of Thomas Pierce, who helped settle the Massachusetts Bay Colony in 1634. The future president attends Philip Exeter Academy and then Bowdoin College in Maine. There, he develops a reputation for being "chivalrous, manly, and warm-hearted."

"He was one of the most popular students in the whole college," says a friend. One of Pierce's fellow students and best friends is Nathaniel Hawthorne, a writer also descended from America's first settlers.*

Law studies and a career in the courtroom soon follow. By his mid-twenties, Franklin Pierce is actively moving toward a career in politics. He campaigns on behalf of Andrew Jackson in 1828 and soon finds himself elected to the New Hampshire House of Representatives. He is at the fore-

---

* In addition to writing *The Scarlet Letter* and *The House of Seven Gables*, Hawthorne will pen an 1852 biography of Pierce in which he will allude to Pierce's mental health, describing him as a "young man vigorous enough to overcome the momentary depression."

front of turning the state into a reliably Democratic area. By 1833, he is serving in the US Congress.

Just after he moves to Washington, Franklin briefly returns to New England and marries twenty-eight-year-old Jane Appleton. She is a melancholy woman who despises the swamps and politicians of Washington. While her husband serves in Congress, Jane remains on the New Hampshire farm. Alone in the capital, Franklin Pierce begins to drink even more heavily. Over the next few years, he will attempt to give up drinking, succeeding for a time.

But the new president will never fully kick his addiction to alcohol.

The two key factors in Pierce's surprising rise to the presidency are his friendship with President James K. Polk and the Mexican-American War. Jane has never enjoyed Washington, so Pierce leaves the Senate in 1842, returning to his New Hampshire law practice. When Polk takes office in 1845, he asks Pierce to be his attorney general. The former congressman says no, having promised Jane he would stay out of politics. But he has also begun drinking heavily again and fears his alcohol intake would become a public issue, which would embarrass the president.

Pierce, a long-standing member of the New Hampshire militia, seeks a US Army commission. So, President Polk names him a brigadier general and sends him to Mexico.

Future American general Ulysses S. Grant, serving as a captain in Mexico, will remember Pierce as a "gentleman and a man of courage" while observing him in battle. Indeed, despite a severe case of dysentery and a horse falling on top of him, Franklin Pierce responds well to the military. Drinking does not openly affect his leadership, but an anonymous 1852 letter to a New Hampshire newspaper refers to Pierce as the "hero of many a well-fought *bottle*."

Baltimore, 1852. Democratic Convention. Four candidates vie for their party's nomination. But after thirty-four ballots, neither James Buchanan, Lewis Cass, William Marcy, nor Stephen A. Douglas have enough votes. Franklin Pierce's name is then added for the thirty-fifth ballot. Pierce's long loyalty to Andrew Jackson and James K. Polk is fueling rumors that he is a pro-slavery northerner. Seizing the moment, Pierce's supporters continue to spread the theory. New Hampshire Democrats place him on the ballot as a "favorite son" candidate, extended as a courtesy by his home state rather than a serious bid for the presidency. At the time, Pierce had been out of elected office for ten years. Yet Virginia quickly casts all fifteen votes for the northerner with southern sympathies. On the forty-ninth ballot, he wins the nomination. Alabama's William R. King is attached to the ticket as vice president to secure even more "Dixie" votes in the general election.*

On June 5, 1852, Franklin Pierce is enjoying a carriage ride with his wife. A messenger gallops to them, bringing exciting news: "Sir, the Democrats have nominated you for president!"

Pierce, who has not told his wife he is returning to elective politics, cheers.

Jane faints.

Franklin Pierce's opponent is fellow Mexican-American War hero General Winfield Scott, a Whig. But old "Fuss and Feathers," a sixty-six-year-old military hero, runs such a poor campaign that many will claim Franklin Pierce does not win the election so much as Scott loses it by supporting the hated Compromise of 1850.

"We Polked you in 1844, we will Pierce you in 1852!" is the Democratic slogan.

Franklin Pierce wins in a landslide. He captures 50 percent of the popular vote and wins all but four states in the Electoral College. This makes him America's youngest president until that time at age forty-eight.

Jane Pierce is horrified by the turn of events. She is appalled that her husband is returning to politics because he promised he would *not* seek

---

* William Rufus King dies forty-five days into his term as vice president. Pierce does not fill King's job, because there is no constitutional provision for filling the office until the Twenty-Fifth Amendment in 1967, leaving the vice presidency empty until 1857. The term *Dixie* is a play on the Mason-Dixon Line, the 1767 surveyor's demarcation that separated North from South.

the nomination. Moving back to Washington from the quiet confines of their farm near Concord does not please her.

Benny's death makes this worse. "I hope he won't be elected for I should not like to be at Washington, and I know you would not either," the boy had written to his mother a few months before the train accident.

Now, Jane is trapped and all but disappears from public view. She suffers a mental breakdown and wears black as a sign of mourning, leading many to call her the "Shadow of the White House." She spends her days upstairs in the executive bedroom, writing letters of apology to her dead son. The Pierces do not entertain. One official will journal that "everything in the mansion seems cold and cheerless."

In his own ongoing state of mourning, President Pierce's drinking again escalates. Alcohol makes him gregarious. The White House is stocked with liquor for use during social occasions, so there is no lack of supply. Pierce consumes bourbon, rum punch, and Madeira wine—or anything else put before him. He is prone to begin drinking downstairs in the White House after dinner while his wife remains upstairs, not monitoring his consumption. Sometimes Pierce leaves the premises to imbibe with friends. In one embarrassing 1853 incident, a carriage he is driving strikes an elderly woman as he returns to the White House from an evening of drinking. Pierce is released from custody because he is president.*

As the year 1854 begins, slavery finally catches up with Franklin Pierce. Thus far he has avoided defining his personal feelings about the enslavement of 3.2 million human beings. However, the pressure is building. The South asks Congress to repeal the prohibition against slavery in new states below a certain latitude and in new territories. Northern anti-slavers oppose that vehemently. President Pierce must make a decision.

But he does not.

He is nicknamed "doughface," the term applied to northerners who sympathize with slavery. Pierce is easily swayed and has a hard time telling people no. It is well known in Washington that he often changes his opinion based on to whom he last spoke.

---

* There is no police report. History does not record what happened to the injured woman.

Finally, the proposed new law is a direct insult to federal power. Voters in each state, not Congress, would decide whether or not a territory adopts slavery. The focus of the legislation is on the territories of Kansas and Nebraska.

Finally, in May 1854, President Pierce signs the Kansas-Nebraska Act.

Almost immediately, pro-slavery white men flood into Kansas to stuff the ballot boxes. Abolitionists then adopt the same policy. In a prelude to Civil War bloodshed, this controversy leads to massive violence as the town of Lawrence is looted and burned by groups *supporting* slavery. "Bloody Kansas" will go down as a huge deficit for the Pierce administration.*

Franklin Pierce's presidency limps to a finish. He is ineffective in confronting critical problems, and his alcohol-fueled indecision hurts the nation. Ironically, given his own depression and that of his wife, Pierce vetoes America's first major mental health bill in 1854. The Land-Grant Bill for Indigent Insane Persons passed the Senate by a significant majority and is supported by his own party, so the veto is confusing. Pierce believes the federal government is not responsible for the social welfare of citizens, thinking this is for states to decide. No mental health legislation will be passed for almost a century.

The Democratic Party is clearly done with Pierce. And, in 1856, Democrats turn to James Buchanan in the upcoming election. Thus, Franklin Pierce is denied his party's renomination.

"There's nothing left to do but get drunk," states Pierce as he moves out of the White House.

And so, he does.

Jane Pierce dies in 1863 and is buried next to Benny in the Old North Cemetery in Concord, New Hampshire. By this time, America is em-

---

* On May 21, 1856, three hundred pro-slavery guerillas under the leadership of Sheriff Samuel T. Jones of nearby Douglas County attacked and looted Lawrence. The town had been founded by anti-slavery settlers from Massachusetts who were attempting to make Kansas a free state. Only one person died, but much of the town was destroyed.

broiled in the Civil War. Franklin Pierce fiercely opposes the policies of Abraham Lincoln, particularly the suspension of habeas corpus.*

Pierce also believes the Emancipation Proclamation, in which President Lincoln frees some of America's slaves, is a violation of states' power "and the rights of private property." Throughout the war, Pierce maintains his long friendship with Jefferson Davis, exchanging letters with the Confederate president. Already reviled in New Hampshire for his pro-slavery beliefs, Pierce is publicly disgraced after Union troops capture Davis's Mississippi plantation and discover bundles of treasonous correspondence.†

But by then, nobody is listening to Franklin Pierce. Devastated by Jane's death, his chronic alcoholism leads to gastritis, malnutrition, and, finally, liver damage. Abdominal fluid accumulation caused by cirrhosis of the liver kills President Pierce. He dies alone at 4:35 a.m. on Friday, October 8, 1869, in Concord. He is sixty-four years old.

The failure of the Pierce administration is not fully recognized by American voters. Violence is in the air. While Washington awaits a new president, forces of rebellion and sedition are gathering strength in the South,

To confront those forces, Pennsylvanian James Buchanan steps into the arena.

He will become an even worse leader than Franklin Pierce.

---

* This is a writ demanding a person arrested and accused of a crime must be brought before a judge and jury. Lincoln's decision allowed individuals to be held in jail indefinitely.

† One of the letters, written just before the war breaks out, encourages Davis and the Confederacy: "I have never believed that actual disruption of the Union can occur without blood. . . . We can overthrow political Abolitionism at the polls, and repeal the unconstitutional and obnoxious laws which in the cause of 'personal liberty' have been placed upon our statute-books."

Chapter Fifteen

MARCH 4, 1857
WASHINGTON, DC
NOON

The James Buchanan presidency is already unraveling.

And it hasn't even started.

As the inaugural festivities begin with the opening prayer, president-elect Buchanan leans over to Supreme Court chief justice Roger B. Taney to discuss one of the most important cases ever tried before the court. Such a conversation is a breach of ethics. Buchanan does not care. For the past two months, he has been secretly sending letters to Taney's fellow jurists wishing to know if the explosive *Dred Scott* decision will be settled before he becomes president. But on Inauguration Day, no verdict has been reached. So, Buchanan has to adjust his address accordingly. Thus, his overture to Justice Taney.

Buchanan looks out at the crowd of fifty thousand. Barricades hold them back. It is a day cold enough for jackets, gloves, and hats. He is exactly six feet tall, with a shock of white hair and a lantern jaw. He wears his collars high to hide his thick neck. Buchanan's victory in the November 1856 election is not large enough to be a mandate, but the margin is a significant 174–114 electoral win over California's John C. Frémont. Buchanan swept the South but was almost shut out in the North, despite being from Pennsylvania. It is well known that he is an advocate of

George Washington

Martha Washington

John Adams

Abigail Adams

Thomas Jefferson

Martha Jefferson Randolph

James Madison

Dolley Madison

James Monroe

Elizabeth Monroe

John Quincy Adams

Louisa Catherine Johnson
Adams

Andrew Jackson

Emily Tennessee Donelson

Rachel Donelson Jackson

Sarah Yorke Jackson

Martin Van Buren

Angelica Van Buren

William Henry Harrison

Anna Tuthill Symmes Harrison

Jane Harrison

John Tyler

Julia Tyler

Letitia Christian Tyler

Priscilla Cooper Tyler

James Polk

Sarah Polk

Zachary Taylor

Margaret Mackall Smith Taylor

Mary Elizabeth Bliss Taylor

Millard Fillmore

Abigail Powers Fillmore

Franklin Pierce

Jane Means Appleton Pierce

James Buchanan

Harriet Lane Johnston

Abraham Lincoln

Mary Todd Lincoln

Andrew Johnson

Eliza McCardle Johnson

Ulysses S. Grant

Julia Dent Grant

Rutherford B. Hayes

Lucy Webb Hayes

James Garfield

Lucretia Garfield

Chester A. Arthur

Mary McElroy Arthur

Grover Cleveland

Frances Folsom Cleveland

Rose Cleveland

to Great Britain. He previously served as secretary of state under James K. Polk and minister to Russia for Andrew Jackson. This has the fortunate consequence of keeping him out of American politics as the issues of slavery and secession heat up.

It also gives him a chance to mourn the loss of William R. King, Pierce's vice president, who dies on April 18, 1853, from tuberculosis.

Buchanan's only comment is that his longtime colleague was "among the best, the purest, and most consistent public men I have ever known."

President Buchanan starts his day early, reading the newspapers and eating breakfast before stepping into the office. He reads voluminously and often takes a walk during the day. Buchanan prefers a simple dinner with drinks on nights there are no social functions.

The president's favorite foods are sauerkraut, ice cream, strawberries, and a fish known as Delaware shad. He drinks whiskey, wine, and port in volumes large enough to cause him crippling pain from gout, requiring lengthy foot baths in warm water to ease the suffering. Indeed, prior to becoming president, James Buchanan purchased gallons of whiskey every week from a Washington merchant. He prefers alcohol because he does not trust the local water supply. There is also a widespread belief that spirits are *good* for a person's health. The average American in the mid-nineteenth century consumes nine and a half gallons of whiskey per year. A jovial drinker, Buchanan is even known to visit local taverns to socialize when spending time at Wheatland, his estate in Pennsylvania.

On those nights when the White House hosts a social function, the president prefers small gatherings rather than large events. He is a great storyteller, fond of regaling guests with lengthy yarns.

But those affairs usually end at an early hour. The president likes to be asleep around 10:00 p.m., which he considers "the time for all good Christians to be in bed."

James Buchanan is fastidious in his dress and a pet lover. His almost constant companion is a Newfoundland dog named Lara who weighs seventy pounds.

She romps around the White House, even attending high-level meetings.

Buchanan is also gifted two bald eagles by an admirer in the West. But the birds cause so much trouble on the White House grounds that they are soon deported to Pennsylvania.

★★★

It doesn't take long for James Buchanan to realize he needs a "First Lady."

So, his niece is summoned.

Harriet Rebecca "Hal" Lane is twenty-six as her uncle takes office. Buchanan has raised his niece since she was ten, sending her to the best boarding schools and even bringing her to London when he serves as minister there.

Queen Victoria finds Harriet delightful and gives "dear Miss Lane" the title of "ambassador's wife" during Buchanan's many social visits to Buckingham Palace. The queen even gives approval to a marriage proposal by British attorney general Sir Fitzroy Kelly because it would keep her in England. Harriet Lane declines.

Miss Lane is spontaneous and poised, with golden-brown hair and a talent for putting even the most high-ranking diplomat at ease. Despite this, hers has been a life of immense grief. Her mother, father, and two brothers died of tuberculosis, leaving her and her sister, Mary, to be raised by Uncle James. But Mary dies in 1855, shortly before Buchanan and Lane's return from London. A devastated Harriet throws herself into her uncle's presidential campaign and then her new role in the White House.

The "Democratic queen," as Harriet Lane is soon known throughout America, is the opposite of Jane Pierce. She wears bright clothing and decorates the mansion with cut flowers. Harriett holds weekly formal dinner parties, where prominent musicians and artists are invited to dine with politicians and diplomats. She takes great care to seat political enemies apart—no easy task as America becomes more divided. Her uncle has cautioned her against marrying too young, a warning she follows throughout his administration despite a large number of suitors, all of whom she considers "pleasant but dreadfully troublesome."

As President Buchanan's popularity slips, Harriet's soars. She becomes an advocate for social causes, including better conditions on Indian reservations. She becomes such a famous national figure that the Revenue-Marine—later to be known as the Coast Guard—names the cutter *Harriet Lane* in her honor. When needed, this vessel serves as the presidential yacht.

President Buchanan prefers black slaves to serve as his personal help, known as "body" servants. But his time in London led to an appreciation for highly trained British butlers and footmen. Thus, Harriet Lane's soirees are staffed by white Englishmen brought over specifically to work in the White House.

So it is that President Buchanan and First Hostess Harriet Lane return Queen Victoria's many favors in October 1860 by hosting Prince Edward. This involves two formal dinners, a fireworks display, and a visit to Mount Vernon. Most auspiciously, a public reception is held on October 4 to welcome the royal heir.

It is a fiasco.

When the East Room doors are flung open at noon, a mob representing all societal levels rushes into the White House to meet the prince and President Buchanan. Quickly, things get out of control. Furniture is smashed. Food and drink wind up on the walls and carpets.

Prince Edward is appalled.*

While the White House is prospering socially, James Buchanan is failing as a president. In 1857, banks begin to fail due to lack of international trade. This starts the Panic of 1857, a financial crisis that lasts deep into the Buchanan administration.

In addition, the president aligns with pro-slavery groups attempting to bring Kansas into the Union as a slave state. The Republican Party, which wins the House majority after the 1858 midterms, blocks this. A few months later, Minnesota is admitted as a free state, enraging the South.

Kansas is finally accepted for statehood, but as a free state, in January 1861. Oregon also is admitted. This leads southern slave owners to meet in Vicksburg, Mississippi, and lobby for the reopening of the African slave trade.†

---

* The incident did not affect the friendship between Queen Victoria and James Buchanan. On August 16, 1858, she telegraphs a ninety-eight-word message to the president. This is the first use of the new transatlantic cable connecting the United States and Great Britain.

† The African slave trade was banned in 1808.

★★★

On October 16, 1859, violence breaks out. Abolitionist John Brown seeks to form an anti-slavery republic in the Appalachian Mountains and emancipate slaves through armed rebellion. He comes from Kansas, where he killed five pro-slavery settlers in the Pottawatomie Massacre of May 1856. This action was in response to the sacking of Lawrence. Now he brings his violence to Virginia.

"I want to free all the negroes in this state," Brown states as he leads a raid on the armory at Harpers Ferry. "If the citizens interfere with me I must . . . burn the town and have blood." He leads a group of white men, four freed slaves, and another who has escaped from slavery, to procure weapons for his uprising. But the raid goes poorly. Soon Brown and his men are trapped in the armory building. The cornered abolitionists fire their weapons. Then two of Brown's men step outside under a flag of truce but are shot dead.

At 11:00 p.m. the following night, ninety US Marines under the command of Colonel Robert E. Lee arrive by train from Washington. Brown refuses to surrender. The siege lasts until dawn, when the marines storm the armory. Several abolitionists are killed. John Brown is beaten with a sword and taken into custody. In all, sixteen people are killed in the conflict, ten of those men under Brown's command.

Quickly, John Brown is sentenced to hang. "I, John Brown, am now quite certain that the crimes of this guilty land will never be purged away but with blood," he states as he is led to the gallows. These are his final words.

Brown becomes a hero to anti-slavery proponents—among them a former Illinois congressman named Abraham Lincoln. Many see Harpers Ferry as a harbinger of violence to come.

Reacting to the carnage, President Buchanan tells Congress that the abolition of slavery is a "disease" that may result in "an open war by the North to abolish slavery in the South."

In the year that follows, 1860, Abraham Lincoln becomes the front-runner for the Republican nomination, speaking out frequently against slavery. The Democrats, divided into northern and southern factions, turn their backs on James Buchanan, selecting anti-slavery northerner Stephen Douglas as their nominee.

Thus, James Buchanan becomes the third sitting president not to be renominated by his party.

On November 6, 1860, Abraham Lincoln is elected president.

But it's too late for him to stop the war.

South Carolina secedes on December 20, bringing an end to the Union formed eighty-four years ago with the Declaration of Independence.

Mississippi leaves on January 9, 1861.

Florida follows one day later.

Alabama the day after that.

Then Georgia.

Louisiana.

On February 4, 1861, meeting in Montgomery, Alabama, delegates from the seven secessionist states form the Confederate States of America. Jefferson Davis is chosen their president.

All of this, and James Buchanan's term *still* has one month left.

Texas secedes on February 23, 1861.

Meanwhile, off the coast of South Carolina, the United States Army maintains a garrison on an island known as Fort Sumter. Confederates target the fort. In New York City, a cargo ship is ready to sail forth to resupply the federal troops with food and ammunition.

President James Buchanan does *not* give the order to launch.

On April 12, 1961, one month after Buchanan and his niece vacate the White House to the Lincoln family, Fort Sumter is struck by heavy cannon fire. The garrison falls.

The American Civil War has begun.

After returning to Wheatland, Buchanan suffers bouts of depression. He begins writing a book titled *Mr. Buchanan's Administration on the Eve of Rebellion* to explain himself. On page 134, Buchanan says, "Congress deliberately refrained throughout the entire session to pass any act or resolution either to preserve the Union by peaceful measures, or to furnish the president or his successor, with a military force to reject any attack which might be made by the cotton states."

The entire book is essentially making excuses and sells poorly. For the rest of his life, James Buchanan remains on his estate as a defeated man.

On June 1, 1868, Buchanan dies of a respiratory ailment. He is seventy-seven years old. His niece, Harriet Lane, fares better. She marries at the age of thirty-six. After her husband and two sons die of disease, she devotes the rest of her life to charitable causes. The Harriet Lane Outpatient Clinic at Johns Hopkins University in Maryland cares for thousands of children to this day.

History has not been kind to James Buchanan, and that is fair. Under his leadership, there were few policy accomplishments, and the nation descended into a brutal war.

Because of Buchanan's ineptitude, Abraham Lincoln is handed the worst crisis in American history. A war that almost destroys a country created under the banner of "All men are created equal."

A war that does eventually destroy the man from Illinois.

Chapter Sixteen

A braham Lincoln is furious.

The battle that could decide America's future is taking place this morning, seventy miles northwest of the nation's capital—and his top general is afraid to fight.

Lincoln stands in his second-floor White House office—"the shop," as he calls it. He is six feet four, wiry, and wearing a shabby black suit with frayed cuffs, blue socks in need of darning, and bedroom slippers. A glance outside the tall southside windows shows the Potomac River rolling lazily alongside the capital on this foggy morning. Directly ahead, the unfinished Washington Monument rises like an enormous stone sequoia. And, as a constant reminder of America's Civil War, the president clearly sees Arlington Heights, where the former home of Confederate general Robert E. Lee is perched on a hill. Union troops occupy it now.

The shop is decorated in worn furniture from previous administrations, with Lincoln unwilling to spend government money on private amenities during this horrendous time. There is a mahogany stand-up desk, a fireplace with a white marble mantel, green-and-gold wallpaper, and dark-green carpet with a gold diamond pattern. The curtains still smell of former president James Buchanan's cigars.

On a corner table stands a bust of Franklin Pierce. Just like the former president, Abraham Lincoln suffered the death of an eleven-year-old son. Willie Lincoln died seven months ago from typhoid fever. The president's grief is enormous, but he cannot let that distract him from winning the war. The bust is a reminder that Lincoln's presidency must not succumb to loss.*

The room is full of maps, placed on the long wooden table inherited from John Quincy Adams and even littered about the floor. Lincoln is obsessive about troop movements, studying these charts late into the night, the great table receiving illumination from an enormous glass chandelier. A gas hose leading down from the light feeds into a small lamp, allowing for more detailed study.

Those maps tell Abraham Lincoln one thing: General Robert E. Lee is on the march.

Throughout the spring and long humid summer, an aggressive Lee has won battle after battle over Lincoln's Union troops. The wily Virginian's army recently crossed the Potomac River into Maryland, bringing it one step closer to Washington. If the capital falls, the war will be over.

The fifty-three-year-old Lincoln is determined that will not happen. "In your hands, my dissatisfied fellow countrymen, and not in mine, is the momentous issue of civil war. The government will not assail you," he warned the Confederacy in his inaugural address. "You have no oath registered in Heaven to destroy the government, while I shall have the most solemn one to preserve, protect, and defend it."

The president's intense commitment is not fully shared by his top commanders. Thirty-four-year-old Union army major general George B. McClellan has used the past year to turn thousands of volunteer soldiers into a disciplined fighting force. But McClellan is overly cautious, as a frustrated Lincoln is well aware, and refuses to aggressively confront Confederate forces.

---

* While Pierce opposed many of Lincoln's policies, he wrote a letter of consolation to the president two weeks after Willie's death. Referring to the loss of his own son and the "crushing sorrow which befell me," Pierce added, "Even in this hour, so full of danger to our country, and of trial and anxiety to all good men, your thoughts will be of your cherished boy, who will nestle at your heart until you meet him in that new life, when tears, and toils, and conflict will be unknown."

Union troops outnumber the rebels, but McClellan is convinced that Lee's army is more powerful. Thus, he does not go on the offensive. "If McClellan is not using the army, I should like to borrow it for a while," Lincoln remarks icily.

The truth is, President Lincoln no longer trusts McClellan. He wants to fire the small, arrogant man who fashions himself after Napoleon Bonaparte. The general is equally disdainful of Lincoln and will run against him for president two years hence.

Today's battlefield is known as Antietam. It is McClellan's last chance to prove himself. His career is on the line in Maryland.

All Lincoln can do is sip his morning coffee, eat his daily hard-boiled egg, study his maps, and wait for a cable from the front lines.

The bloodiest day in American history is about to begin.

Stars are still shining as troops move into position. Muskets and canteens rattle as blue-uniformed Union soldiers advance on foot through rolling forest. They leave the woods and enter a cornfield where the crop is ready for harvest; ears of corn hang heavily on tall green stalks. These soldiers have spent the night in the open, rain falling off and on, sleeping fitfully as they await the dawn. They know Confederate artillery on a distant rise is aimed right at them. Today is going to be savage. "All realized that there was ugly business and plenty of it just ahead," one private will remember of the tension.

Suddenly, cannon fire breaks the calm. "The air is full of explosions and smell of brimstone," writes a northern soldier. "I was exposed to the fire of slavery."

The cornfield becomes bloody as shells explode. "Artillery hell" is how a Confederate officer describes the carnage. There is nowhere to hide. Foot soldiers advance through the tall stalks of corn, bayonets gleaming as the sun rises. Thick rows of vegetation make for poor visibility. Fighting takes place at close range as men chance upon one another. Fists, gun butts, bullets. The air is rent by the crackle of ammunition snapping through leaves and the constant bellow of cannon fire.

Bodies lie everywhere, wounded men screaming loudly in pain. At times, their cries are cut short by a quick bayonet thrust from an opponent. Major General Joseph Hooker, field leader of the Union troops, marvels that "every stalk of corn in the northern and greater part of the field was cut as closely as could have been done with a knife, and the slain lay in rows precisely as they had stood in their ranks a few moments before."

Next to the cornfield, Union troops take fire in a thick grove of trees known as the East Woods. Confederate soldiers hide among the dense forest's roots and fallen logs. The brambles are so thick that men from the same side mistakenly fire on one another.

Thousands of dead bodies now litter the forest floor and the cornfield. It is not even 7:00 a.m.

Union troops hold the advantage in numbers, but Confederate general Robert E. Lee's skillful movement of men and cannon means that some northern units are taking more than 50 percent casualties. Six generals will be killed in action today, the most such casualties in one day of the entire war.

The fighting goes back and forth all morning, casualties mounting. One half-mile stretch of sunken dirt road becomes a cemetery, with 5,600 dead and wounded.

It is here, a place that will go down in history as "Bloody Lane," that Major General McClellan makes a crucial blunder. The Confederacy is out of reinforcements. As this stretch of rebel line is broken, McClellan has fresh backup troops ready to rush in and win the battle.

But "Little Mac" stands still.

The fighting continues through the afternoon. At 5:30 p.m., a truce is called so both sides can collect their wounded. General Lee then waits through the night for the inevitable Union attack. But it never comes. Once again, Major General McClellan does nothing.

Relieved, Lee retreats. Both sides suffer a combined 22,727 killed and wounded in one day of fighting. Thousands more will die later from their wounds. On this single day, the number of Americans killed and wounded is the highest in the nation's war history.

General Lee continues retreating for the next five weeks, pulling his army back across the Potomac into Virginia. The Confederates are decimated, having lost 31 percent of their total force at Antietam. But to President Lincoln's chagrin, Major General McClellan refuses to pursue the enemy force. Lincoln grows angrier with every passing day, continuously telegraphing McClellan to get his army on the move.

Finally, the president can take no more. On November 5, 1862, Major General George B. McClellan is relieved of command. Lincoln has no choice. It is still possible for the North to lose the war.*

It has been a long journey for Abraham Lincoln.

"I was born Feb. 12, 1809, in Hardin County, Kentucky. My parents were both born in Virginia, of undistinguished families," Lincoln writes in a sketch of his life, five months before accepting the Republican Party's presidential nomination. His place of birth is a log cabin. The Lincoln family has little money. Thomas Lincoln, the future president's illiterate father, is descended from Puritan settlers who arrived in America in 1637. Young Abe's namesake is his grandfather, who fought in the Revolutionary War and was later killed in a Native American attack on their Kentucky homestead. Daniel Boone is a distant relative.

Thomas Lincoln moves the family to Indiana when Abraham is eight. "A wild region, with many bears and other wild animals still in the woods," Abe writes. "There I grew up."

The future president is raised in a Baptist household, with his parents abstaining from alcohol, dancing, and purchasing slaves. He educates himself, learning to read and poring through books. Lincoln's mother dies from drinking poisoned milk two years after arriving in Indiana, causing his father to remarry one year later.†

Life on the farm does not suit Abraham Lincoln, who is derided as lazy due to his preference for reading and writing. He performs manual labor reluctantly. However, Abe develops a talent for wielding an axe to split rails for fences and grows into a strong, tall young man. He is athletic and wins the county wrestling championship at age twenty-one.

Eleven years later, as Lincoln is trying to move up in the political

---

* On November 7, Lincoln replaces McClellan with General Ambrose E. Burnside, a man known for his distinct facial hair. His facial hair introduces the term *sideburns*. Lincoln replaces him two months later with General Joseph Hooker, whose last name is synonymous with prostitution. Unlike Burnside, however, this term has been in use since the fifteenth century. Both generals failed to distinguish themselves in the field.

† Milk poisoning is caused by a cow that has eaten the white snakeroot plant, which contains the fatal ingredient tremetol.

world, he has an enormous setback. Though he has become a success, serving in the Illinois state legislature and practicing law, he is prone to bouts of deep depression. The worst comes in January 1841. He is engaged to be married to a woman named Mary Todd. But suddenly, she breaks off the engagement, sending Lincoln into such despair that friends fear he will commit suicide. It is months before the young politician steadies himself.

But Lincoln's mental state continues to be a problem. Black moods will follow him for the rest of his life. His remedies for depression are reading works of humor and taking mercury pills.*

On November 4, 1842, Lincoln finally marries Mary Todd after a stormy three-year courtship. Blue-eyed and five feet two, the twenty-four-year-old Mary is intelligent, eccentric, and self-absorbed—in every way the opposite of the witty, practical, self-effacing Abe. But Mary's faith in her new husband's talent is indefatigable. She becomes his biggest supporter and chief adviser. The Lincolns soon have four sons, among them Eddie, who dies at three from tuberculosis. Twelve years later, Willie will succumb to typhoid fever at age eleven. The eldest boy, Robert, will go on to serve in the Union army during the Civil War. Tad, the youngest, dies from tuberculosis at the age of eighteen, six years after the war ends.

February 27, 1860. Abraham Lincoln, a former Whig, is now a rising star in the Republican Party. He has come to New York City to speak at Cooper Union, a private college located in a lower Manhattan brownstone building. Lincoln wishes to run for president but is reluctant to declare his candidacy, even though the nominating convention is just three months away. Tonight will decide his fate.†

This is the first time Abe Lincoln gives a speech in New York. He will be the third and final orator this evening. Among the crowd in the

---

* Pills known as "blue mass" were commonly prescribed for depression. The active ingredient is the neurotoxin mercury, which can have negative long-term effects. Fearing it would impair his thinking, Lincoln stopped taking the pills soon after his inauguration in 1861.

† Lincoln served as a US congressman from 1847 to 1848, representing the Seventh District of Illinois. He was unhappy with the job and returned home after one term.

packed auditorium are several prominent journalists. A good performance before these influential men will go a long way toward raising Lincoln's national profile.

Slavery, of course, is the primary issue. Lincoln believes it is a blemish on America. He has stated that the *Dred Scott* decision is at odds with the Declaration of Independence and its promise of equal rights for all. Lincoln articulated his belief system while running against Stephen A. Douglas for the Senate in 1858. Abe would go on to lose that election, but his quick wit and ability to explain his ideals win him many new supporters.

Yet Abraham Lincoln is still a regional novelty, popular in Illinois but unknown in the big eastern communities. So it is that he has been invited to New York City. Lincoln is introduced by white-bearded poet William Cullen Bryant, editor of the *New York Evening Post*. Those who have seen Lincoln in public before are not startled by his appearance and vocal pitch, but to those who have not, Lincoln is an awkward surprise. His suit fits poorly, his shoes appear shabby, and he speaks in a high-pitched voice. Some will later claim that the gangly speaker is actually "ugly."

But Lincoln's words are powerful.

He scolds pro-slavery Democrats for ignoring the wishes of the Founding Fathers in his argument that the federal government can prohibit slavery in territories—but not states. Lincoln also takes a stand against radical abolitionists like John Brown, distancing the Republicans from violence. He compares southern states wishing to secede with thieves trying to steal from the Union.

Lincoln's most powerful moments come at the end, in words reserved for members of his *own* party. He is fearful that America's experiment with democracy will fail if secession divides the nation—and it is incumbent upon good men to support the Union.

"Let us have faith that right makes might," he tells Republicans. "And in that faith, let us, to the end, dare to do our duty as we understand it."

The Cooper Union speech, as it will become known, is an extraordinary success. Horace Greeley praises Lincoln in the *New York Tribune*, calling his oration "one of the most happiest and most convincing political arguments ever made in this city."

★★★

Three months later, Abraham Lincoln is named the Republican Party's presidential candidate. On November 6, 1860, he is elected president of the United States. In a four-way contest against a Democratic Party divided by slavery, he defeats constant Democratic adversary Stephen A. Douglas, Southern Democrat John Breckinridge, and the Constitutional Union's John Bell. Lincoln's Electoral College tally is 180, more than the other three candidates combined.*

Abraham Lincoln's victory shows how deeply divided America has become. He sweeps the North plus the free states of California and Oregon, Bell and Breckinridge split the South, and Douglas wins only Missouri. Punctuating the division is Lincoln's vice president, Senator Hannibal Hamlin from Maine. The dour Hamlin was specifically chosen by the Republicans to secure abolitionist northern votes.

The secession of southern states begins almost immediately after Abraham Lincoln's victory. South Carolina goes first on December 20, 1860.

Mary Todd Lincoln understands the South.

She was born a Kentucky belle in a slave-owning family. Eight of her siblings support the Confederacy, including one half brother who abuses Union prisoners in a Confederate jail. Mary is considered a traitor by southerners and viewed with suspicion by northerners. Throughout her two decades of marriage to Abe, her high social aspirations have been unfulfilled.

So, when the Lincolns move into the White House on March 4, 1861, the First Lady eagerly begins redecorating and entertaining. Her husband intentionally fills his office with old furniture while she enjoys lavish shopping sprees. The funds come from a congressional remodeling appropriation, but Mary ignores the budget and spends at will.

She is fond of throwing lavish dinners, including one party for six hundred guests. Her critics label her extravagant and deride her fashion taste. Yet in March 1862, when eleven-year-old Willie dies after con-

---

* Abraham Lincoln wins the popular vote with over 1.8 million to Stephen A. Douglas's over 1.3 million. The two southern candidates run far behind.

tracting typhoid fever from drinking fetid Potomac River water, these same individuals complain when Mary mourns instead of entertains.

Mary Todd Lincoln is a devoted wife, refusing to leave Washington and her husband, despite the risk of Confederate invasion. She visits military camps, volunteers in hospitals, and supports causes to help formerly enslaved men and women.

Through it all, the First Lady has the full support of her husband. "My wife is as handsome as when she was a girl, and I . . . fell in love with her; and what is more, I have never fallen out," he remarks one evening as she greets guests.

Although his wife likes to socialize, President Lincoln prefers to work.

He sleeps down the hall from his office in quarters accessed by a private passage. Mary's bedchamber is across the corridor in what is known as the Prince of Wales suite, a nod to the royal visit of 1860. Up at 7:00 a.m. after a typically restless night, Lincoln works for an hour before enjoying his daily walk around the mansion's expansive grounds. Then it is breakfast in his office, often with a fire in the marble hearth. Andrew Jackson, whose portrait hangs above the mantel, looks down as Lincoln enjoys a spartan meal.

"The pleasures of the table had few attractions for him," private secretary John Hay will write. "His breakfast was an egg and a cup of coffee; at luncheon, he rarely took more than a biscuit and a glass of milk, a plate of fruit in its season; at dinner, he ate sparingly of one or two courses."

★★★

While the Lincolns' marriage is steady, problems are developing. Always unpredictable, Mary has developed such a terrible temper that her nickname among White House staff is "hellcat." She makes frequent trips to New York and Philadelphia to purchase dresses, furs, and earrings

---

[*] To keep Mary happy, Abraham Lincoln attends the events, in particular her regular Tuesday and Saturday receptions open to the public. He did not, however, want to be the center of attention. "He would shake hands with thousands of people, not even conscious of what he was doing, his eyes dim, his thoughts withdrawn," aide secretary John Hay wrote. "Then suddenly he would see some familiar face . . . he would greet the visitor with a hearty grasp."

that the Lincolns cannot afford. For one four-month span, she purchases three hundred pairs of gloves. More troubling, Mary's gait has become wobbly, her skin pale, and she suffers from hallucinations.*

To distract himself from Mary's behavior, Lincoln is focused on a Union victory. Once in a while, he takes a break to joke with some of the younger members of his staff, but Lincoln's set of daily problems require the solitude that promotes reflection. It is the war, above all, that defines the president's days. He is consumed with finding the right generals, building a wartime economy to meet the army's needs, and preventing recognition of the Confederacy by foreign nations.

Throughout the conflict, Lincoln is sure of Union victory—though that is in the balance until the 1863 Battle of Gettysburg. He is determined that when peace arrives, terms with the South will not be onerous. Lincoln's great wish is that the nation heals and unites.

Yet Abraham Lincoln's compassion only goes so far. When he finally settles on General Ulysses S. Grant to lead his Army of the Potomac, critics claim that Grant is a "butcher." They rail against his aggressive battlefield tactics and the high body count of fallen Union soldiers under his command.

Abraham Lincoln does not care. "I can't spare this man," the president states. "He fights."

Lincoln has become hardened and practical. Every dead rebel brings the nation closer to peace. This policy does not change when General William Tecumseh Sherman rampages through the South, his army setting fire to Atlanta and destroying farms and plantations on his March to the Sea.

In November 1864, as the tide of the war turns irrevocably toward the North, Abraham Lincoln runs for reelection. Hannibal Hamlin is out as vice president. Anticipating the coming reconciliation with the South, Lincoln's new second is southerner Andrew Johnson from Tennessee. The former tailor is fond of drink but showed his courage by remaining in the Senate after his home state seceded from the Union.

Should anything happen to Abraham Lincoln, the weight of the presidency will fall on this simple man's shoulders.

---

* Some scholars believe Mary Todd Lincoln suffered from pernicious anemia, which is brought on by a lack of vitamin B12. The brain shrinks, causing a loss of cognitive function and paranoia. However, the condition is not discovered until 1874.

★★★

The election of 1864 is brutal. The Democrats nominate General George B. McClellan, who despises Lincoln for firing him.

Although fighting for the Union, McClellan is an ardent racist, campaigning throughout the North on a platform of suppressing freedom for black people. One campaign poster he approves stands out.

Elect Lincoln
And the
Black Republican Ticket
You will bring on NEGRO EQUALITY,
more DEBT, HARDER TIMES, another
DRAFT!
UNIVERSAL ANARACHY AND ULTIMATE
RUIN

ELECT
M'CLELLAN
AND THE WHOLE
DEMOCRATIC TICKET
You will defeat NEGRO EQUALITY,
Restore Prosperity, re-establish the
UNION!
In an Honorable, Permanent, and happy
PEACE

Abraham Lincoln easily defeats McClellan, who then temporarily moves to the South of France. By 1877, though, he is back in the United States and wins the governorship of New Jersey.

★★★

It is April 9, 1865, when the Civil War ends. Washington is the scene of great revelry.

Abraham Lincoln does not live to see the party.

Six days later, he is shot in the head while watching a play with his wife in a place called Ford's Theatre. General Grant and his wife, Julia, who does not like Mary Todd Lincoln, were supposed to be in attendance but canceled. Assassin John Wilkes Booth, a well-known actor and Confederate supporter, pulls the trigger. Though Lincoln survives for hours, he dies at 7:22 a.m. on April 15.[*]

A distraught Mary Todd Lincoln is never the same. Ten years later, she is declared mentally insane.[†]

Abraham Lincoln was perhaps the greatest president. Critics complained he was too impatient with his generals. Others were offended when he suspended the writ of habeas corpus, even though the Constitution proclaims this legal in times of rebellion. But for the most part, history agrees with the way Lincoln performed the mammoth task of conducting a war that pitted friends and neighbors against one another.

The greater, unanswered question is how Lincoln would have governed during his second term. More specifically, would he have brought the nation together?

Conjecture is a fool's errand. What history does demonstrate is Abraham Lincoln's superior character. Above all, he was anguished over a fractured country and millions of enslaved human beings. On January 1, 1863, President Lincoln freed the black slaves by issuing the Emancipation Proclamation—and leading to his death at the hands of a secessionist fanatic who opposed black suffrage.

No president was ever confronted with more turmoil than Lincoln. But he handled it.

Perhaps his greatest words are from the Second Inaugural: "With malice toward none, with charity for all, with firmness in the right as God gives us to see the right, let us strive on to finish the work we are in, to bind up the nation's wounds, to care for him who shall have borne the battle, and for his widow and his orphan, to do all which may achieve and cherish a just and lasting peace among ourselves and with all nations."

---

[*] More details on the Lincoln assassination can be found in the authors' *Killing Lincoln.*

[†] Mary Todd Lincoln survived her husband by seventeen years. Concerned about his mother's mental health in 1875, son Robert Lincoln sought to place her in an Illinois insane asylum. Mary was not informed about the hearing until the day it took place. A judge ruled that she should be sent to the Bellevue Place sanatorium in Illinois, where she spent three months. Ten years later, on the anniversary of son Tad's death, Mary collapsed and fell into a coma. She died the next day, July 16, 1882, from a stroke. She is buried with Abraham Lincoln in Oak Ridge Cemetery in Springfield, Illinois.

Chapter Seventeen

APRIL 15, 1865
WASHINGTON, DC
11:00 A.M.

Andrew Johnson should be dead. Just like Abraham Lincoln.
But he's not.

And now he is the leader of the country.

Flags are lowered to half-mast as news of President Lincoln's death spreads throughout the city. Supreme Court chief justice Salmon P. Chase makes his way to the Kirkwood House, a hotel on 12th and Pennsylvania, where Vice President Andrew Johnson maintains a suite. The Tennessean already knows of Lincoln's assassination, having visited the unconscious dying president earlier that morning. The vice president is grief-stricken, much like Chase and the other cabinet members filing into the room. Soon, the "small parlor," as it is known, lives up to its name. There is little space to spare as ten witnesses pack the suite and Chase begins administering the oath of office.[*]

The assembled dignitaries do not have a favorable impression of Andrew Johnson. His drunken speech at Abraham Lincoln's second inau-

---

[*] Attorney General James Speed, Treasury secretary Hugh McCulloch, Postmaster-General Montgomery Blair, Blair's father Francis Blair Sr. of Maryland, US senator Solomon Foot of Vermont, US senator Alexander Ramsey of Minnesota, US senator Richard Yates of Illinois, US senator William M. Stewart of Nevada, John P. Hale of New Hampshire, and US representative John F. Farnsworth of Illinois were in attendance.

guration embarrassed the president and everyone in attendance. But Johnson now appears to be a different man. Like Secretary of State William Seward, absent because he was severely injured in the assassination plot against Lincoln, the new president was also a target.

John Wilkes Booth, the actor who shot Lincoln, hoped Johnson and Seward would be murdered at roughly the same moment. Coconspirator Lewis Powell burst into Seward's home and slashed his face with a knife before fleeing.

George Azterodt, the German immigrant tasked with killing Andrew Johnson in his hotel room, panicked and never carried out the act. Nevertheless, Azterodt will hang for his role in the plot, as will Powell.

But that is all to come. For now, Andrew Johnson has no idea he was an assassination target. So rather than being rattled by a near-death experience, Johnson appears calm. He requests the cabinet stay on rather than resign, helping him continue Lincoln's policies.

"We all felt as we left him, not entirely relieved of apprehensions, but at least hopeful that he would prove to be a popular and judicious president," writes Treasury secretary Hugh McCulloch.

Those hopes will not be realized.

★★★

Andrew Johnson is fifty-six when the presidency is thrust upon him. He was born into poverty on December 29, 1808, in Raleigh, North Carolina. His mother, Mary "Polly" McDonaugh, works as a washerwoman, an occupation that takes her alone into the homes of wealthy citizens. Young Andrew bears little resemblance to his father, Jacob, leading to rumors that some other man had his way with Polly. When Jacob dies of a heart attack before Andrew turns four years old, his widow remarries and, years later, apprentices her uneducated son to a local tailor.

Though Johnson dislikes the work, one benefit is that benevolent citizens visit the shop and read aloud to the workers as they perform their cutting and sewing. In this way, the illiterate boy develops not only a passion for knowledge but also a gift for phrasing the spoken word that will one day make him a powerful public speaker.

After five years, Andrew Johnson flees his apprenticeship. Fearing arrest when his employer offers a reward for his return, the teenager travels deeper into the South. At seventeen, Johnson settles in Greeneville, Tennessee, and marries the sixteen-year-old daughter of a local cobbler. In so doing, Eliza McCardle becomes a bride at a younger age than any First Lady in history. In what will prove an amazing coincidence, Mordecai Lincoln, a cousin once removed from Abraham, performs the ceremony.

The couple soon move into a two-room home, where Johnson opens his own tailor shop. Together, they raise five children. All survive to adulthood. Eliza is educated and teaches her husband how to read and write. Despite suffering off and on from tuberculosis through much of her adult life, Eliza also manages the family finances as the business expands. In time, the Johnsons become prosperous enough to buy a male slave named Sam and a woman named Dolly—who soon gives birth to children Liz, Florence, and William.

Andrew Johnson does not own a plantation, so these slaves are used for domestic labor. Dolly is a teenager when Johnson purchases her for $500 in 1842. Records list her as "black" while her children are labeled "mulatto," leading historians to suggest Andrew Johnson is the father of the mixed-race offspring.*

In addition to wealth, Andrew Johnson is developing an interest in politics. He joins the Tennessee militia, attaining the rank of colonel, by which he is often addressed for the rest of his life. Much like fellow Tennessean Andrew Jackson, the tailor from Greeneville uses his military background to fuel his political rise. By 1843, the Democrat is elected to Congress, where he serves ten years. Throughout his time in the House of Representatives, Johnson toes the southern position that slaves are private property and their ownership is protected by the Constitution.

In 1853, the five-foot-ten Johnson is elected governor of Tennessee. He remains a common man and often tells voters about being born in a log cabin. Johnson is known to be kind, never condescending. His skills as a tailor mean that his clothing fits impeccably. By now a very wealthy man, Johnson is still popular with working-class voters who identify with his poor roots. However, the governor is often looked down on by those born into money. He takes advantage of that, proclaiming himself a man of the people during campaign speeches and vilifying wealthy

---

* Andrew Johnson's son, Robert, is also rumored to be the father of Dolly's children. When the freed slave William dies in 1943, "Robert Johnson" is listed as the father on his death certificate.

plantation owners. "I have not got many slaves; I have got a few; but I made them by the industry of these hands," he says.

So, it comes as no surprise when Andrew Johnson is elected to the US Senate in 1857. The former tailor continues to support slavery, speaking out against those who would attempt to end the practice. Johnson's one key piece of legislation is a bill that would provide free farmland for white men. This Homestead Act fails in the Senate. However, he becomes an unlikely hero to abolitionists after refusing to leave the Senate when Tennessee secedes, a public statement of his strong support for the Union.

Even after the Civil War begins, Johnson remains in Washington while his family and slaves stay home in Tennessee.

As the Union army takes control of his home state, Abraham Lincoln appoints Johnson its military governor. Thus, he returns to Tennessee in 1862. Johnson's growing influence makes it possible for him to make a special request of President Lincoln. When the Emancipation Proclamation is issued, Lincoln *exempts* Tennessee. So, while slaves are free everywhere in the Confederacy, an exception is Johnson's home state.[*]

Johnson is a political animal and knows he can no longer support slavery. He now wishes to align himself more closely with Abraham Lincoln. It is also becoming clear that the North will win the war and slavery is doomed, so there is little sense in supporting it. On August 8, 1863, Johnson frees his own slaves. Most choose to remain with him as paid employees.[†]

He states, "I, Andrew Johnson, do hereby proclaim freedom to every man in Tennessee. I will indeed be your Moses and lead you through the Red Sea of war and bondage, to a fairer future of liberty and peace."

Yet Andrew Johnson is *not* a believer in equality. "Everyone would and must admit that the white race was superior to the black," he writes a friend.

---

[*] Though it is commonly believed that the Emancipation Proclamation freed all slaves, the directive applied only to border states and states actively rebelling against the Union. Louisiana, Tennessee, and portions of Virginia were by then occupied by federal troops and were exempt.

[†] To this day, Tennessee celebrates August 8 as Emancipation Day.

It is a quick rise for Andrew Johnson. Abraham Lincoln serves only six weeks of his second term. Now Johnson must run the country.

As a favor to Mary Todd Lincoln, the new president and his family do not move into the White House for six weeks. Johnson continues living at the Kirkwood Hotel, using space in the Treasury Building for his temporary new office. It is there that he holds his first reception for foreign dignitaries.

After taking up residence in the White House, the new president entertains frequently, despite the deep postwar tensions. His wife, Eliza, is confined to her bedroom on the second floor with tuberculosis, so Johnson appoints his eldest child, Martha Johnson Patterson, to serve as First Hostess. Her husband is David Trotter Patterson, who will become a senator in 1866 when Tennessee formally joins the Union.

"We are plain people, from the mountains of Tennessee, called here for a short time by a national calamity," states thirty-six-year-old Martha. But the truth is somewhat different. She attended Miss English's Seminary in Washington and was often seen at social functions in the Polk White House.

It is Martha Patterson, dressed tastefully in a black dress, her dark hair in curls adorned with flowers, who greets guests as they enter a function. And it is also Martha who continues the renovation begun by Mary Todd Lincoln, spending $30,000 to update the aging White House building.*

She orders the demolition of the East Wing, updates sanitary conditions in the kitchen, and even oversees the feeding and care of cows wandering the White House grounds. Martha also expands the practice of hanging portraits of previous presidents on the White House walls to convey the building's history—a tradition that continues to this day.

The day begins at 4:00 a.m., when the president's freed slaves and others build fires in the kitchen.

The president awakens at dawn. He does not have a routine but enjoys having a manservant dress him and wait his table at breakfast. The president works through the day and late into the night. He has long

---

* $2.6 million in modern currency.

conversations with old friends from his many years in Washington, and he takes occasional trips to the circus and watches minstrel shows. Checkers are Johnson's game of choice, often enjoyed with a glass or two of Tennessee bourbon. When he attends church, which happens sparingly, he and Eliza prefer the Methodist service—though Johnson is also drawn to Catholicism, if only because there is no charge for the pew.

At first, everyone in Washington is President Johnson's friend.

But that support begins to erode quickly. Johnson does as he pleases his first eight months in office, with Congress in recess before the return of southerners to the chamber. In the absence of opposition, he sets forth his own policies on Reconstruction, as the postwar reunification of America is known. Despite his claims of being a "Moses for freed slaves," he opposes full equality for black people as well as their right to vote. In this way, Johnson alienates many in the North. Senator Charles Sumner of Massachusetts says, "Johnson is an insolent drunken brute in comparison with which Caligula's horse was respectable."

The criticism is not wholly unjustified. Andrew Johnson allows the South to install "Black Codes"—new laws that are slavery by another name. He also pardons thousands of southerners who committed treason against the United States, many of them the same wealthy planters he once despised.

Congress soon fights back.

Upon its return, Republicans pass a series of sweeping measures designed to ensure black civil rights. This includes the Fourteenth Amendment to the Constitution, guaranteeing freedom to all. President Johnson vetoes each bill only to see Congress override him. It is an embarrassing display.

Soon, a furious Johnson undertakes a lengthy series of campaign speeches during the midterm elections of 1866. His attacks on Republicans are vile and coarse. Very often he is drunk. Whatever popular appeal Johnson once possessed disappears. It is estimated that one million northerners turn against him after those speeches, all but ensuring he will not be renominated in 1868.

In February of that year, the House of Representatives votes to impeach Andrew Johnson—the first time such a thing occurs to a president in American history. The charge is "high crimes and misdemeanors." When the motion goes to the Senate, thirty-six votes are required to convict the president. But only thirty-five senators are in favor, sparing Johnson's presidency by one vote.[*]

The impeachment crisis ends on May 26, but the bitterness continues. Johnson's antiblack policies are already sabotaging Reconstruction. Violent pro-white groups such as the Ku Klux Klan are emerging in the South, physically attacking freed slaves. This secret society composed of former Confederate soldiers uses the cover of darkness to whip, torture, and murder. They also attack white schoolteachers who tutor black children.

Though clearly a failed president, Andrew Johnson is defiant to the end. He claims unjust Republican policies have victimized the South and offers unconditional amnesty to all Confederate soldiers. He argues against black voting rights, a privilege that will be ensured with the Fifteenth Amendment in 1870. Johnson insists his version of Reconstruction would have worked if only the Republicans had not gotten in the way.

But it really doesn't matter what President Johnson says—the Republicans refused to consider him for nomination, instead nominating General Ulysses S. Grant.

On March 4, 1869, Andrew and Eliza Johnson leave Washington and return to Tennessee. The new president, Ulysses S. Grant, supported efforts to impeach Johnson and publicly announces that he will not allow him to ride in his carriage on Inauguration Day. Rather than travel to the ceremony in a separate carriage, Johnson does not go at all. He remains in the White House, signing bills and issuing last-minute pardons. At noon, as Grant is being sworn in, Johnson stands from his desk, shakes hands with his cabinet members, and states, "I fancy I can already smell the sweet mountain air of Tennessee" as he walks out the door for the last time.[†]

---

[*] The primary charge against President Johnson was that he violated the Tenure of Office Act by firing Secretary of War Edwin Stanton. This law, which required Senate approval for removal of a cabinet officer, was passed in 1867. However, this was just a pretext for removing Johnson from office for disagreeing with the Republican congressional majority over Reconstruction.

[†] John Adams, John Quincy Adams, and Martin Van Buren also chose to avoid their successor's inauguration. After Andrew Johnson, it will be 152 years before Donald Trump becomes the next president to refrain from attending.

Upon returning home, there is disarray. The impeachment humiliation is still fresh in the former president's mind. His sons Charles and Robert are dead from alcohol-related incidents, and his youngest child, Andrew Jr., is headed toward the same fate. It is his daughters, Martha and Mary, who welcome the former president and First Lady back to Tennessee.

Andrew Johnson is relieved to be home. "I have performed my duty to my God, my country, and my family. I have nothing to fear," he reflects in a note that will be found among his papers after he dies.

Yet he longs to return to Washington and runs unsuccessfully for the House and Senate. Finally, in 1875, Johnson is chosen by the Tennessee state legislature to return to Congress. "I'd rather have this information than to learn that I had been elected President of the United States. Thank God for the vindication," he states.

During his brief return to the Senate, Andrew Johnson is a very vocal critic of his successor, Ulysses S. Grant. He rails against the corruption that is sullying his administration. But Grant ignores him. As do most other senators.

In July of that year, Johnson suffers a stroke while returning to Tennessee for a visit. His former slave, William, is at his bedside as he dies. Eliza Johnson succumbs to tuberculosis six months later at the home of her daughter Martha.

Perhaps the only positive of the Johnson administration is the purchase of Alaska from Russia in 1867. Secretary of State William Seward, now recovered from the assassination attempt on the night Lincoln was attacked, brokers the sale. The US government gives the Russians $7.2 million ($149 million today), and residents are granted three years to decide whether they would like to remain in Alaska as American citizens or go to Russia.

With that as one of his few accomplishments, Andrew Johnson goes down in history as the first president ever impeached.

And little more.

Chapter Eighteen

MAY 3, 1871

WASHINGTON, DC

DAY

President Ulysses S. Grant is out for blood.

And the longtime military man has seen a lot of it in his forty-nine years.

White supremacists rampage through the South, terrorizing black citizens. The worst of these vigilante groups is named the Ku Klux Klan, founded in 1865 by Confederate general Nathan Bedford Forrest. This is the fault of former president Andrew Johnson, whose Reconstructionist policies are very lenient to Southern rebels.*

The Klan's goal is to roll back the freedoms gained by former slaves. Their methods are violence and intimidation. By day, these marauders are doctors, lawyers, policemen, and other respectable occupations. At night, they turn into killers.

This anonymity leads them to use code to confirm their membership. Each chapter is autonomous, so all are suspicious of outsiders. "Who goes there?" is a simple introduction.

"A friend."

"Friend to whom?"

---

* Ku Klux Klan is a variation on the Greek word *kyklo*, meaning "circle." This emphasizes the tight bond of family but also the need for complete trust and secrecy within the circle.

"Friend to our country," comes the appropriate response.

But the Klan is no friend to the United States of America or President Ulysses S. Grant.

Among the worst of their attacks takes place in the South Carolina backcountry. Fifty Klansmen ride into small settlements on horseback. They storm into houses just after midnight. Black men are dragged outside, beaten in front of their families, and then forced to swear an oath that they will never vote at all.

The log cabin of Jim Williams is besieged. The Klan singles out the former slave because he ran away from his owner during the Civil War and fought for the North. This is a cardinal sin to the Klan, whose leader, General Forrest, led the massacre of Union troops during the Battle of Fort Pillow—of whom two hundred are black soldiers.

Locating Williams's cabin in western South Carolina in the dead of night, the Klansmen find only his wife and children. But after tearing up the floor, they discover Williams crouching beneath. They then drag the terrified man from his home, slide a noose around his neck, and hang him from a pine tree as his family watches. When Williams grabs a tree branch to block his fall, his fingers are hacked off with a knife, forcing him to drop to his death. For good measure, the Klansmen riddle his body with bullets.

President Grant has had enough. He signs an act of Congress stating that his administration will not tolerate these hate groups. Reconstruction is his top priority, and the Klan stands in the way. Local southern law enforcement is doing nothing to stop the terrorists, so Grant deploys federal troops and special prosecutors to bring the Klan to justice. The president suspends habeas corpus, leading many to call him a dictator. Grant does not care. His goal is nothing less than complete destruction of the Ku Klux Klan.

It has been just over two years since the Civil War general took office. He is small in stature and known for his skills on horseback and his aggressive battlefield strategies. He has been busy these past fourteen months, overseeing the ratification of the Fifteenth Amendment and creating a new cabinet office known as the Justice Department. Grant knows the South could very well get out of control again. He has to stop that.

The attack on the Klan works. When Forrest is called to appear before Congress, he denies being a Klansmen. By 1872, the Ku Klux Klan is in disarray.

The key moment comes after the death of Jim Williams. On orders from President Grant, Union troops led by Major Lewis Merrill infiltrate the Ku Klux Klan in Yorkville, South Carolina. In 1871, Klansmen throughout the region are arrested and the leaders brought to trial. Town doctor James Rufus Bratton is found to be the local leader. He escapes to Canada after being convicted of Williams's murder.

This is a high point in the up-and-down Grant presidency. His two terms in office take place at a pivotal time in American history. The president is an old soldier so principled that he refuses to use profanity. Unfortunately, those around him do not share his principles.

As with many early presidents, Ulysses S. Grant can trace his lineage to America's first settlers. Matthew and Priscilla Grant arrived in the Massachusetts Bay Colony in 1630. Over the centuries, the family moved west. It is 1822 when the future president, Hiram Ulysses Grant, is born in Point Pleasant, Ohio. His father, Jesse, is a tanner. His mother, Hannah, descended from Irish immigrants.

From a young age, "Ulysses," as his father calls the boy, shows a talent for riding horseback. He attends a local school and is an average student, but, in 1839, he is accepted into the US Military Academy at West Point. A mistake is made on his records, stating that his initials are "U. S. Grant," earning him the nickname "Uncle Sam" Grant—or just "Sam." He would answer to that name the rest of his life.

This same error leads to him being officially known as Ulysses S. Grant. He will never use the name Hiram again.

Upon graduation in 1843, Grant is assigned to the Jefferson Barracks outside St. Louis. There, he meets Julia Dent, a local beauty whose brother is a young lieutenant who also attended West Point. Julia is charismatic and outgoing, the opposite of her beau. Her distinguishing physical characteristic is one eye that has an opaque white iris—"wall eyed," as it is known. The couple marry in 1848, having four children who will go on to live long and healthy lives.

Soon, the Mexican-American War arrives, and Captain Grant is pressed into foreign service. He is unhappy to be away from Julia. But Grant distinguishes himself in battle, riding bravely through the streets of Monterrey on horseback to deliver a crucial message to a besieged unit, all the while taking sniper fire. He also befriends several fellow lieutenants who will later become Confederate army generals, such as James "Pete" Longstreet.

It is during the Mexican-American War that Grant meets Brevet Colonel Robert E. Lee, destined to become his battlefield adversary in the Civil War. Their lone encounter is not pleasant. Lee upbraids Grant for his slovenly appearance. It is a slight the young lieutenant will never forget.

Grant musters out of the army after the Mexican-American War, done in by the burden of a posting in California far from his family. He resigns his commission after repeated instances of drunkenness and returns to St. Louis. There he and Julia suffer seven years of hardship; Grant is unable to make a living outside the military. So, when the Civil War begins in 1861, the former soldier is eager to fight once again. However, his request for a new commission in the US Army is rejected by Major General George B. McClellan. Grant instead volunteers for the Illinois militia. From this simple beginning, he rises to become Abraham Lincoln's top general and proves to be the only Union commander capable of defeating Robert E. Lee.

In April 1865, Ulysses S. Grant accepts Robert E. Lee's surrender at Appomattox Court House in Virginia. At that famous meeting, Grant will remind Lee of their conversation long ago in Mexico. In typical fashion, the Confederate general's uniform will be spotless on that day while Grant's will be mud-spattered from a long ride on horseback.

Given the American public's fondness for voting top generals into the White House, U. S. Grant's decision to run for the presidency in 1868 is no surprise. His interest in politics comes from a lengthy speaking tour in 1866. The general-in-chief, as Grant was titled after the war, accompanies President Andrew Johnson through several northern cities. Grant is so disgusted by Johnson's pro-southern Reconstruction plans and drunken tirades that he abruptly goes home.

The president senses Grant's opposition to his policies and attempts to have him replaced. He fails. Sam Grant then gets his revenge—announcing his bid for the presidency.

On May 21, 1868, Grant is chosen as the Republican candidate. Schuyler Colfax from Indiana, Speaker of the House of Representatives, is his running mate. The contest pits Grant against Democrat Horatio Seymour, who is heavily backed by the Ku Klux Klan. The general wins easily, capturing 52 percent of the popular vote and winning the Electoral College by a margin of 214–80.

Thus, Ulysses S. Grant becomes one of the youngest presidents in American history at age forty-six. Ironically, Grant hates politics and has little skill as an orator. But that does not matter because his battlefield success captures the imagination of the American voter.

In Washington, Grant no longer has to worry about bad food.

Breakfast during the Civil War was strong black coffee and cucumber soaked overnight in vinegar—a pickle. But the president lays on the feedbag now that he is in the White House. Typical morning fare is broiled Spanish mackerel, bacon, eggs, buckwheat cakes, steak, and coffee.

The years away from family during his military service have given the president an appreciation for home life. Now, he dotes on his two youngest children, rolling pieces of bread into small "musket" balls and flicking the "ammunition" playfully at teenaged Nellie and eleven-year-old Jesse while seated at the dining room table.

Upon first taking office, Grant hires an army cook to serve as White House chef. But Julia is appalled that turkey is served at each state dinner. So Italian immigrant Valentino Melah, with a background in the hotel business, is brought in to oversee a revamp of the kitchen. Thus begins the five-foot-ten Grant's transition from a wartime 135 pounds to the portly president he becomes over two terms in office.

Turkey is replaced by twenty-nine-course dinners featuring French vegetable soup, a croquette of meat, steak served with mushrooms and potatoes, and leg of partridge—all washed down with fine European wine. Grant demands that his own beef be cooked until charred. He also insists that the chef serve no dessert other than rice pudding, about which he is fanatical.*

Two moments define the social White House under Grant. The first comes on March 4, 1873, during the grand dinner following the president's Second Inaugural. Grant's swearing-in ceremony is one of the coldest on record, with a temperature of six degrees. After a parade on the newly paved Pennsylvania Avenue, the festivities move to a temporary building holding six thousand revelers. But the night is cut short when the food and champagne freeze.

The second moment is the marriage of Nellie Grant. The president and First Lady are not in favor of the wedding, believing their nineteen-year-old daughter too young and their potential British son-in-law too much of an entitled layabout. But they splurge lavishly, making plans to redecorate the White House for the ceremony in the East Room.

However, the sudden death of Millard Fillmore on March 4, 1874, derails the plans. It is traditional to drape the Executive Mansion for thirty days of mourning after a past president dies. All mirrors and chandeliers are rimmed in black crepe, as are the front door and all window frames. In contrast, Grant's plan to redecorate the East Room features an all-white motif.

At precisely thirty days, the crepe is removed and a hurried construction crew races to complete the new design, adding a temporary wedding platform. On May 21, 1874, Nellie Grant marries English singer Algernon Sartoris.

The wedding is a national sensation. Nellie wears a white satin dress trimmed in Belgian lace and is lauded from coast to coast for her fashion sense. She and her eight bridesmaids descend the grand staircase as 250 guests look on. Army and navy officers in full dress uniform stand at attention, lining the final steps to the East Room altar. The *Daily Graphic* splashes the nuptials on page one. Security is tight due to the overwhelming demand for invitations.

Julia Grant, who has known years of deprivation and hardship during

---

* The reason Grant was so fond of rice pudding is unknown, but he enjoyed this dessert since his childhood.

her marriage, calls the White House years "the happiest period" of her life.[*]

★★★

It is not so happy for Sam.

The year is 1869. Grant is just a month into his presidency. Jay Gould and James Fisk, speculators from New York, have conceived of an outrageous plan to corner the gold market. The two men are well-known scoundrels with a history of committing fraud. Their plot is to convince the Grant administration not to sell any government gold. This will make the private supply of the precious metal more valuable. The two men enlist the help of Abel Rathbone Corbin, a financier married to President Grant's sister, Virginia.

Soon, Grant becomes suspicious. In the decades he has known Corbin, his brother-in-law has never shown interest in the gold market. And appearances can mean everything. If the public comes to believe that Grant is conspiring with a family member to help Gould and Fisk control gold prices, the implications could be disastrous. Grant is an honest man. He does not attend church but has a deep personal faith in God. His bouts of drinking in his younger days still dog his reputation, but no one has ever accused Grant of being deceitful.

On Friday, September 24, 1869, Grant orders $4 million of government gold to be sold on the open market.[†]

The president's goal is to break the speculators. He succeeds. The price of gold plummets and leads to financial ruin for many investors. This event is known as Black Friday. Despite Grant having no involvement in the sale, many Americans believe he stands to profit.[‡]

---

[*] Immediately after the wedding, Nellie Grant and her new husband moved to his home in England. A devastated President Grant went to Nellie's White House bedroom on the day of her departure and broke down sobbing. Ultimately, the predictions he and Julia made about the marriage are proven true. Though Nellie bears four children, Sartoris begins drinking heavily. She leaves him in 1889, receives a generous alimony settlement, and returns to the United States with the children. Nellie Grant marries again in 1912. She suffers a stroke three months later that leads to paralysis and ultimately her death in 1922 at sixty-seven.

[†] $92 million today.

[‡] Gould and Fisk anticipated Grant's maneuver and managed to emerge from Black Friday with their fortunes intact. In 1872, Fisk is shot and killed by his mistress's lover. Gould would be bilked out of $1 million by an investor in a subsequent investment scheme but ultimately made a second fortune in the railroad business.

★★★

Black Friday is just the beginning of Grant's scandals. His attempts to treat Native Americans more humanely are undone by unscrupulous individuals who steal government supplies from the Indians. The Credit Mobilier scandal sees railroad companies drastically overcharge the Treasury for services—and then bribe federal officials to keep it secret.

Distillers in the Midwest are swindling the government out of excise taxes. When the "Whiskey Ring" is finally prosecuted, Orville Babcock, Grant's private secretary, is arrested. Insisting Babcock is innocent, Grant becomes the only sitting president to voluntarily testify in court as a defense witness. Babcock is cleared of all charges.

In New York City, the Custom House is illegally charging outrageous fees to lease federal warehouses.

Then comes the Panic of 1873, which sees Wall Street shut down for ten days.*

At a time when America is still reeling from the Civil War, these scandals become a constant distraction. Grant is often accused of being gullible. The president believes in the power of the legislative branch—Congress—intentionally weakening the office of the presidency in a way that will remain in place until Theodore Roosevelt, thirty years later.

Overall, U. S. Grant does succeed on a number of fronts. He advances Reconstruction in the South, fights for equal rights for all, and remains an honest man.

In his 1877 farewell address to Congress, his Eighth Annual Message, a humble Grant admits his shortcomings, speaking of his "misfortune to be called to the Office of Chief Executive without any political training."

In closing, the outgoing president apologizes for his "errors of judgment."

Upon leaving office on March 4, 1877, U. S. Grant's popularity is high. He and Julia undertake a two-year trip around the world, where they are greeted by royalty wherever they go. Upon their return, Grant decides

---

* The Panic of 1873 was a nationwide depression brought on by the crash of the European stock market. One hundred US banks failed as a result.

to run once again for the White House. But the Republican Party is now split into liberal and conservative factions. Neither is particularly fond of Sam Grant. Thus, the nomination goes to another Civil War veteran, James A. Garfield.

Now in his sixties, Ulysses S. Grant is broke. A series of bad investments have badly hurt him and Julia. So, Grant decides to write his memoirs, and he enlists the famous Mark Twain to help him. At first, the writing goes well. But then, Grant is diagnosed with throat cancer—he was a daily smoker of cigars almost his entire adult life. Struggling mightily, Grant completes the book just days before his death. He is sixty-three years old and has wasted away to one hundred pounds.

Grant's funeral in New York City on August 8, 1885, draws one and a half million citizens.[*]

Eight years is not a long time in history, but many things changed in the Grant administration. He created Yellowstone National Park. Oversaw the completion of the transcontinental railroad. Advocated for legal reforms that benefit women.

But there was bad news as well. The Sioux wiped out General George Custer and his forces in Montana on June 25–26, 1876, forever escalating the conflict between white settlers and Indians. Although sympathetic to Native Americans, President Grant could do little to stop the bitter conflicts.[†]

By 1877, memories of the Civil War are fading. Economic expansion is on the rise. There are now thirty-eight states, and everything seems possible in the home of the free. Into this benign time steps a man so opposite Sam Grant it is hard to believe.

His name is Rutherford.

---

[*] Julia Grant lives to be seventy-six, dying of complications from heart and kidney disease on December 14, 1902. She is buried with her husband in Grant's Tomb in New York City. Mark Twain was an unknown reporter when he first met Grant in 1867. Their friendship grew over the next two decades, leading Twain to offer his advice for writing and editing the president's memoirs.

[†] More details about the Battle of the Little Bighorn can be found in the authors' *Killing Crazy Horse.*

Chapter Nineteen

R utherford B. Hayes senses disaster.

Election night. "Rud," the Republican candidate for president, believes he has no shot of winning. Family and friends gather here in his rented mansion to await the results on a cold and stormy night. Lucy Hayes, Rud's wife of twenty-three years, has already gone upstairs to lie down, claiming a headache. One by one, as telegrams arrive bearing bad news, guests pull on scarves and thick coats, heading home.

Hayes says his goodbyes. Rather than stay up waiting for the bad news, he joins Lucy in the bedroom.

The campaign of 1876 has been brutal—a contest so tight Hayes predicts that if he loses it will be the result of "violence and intimidation" in the South. It is a battle of governors: Hayes, the two-term leader of Ohio, and Democratic opponent Samuel J. Tilden, a bachelor and former corporate lawyer who runs New York. Tilden is a War Democrat. His election could derail a decade of Reconstruction.

Both candidates say they are reformers, vowing to halt the corruption of the Grant administration. Hayes, with a long beard down to his chest, is a diehard Republican. He is fearful of resurgent white supremacist groups in the South. Hayes supports suffrage and other civil rights for blacks.

That is a ruse.

It has been sixteen years since a Democrat lived in the White House, but the Republican streak appears to be over. Tonight's early election returns make it clear that Hayes will not win. He lost New York City in a landslide. Nationwide, Hayes is thousands behind in the popular vote. The pro-Republican *New York Tribune* has already headlined the morning edition "Tilden Elected."

The *Chicago Tribune*'s banner is even more blunt: "Lost."

Yet five hundred miles east of where Rutherford Hayes now sleeps, Medal of Honor honoree Daniel Sickles pays a late-night visit to Republican Party headquarters at the Fifth Avenue Hotel in New York City. President Grant's former minister to Spain has just returned from Europe and is nervous about tonight's election. Expecting a room full of enthusiastic supporters, Sickles finds the hotel almost empty. He begins sorting through election returns. Doing quick math, Sickles realizes Rutherford B. Hayes is not yet out of the race. Though behind in the popular vote, the Ohio governor can still be elected if he wins South Carolina, Louisiana, Oregon, and Florida.

"Stand firm," Sickles cables Republican leaders in those states. "Hayes has 185 votes."*

And 185 is precisely the number needed to win.

Sickles's amazing prediction comes true. When all the votes are counted, Democrat Samuel Tilden wins the popular vote 4,286,808 to 4,034,142—a victory of 50.9 percent to 47.9 percent.

Yet the Electoral College is a different story.

Tilden: 184.

Hayes: 185.

Immediately, there are widespread reports of election cheating. Democrats in Congress seek to block the counting of electoral votes. The final result is delayed for months as a special bipartisan commission investigates. Hayes is finally named president on March 2, 1877, just three

---

* Dan Sickles is projecting wins for Hayes in those four states.

days before the inauguration. Democrats still refuse to believe he won, pointing to Tilden's enormous advantage in the popular vote. They nickname Hayes "Rutherfraud" and "His Fraudulency."

Southerners call Hayes's victory "the fraud of the century." However, this "Compromise of 1877" means he agrees to withdraw federal troops from the South, effectively ending Reconstruction.

For this reason, hoping to restore faith in the voting process, Rutherford B. Hayes vows to serve just one term in office.

It is a promise he will regret.

The new president was born in Delaware, Ohio, on October 4, 1822, 145 miles north of where fellow Ohio native Ulysses S. Grant came into the world nearly six months earlier. The two men would appear to have many similarities throughout their lives: both are descended from America's earliest settlers, have relatives who fought in the Revolutionary War, and served as Union generals in the Civil War.

But they have little else in common. Grant's is a life of hardship while Hayes comes from wealth, despite a tragedy before he is even born. Their presidencies would be equally divergent. Hayes is intent on cleaning up every controversy made by his disorganized predecessor.

Rud, as he is called, is the fifth child born to Rutherford and Sophia Hayes. He never knows his father, a successful whiskey distiller who dies of a fever two months before his son's birth, leaving the child to be raised by his single mother and his sister, Fanny.

Success and affluence follow Hayes the rest of his life. Wealthy relatives fund Rud's education at Kenyon College in Ohio as well as Harvard Law School. Upon graduation, the future president establishes a thriving criminal law practice in Cincinnati. In 1852, at age thirty, he marries Lucy Ware Webb, an ardent Methodist and abolitionist who abstains from alcohol. She influences Hayes. He drinks a beer occasionally but little else. He also takes a hard anti-slavery stance, even defending runaway slaves as part of his law practice. The couple have eight children, five of whom live to adulthood.

Rutherford B. Hayes is almost forty years old when the Civil War begins. He stands five feet nine, with a medium build. Blue eyes and brown hair. As a child, his mother refused to let him engage in rough sports or fisticuffs, yet Rud has grown into a rugged individual, at ease on horseback and firing a gun. Rather than remain at home during the war, he uses political connections to arrange an officer's commission in the Twenty-Third Ohio Volunteers, ultimately rising to general. Though militarily inexperienced at the outset, Rud Hayes distinguishes himself as a leader. He is calm under fire. "His whole nature seemed to change in battle. From the sunny, agreeable, the gentle gentleman," future president William McKinley, who enlisted then rose to brevet major in the Twenty-Third, will remember, "he was, once the battle was on, intense and ferocious."

Hayes is wounded five times, including a moment when his left arm is fractured by a bullet. A horse is shot out from under him at the 1864 Battle of Cedar Creek in Virginia. There, he is also hit in the head with a spent musket ball that has already passed through the body of another soldier.

The Ohio Volunteers fight in several major engagements, including the bloody battle at Antietam, which Hayes misses while recuperating from one of his many wounds. Very often, "Mother Lucy" joins her husband in camp, earning the affection of the men as she tends to wounded soldiers.

In 1863, it is Lucy's turn to be consoled. Their fourth son, Joseph, dies of dysentery while visiting his father's encampment in the new state of West Virginia. He is not yet two years old. The Hayeses are devastated, Lucy calling the moment "the bitterest hour" of her life.

The couple's fifth son, George, is born one year later. He also dies in infancy from scarlet fever.

Politics arrives in 1864, even as the Civil War continues. Rutherford B. Hayes is nominated as the local Republican candidate for Congress. He accepts but refuses to campaign, stating that "an officer fit for duty who at this crisis would abandon his post to electioneer for a seat in Congress ought to be scalped."

Rud wins.

He is later elected governor of Ohio, during which time he founds Ohio State University. But in 1872, at age fifty, Hayes leaves politics of his own accord. However, he soon tires of having little to do. Three years later, in desperate need of a candidate, the state's Republican Party asks him to run for governor once more.

He wins again. Coincidentally, Cincinnati is home to the 1876 presidential convention. Former Speaker of the House James G. Blaine is the Republican front-runner but does not get the 378 delegates required to secure the nomination. Because he is a local politician, Hayes's name has been added to the list of six candidates as a courtesy. But he soon gains momentum, and on June 16, 1876, after seven ballots, he overtakes Blaine to win the nomination.

The war hero does not lobby for the nomination, but he accepts it. Hayes's running mate is chosen by the convention later the same day. The vice presidential candidate is Representative William A. Wheeler of New York. Hayes has never met the man. "I am ashamed to say: who is Wheeler?" he asks friends.

On March 5, 1877, Rutherford B. Hayes is sworn in as the nineteenth president of the United States.

Lucy Hayes, thrilled at her husband's success, eagerly takes to White House life. She soon becomes one of the most popular First Ladies in history. Technically, she is also the *original* First Lady. Though the term has been in casual use since the Washington administration, the Hayes presidency is the first time that term becomes an official title.

Lucy is the first wife of a president to graduate college. She is also an advocate for integration, inviting black musicians to play in the White House for the first time. Hayes says of his wife, "She is a genuine woman, right from instinct and impulse rather than judgment and reflection."

The nation has just come off a dizzying year of centennial celebrations, citizens everywhere marking the one hundredth anniversary of the United States. Indian wars in the West are bloodier than ever. California seethes with anti-Chinese sentiment. On the Mexican border, desperados ride into America to plunder towns and homes. And, as millions of Americans struggle with financial hardship, a handful of powerful corporate barons are stealing millions.

In addition, the North and South are still deeply divided by race.

Much to Hayes's disadvantage, the Democratic Party is regaining control of southern legislatures and congressional seats by intimidating black voters. Federal troops have occupied the South since the Civil War to prevent injustice. The bulk of the twenty-five-thousand-man US Army withdraws as stipulated in the Compromise of 1877 and has now moved west to fight Indians. The House of Representatives is overwhelmingly Democrat and refuses to fund the army if federal troops continue to patrol the South.

President Hayes thinks he has a solution. Should it succeed, Reconstruction will be complete. He agrees to remove the US military from Dixie if Democrats guarantee to uphold civil rights for all. They promise to do so, a vow quickly broken. White officials throughout the South soon use poll taxes, literacy tests, intimidation, and violence to deny black men the right to vote. These practices will continue for another century.

Back in the White House, President Hayes is under siege. The Democratic House attempts to alter election laws made after the Civil War. They believe repealing these statutes will lead to victory in the South and win them the presidency in 1880. One adviser tells Hayes, "They want to kill with impunity so many negroes as may be necessary to frighten the survivors from the polls in the south."

When the Republican Senate refuses to pass the antiblack legislation, the House attempts to shut down the entire government. Democrats defund the military and civil service. To make matters worse, the House of Representatives adjourns, and its members return home.

President Hayes is furious. He calls this behavior "Democratic attempts to revolutionize the government of our fathers" and demands that Congress return for a special session. They do.

After contentious debate, Congress *does* agree to keep the government open. But Democrats add a cunning stipulation: federal troops can *never* be used to keep the peace at polling places.

Hayes considers this an attack on the Constitution. His posture is that "it is the right of every citizen to cast one unintimidated ballot and have his ballot honestly counted."

So, he vetoes the military polling place bill.

The Democrats don't have the votes to override the veto.

But it's not over. The House tries again. Tensions mount between the North and South. Democrats even label the new legislation a "war measure."

Hayes does not back down. He vetoes the second bill, too. Finally, the president wins the day.

★★★

And then there is the matter of wealth.

The depression begun by the Panic of 1873 continues, with high unemployment and falling crop prices. Rail workers stage a massive strike in 1877 seeking better wages, forcing President Hayes to send in federal troops to quell rioting.

Yet for all the poverty in America, there exists a group of powerful men with more money than they can ever spend. The Hayes administration marks the rise of what will become known as the Gilded Age. The United States is being transformed into a new commercial society. Corporations control vast industries. The small local factories that once defined the American economy are being replaced.*

Rutherford B. Hayes sees the danger. America's richest man, Cornelius Vanderbilt, dies just before Hayes takes office, leaving a fortune of $105 million ($2.9 billion today). But other rich men, such as Andrew Carnegie and John D. Rockefeller, are proving that America is now being exploited by men of great wealth.

Hayes worries that the country might become a "government of corporations, by corporations, for corporations."

The president writes in his diary, "It occurred to me that it is time for the public to hear that the giant evil and danger in this country, the danger which transcends all others, is the vast wealth owned or controlled by a few persons. Money is power."

He continues, "Excessive wealth in the hands of the few means extreme poverty, ignorance, vice, and wretchedness as the lot of the many."

★★★

In these turbulent times, Rutherford B. Hayes finds tranquility in the White House. He travels extensively during his term, delivering short speeches around the country to sway voters. But returning home is always

---

* The term *Gilded Age* is coined by author Mark Twain in an 1873 novel by the same name. This is a time of materialism and political corruption defined by the gross excess of individuals who grow rich creating monopolies in steel, petroleum, and railroads.

a pleasure, for the Hayes Executive Mansion is one of the most relaxed in history.

The president's two youngest children, ten-year-old Fanny and five-year-old Scott, have the run of the White House. They have no lack of playmates, for Hayes has brought an astonishing eight dogs to Washington. There is also a cat named Piccolomini.

First Lady Lucy Hayes presides over all this. A short brunette with a quick wit, she is outgoing and fun loving, at ease making conversation with diplomats and household staff alike. There is no money to remodel the White House, so she makes sure the furniture is arranged to cover the holes in the carpet. It is Lucy who oversees the addition of running water to the mansion. She also adds the first telephone, typewriter, and phonograph.

The house is so full of guests at Christmas that the three oldest Hayes boys—Webb, Rutherford, and Joseph—are forced to sleep in bathtubs when they come home from college. The First Lady's decision to ban alcohol in the White House has given her the new nickname of "Lemonade Lucy." Her husband doesn't mind that at all, believing it will give him political currency with the growing Prohibition movement.

By year two, Rutherford B. Hayes is solving America's problems one by one.

Diplomatic discussions with China defuse tensions about immigration. Hostility at the Mexican border comes to an end as Hayes threatens to send soldiers into that country. Fighting with Native Americans in the West slackens as the frontier grows smaller.

The more difficult problem is corruption. Hayes is outraged by federal agents stealing money. In one major situation, he fires future US president Chester A. Arthur as collector of the Port of New York, a notorious place of corruption. For that, Rutherford B. Hayes earns the enmity of New York's powerful boss, Roscoe Conkling.

But perhaps the most important issue Hayes deals with is the fight for black voting rights in the South. There, he is not able to improve things.

After four years, President Hayes keeps his promise. He will not run for reelection in 1880. Another Republican, James A. Garfield, also from Ohio, secures the nomination.

On March 4, 1881, Rud and Lucy Hayes gather their kids and pets for the journey home to Ohio. The president essentially retires and does very little, completely staying out of national politics.

Lucy Hayes dies of a stroke on June 25, 1889, at age fifty-seven. Four years later, Rutherford Hayes passes away from a heart attack. He is seventy years old. In the last decade of his life, he continues to fight for black civil rights and prison reform. His writings reflect that his animosity toward corporate corruption does not diminish.

For now, the United States remains a rapidly changing nation in search of a positive direction.

Chapter Twenty

JULY 2, 1881
WASHINGTON, DC
9:00 A.M.

Death is stalking President James A. Garfield.

Saturday morning. Sun shining. The first day of the president's summer vacation. An eager Garfield rides in a small carriage to the Baltimore and Potomac Railroad Station. Secretary of State James Blaine drives the buggy. Garfield is six feet tall with a full beard. The coming journey has him energized. He amazed his teenaged sons just moments ago by performing a backflip while leaving the White House.

Garfield's boys, James and Harry, now ride behind the president in a second carriage. They will travel with their father. The first stop will be Williams College in Massachusetts, where Garfield will address his alma mater. Then the entourage will take the train to Long Branch, New Jersey. The president's wife, Lucretia, awaits in a rented cottage near the shore. The ocean air is thought to be good for her recent bout of malaria.

President Garfield does not have a bodyguard. It has been sixteen years since Abraham Lincoln's assassination, but a presidential security detail is still thought to be unnecessary. He is unconcerned.

A lone policeman greets Garfield as his carriage pulls up to the station. The president calls out to Officer Patrick Kearney, wondering how much time there is before his train leaves. A stoic Kearney shows Garfield his watch. Having ten minutes to spare, Garfield takes his time concluding a final conversation with James Blaine.

Finally, the president places one hand on the secretary of state's shoulder and says goodbye. Blaine, realizing the president of the United States does not have an escort, steps out to walk Garfield into the station, and the president's teenagers, Harry and Jim, follow behind.

Suddenly, remembering Officer Kearney's assistance, the president turns and tips his hat to the policeman, who waves from the street.

Everything is calm. Yet Garfield has no idea a killer is watching his every move. This would-be assassin has, in fact, been stalking the president for weeks.

Charles J. Guiteau, thirty-nine years old, is a former law clerk who has tried and failed several times to secure a job in the Garfield administration. That disappointment has left him angry and destitute. Guiteau's shoes are worn, his jacket threadbare. He is such a pest that White House officials have banned him from the grounds.

The Illinois native has known a life of failure. During one phase in the 1850s, he joined a utopian religious sect known as the Oneida Community. Among its beliefs was polygamous marriage. But the women of the group disliked Guiteau's sexual advances so thoroughly they rhyme him "Charles Git Out."

When Guiteau leaves the sect and marries, his wife soon asks for a divorce on the grounds of infidelity. She calls for a prostitute to testify in court. In addition to this embarrassment, Guiteau has no money. His life is falling apart.

Guiteau has gone from job to job, woman to woman. Delusional, he now believes his future lies in politics. After backing Garfield's presidential bid, the drifter feels he is owed a favor—and not just any favor. Guiteau believes it is his destiny to serve as a US consul in Paris. On March 5, 1881, he arrives in Washington, twenty-four hours after President Garfield's inauguration. Three days later, Guiteau attends a public gathering at the White House, where he actually meets the new president. Rambling, Guiteau explains that he campaigned vigorously on Garfield's behalf and would like a job.

President Garfield promises nothing.

In the three months since then, Guiteau has wandered Washington seeking to convince officials to employ him. No one will. Rejections pile up. So, a furious Guiteau decides he must *kill* Garfield in order for a new president to give him a job.

The would-be assassin first envisions using a knife. But he is not a tall or strong man. The would-be assassin immediately rejects that weapon, sure the president would overpower him.

So, Charles Guiteau buys a gun. Now, clutching his new .44-caliber British Bulldog pistol, the bearded Guiteau watches the president's carriage arrive on the corner of Sixth Street NW.

James A. Garfield steps into the train station. He turns right, his back to the would-be assassin, who stands three feet away.

Charles J. Guiteau places his forefinger on the trigger.

The man about to die has a dubious past. After marrying Lucretia Randolph in 1858, the Garfields do not honeymoon due to lack of money. They move into a boardinghouse and, though wed, begin living separate lives. "Crete" Garfield writes a friend that hers is a marriage of "duty."

This is because James A. Garfield still pretends he is single. The young academic is charismatic and handsome. Dark hair, blue-gray eyes. He complains to friends of being "restless and unsatisfied" with marriage.

Born in 1831, James Garfield is the last of the log cabin presidents. His heritage is descended from America's first immigrants, with Edward Garfield arriving in Massachusetts from England in 1630. The future president is the son of farmer Abram Garfield, the youngest of five children. But Abram dies of pneumonia shortly before James's second birthday. The boy is raised by his widowed mother, Eliza, with whom he is very close.

The future president's childhood is spent in such great poverty that Garfield is the butt of jokes from local children who make fun of his single mother, his unwashed hands and face, and his dirty, tangled hair. He is so prickly about the family's lack of money that "sensitive as a girl" is a frequent insult. James Garfield will become one of the poorest men in history to rise to the White House.*

"Poverty is uncomfortable," Garfield remembers one day. "But nine times out of ten the best thing that can happen to a young man is to be tossed overboard and compelled to sink or swim."

The Ohio frontier is a hard place. Thick woods, deep ravines, powerful rivers, hardscrabble living. Before he is ten, Garfield learns to hunt because it means meat on the table. As he grows to full height, revenge comes into play. The future president picks fights with those who once taunted him, taking delight in thrashing his enemies. Some say he lives in a fantasy world, with one cousin accusing him of "building lofty air castles." As he grows into a man, Garfield distances himself from the hardship of day-to-day life so completely that he actually falls into a well while lost in thought.

Young James Garfield dreams of running away to sea. That thought comes to an end when he attempts to find work on a sailing ship in Cleveland. The drunken captain verbally embarrasses Garfield, so much so that he flees the laughter of the crew—shaming him as he steps back on the shore.

Eventually, Garfield finds salvation in reading. Nothing makes him happier than opening a book. Garfield enjoys history but is most fascinated by the fictional story of Robinson Crusoe. He reads by firelight, often poring over the same book repeatedly because he cannot afford new ones.

Hard work, education, and desperation fuel Garfield's rise. He labors as a janitor, carpenter, and mule driver on a canal boat to pay for college. At seventeen, he begins attending Geauga Academy in Chester Township, where he meets his future bride. Lucretia Randolph is a petite brunette with dark eyes and a frail demeanor. The ebullient Garfield is smitten, though nothing comes of their acquaintance at first. He is outgoing, thickly muscled, and still fond of using his fists. Lucretia is intent on getting a strong education and focuses more on her studies than finding a husband.

Yet James Garfield slowly becomes more polished. The young scholar seeks higher education at what will become known as Hiram College in Ohio. Upon arriving, he is surprised that Lucretia is also enrolled. The

---

* Virginia likes to claim itself the "Mother of Presidents," but Ohio is home to an equal number. Garfield is the fourth of eight men from the Buckeye State, as he was born in Cuyahoga County in 1831. Virginia and Ohio both claim William Henry Harrison as a native son, as he was born in the former and later moved west.

future president becomes so exceptional at his studies the school makes him a teacher of the Classical Greek language. He is equally stunned when Lucretia is one of his students.

The couple begin courting.

The romance continues until Garfield leaves Ohio for two years to attend Williams College in Massachusetts. Lucretia waits patiently for his return. Eagerly, she takes the train to his graduation, only to notice another young lady vying for Garfield's attention. Heartbroken, she confronts James, who admits to the relationship. Not for the first time, he swears to end the affair and be faithful.

That promise turns out to be false. However, Garfield's career continues to rise. He is named principal of Western Reserve University and then elected to the Ohio state senate, a job that keeps him from home for months at a time. When the Civil War begins, Garfield continues his long absences from his wife by joining the fight. After leading a successful charge against Confederate forces at the Battle of Middle Creek in Kentucky, James Garfield is named brigadier general. This success, in turn, leads to his election to Congress in 1862. Lucretia does not follow her husband to Washington, preferring to stay at home in Ohio.

All this takes a toll. In the first five years of their marriage, James and Lucretia are together less than twenty weeks. The future president has many extramarital liaisons, even while the couple give birth to a baby named Eliza. But, in 1863, Eliza dies from diphtheria. That deteriorates the marriage even further.

In all, James Garfield serves eighteen years in the House of Representatives, and, in 1880, he is elected to the Senate—but he never serves.

The presidential election intervenes.

It is a troubling time for the Republican Party, which has not lost a presidential election in twenty-four years. Rutherford Hayes is retiring, and former president Ulysses S. Grant is seeking a comeback. This infuriates candidates who have been patiently waiting their chance to run. As the June 1880 convention in Chicago goes through one ballot after another, there is no clear majority candidate. James Garfield stays out of the race, supporting fellow Ohio politician John Sherman.

But Sherman, the younger brother of Union general William Tecumseh Sherman, gets nowhere in the presidential process.*

Finally, after thirty-three ballots, supporters add Garfield's name. He gets seventeen votes on the subsequent ballot. Exhausted, Republicans rally to the former brigadier general. After thirty-six ballots, Garfield emerges victorious.

Controversial New Yorker Chester A. Arthur, who was fired by President Hayes for corruption, is added to the ticket as vice president with the hope that he will deliver his home state to the Republicans.†

Lucretia Garfield, who was once so miserable in Washington, now thrills to the idea of living in the White House. She campaigns aggressively for her husband, even allowing people to gather on their front porch to debate issues.

Opposing Garfield is Winfield Scott Hancock, a Democrat and former army officer. Hancock fought in the Mexican-American and Civil Wars and is considered a hero for his leadership during the 1863 Battle of Gettysburg.

Knowing they cannot attack Hancock's patriotism, the Republicans instead portray the general as an enemy of the working man because he opposes tariffs that protect jobs. The strategy works. On November 7, 1880, James A. Garfield wins by fewer than ten thousand votes, and the electoral count is 214 for Garfield, 155 for Hancock.

Charles J. Guiteau wants to be remembered for killing a president.

He chose his British revolver because he "thought it would look nice in a museum." Now, President Garfield is just three feet away. Yet even

---

* John Sherman did not win the nomination because he was a poor public speaker, "thin as a rail, over six feet high, with close cropped beard and possessed of bad teeth." Even his home state of Ohio was against his nomination.

† Also on the vice presidential ballot in 1880 is Senator Blanch Kelso Bruce of Mississippi, who receives eight votes. Bruce becomes the first African American to win votes at a major party's convention. He is also the first of his race to serve a full term in the Senate. There was one ballot for vice president at the Republican Convention and Bruce won eight votes, making him the first African American to receive votes for an executive branch office—the vice presidency—at a national party convention.

at that short distance, Guiteau misses the first shot, the bullet slamming into Garfield's right arm, passing through flesh and suit jacket.

"My God, what is this?" demands the surprised president.

Garfield twists his head around to see who shot him. Then Guiteau fires again, his second round striking the taller man in the back. The president drops face down to the carpeted floor. He vomits. The entry wound on the back of his gray jacket spreads into a broad crimson stain. Screaming breaks out in the railway as the crowd hears gunfire and witnesses the fallen Garfield. Among the onlookers is Robert Todd Lincoln, son of the former president, who has come to board the train with his boss. The thirty-seven-year-old Lincoln is Garfield's secretary of war.

The assassin makes a run for it. But Officer Kearney, reacting to the gunshots, grabs the shooter. In his extreme panic, the policeman forgets to take Guiteau's gun, a fact he will only discover at the police station.

Soon, the streets of Washington fill with lynch mobs eager to avenge the shooting. Garfield has only been in office four months but is already popular. Washington police must hide Guiteau for his own safety.

But President Garfield is not dead. The second shot missed his spine but broke two ribs. The bullet is hidden somewhere near his pancreas. Within five minutes, the president is under a doctor's care. A horsehair mattress is found in a back room. Garfield is laid upon it, barely conscious and in great pain. A surgeon who happens to be in the station joins the growing number of medical professionals attempting to help. He enters the upstairs room and bends over to check Garfield's condition, making Charles Purvis the first black doctor in history to treat a president of the United States.

A telegram is immediately sent to Lucretia, telling her of the shooting. Coincidentally, former president Ulysses S. Grant is staying in a nearby cottage at the Jersey shore. He arrives to check on the stunned First Lady, even though he is also distraught.

But Grant delivers some good news: friends in Washington say the president's wounds are not fatal.

Immediately, Lucretia returns to the White House by special train.

Then she waits.

★★★

Two months later, James Garfield is still alive. He has been moved from the White House to the Jersey shore to convalesce. Charles Guiteau remains in a Washington jail, charged with attempted murder.

The bullet from Guiteau's second shot remains hidden in Garfield's torso. Despite a team of nine doctors attending to the president, none has been able to extract the round.

That situation leads to blood poisoning and infection. On September 19, 1881, James A. Garfield dies. He served just six months as president.[*]

The nation is shocked by the assassination of President Garfield. Immediately upon the president's death, the charge against Charles Guiteau is elevated to murder. He pleads not guilty, representing himself. The court appoints a defense lawyer anyway. It doesn't matter. On June 30, 1882, the assassin is convicted and sentenced to death. Expecting to win the verdict and already planning a national speaking tour, Guiteau rises to his feet after the sentencing and screams at the jury, "You are all low, consummate jackasses!"

Five days later, Charles Guiteau is hanged. He waves and smiles to spectators on his way to the gallows, believing himself a hero. He dances up the hanging steps and then recites a poem he has written as his last words. A hood is placed over his head. The hangman pulls his deadly lever. The floor drops. Rope stretches.

Guiteau's neck snaps.

Vice President Chester A. Arthur is sworn in on September 20, 1881. He is amazed by this turn of events, having enjoyed the relative anonymity of the vice presidency. Few in America even know his name. Arthur's wife died shortly before he and Garfield won the election. Devastated, he virtually disappeared from public life.

But now, Chester A. Arthur is back.

And things will not go well.

---

[*] Lucretia will go home to Ohio with her family, where she will live thirty-six more years before dying of pneumonia on March 14, 1918.

Chapter Twenty-One

MARCH 2, 1882

WASHINGTON, DC

2:00 A.M.

President Chester A. Arthur is up late.

The fifty-two-year-old widower walks the streets of Washington with friends. Thursday night. Dead of winter. Moon almost full. Dewitt "Clint" Wheeler and Stephen French are visiting from New York. There is no security detail, though that does not really matter—right now the capital's broad boulevards are empty.[*]

Arthur is six feet two, impeccably dressed in a silk top hat, gloves, and a warm coat bought from an expensive Manhattan tailor. He is well known for his polished manners. The president owns *eighty* pairs of pants and wears a tuxedo every time he attends a play. Arthur is an amiable man who enjoys engaging complete strangers in conversation, unlike his predecessors. U. S. Grant simply tipped his hat and said nothing while President Garfield rarely left the White House at all.

President Arthur enjoys lavish meals, conversation that avoids politics, and staying up until the early morning hours. Other than the occasional horseback ride, walks are his only exercise. Tonight's dinner is served just before midnight. Typical fare is seafood and steaks, beef,

---

[*] Clint Wheeler and Steve French were well known to the press as two of the top officials in the New York City Republican Party.

lamb, or turtle. The meal is followed by a card game played while smoking cigars and drinking claret.

During Arthur's days working in New York City, such a feast would have been followed by a night of carousing, a major source of contention between Arthur and his wife during their twenty-one-year marriage, despite the fact that he was not a skirt chaser. "Arthur was always the last man to go to bed in any company and was fond of sitting down on his front steps at 3 a.m. and talking," one friend will remember.

Nell Arthur, a Virginian, raises the couple's two children in style. She likes the finer things in life and is generally a good companion for her husband. However, Nell dies from pneumonia on January 12, 1880, at age forty-two. She does not live long enough to see Chester become president. In her honor, Arthur pays for a stained-glass window dedicated to her at nearby St. John's Episcopal Church. From his second-floor White House bedroom, the president can see the distant light shining through this memorial.

It has been a time of grief for Chester A. Arthur. In addition to losing his wife, the assassination of James Garfield remains shocking. The leap from vice president to president has caught Arthur completely by surprise.

In truth, Chester Arthur dislikes being president. He procrastinates, does as little work as possible, and detests not being able to delegate hard decisions to subordinates—as he did while running the Custom House in New York City.

The president also hates living in the White House. Working in an office just down the hall from his bedroom is claustrophobic and isolating. With the exception of the window dedicated to Nell, the view from Arthur's quarters is dark government buildings instead of New York City's bustling streets.

So, Chester Arthur is bored with Washington. His ten-year-old daughter, also Nell, remains in their Lexington Avenue home in New York, cared for by servants. His son, Chester, is studying at the College of New Jersey. Other than a cook and a steward, Arthur is by himself each night in the Executive Mansion, often waking up sad. "President Arthur has found himself the loneliest man who ever occupied the White House," writes the *Buffalo Commercial*.

So tonight, the president is happy to be walking around Washington with his old friends. They run into a reporter, who is startled the three men are simply wandering.

The late night is no problem because Chester Arthur often sleeps until 10:00 a.m. Then he will put on a suit of the finest tweed and drink coffee and eat a buttered roll for breakfast in his private dining room on the first floor. After that, the president will walk upstairs to his office, conduct cabinet meetings, and then wait impatiently for dinner.

Former president Rutherford B. Hayes is outraged by President Arthur. He does not like that the ban on alcohol in the White House has been lifted. Hayes cannot believe that a man he once fired for "corruption" has ascended to the highest office in the land. And he certainly does not approve of the lavish entertaining that dwarfs anything he ever did. "Nothing like it ever before in the Executive Mansion," Hayes rails. "Liquor, snobbery, and worse."

Yet the wealthy lifestyle Hayes rebukes is something Chester Arthur has always wanted. For he was born in far less luxurious circumstances. Arthur's roots are in the woods of Vermont and the Baptist church, in which his father was a minister. The family is transient as he grows up, moving from one town to another while the Reverend William Arthur preaches throughout the Northeast. Chester, born in 1829, is the fifth of nine children. He learns his lessons but rejects the rural life.

Arthur's dream is to become a wealthy New York lawyer. After graduating third in his class at Union College, he earns a job as a Manhattan law clerk in 1854. Throughout his twenties, Arthur lives in a boardinghouse on Broadway and makes a name for himself defending runaway slaves. His father was a staunch abolitionist.

Along the way, a roommate from Virginia named Dabney Herndon introduces him to his cousin Ellen Herndon, also known as Nell. Things progress. She is twenty-two years old and Arthur twenty-nine when they marry in 1858.

Conflict arises between the couple as the Civil War looms. Chester Arthur has been appointed quartermaster of the New York State militia, a task he performs so well that he rises to the rank of brigadier general. Arthur chooses not to join the fighting, instead spending the war building a law practice. His specialty is representing clients suffering personal or property loss due to the war. This makes him rich.

It is also during this time that Chester Arthur comes under the thrall of Roscoe Conkling, the feared boss of New York's Republican political machine. Conkling is the same age as Arthur but far more conniving. An attorney and US senator, he uses patronage and strict adherence to the party line as a means of achieving power. Arthur becomes a top Conkling lieutenant, rewarded with the plush job of chief counsel to the New York City Tax Commission in 1869. The job pays $10,000 per year at a time when an average worker makes less than $500.*

In 1871, Chester Arthur gets a promotion. Conkling arranges for President Grant to appoint Arthur to the position of collector of the Port of New York. It becomes his job to supervise the 1,300 agents gathering import duties. As part of the position, Arthur receives a portion of all fines assessed against undervalued imports. He also accepts kickbacks and bribes, which are immediately sent to Boss Conkling to fund the Republican machine.

For seven years, Chester Arthur receives a total income equivalent to $2 million in today's money. New York's port is the lucrative heart of the nation's shipping and immigration. He and Nell own a comfortable home at 123 Lexington Avenue, a five-story brick building in the Romanesque Revival style. The collector has little to do at work, as his job is entirely run by underlings. The minister's son, now in his early forties, enjoys the best of everything. At Nell's encouragement, he begins attending the theater and polishing his manners to better enjoy upper society.

The election of Rutherford B. Hayes in 1876 brings an end to Chester Arthur's reign over the ports. Almost immediately, Hayes attacks corruption and tries to bring down Roscoe Conkling. Arthur is removed from his job in 1878.

It gets worse three years later. The truth is that Chester Arthur is an absentee father. He often travels, leaving his wife and two children alone.

In early January 1880, Arthur is in Albany, the New York state capital. While he is away, Nell attends a concert and is caught in a downpour

---

* $300,000 in modern currency.

while waiting for a carriage. She falls ill with pneumonia. Arthur receives the news and rushes back to be with his wife. He finds her lying in bed, unconscious. Her lung condition has been compounded by a heart ailment, and a physician has sedated her with morphine.

Chester Arthur sits with his wife around the clock. He speaks to her and holds her hand. Yet Nell never wakes up.

Arthur is shattered. A friend describes him as "completely unnerved." Nell is buried four days later at the Arthur family plot in Albany.

Chester A. Arthur's road to the White House is strange. He doesn't know the Republican presidential nominee, James Garfield, at all. Garfield chooses him because the party needs to carry the state of New York. Although Arthur did not campaign to be the vice presidential nominee, he is very pleased.

"The office of the vice president is a bigger honor than I have ever dreamed of attaining," Arthur states.

The new president moves into the White House three months after President Garfield dies of his gunshot wounds.

The mansion is once again falling apart. Arthur delayed his presence until renovations could take place. Louis C. Tiffany, son of the famous New York jeweler, is brought in to undertake a drastic redesign. The East Room is completely redone, but Arthur's greatest focus is his personal dining room, where the walls are painted in gold and pomegranate. A fireplace and new sideboard are added. When he finally moves in, President Arthur asks his youngest sister to spend four months a year serving as official hostess. Mary Arthur McElroy, the forty-year-old wife of an insurance salesman, agrees.

This proves quite necessary: Chester Arthur will hold fifty state dinners during his short term in office and host dozens more private functions. The Arthur White House will gain an unmatched reputation for the finest food and wines, the best cigars, and a cosmopolitan atmosphere.

"I dined at the White House yesterday," writes the wife of Secretary of State Blaine. "The dinner was extremely elegant, hardly a trace of the old

White House taint anywhere, the flowers, the damask, the silver, the attendants, all showing the latest style and an abandon in expense and taste."

In time, President Arthur's meals get longer, his waist wider. He has grown muttonchop sideburns, and his hair is graying. His walks become less frequent. The nights grow later, with dinner never starting until at least 10:00 p.m.

But high living will soon catch up with Chester Arthur.

On August 1, 1882, Dr. Brode Herndon, Arthur's longtime friend, writes in his private diary, "The President sick in body and soul."

President Arthur has Bright's disease, a fatal kidney ailment. Doctors expect his health to deteriorate rapidly. Arthur is in constant pain.

Yet the president will finish his term, never telling the public about his illness.

As he is ailing, Arthur's presidency becomes largely ceremonial.

He is present at the opening of the Brooklyn Bridge in 1883, begins diplomatic relations with Korea, authorizes the building of the United States Navy's first steel ships, and accepts the Statue of Liberty as a gift from France.

The biggest controversy that envelops the Arthur administration is Chinese immigration. In the mid-nineteenth century, Chinese men begin immigrating to California in order to work on the transcontinental railroad. When that is completed in 1869, many Chinese immigrants turn to mining. White settlers see them as a threat. In addition, the Naturalization Act of 1790 does not allow Chinese immigrants to seek citizenship, which is limited to "free white persons."

Vigilantes throughout California start terrorizing the immigrants. In Los Angeles, nineteen Chinese people are shot or hanged in a single night, including a fourteen-year-old boy. "The Chinese must go!" is a common refrain throughout the West.*

---

* The Los Angeles Chinese Massacre of 1871 was an attack by an estimated five hundred white and Latino Americans based on rumors that Chinese gangs were killing local citizens. Eight men were convicted of manslaughter for the murders, although all the convictions were overturned on a legal technicality.

In response, Congress passes a bill stipulating that no Chinese person be allowed to enter the United States for a period of twenty years. This was the Chinese Exclusion Act of 1882. It bans laborers from immigrating but makes some exceptions for "non-laborers" such as diplomats and merchants.

President Arthur vetoes the legislation.

He ultimately gives in when a bill reducing the exclusion to ten years is placed before him.

The *New York Times* congratulates Arthur on his "firmness and wisdom."

Another newspaper, however, is not impressed with Arthur's presidency. The *Chicago Tribune* writes, "Mr. Arthur's temperature is sluggish. He is indolent. It requires a great deal for him to get to his desk and begin the dispatch of his business. Great questions of public policy bore him. No president was ever given to so much procrastination as he is."

Arthur does manage to get an anti-corruption law passed, called the Pendleton Civil Service Reform Act. It demands that merit, not patronage, will be the basis for federal hiring.

But the truth is that President Chester A. Arthur is not strong enough to rein in bigotry and other wrongs. So, there is not much enthusiasm for his reelection. In fact, he loses the nomination to former secretary of state James Blaine on June 6, 1884.

But Blaine does not carry the day. Instead, it is New York governor Grover Cleveland who is elected president. Cleveland is the first Democrat to win the presidency in twenty-eight years.

And he is a man with a past.

Chester Arthur goes down in history as a mystery. No great achievements in office, no indelible profile. He dies on November 18, 1886, in New York City at the age of fifty-seven. Friends and family surround his bedside. He is buried in Albany next to his wife.

While the nation deeply mourned his assassinated predecessor, James A. Garfield, little notice is taken of Chester Arthur's demise.

Chapter Twenty-Two

G rover Cleveland has a secret.

It has been ten days since the governor of New York was selected as the Democratic candidate for president at the party's national
convention in Chicago. He has kept his dark past hidden for a decade.
But now the scandal is revealed in black and white as the readers of the
Buffalo *Telegraph* open their morning newspapers. Immediately, the city
is awash in shock and indignation.

"A Terrible Tale," screams the headline.

"A Dark Chapter in a Public Man's History."

The presidential campaign of Grover Cleveland—a candidate whose
slogan is "Grover the Good"—may be over before it has even begun.

The situation begins on December 15, 1873.

Thirty-eight-year-old Maria Halpin is leaving work on a cold night
in Buffalo. After stepping outside the Flint & Kent Department Store,
Maria encounters Grover Cleveland. Nearly six feet tall and powerfully
built, he is a bachelor who has been pursuing her romantically for six
months. Cleveland is also the Eric County sheriff. Halpin is a regular

churchgoer and already the mother of two children by her deceased husband. She has little interest in the lawman, but he is relentless.

Maria Halpin's plans for the night change when Cleveland invites her to dinner. She says no at first, but he is "persistent," in her words. They walk together to the Ocean Dining Hall and Oyster House. Afterward, the burly sheriff accompanies the trim brunette back to her boardinghouse.

What transpires next becomes an object of contention. Maria alleges Grover Cleveland pushes his way into her bedroom for sexual activity "by force and without my consent." Through surrogates, Sheriff Cleveland acknowledges that he and Halpin were "illicitly acquainted" but that the act was consensual.

Nevertheless, Halpin refuses to see Grover Cleveland again.

Six weeks later, her pregnancy is confirmed. She informs Cleveland that he is the father and requests that he marry her so she might avoid the shame of giving birth to an illegitimate child. The sheriff does not give Halpin an answer, repeatedly putting her off.

On September 14, 1874, Maria Halpin gives birth to a boy at Buffalo's home for unwed mothers. Cleveland takes responsibility for the baby, naming him Oscar Folsom Cleveland. But then, the sheriff pays a group of men to abduct the child. And not only that, but he also uses his political influence to have Halpin thrown into the Providence Lunatic Asylum.

Treating Maria Halpin is Dr. William G. King. The *Chicago Tribune* reports King's story: "She was brought to the asylum without warrant or form of law. When he examined her he found that she was not insane, though she had been drinking. The managers of the asylum had no right to detain her."

Maria Halpin is released five days later. She hires an attorney to help her regain custody of her son. This is successful. However, Cleveland knows she cannot afford to care for the boy. In an effort to distance himself from Halpin and his son, Grover Cleveland offers her $500 to give the child up for adoption. Additionally, Maria Halpin can make no further financial claims against the sheriff. She signs a document making the transaction official and accepts the money.*

---

* $15,000 in modern currency. The details of the Cleveland-Halpin affair can be found in the September 26, 2013, issue of *Smithsonian Magazine*.

The baby is adopted by the same Dr. King of the Providence Asylum, who changes the child's name and raises him as his own. Maria Halpin leaves Buffalo shortly afterward, moving close to New York City.*

With Maria Halpin departed, Grover Cleveland sets his sights on higher political office. In 1881, seven years after the scandal, he is elected mayor of Buffalo. The next year, Cleveland successfully campaigns for governor of New York. In 1884, he wins the Democratic nomination for the presidency, running on reform. His Republican opponent, James G. Blaine, has had a career fraught with bribery scandals. Despite the Halpin situation, Cleveland campaigns as the "honest" candidate.

Republicans scorn him. The story is dredged up, and reporters track down Halpin, who is now living in New Rochelle, New York. Partisan newspapers both condemn and defend Cleveland's behavior.

The American public makes the ultimate decision. The campaign is one of the dirtiest in history. A Republican slogan directed at Cleveland says, "Ma, ma, where's my pa?"

But in the end, the New Yorker prevails.

The margin is extremely close, with Cleveland winning 48.8 percent of the popular vote to James G. Blaine's 48.3 percent. On November 4, 1884, Grover Cleveland is elected the twenty-second president of the United States, which conjures up a new chant, this time from the Democrats:

"Hurrah for Maria.

Hurrah for the kid.

We voted for Grover,

And we're damn glad we did."

Knowing he remains under the umbrella of scandal, President Cleveland decides to get married. But his choice of brides is startling.

On June 2, 1886, thirty-one guests at the White House look on as the president marries Frances "Frank" Folsom. She is the daughter of Oscar Folsom, the president's former law partner. The portly forty-nine-

---

* History does not record the child's fate. Some believe he grew up to become a Buffalo gynecologist, but that is not certain. Also not certain is whether Maria Halpin had contact with her son. It is known that she put her two previous children up for adoption.

year-old president has known his dark-haired new bride since she was an infant, for Frances is only twenty-one years old. She is so young that Grover Cleveland bought her first baby carriage.

Nevertheless, the union will succeed. The couple have five children together, including their oldest daughter, Ruth. In what will become legend, the Baby Ruth candy bar is named after her. It is one of the bestselling chocolate confections in history.

America is fascinated with the beautiful new First Lady. Articles about Frances Cleveland fill the pages of magazines and newspapers. Americans purchase dozens of products bearing her likeness, from scarves to postcards, as she becomes the most popular president's wife since Dolley Madison.

Soon, the Halpin scandal is forgotten.[*]

Grover Cleveland's unconventional behavior is a lifelong pattern. His given name is Stephen, named for an influential pastor in Caldwell, New Jersey, where the future president was born in 1837. In adulthood, Cleveland decides to go by the name Grover.

He is the fifth of nine children. Money is tight, and the family moves often.

His father, a Christian missionary, dies of a gastric ulcer when his son is sixteen. Shortly afterward, Cleveland leaves home, moving to Buffalo in search of work. He finds employment at a law firm where former president Millard Fillmore was once a partner. After a short time, Cleveland is admitted to the New York bar. Three years later, in the midst of the Civil War, he pays a Polish immigrant $150 to perform his military service rather than do the fighting himself. This is legal, allowing many affluent northerners to avoid the draft.[†]

Throughout the early years of his legal career, Grover Cleveland lives in a boardinghouse and sends money to support his mother and sisters. However, he does not live a spartan lifestyle, regularly frequenting the saloons of Buffalo. Cleveland stands five feet eleven and weighs 260 pounds. Despite his girth, he is an avid outdoorsman, fond of tramping

---

[*] Maria Halpin dies in 1902 at age sixty-six.

[†] Equivalent to $3,500 in modern currency. Cleveland's substitute, thirty-two-year-old George Benninsky, survives the war.

through the woods to hunt or cast a fishing line. He prefers dark suits and bow ties. Cleveland's first foray into politics comes in 1870, when he is elected sheriff of Erie County.

Grover Cleveland's rise from county sheriff to president of the United States is rapid—and unlikely. He is conservative in his views, focusing on growing American business and ending the depression the nation has endured since 1882. As he settles into the White House, he faces a rapidly changing America. Out his office window, he can see the Washington Monument, finally completed after decades of work. Alaska is now a United States territory, one step away from statehood. The first ever baseball World Series takes place in 1884; the Providence Grays defeat the Cleveland Blues for the title.

Cleveland's vice president is Thomas Hendricks from Indiana, who dies less than a year after taking office. Keeping with precedent, that position is not filled during Cleveland's first term. But Hendricks's death spurs the Presidential Succession Act, formalizing who is next in line if a president and vice president die.[*]

The stocky Cleveland starts each morning with oatmeal, steak, and eggs and washes it all down with coffee. He reads several newspapers while eating. As for dinner, Cleveland does not like the meals cooked by Madame Petronard, the French woman serving as White House chef. He prefers fare like a lamb chop and pickled herring to the heavy sauces and European cuisine she serves. His favorite meal is corned beef and cabbage. Cleveland does not exercise at all—the first chief executive to not include some form of physical activity in his day. He believes that "body movement . . . is among the dreary and unsatisfying things of life."

As for governing, President Cleveland still has a Native American problem on his hands. There is brutality and corruption in the West, so he signs the Dawes Act of 1887 into law. This divides tribal reservations into individual allotments of 160 acres per family. The well-meaning legisla-

---

[*] The Speaker of the House is first up after the president and vice president, and then the president pro tem of the Senate.

tion is intended to empower Indians and help end their abuse by federal officials who have a long history of cheating and swindling the tribes.

However, the Dawes Act fails. It ends the traditional tribal structure that is the foundation of Native American culture. It also robs many tribes of their land—property that is quickly snatched up by the railroads and white settlers.

Despite this and other failures, Grover Cleveland grows in popularity with the American electorate. His administration presides over relative economic calm. He and Frances are happy in the White House.

In 1888, Grover Cleveland once again accepts the Democratic nomination for the presidency. His Republican opponent is Benjamin Harrison of Indiana, a US senator, Civil War general, and grandson of former president William Henry Harrison.

The main issue in the campaign is tariffs. Harrison supports high protections while Cleveland wants to increase foreign trade by lowering them.

It is Grover Cleveland who gets the most popular votes on Election Day, but he loses the Electoral College by a wide margin.*

So it is that Benjamin Harrison—a man who starts each day with a large piece of pie—is chosen as the twenty-third president of the United States.

Shortly before leaving office, Grover Cleveland signs a bill adding North Dakota, South Dakota, Montana, and Washington State to the Union. This brings the total number of states to forty-two.

Cleveland works feverishly to the end of his term.

It is, however, his wife who has the last word as the couple depart the White House on March 4, 1889. Says Frances Cleveland to White House butler Jerry Smith, "I want you to take good care of all the furniture and ornaments in the house, for I want to find everything just as it is now when we come back again. We are coming back four years from today."

---

* The electoral vote in favor of Harrison is 233–168. The popular vote for Cleveland is 5,534,488 to 5,443,892.

Chapter Twenty-Three

President Benjamin Harrison will see Theodore Roosevelt.

Harrison, fifty-five, is a cold, imperious man who owes his election to backroom deals. Roosevelt is an energetic thirty-year-old with a high-pitched voice and a passion for political reform. The younger man has come seeking a job as a civil service commissioner. The position pays $3,500 a year, just enough for Roosevelt to keep his family afloat.*

The president's office on the second floor of the White House has changed little since the days of Abraham Lincoln. However, Harrison is not pleased with it. The Executive Mansion is now full of relatives who have come to live with him, so he is eager to see a separate building constructed on the White House grounds. This would allow him to work in a space far from social chatter.

On this Tuesday, the president focuses on the ambitious man sitting before him. Harrison will long remember Roosevelt as a person "who wanted to get rid of all the evil in the world between sunrise and sunset."

He will also quickly offer him the civil service commissioner job.

Stunned, Roosevelt accepts. He campaigned vigorously for Harrison

---

* A civil service commissioner is responsible for the hiring of federal employees, investigating fraud, and confronting political abuses of power.

and is a loyal Republican. The New Yorker is hoping to resume a career in politics, and this is a strong start.

Harrison has already made another key hire—that of Philadelphian John Wanamaker to postmaster general. No one raised more money for Benjamin Harrison's campaign than this department store owner. Such is his influence that he shrewdly turns down the job of secretary of the navy in favor of the Post Office.

Wanamaker knows the power of patronage. He controls fifty-seven thousand key postal jobs across America, with tentacles in every congressional district. Immediately upon taking office, he fires twenty-five thousand Democrats, replacing them with Republicans.

If Teddy Roosevelt knows about this, he does not say, but he surely understands that powerful forces control Benjamin Harrison—and the president is fine with that.

However, Roosevelt will eventually turn on Harrison, publicly accusing him of lacking backbone.

"Damn the president! He is a cold-blooded, narrow-minded, prejudiced, obstinate, timid, old psalm-singing Indianapolis politician," Roosevelt writes in an 1892 letter to fellow Republican Henry Cabot Lodge.

Yet Harrison makes no effort to muzzle young Teddy.

He has more important things to think about.

Benjamin Harrison is the grandson of a president. He was born in North Bend, Ohio, in 1833. Three generations of the Harrison family hail from this small town in the southwest corner of the state. He is named for a great-grandfather who signed the Declaration of Independence.

The boy is seven when his grandfather William Henry Harrison is elected America's ninth president. But he does not travel to Washington for the inauguration. Benjamin does, however, attend his grandfather's funeral when the coffin is transported to Ohio for burial in July 1841.

Benjamin grows up in a warm home, with his father, John, and mother, Elizabeth, placing a great value on education for their ten children. He attends college at Miami of Ohio University and then studies law with a Cincinnati judge. Harrison grows into a distant man with a disinterested handshake. His political career will be marked by passionate speeches that bring audiences to their feet. He is comfortable speaking to groups, but not one-on-one.

At age thirty, Harrison marries Caroline Scott, a music teacher and daughter of a Presbyterian minister. She is small, brown-haired, and attractive, her playful sense of humor a contrast to her husband's icy demeanor. The couple have a boy and a girl. They move to Indianapolis one year after the nuptials, where Harrison works in a series of legal positions.

The Civil War is the making of Benjamin Harrison. His unit, the Seventieth Regiment Indiana Infantry, participates in several key campaigns, including General William Tecumseh Sherman's infamous burning of Atlanta. Abraham Lincoln personally promotes Harrison to the rank of brigadier general.

Upon his return home, the general becomes a pillar of the Indianapolis community. His law practice flourishes as his battlefield reputation becomes known. Eventually, Benjamin and Caroline build a brick mansion. He is known as a quick-thinking attorney, winning most of his cases.

But politics is in Harrison's blood. He runs for governor of Indiana in 1872 and loses, yet he remains active in the local Republican Party, campaigning for other candidates. He runs for governor a second time and loses that race as well. In 1881, however, his party loyalty leads to election from the state legislature to the United States Senate. Seven years later, he becomes the Republican candidate for president.

A ruthless bargain makes that happen. One of the great powers a president enjoys is dispensing jobs through appointment—a process known as patronage. During the Republican presidential convention in Chicago, Harrison's handlers make bold promises to rich men. If the candidate is elected, Big Business will have access to the White House.

Harrison's strategy works—money and support flow in. He easily defeats Ohio senator John Sherman for the Republican nomination.

On the personal front, Benjamin Harrison stands five feet six inches tall. His opponents call him "Little Ben" for his height and "Kid Gloves" because he wears gloves on his hands to prevent infection, even on warm days. He is stout, with a flowing gray beard, and leads a Bible study group at the local Presbyterian church where Caroline teaches Sunday school.

★★★

Life in the White House is different.

The new president and First Lady take up residence quickly, along with Caroline's father, her widowed niece, and her daughter, Mary, and her husband, as well as two of their children. Occasionally, their thirty-five-year-old son, Russell, and his wife visit from their home in New York City.

Yet it is the president's wife, "Carrie," who is very much the lady of the mansion.

Once again, Congress is allocating money for a refurbishment. Caroline is cautious with the allotted $35,000, wanting to make the funds last. She studies the history of the building to let the past inform her decorating. Rather than focus on public spaces, her emphasis is the residence. The bathrooms are a highlight, completely redone with white tile, marble, and porcelain bathtubs.

And then there are the new touches. Many American homes now feature telephones. Automobiles are a new novelty, though not yet replacing horses as the main mode of transportation. The nation is modernizing at a brisk pace.[*]

So, the First Lady splurges on the amazing new invention sweeping the country: electric lighting. Wires are embedded in the plaster walls throughout the Executive Mansion, and a round switch is placed in each room.

However, the Harrisons are terrified of the new system.

The president and First Lady are so afraid of being electrocuted that they hire a man whose only job is to turn the lights on and off. They refuse to touch a switch. Ike Hoover, the new employee, will go on to work in the White House for the next forty-two years, rising to chief usher.

Yet Hoover cannot be present at all times. When he is away, the lights blaze. Rather than risk "death" by turning off the bulbs before going to bed, President Harrison sleeps with them on.

---

[*] The first patent for a telephone was filed by Alexander Graham Bell on March 7, 1876. The American Telephone and Telegraph Company (AT&T) is founded nine years later. The first pay phone was invented in 1889. There were forty-eight thousand phones in the United States in 1880, a number that grew to six hundred thousand by 1900.

In the kitchen, Caroline hires former slave Dolly Johnson, a Kentucky native recommended by Teddy Roosevelt. Maryland oysters, consommé, bouillon, terrapin, lettuce salad, corn, fig pudding, sausage rolls, chicken salad, and macaroni soon become standard in the White House. President Harrison is fond of eating a slice of pie each morning for breakfast, with Chef Dolly surprising him with a new flavor every day.*

Tragedy strikes in December 1889. Caroline's sister and the president's twenty-five-year-old nephew die of fever within the span of three days. It is Christmas time. Despite their grief, the president and First Lady are determined that mourning will not interfere with the celebration. Harrison is struck by an inspiration: "We shall have an old-fashioned Christmas tree for the grandchildren upstairs and I shall be their Santa Claus."

So it is that the first decorated Christmas tree is set up in the second-floor library. Every year, for the rest of his term, the tree will be the centerpiece of the Harrison White House. It is a tradition that continues to this day.

On the job, President Harrison is largely a failure. He works long hours but gets little accomplished. He defers most problems to Congress, which continues the high tariffs and increases the price of silver to please the mining states. The Sherman Silver Purchase Act will lead to the financial crisis known as the Panic of 1893.

Harrison's mistake is switching government purchases from gold to silver. As the gold market falters, anxious Americans withdraw their funds from banks. More than four hundred financial institutions close. Thousands of Americans are thrown out of work. That dooms the Harrison administration.

And there's more.

President Harrison ignores the Battle of Wounded Knee, where three

---

* Dolly Johnson joined the White House staff in December 1889. The Kentucky native received a salary of seventy-five dollars per month. The former slave cooked "bluegrass cuisine" and as the first black head chef at the White House was considered an inspiration to other members of the staff. Longtime White House butler Jerry Smith called her hiring "one of the greatest acts of the present administration."

hundred Lakota Sioux are massacred by the United States Army in 1890. He also allows Stanford Dole, cousin of the future pineapple baron, to overthrow Queen Lili'uokalani in Hawaii, thereby setting up a system where an American corporation exploits the native population.

Taking everything into account, Benjamin Harrison's record on protecting minorities is abysmal.

Nevertheless, the Republicans renominate Harrison in 1892. In a repeat of the previous presidential election, the Democrats select Grover Cleveland, who has kept a low profile in New York City, practicing law.

On October 25, 1892, two weeks before the election, Caroline Harrison dies from tuberculosis at the age of sixty. The First Lady's funeral service takes place in the East Room. Devastated, Benjamin Harrison ends his campaign.

On November 8, 1892, Grover Cleveland wins in a landslide.

Benjamin Harrison dies from pneumonia on March 13, 1901, at his home in Indianapolis. He is sixty-seven years old. After leaving office, he marries Caroline's niece, thirty-seven-year-old Mary Scott Lord Dimmick. This causes a rift between the former president and his son, Russell, who is four years older than his father's new bride.

The twenty-third president's legacy is scant. Detractors called him "the human iceberg." Supporters liked what he could do for them.

By most accounts, Harrison was an honest man but had little ambition to improve the lives of ordinary Americans. His focus was on helping powerful men. One of the few Benjamin Harrison quotes that endure is this: "The indiscriminate denunciation of the rich is mischievous. It perverts the mind, poisons the heart, and furnishes an excuse to crime.

"No poor man was ever made richer or happier by it."

Chapter Twenty-Four

MARCH 4, 1893
WHITE HOUSE
DAY

He's back.

It doesn't take long for President Grover Cleveland and his family to settle into the White House. As First Lady Frances predicted, the Clevelands are returning exactly four years to the day since leaving. Butler Jerry Smith, dressed in formal wear, welcomes them home.

The fireplaces are roaring. Rain, snow, and sleet cover Washington, but the president has insisted on holding his inauguration outdoors. The wind blows hard throughout his twenty-minute speech, making it difficult for the audience to hear his words. Then comes the four-hour inaugural parade, featuring, for the first time, women.

By the time the day is over, the Cleveland family is wet and chilled. The president's mustache is actually coated with ice. Now, as the group steps inside and removes heavy, long coats, the fires are welcome.

To Frances Cleveland's disappointment, the mansion is very different than when she left it—Caroline Harrison's renovations can be seen throughout the residence.

The Cleveland family has also changed. The First Lady is pregnant with their second child. Baby Ruth, born between terms, is almost two. The president's fondness for beer has seen him gain fifteen pounds. At fifty-five, Cleveland's walrus mustache is gray. He is also having trouble enjoying his cigars because the roof of his mouth is starting to feel "rough"—a condition he will soon see a doctor about.

The president's second term will be just as stormy as today's foul weather. America is still experiencing a financial panic, labor unions are threatening to strike, and policies such as high tariffs and the silver standard are wreaking economic havoc.

Three months pass. The date is June 18, 1893. White House physician Dr. Robert O'Reilly requests a moment with the president. Grover Cleveland is busy but makes time. He sits behind a massive oak desk in his second-floor office, a gift from England's Queen Victoria.*

O'Reilly requests that the president open his mouth so he might look at a troubling lesion noticed by Cleveland's dentist.

The president is distracted. He's been busy since the day after the inauguration, undoing problems created by the Harrison administration. Hawaii is first on Cleveland's agenda, with the president refusing to annex the islands, aware the local population is angry about being governed by corporations.

The truth is, America is in deep financial trouble. Banks are closing, and two important railroads have gone bankrupt, causing a "Black Friday" stock market crash. Cleveland understands the situation and works to return America to the gold standard.

Yet the painful spot on his hard palate has been keeping the president up nights. So, he opens his mouth. O'Reilly discovers a spot the size of a quarter that looks troubling. He correctly predicts that it is cancerous and must be removed. The tumor appears to be the result of the cigars Cleveland clamps into the corner of his mouth for hours on end.

However, the doctor is not sure Grover Cleveland can survive a major operation. The president's neck is thick, he has gout and sleep apnea, and he is so corpulent that his nieces and nephews call him Uncle Jumbo.

In addition, there are the political implications of performing surgery. The procedure will hinder the president's ability to speak. In August, he

---

* The Resolute desk is so named because it was built from the timbers of a British ship of the same name.

is due to address Congress about repealing the Sherman Silver Purchase Act. Cleveland is also concerned that news of his surgery might have a further negative effect on the stock market. Yet the operation cannot wait—so it will be performed in total secrecy.

Two weeks later, on July 1, President Cleveland boards the yacht *Oneida* on New York's East River. The press and White House staff are told nothing. He is sedated. Two molars are removed. The surgeons cut into his palate, where it becomes clear that the tumor is larger than believed. The roof of Cleveland's mouth and part of his jaw are removed. A piece of vulcanized rubber is inserted to fill the hole.

Several days later, a second surgery is performed to remove another tumor.

In the meantime, America begins wondering *where* the president is. From July into August, Cleveland is invisible. Official reports say he has a toothache. As the Panic of 1893 rages, no one seems to be in charge. Frances Cleveland, making excuses for her husband, simply states that he is suffering from rheumatism. The president recuperates far from Washington in Cape Cod, Massachusetts, not even telling Vice President Adlai Stevenson about the surgery.*

In fact, Grover Cleveland is having a hard time speaking, has lost hearing, is irritable, and suffers from depression brought on by anesthesia. Yet, on August 7, he reappears to successfully lobby a special session of Congress about repealing the silver act. However, his speech is muddled and slow.

It is not until 1917, nine years after Grover Cleveland's death, that the full story of the vanishing president will finally be released to America.

First Lady Frances Cleveland has health issues of a more positive sort. She gives birth to daughter Esther in 1893, the first and only child of a president ever born in the White House. Another girl, Marion, comes along in 1895. Fearing public demand for information about

---

* Cleveland purchased a home in Bourne, on Buzzards Bay, between his first and second terms. Gray Gables consisted of a main house, a hunting lodge, and 110 acres of beachfront. The cost was $20,000 (nearly $600,000 in modern currency). It burned down in 1973.

the children is too intense, the Clevelands close the White House to the public.

Grover Cleveland's second term is one setback after another. He vetoed an astounding 414 bills during his first term and now rejects another 170 more in the second. Congress loathes him. In addition, he capitulates on the issue of Hawaii, recognizing it as a sovereign American territory. He originally opposes annexation of Hawaii as he is an "anti-imperialist" in the sense that he is against the US becoming a colonial power. He establishes diplomatic relations with the Republic of Hawaii under the presidency of the fruit magnate, Sanford Dole. The fruit barons who run the place are ecstatic.

President Grover Cleveland's downfall begins on June 16, 1896, when William McKinley of Ohio is nominated as the party's next presidential candidate. The Ohio governor will be opposed by William Jennings Bryan of Nebraska, a staunch advocate of silver. Democrats unhappy with Bryan's monetary policies ask President Cleveland to represent a *third* party in the coming election. He turns them down.[*]

On November 3, 1896, William McKinley is elected president.

On March 4, 1897, Grover Cleveland and his family move out of the White House—this time for good. Frances, who is relieved to be done with the enormous demands placed on the First Lady, weeps as they depart.

Not so President Cleveland. He has had enough.

President Cleveland dies on June 24, 1908, at age seventy-one. The cause of death is Alzheimer's disease and a heart attack. Frances Cleveland marries again in 1913. This makes her the first presidential widow to remarry. Her husband, Thomas Preston, is an archeology professor at Princeton University. She dies in her sleep in 1947 at age eighty-three and is buried with the president in Princeton, New Jersey.

---

[*] Presidential terms will not be limited to two until the Twenty-Second Amendment is ratified in 1951.

Cleveland is the only man to serve nonconsecutive terms as president. He accomplished little of lasting importance but held the affection of many Americans.

Cleveland's second term was marred by physical infirmities that sapped his strength. As a result, the Republicans have a relatively easy time capturing the White House in 1896. Said incoming president McKinley about Cleveland, "What in the world has Grover Cleveland done? Will you tell me?"

No one could.

Chapter Twenty-Five

FEBRUARY 15, 1898
HAVANA, CUBA
9:40 P.M.

The USS *Maine* is sinking.

An explosion rocks the tropical night, eventually killing hundreds of American sailors. It is too late to seal the 214 watertight compartments, so the ocean rushes in belowdecks and floods the vessel. The scene is a cauldron of death, with sailors screaming for help while fires and smoke envelop them. More explosions ripple through the ship as ammunition stores detonate. Boilers explode, fatally scalding men in the engine room. The steel deck is too hot to stand on. No one knows who detonated the bomb, but it is clear that this six-thousand-ton battleship is heading to the bottom of Havana Harbor. Only her mast will remain above the surface.

In all, 261 men will die tonight. Twenty-two of these are African Americans on this integrated ship. Because of the bomb's forward location beneath enlisted sailors' quarters, only two officers will perish.

The *Maine* has been sent to Havana by President William McKinley to keep the peace. Since 1895, Cubans have been rioting against Spain, which has ruled the island since the time of Christopher Columbus. The president has been under pressure for months to formally declare war on the Spanish but has resisted. As a veteran of the Civil War who enlisted at age eighteen, McKinley knows the horror of combat.

He does not want to fight Spain.

But now the president has no choice. In his mind, there is little doubt that Spain is the belligerent. That country has forced his hand by sinking a US warship. America has not fought a major conflict since the Civil War. The nation is still very much divided between North and South.

But now it unites.

"Remember the *Maine*!" will become a popular rallying cry.*

William McKinley is a complex man.

He stands five feet seven and has an incredible memory. He is sedentary; his only form of exercise is stepping outside to smoke. White House usher Ike Hoover states that "one never saw him without a cigar in his mouth except at meals or when asleep."

However, the president does not allow himself to be photographed with a cigar, believing the habit makes him look bad.

The former Ohio governor has a dour face with an intimidating brown-eyed gaze and eyebrows almost as long as Grover Cleveland's mustache. Despite his intense look, he conveys an easy manner that draws people to him.

William McKinley was born in Niles, Ohio, in 1843, the son of a successful pig iron manufacturer of the same name. He is a bright child, and by his teenage years, he is teaching school. The outbreak of the Civil War leads him to volunteer as a private, and he serves in the Twenty-Third Ohio Infantry under Major Rutherford B. Hayes. McKinley fights all four years of the conflict, rising to the rank of brevet major.

Law studies follow the war. Then marriage to Ida Saxton, an auburn-haired, blue-eyed daughter of a prominent Ohio banker. She is twenty-three when they wed and gives birth to two daughters. But soon Ida begins having epileptic seizures. She loses consciousness for brief periods of time, staring blankly into space. When this happens at a public function, such as a dinner, McKinley hides the affliction by quickly placing a napkin over her face until she regains consciousness.

Ida's health problems worsen. Their daughter Katie dies at age three

---

* A 1976 United States Navy investigation found that the explosion was caused by coal dust igniting onboard ammunition. A separate study twenty years later, commissioned by *National Geographic* magazine, stated that a mine caused the explosion. The mystery of the *Maine* remains unsolved.

from a typhoid infection. The baby, Ida, passes away from a fever. The combination of these deaths and her own afflictions result in Ida becoming a recluse before she is even thirty. She cuts her hair short, hoping it will end her chronic migraine headaches. However, William McKinley's devotion never wavers. As her epilepsy gets worse, Ida spends her days crocheting bedroom slippers in a rocking chair. Over the course of her lifetime, she will construct more than three thousand pairs as gifts.

Through his longtime friendship with former president Rutherford Hayes, McKinley combines his law practice with politics. In 1876, he successfully runs for Congress, serving in the House for six terms. McKinley's affable manner propels him to the chairmanship of the powerful Ways and Means Committee.

By age forty-six, William McKinley is a rising star in the Republican Party. He successfully runs for governor of Ohio in 1892. Whether in Washington or Columbus, Ida remains at his side even though she could "seize" at any time.

It is 1896 when William McKinley successfully runs for president. His opponent is William Jennings Bryan of Nebraska, a man known for his oratory. Indeed, Bryan's eloquent "Cross of Gold" speech during the Democratic Convention will be remembered as one of the most powerful political addresses in history.*

But while Bryan travels the country by train, delivering speeches on railway platforms, McKinley prefers to remain at home in Ohio with Ida. His campaign strategy is a series of "Front Porch" speeches, with voters standing on his lawn to hear what the Republican candidate has to say.

Ida McKinley proves useful. She often sits outside her husband's office to listen in on campaign meetings. Afterward, she offers her advice to the "major," as she calls him. Newspaper reporters are aware of Ida's condition but do not write about it. The Democratic Party is not so kind, labeling Ida a "lunatic" and seeking to drag her illness into the presidential campaign.

In the end, Williams Jennings Bryan captures the thinly populated

---

* Bryan, an advocate of a currency based on silver, brought the convention to its feet during his stirring thirty-five-minute oration. The speech gets its name from the final line: "You shall not crucify mankind upon a cross of gold."

southern and plains states, which offer little in the way of Electoral College votes. McKinley wins the industrial Northeast, the Midwest, and California, beating Bryan 271–176. Garrett Hobart of New Jersey becomes vice president at age fifty-two. Three years later, Hobart will become the sixth vice president to die in office.[*]

On March 4, 1897, William McKinley is sworn in as the twenty-fifth president of the United States. Ida attends the inauguration. She even makes an appearance at the evening ball but leaves abruptly after fainting.

The McKinley administration gets off to a brisk start. World events demand nothing less. Gold is discovered in Alaska, striking coal miners in Pennsylvania turn violent, the first Boston Marathon is run, and Americans are being threatened in Cuba.

McKinley's workday begins early, with eggs for breakfast. He is not productive with his time, stepping away from the office quite often to indulge Ida's requests. To please his wife, the president stops drinking but continues to smoke cigars. He often breaks these in two and stuffs the tobacco in his mouth to get the desired calming effect rather than light up in Ida's presence.

The fight in Cuba defines William McKinley's presidency. The explosion of the *Maine* comes less than a year into his first term. The year 1898 will be spent lobbying Congress for war funding as Havana is blockaded. On April 25, Congress votes to declare war on Spain. The First United States Volunteer Cavalry is formed, led by Lieutenant Colonel Theodore Roosevelt. These "Rough Riders" will earn fame for a key victory at a place known as San Juan Hill.

The war spreads to the Philippines, also controlled by Spain. There, the United States Navy destroys an outmatched Spanish fleet. The fighting then spreads to Puerto Rico.

After seven months, Spain surrenders. The Treaty of Paris is signed

---

[*] Hobart, who made his name as president of the New Jersey Senate, dies at age fifty-five from heart disease. The illness consumed the last year of his life. In expectation of the vice president's death, the McKinley administration announced his retirement from public life three weeks before he passed.

on December 10, 1898, giving the United States control of Cuba and the other territories.[*]

President McKinley then turns his attention to more trivial matters, such as becoming the first president to ride in a motorcar. On July 13, 1901, he enjoys a short journey in a Stanley Motor Carriage steam-powered vehicle known as a Stanley Steamer.

On November 6, 1900, William McKinley is reelected to a second term. His new vice president is war hero Teddy Roosevelt. Once again, McKinley's opponent is William Jennings Bryan of Nebraska, who loses by an even greater electoral margin than in the previous campaign: 292–155.

As the new century begins, all appears to be going smoothly for the president. The press generally likes him—stories abound about his remarkable memory for names and faces. Everywhere he goes, William McKinley shakes as many hands as he can, a large smile always on his face.

Change in America is coming fast: cities see their first "skyscraper" buildings, a new form of entertainment known as "moving pictures" is growing in popularity, and two inventions soon to change the world—the radio and the airplane—are almost perfected.

To display all the innovation, a Pan-American Exposition is scheduled for September 1901 in Buffalo, New York. President William McKinley will make the trip to give a speech.

His *last* speech.

Leon F. Czolgosz despises the president.

On September 6, 1901, the twenty-eight-year-old drifter from Ohio leaves his room at Nowak's Hotel on Broadway in Buffalo. He is an extreme anarchist who believes America and the world can only be

---

[*] By the war's end, Cuba, Guam, the Philippines, and Puerto Rico will be taken from Spain and placed under US protection. Guam is now a US territory, Puerto Rico is an American commonwealth, and the Philippines is an independent nation. Cuba is also independent, though with a US naval base at Guantanamo.

changed by anarchy. Czolgosz lives on a large farm but spends most of his time alone, reading books about violence. The recent assassination of Italy's King Umberto I inspires him.

Concealed in Czolgosz's large handkerchief is a .32-caliber revolver loaded with five bullets. He travels to the Pan-American Exhibition, seeking out the venue where President McKinley will be speaking.

Czolgosz gets in the receiving line where the president is expected to shake hands. Earlier, he wanted to shoot McKinley as the president arrived in Buffalo by train, but he could not get close enough to take a shot. Now the situation is different. The crowd is large and excited. Czolgosz waits patiently. At 4:06 p.m., McKinley appears. The president looks his killer directly in the eye and reaches out to shake hands. Czolgosz immediately pulls his revolver and shoots twice from a foot away. Amazingly, the first bullet ricochets off a suit button and lodges in the folds of McKinley's jacket.

But the second round pierces the president's stomach. McKinley falls backward to the ground.

The crowd is on Czolgosz in an instant. He is hurled down, kicked, and beaten. Police immediately take him to the Thirteenth Precinct House, where he is interrogated. On September 23, 1901, Czolgosz pleads guilty and declines counsel because he does not acknowledge the right of the court to try him. It doesn't matter. Proceedings are swift, as the jury takes just nine hours to find him guilty of murder.

On October 29, Czolgosz is placed in the electric chair at Auburn State Prison, telling onlookers, "I killed the president because he was the enemy of the people."

Sulphonic acid is then poured over his corpse to accelerate decomposition.

★★★

President McKinley, however, is not dead. But doctors cannot find the bullet that is lodged in his lower back. He is wheeled into surgery. Lead physician Herman Mynter gives McKinley an injection of morphine for his pain. During the ordeal, the president says this about his assassin: "He didn't know, poor fellow, what he was doing. He couldn't have known."

Finally, the surgical team gives up and the wound is closed. The bullet is still inside McKinley. Word is passed to Vice President Roosevelt, who hurries to Buffalo. Ida McKinley is also told of the shooting. She takes the news calmly.

For a time, it appears the president will survive. Roosevelt departs Buffalo. But then, a turn.

The bullet has passed through the colon, peritoneum, pancreas, and kidney. Gangrene quickly sets in, the same condition that killed President James Garfield. Theodore Roosevelt is recalled to Buffalo.

Nine days after he was shot, at 2:14 a.m. on September 14, William McKinley dies of infection. A death mask is taken. Ida halts the autopsy after four hours and orders that her husband's body be taken home to Ohio.

At 3:00 p.m. on this same Saturday, Theodore Roosevelt is sworn in as the twenty-sixth president of the United States.

Five days later, America comes to a stop for five minutes to mourn William McKinley. Trains halt. Business ceases. People pause to pay respects.

President McKinley is buried on September 19, 1901. Ida is too distraught to attend the funeral.

Ida McKinley will spend the rest of her life overseeing the construction of a memorial in her husband's honor in Canton, Ohio. But Ida will not live to see its completion.*

The presidency of William McKinley was largely unexceptional. He is remembered most for the US victory over Spain.

On September 27, 1901, forty-two-year-old Teddy Roosevelt, his wife, Edith, and their six children move into the White House.

The building will literally never be the same again.

---

* Ida McKinley died on May 26, 1907, in Canton. Her cause of death was the flu.

Chapter Twenty-Six

Theodore Roosevelt does not like to be called Teddy.

Mr. President, Colonel, or even T. R. are fine. Uttering the nickname "Teddy" in his presence will get you a cold stare.

It has been fifteen months since Roosevelt assumed the presidency. He is forty-four years old, a burly, athletic man of high energy and even higher aspiration. He was a cowboy, a boxer, a former New York City police commissioner, and the governor of New York. He has wire-rim glasses, short brown hair, and a jutting jaw—a face of constant emotion, flashing from high spirits to rage in an instant. The president stands five feet ten inches tall and weighs 210 pounds.

Shortly after taking office, on October 17, 1901, Roosevelt directs his personal secretary, George B. Cortelyou, to change "the headings, or date lines, of all official papers and documents requiring his [Roosevelt's] signature, from 'Executive Mansion' to 'White House.'" Presidential stationery was also changed to reflect the name.

Tonight, an ebullient Roosevelt welcomes guests to the new White House dining room. He has changed everything in the Executive Mansion. Instead of portraits decorating the walls, enormous buffalo, moose, and elk heads, all shot by Roosevelt, look down on the seventy-five guests. Walls of dark carved oak, waxed to a shine, replace simple plaster. Electric crystal chandeliers flood the room in light.

At First Lady Edith Roosevelt's insistence, the decor is softened by a dinner table decorated in pink tablecloths, napkins, candles, and roses. She also wears pink, with almost every other female guest dressed in white satin or silk.

The lavish dinner this evening is in honor of Roosevelt's cabinet, but it is really being held to show off the new room.

★★★

President Roosevelt and his advisers have been extremely busy since William McKinley was assassinated. Tonight, the talk around the crescent-shaped table is of the new canal across Panama, soon to begin construction. In addition, "Teddy's Bear" is an object of humor. The new term is coined after a recent presidential hunting trip to Mississippi, where Roosevelt refused to shoot a captive brown bear. Cartoonist Clifford Berryman drew a picture of the moment, leading a candy-store owner to sell a toy with the name Teddy Bear. It is now a global sensation.

Roosevelt offers a toast to his cabinet, all of whom sit with their wives. The most important of tonight's guests are railroad baron E. H. Harriman and Pittsburgh industrialist Henry Frick. Glasses clink, and cries of "hear, hear" fill the room. Theodore Roosevelt is the youngest president in history, two decades junior to most of his advisers.

Yet there is no deference in Roosevelt's behavior—and no doubt about who is in charge. "I did not usurp power," he will write of his presidency, "but I did greatly broaden the use of executive power."

After a series of bland presidents, Roosevelt has changed the federal system in many ways. The new grandeur of the White House is just one example. With an eye toward history, the First Couple sleep in the large 1861 "Lincoln Bed," but most everything else is brand-new. Gone are the gas chandeliers dating back to a time before electricity. Roosevelt has torn up dilapidated wooden floors and replaced them with marble, knocked down walls, ripped out the grand staircase, and moved the servants' quarters to the attic.

In addition, the president has built a brand-new office on the lawn.

For the first time in history, the chief executive does not work in the main building, as his six children and the thirty staff make the residence too cramped. The new West Wing allows President Roosevelt to labor without interruption.

Tonight's party ends just after 10:00 p.m. It is a Thursday, and tomorrow morning comes quickly. Roosevelt will be up for breakfast at 7:00 a.m. and in the office by 7:30 a.m. His day will be cut short by a train trip to New York City for the funeral of former First Lady Julia Dent Grant. She is being laid to rest alongside her husband in Grant's Tomb overlooking the Hudson River.

T. R. was born into privilege in 1858, the son of New York philanthropist Theodore Roosevelt Sr. and his wife, Martha. As a boy, Teddy suffers from severe asthma that makes him feel like he is drowning. He develops unique passions, such as taxidermy, after coming across a dead seal in a fish market. In 1865, young Roosevelt witnesses Abraham Lincoln's funeral procession as it passes through New York City. In time, Theodore becomes a staunch advocate for physical fitness, using exercise to treat his asthma. After being threatened by bullies, he hires a boxing coach to teach him self-defense. He later adds judo to his regimen.

Roosevelt is homeschooled as a child, lacking ability in math but good in history, biology, and French. His father dies soon after Teddy begins college at Harvard, devastating the young man. He feels like he gets little out of school, as he is fonder of physical activities like rowing and boxing. His inheritance of $65,000 ($1.9 million today) is enough for him to begin a political career. The bulk of the Roosevelt money comes from his grandfather Cornelius, who, as a bank executive in New York, earned millions of dollars.

In 1880, Theodore Roosevelt marries Alice Hathaway Lee, the daughter of a Boston banker. "As long as I live, I shall never forget how sweetly she looked, and how prettily she greeted me," is his memory of their first meeting. On April 12, 1884, Alice gives birth to a daughter—also named Alice.

Then, something terrible happens. Doctors who deliver the Roosevelt baby have absolutely no idea Alice is gravely ill during the birthing.

Unbeknownst to her or anyone else, she has Bright's disease, an affliction of the kidneys.*

Two days after the birth, Alice Roosevelt suddenly dies. She is just twenty-two years old.

On the same day, Teddy Roosevelt's mother passes away from typhoid fever. These medical catastrophes overwhelm the strong-minded future president.

"The light has gone out of my life," he writes in his diary.

Theodore Roosevelt does not get over the tragedies quickly. He decides to move to North Dakota, where he owns a ranch. Baby Alice, two years old, is left behind to be raised by an aunt. He prefers to call her Baby Lee so he will not be reminded of his departed wife.

For the next few years, Teddy Roosevelt travels back and forth from New York to North Dakota. Slowly, his eastern manners are tempered by the West. The New Yorker is out of place on the plains, a man of education and entitlement surrounded by cowboys raised in a hard frontier lifestyle. But Roosevelt transforms himself, spending his days on horseback, roping cattle and hunting for his dinner. He embraces a new sensibility about how America should be run. Not by "emasculated, milk-and-water moralities admired by the pseudo-philanthropists," Roosevelt writes, but by "the stern, manly qualities that are invaluable to a nation."

This new political theory becomes an obsession. For the rest of his life, Theodore Roosevelt will present himself in a confrontational, machismo style.

During a visit to New York City, he rekindles a relationship with childhood friend Edith Carow. She is a patrician woman standing five feet seven, with auburn hair, square shoulders, and a fondness for decoration. Their fathers knew each other, and the two played together as children.

Teddy actually courted Edith before marrying Alice, but the families objected, and they broke it off. However, in September 1885, one year after the death of Alice, T. R. sees Edith again. Surprised to find himself

---

* At the time, the symptoms of Bright's disease were unknown. Alice Roosevelt delivered the baby at home in Manhattan, and all was thought to be relatively well.

still smitten, Roosevelt proposes two months later. However, the couple agree to keep the relationship secret for fear of more family rejection. Then, Edith's widowed mother suddenly moves the family to London to save money, the family fortune being depleted.

But Teddy Roosevelt will not be denied. He travels to England, even befriending British diplomat Cecil Spring Rice on the ocean voyage, asking him to serve as his best man.

On December 2, 1886, the couple are married in London. The church Teddy and Edith choose is St. George's in Hanover Square. Coincidentally, William Franklin, son of Founding Father Benjamin Franklin, was also married there in 1762.

Theodore Roosevelt's time as a cowboy is over. A hard winter wipes out his cattle herd. So, after three years on the plains, he returns to New York City and begins anew in the political world.

Cuba, 1898. A July day under a scorching tropical sun. Teddy Roosevelt and his Rough Riders of the First United States Volunteer Cavalry prepare to attack a position known as San Juan Heights, where almost six hundred Spanish soldiers defend the summit. They are protected by rock walls, cannon, and barbed wire. The peak is flanked by two hills named Kettle and San Juan. In addition to the Rough Riders, there are 1,250 black soldiers and several other units, bringing the total American force to eight thousand. An official US report states that "blacks and whites, fought side by side, endured the blistering heat and driving rain."

The American fighters are exhausted, forced to march eight miles to a small valley at the bottom of the hill. The Rough Riders are riders in name only, with the military forcing them to leave their horses in America and fight like infantry.

Lieutenant Colonel Theodore Roosevelt is one of the few men with a horse today. His rank is provided by the army because of his political clout. In the past, he served as the assistant secretary of the navy during William McKinley's first term, as well as New York City police commissioner. He is known for his tenacity and unorthodox tactics, such as prowling the New York streets long past midnight to make sure police officers are walking their beats.

Now, a restless Roosevelt once again becomes a man of action. At

1:00 p.m., he gives the order to attack up Kettle Hill. The Rough Riders leave behind the tall grass that has given them cover from Spanish cannon and slowly trudge up the hill under heavy fire. The Spanish artillery soon finds them. The Rough Riders return fire.[*]

Soon, Roosevelt notices that Spanish accuracy is flawed. Their cannons are not positioned to execute "plunging fire," meaning that the rounds will fly over the intended targets. Also, it appears to him that Spanish trenches are not in proper tactical position, making it hard for marksmen to fire down the slope.

So, the colonel orders his men to pick up the pace. Those remaining at the bottom of the hill will surely die. Roosevelt knows things are dicey. Now, believing only an all-out charge can dislodge the Spanish, he gallops his horse toward the enemy lines, exhorting his men to follow.

Soldiers begin sprinting, Roosevelt riding back and forth under a hail of bullets. Kettle Hill is not steep, but it is a long half mile to the Spanish position. A trio of rapid-fire US Gatling guns provide cover for Roosevelt and his assault wave. Men grow exhausted from the heat. The pace slows. At the very top, the fighting is hand to hand. But the hill is taken.

Roosevelt immediately crosses the steep ravine to the adjacent San Juan Hill, where the fighting is still intense. His men are spent, so only five follow. A short time later, San Juan Hill falls.

The final cost is horrific: 144 Americans dead, 1,024 wounded. Spanish casualties number 58 killed and 366 wounded as the Americans take the day. Only 41 Spaniards are taken prisoner, many fleeing as their position is overrun.

"We had a bully fight," Roosevelt says with pride afterward.

Four months later, Colonel Theodore Roosevelt is elected governor of New York. He immediately sets out to reform corruption. That causes concern inside the Republican Party, the beneficiaries of some scandalous graft. Three very powerful men, Standard Oil's John D. Rockefeller, steel magnate Andrew Carnegie, and financier J. P. Morgan, are especially worried. These "robber barons," as they are known, come up with an

---

[*] The Rough Riders take their name from one of Buffalo Bill's traveling shows, "Buffalo Bill's Wild West and Congress of Rough Riders."

ingenious solution to muzzle Governor Roosevelt: get him nominated as vice president.*

The McKinley campaign will benefit from the war hero's popularity while the barons will no longer have an adversary in the New York state house.

All goes according to plan until President McKinley is shot dead.

It is 1903. Life in the Roosevelt White House reverberates with the sounds of children at play. The oldest daughter, Alice, a precocious teenager, is often at odds with her stepmother, First Lady Edith Roosevelt. Their fights are so intense that the president remarks, "I can either run the country or I can attend to Alice, but I cannot possibly do both."

The problem is that Roosevelt's oldest daughter needs attention. So, she takes up smoking cigarettes. The president refuses to allow that in the White House, causing the teenager to smoke outside on the roof. Her rebellious nature vexes the president of the United States.

The five children from the president's second marriage are all under the age of twelve when their father takes office: Theodore Jr., Kermit, Ethel, Archie, and Quentin. On one occasion, five-year-old Quentin rides a pony named Algonquin up the White House elevator so he can entertain Archie, who is sick in bed.†

In addition to five dogs, the Roosevelt menagerie includes a small bear, a lizard, several guinea pigs, a real pig named Maude, blue macaw Eli Yale, Josiah the badger, a rooster, a hen named Baron Spreckle, a hyena, a barn owl, Algonquin the pony, and a rabbit named Peter. The animals are cared for by White House staff on the mansion grounds.

The president dotes on his children, often breaking up his workday to

---

* The term *robber baron* comes from the German *Raubritter* (robber knights), a group of medieval men who charged illegal tolls to cross roads and bridges.

† Alice Roosevelt will marry Nicholas Longworth III, who becomes Speaker of the House. She will have her only child through an affair, become a prominent socialite, and live to ninety-six, dying of pneumonia. Quentin is shot down over France during World War I, dying at age twenty. Archie fights in World Wars I and II, succumbing to a stroke in 1979 at age eighty-five. Kermit kills himself in Alaska in 1943. Theodore Jr. goes ashore on Utah Beach on D-Day as a brigadier general in the army, earning a Medal of Honor for his courage—only to die in France from a heart attack one month later. Ethel serves as a nurse in France during World War I. She lives to eighty-five before dying.

spend time with them. He takes long hikes with his family in local Rock Creek Park, often requesting that foreign dignitaries join them.

And then there is food. Kermit Roosevelt calls his father's morning cup of coffee "more in nature of a bathtub." The president drinks gallons, and he uses *seven* lumps of sugar in every cup. For breakfast, hard-boiled eggs, hominy, rolls, crackers, and cantaloupe are the usual fare.

Roosevelt spends much of his day working on speeches and writing letters. He breaks his routine into small chunks of time, each involving tremendous focus. From the moment he rises in the morning until midnight, T. R. plans every aspect of his schedule down to the minute. And there is always time for a workout.

During his regular judo sessions, the president can be seen grappling with aides and even White House visitors. He calls this lifestyle that of "strenuous endeavor."

On one occasion, he injures his eye while wrestling. The detached retina will not completely heal for the rest of his life.

With his excitable high-pitched voice and fondness for pounding his fist as he talks, few doubt Teddy Roosevelt when he states, "No man has had a happier life than I have led; a happier life in every way."

The first three years of Roosevelt's term are largely successful. He is a direct man, telling the public to "walk softly and carry a big stick." But Roosevelt certainly does *not* walk softly. When the United Mine Workers strike in May 1902, threatening energy delivery to the nation, the president demands the mine owners negotiate a settlement—or else.

"Else" is the federal government seizing and operating the coal mines.

A settlement is quickly reached.

Thus, Teddy Roosevelt goes into the election of 1904 in a strong position. He easily defeats Democrat Alton B. Parker, a chief judge of the New York Court of Appeals, with 336–140 electoral votes.

The president has strong words for Congress.

The date is December 5, 1905, as Roosevelt sends his fifth Annual Message to Congress. The House chamber is packed. A clerk reads it aloud.

The remarks stretch to an hour long, but one sentence in particular stands out: "All contributions by corporations to any political committee or for any political purpose should be forbidden by law."

The robber barons' attempts to corral President Roosevelt have failed. He opens a new cabinet position known as the Department of Commerce and Labor to oversee corporate behavior. Later, he orders the Department of Justice to prosecute a J. P. Morgan company known as Northern Securities for violating antitrust laws. The case is argued in the Supreme Court in December 1903, and a decision is handed down against Northern Securities in March 1904.

Roosevelt goes on to regulate railroad rates and even food, demanding federal inspection of meatpacking plants. He supports the Pure Food and Drug Act of 1906, which allowed Congress to create the Food and Drug Administration.

Robber baron Henry Clay Frick will look back on Roosevelt's accomplishments with regret: "He got down on his knees for us. We bought the son of a bitch. Then he did not stay bought."

There are other matters. In Panama, the canal connecting the Atlantic and Pacific Oceans is being dug through thick jungle. Roosevelt's love of the outdoors leads him to create the national Forest Service to protect vast swaths of American land. And the president is instrumental in brokering peace between Japan and Russia in 1905 after their recent war. He brings both sides to the negotiation table in Portsmouth, New Hampshire—an act that will win him the Nobel Peace Prize.

But domestic peace is elusive in America. The disenfranchisement of black citizens continues. Theodore Roosevelt is aware of the situation and sends a signal by inviting civil rights leader Booker T. Washington to a White House dinner in 1901. This is considered scandalous by some, for segregation is still very much the norm in the American South—and never before has a black man eaten dinner with a president as a guest at the White House.

"No white man who has eaten with a negro can be respected," states

South Carolina governor Miles McSweeney. Many other critics say much worse.

Uncharacteristically, the president backs down, claiming that the meal was lunch instead of dinner and that no Roosevelt women were in attendance. It will be decades before this fact is corrected—and even longer before another black man dines with a president as a White House guest.

Yet Roosevelt's meager attempts to address race are more than any president since Abraham Lincoln. Many in the black community applaud his efforts. Black Tennessee preacher William McGill believes the elevation of Booker T. Washington is a historic moment. He states, "The administration of President Roosevelt is to the Negro what the heart is to the body. It has pumped life blood into every artery of the Negro in this country."

In the end, Theodore Roosevelt is a man of his times and does not believe in the equality of races. He is both progressive and regressive. In 1906, he writes a private letter to his friend Owen Wister about black people: "As a race and in the mass, they are altogether inferior to the whites."

On the subject of Native Americans, Roosevelt is even more scathing. "I don't go so far as to think that the only good Indian is the dead Indian," he states, "but I believe nine out of every ten are, and I shouldn't like to inquire too closely into the case of the tenth."[*]

In addition, Roosevelt extends the Chinese Exclusion Act, originally signed by President Chester Arthur, which keeps Asian laborers out of the United States.

★★★

By the end of Theodore Roosevelt's second term, America's position as a global power is on the rise. On the president's order, America's sixteen great battleships—all painted white—are being sent around the world as a show of force. Roosevelt sees this as a capstone to his many achievements. The purpose of the journey is friendly, visiting other nations in a

---

[*] Roosevelt says this on January 14, 1886, at the Young Men's Institute in New York City, while delivering a speech titled "Ranch Life in the West."

gesture of goodwill. But Roosevelt is also making a point: America is a world power with a navy that can go anywhere on the high seas.

This kind of signal is also displayed domestically—especially by federal regulation of corporations. Says the president, "A man who has never gone to school may steal from a freight car. But if he has a university education, he may steal the whole railroad."

The Roosevelts leave the White House on March 4, 1909. He is only fifty years old and still has boundless energy. But the president believes two terms are enough for any man, thinking that only a dictator would wish to stay on longer.

So it is that, in 1908, William Howard Taft, Roosevelt's secretary of war, is nominated as the Republican candidate for president. Theodore Roosevelt hears the chants of "four more years" from delegates at the convention in Chicago, but he will not be swayed.

The portly Taft defeats Democrat William Jennings Bryan, who is running for a *third* time, by an electoral vote of 321–162. The popular vote is 7.6 million to 6.4 million.

Almost immediately upon leaving office, the young former president travels to Africa, where he shoots big game and collects animal specimens for the Smithsonian Institution. From there, he goes to Europe. But Theodore Roosevelt never loses track of what is happening in America—and what he hears infuriates him. President Taft is reversing many of Roosevelt's progressive measures, favoring corporate power over the needs of working people.*

Roosevelt fumes. A little over a year after leaving office, he begins campaigning for a *return* to the presidency. He becomes a fierce advocate for labor. This leads to Roosevelt's departure from the Republican Party in 1912, when Taft once again wins the nomination. Teddy Roosevelt then forms his own Progressive Party—nicknamed the "Bull Moose Party"—as an alternative, all but ensuring that the Democratic

---

* One item on Taft's agenda was reversing Roosevelt's environmentalism. He allowed much public land to be opened for private use.

Benjamin Harrison

Caroline Harrison

Mary McKee Harrison

William McKinley

Ida Saxton McKinley

Theodore Roosevelt

Edith Kermit Carow Roosevelt

William Howard Taft

Helen Herron Taft

Woodrow Wilson

Edith Wilson

Margaret Woodrow Wilson

Ellen Axson Wilson

Warren G. Harding

Florence Kling Harding

Calvin Coolidge

Grace Coolidge

Herbert Hoover

Lou Henry Hoover

Franklin D. Roosevelt

Eleanor Roosevelt

Harry S. Truman

Bess Truman

Dwight D. Eisenhower

Mamie Eisenhower

John F. Kennedy

Jaqueline Kennedy

Lyndon B. Johnson

Lady Bird Johnson

Richard Nixon

Pat Nixon

Gerald Ford

Betty Ford

Jimmy Carter

Rose Carter

Ronald Reagan

Nancy Reagan

George H.W. Bush

Barbara Bush

Bill Clinton

Hillary Clinton

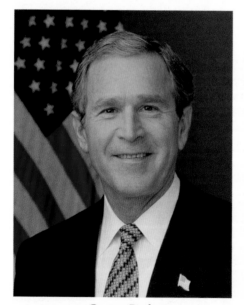

George Bush

Laura Bush

Barack Obama

Michelle Obama

Donald Trump

Melania Trump

Joe Biden

Dr. Jill Biden

nominee, Woodrow Wilson, wins the presidency over the divided Republicans.*

And even as this comes to pass, Theodore Roosevelt is still not through with the White House.

January 5, 1919. Roosevelt is mourning the death of his son Quentin, shot down and killed while flying as an American pilot in World War I six months earlier. It is now Woodrow Wilson who is debating whether or not to run for a third term in office. Should he not, Roosevelt plans to enter the race. His divide with the Republicans is over, and the former president is the most dominant member of that party. His nomination is all but assured.

That night, Theodore Roosevelt is up late, correcting an article for *Metropolitan* magazine. He begins having trouble breathing but continues to work. He and Edith are at their longtime home in Sagamore Hill, Long Island. Finally, Roosevelt goes to bed.

He never wakes up. Just sixty years old, Teddy Roosevelt dies in his sleep from a pulmonary embolism.

Edith Roosevelt passes away from heart failure on September 30, 1948, having outlived her husband as well as her sons Archie, Kermit, and Quentin.

One of her last acts is to burn all the letters she and the president exchanged.

Theodore Roosevelt's presidency defined a new era where protections were mandated for working people. Despite his opinion on race competence—one he shared with Winston Churchill, among others—Roosevelt was a compassionate man. On his watch, the nation became

---

* After losing the Republican nomination to Taft in June 1912, Teddy Roosevelt boasted that he felt "as strong as a bull moose." During a campaign stop in Milwaukee, Roosevelt was shot at by a deranged member of the audience. That did not stop him from finishing his speech and telling the audience that "it takes more than that to stop a bull moose." The nickname stuck. He recovered quickly from the chest injury.

more socially conscious. The National Association for the Advancement of Colored People was founded in the last months of Roosevelt's presidency in order to coincide with the one-hundredth anniversary of Abraham Lincoln's birth.

Theodore Roosevelt ends up on Mount Rushmore in South Dakota alongside Abraham Lincoln, George Washington, and Thomas Jefferson. While he did not achieve the greatness of those men, he will always be remembered as a vibrant president who, above all else, put America first.*

---

* On September 28, 1916, Roosevelt wrote a letter saying, "We are not going to have any real Americanism in this country until we create an effective popular opinion which will insist that the man descended from French, the man descended from English, or the man descended from German ancestry has any business to consider loyalty to any country except the United States." That letter is now in private hands.

Chapter Twenty-Seven

The president of the United States is stuck.

In the bathtub.

He can't get out.

So, William Howard Taft calls for help.

This is not uncommon. White House staff know not to overfill the porcelain tub as they draw a bath, understanding that water will spill onto the floor as the extremely corpulent president steps into his daily soak. They also know that Taft requires assistance to exit. The chief White House usher, Ike Hoover, will long remember that the president "would stick" and needed help "each time."

Responding to Taft's call, Hoover steps into the president's bathroom, where the rapidly reddening chief executive reclines in hot water, his thick neck and gray walrus mustache on display. Taft is a jovial man and, despite his size, an athlete. During his college days at Yale, the president was a champion wrestler. Thanks to Taft, an avid golfer, the sport will enjoy a leap in popularity during his time in office. He will also introduce the "seventh inning stretch" to baseball games. But at 350 pounds and six feet tall, the president challenges his tub.*

---

* While attending a baseball game in Pittsburgh, Taft stood to stretch during the seventh inning. Out of respect, the entire crowd got to their feet. The tradition was born.

The thirty-eight-year-old Hoover, whose White House jobs included turning the lights on and off during the Harrison administration eighteen years ago, is used to performing unusual tasks. He grasps the fifty-two-year-old president's extended fist tightly and pulls until Taft pops loose. Only when he is certain the president is unstuck does Hoover leave the room.

Just another day in the Taft White House.

President William Howard Taft will serve just one term in office, undone by an escalating feud with his predecessor, Teddy Roosevelt. Yet unlike many other men who have been chief executive, the presidency is *not* his dream job. Instead, the conservative Republican harbors hopes of being a Supreme Court justice.

Taft was born in Ohio, the son of President Ulysses S. Grant's secretary of war, Alphonso Taft. The year is 1857. He grows up in Cincinnati and then attends Yale. Taft's popularity and charisma lead to an invitation to join the Skull and Bones secret society, of which his father is a founding member. He has no facial hair at this time and wears his mane slicked straight back. After graduation, Taft studies law and passes the Ohio bar. There is no greatness in his early years to suggest he will rise to national office.*

But Taft's father has shown him the value of hard work, making the right friends, and playing politics. At age twenty-nine, William is appointed to a vacancy on the Superior Court of Cincinnati. In order to keep that spot, he must run for reelection. So, in 1884, Taft enters the world of campaign politics. He wins. This is also the year he marries Helen Herron, a social climber whose family is well connected in Ohio politics.

William Howard Taft's career rise is swift because of his connections. By 1889, the thirty-two-year-old is being considered for the role of US Supreme Court justice by President Benjamin Harrison.

But that ambition is not to be. Harrison instead names Taft as the nation's solicitor general, a rung just below attorney general, which allows

---

* Skull and Bones was founded at Yale in 1832. Dozens of prominent Americans have been members. Presidents George H. W. Bush and George W. Bush are among them. The 2004 presidential election pitted Bush against fellow Bones member John Kerry.

him to achieve prominence by arguing cases before the Supreme Court. This also brings Taft to Washington, where he and Helen immerse themselves in society life. Within two years, Taft accepts a lifetime appointment as a judge on the US Court of Appeals, based in Cincinnati. This is considered a path to the Supreme Court.

Eight years later, Judge Taft is summoned to speak with President William McKinley. Once again, Taft believes he is about to be awarded a spot on the Supreme Court bench. Again, he is disappointed. Taft is a lukewarm supporter of the president, only voting for the Republican because he believes the Democrats and their preference for a currency backed by silver is folly. McKinley requests that the forty-two-year-old Taft travel to the Philippines, newly taken from Spain at the end of the Spanish-American War. There, Taft will install a new government and serve as governor-general.*

The assassination of William McKinley and the inauguration of Theodore Roosevelt cut short Taft's time in the Philippines. Roosevelt and Taft are friends who first met when the new president was a civil service commissioner and Taft an inspector general. President Roosevelt asks Taft to sail home and join his cabinet as secretary of war. If all goes well, Roosevelt promises Taft, he will appoint him to the Supreme Court when the next spot opens.

Observing Roosevelt performing his presidential duties, William Howard Taft begins thinking about the top spot. Publicly, however, he does not acknowledge interest, stating, "I would not run for president if you guaranteed the office."

But Helen Taft dreams of living in the White House and pushes her husband to run.

As Roosevelt's second term winds down, Helen's urging becomes more intense. The president has already declared he will not seek a third term, an admission he regrets but cannot walk back without losing face. Thus, Roosevelt uses all his influence to swing the Republican nomination for his longtime ally.

The Republican National Convention is held in Chicago. Taft wins on the first ballot.

---

* Taft had almost unlimited power to run the Philippines and was reluctant to return to the United States.

His foe in the 1908 race is Democrat William Jennings Bryan, the longtime party stalwart who has already lost the presidential election twice. Taft has, by now, grown into an enormous man with a mustache spreading across almost the entire width of his face. He is fifty-one years old. Throughout the campaign, Taft visits the White House seeking political advice from Roosevelt. He barely wins the popular vote, getting just 51.5 percent of the electorate. But Taft's Electoral College margin is a healthy 321–162 over Bryan.

On March 4, 1909, William Howard Taft is sworn in as twenty-seventh president of the United States. Severe winter weather forces the inauguration to take place inside the Senate Chamber. Nearly ten inches of snow fall, a record for Inauguration Day. It takes six thousand sanitation workers to clear fifty-eight thousand tons of snow from the parade route.

That is just the first storm of Taft's presidency. In a matter of months, a cyclone named Teddy will emerge.

William and Helen Taft have three children as they move into the White House. Their son Robert is away at Yale and their daughter, Helen, is at Bryn Mawr outside Philadelphia, leaving only eleven-year-old Charles at home. Gone are the hijinks of the Roosevelt children, and with them the menagerie. Taft's choice of pets is neither exotic nor numerous but unique in its own way: a cow named Wooly-Mooly. She grazes on the South Lawn throughout the day.

For breakfast, Taft eats a steak every day. The morning meal also consists of grapefruit, grilled partridge, venison, waffles, hominy, rolls, and bacon. The president consumes large amounts of coffee throughout his working hours, tempering his ability to sleep through the night. Starting in October 1909, his workday takes place in a new presidential office with a unique shape. The Oval Office, as it is known, becomes a centerpiece for all executive functions.

Dinner features many things: fish, lamb chops, Lobster Newburg, salmon cutlets, tenderloin, cold tongue and ham, and terrapin soup. All this washed down with persimmon beer or champagne. After the evening meal, President Taft enjoys a cigar.

Eventually, President Taft grows tired of being stuck in the bath and orders the installation of a new tub so large it can fit four people. Also expanding is the president's girth, even though he believes "no true gentleman weighs more than 300 pounds"—a number he is far exceeding.

Helen "Nellie" Taft does not have a weight problem, but she suffers from hypertension. Two months into her husband's presidency, the First Lady suffers a stroke, throwing the White House into chaos.

Helen has long sought the prestige of being First Lady, chafing for the chance to be at the forefront of Washington society. The stroke is a stunning setback. Her speech is impaired. Yet she rallies, recovering within a year. The First Lady begins sitting in on presidential meetings, offering advice. She gets rid of the White House horse and buggy, insisting that the president travel by car. On March 27, 1912, she personally plants the first of three thousand cherry trees sent to Washington by the city of Tokyo, forever changing the capital landscape.*

Helen also has a strong dislike for Teddy Roosevelt's oldest daughter, Alice. It is not known exactly why, but the sentiment is so powerful that she convinces her husband not to bring Nicholas Longworth, Alice Roosevelt's husband, into the Taft cabinet. Helen has been active in selecting many of the president's advisers, overruling suggestions made by former president Roosevelt.

This simple act of shunning Longworth sows the seeds for a bitter feud between Roosevelt and Taft that will change history.

Ultimately, William Howard Taft is not a man of the people. He signs a bill increasing protective tariffs, pleasing America's large corporations. Then he calls for a new constitutional amendment to permit the collection of income taxes. Taft also allows public lands to be used for coal mining, in direct opposition to Theodore Roosevelt's land preservation vision.

It is June 1910 when Roosevelt returns from Africa. He is still a national hero, well regarded by the American people. But, at Helen's suggestion, President Taft snubs T. R., refusing to meet with him.

---

* In 1909, Taft purchases four vehicles for the White House: two Pierce-Arrows, a white Stanley Steamer, and a Baker electric.

Theodore Roosevelt is shocked.

Two days later, as Taft realizes his mistake, he relents and invites Teddy to meet. This time, T. R. turns *him* down.

Soon, Theodore Roosevelt makes a decision: he will seek the presidency once again. He does not make his intentions public, but he travels to Osawatomie, Kansas, where he delivers his "New Nationalism" address, explaining that the federal government should be "socially conscious."

Tension between the two men grows. Five days after Roosevelt's speech, Taft refuses to be present at a dinner held by the National Conservation Congress to honor both men. "He has utterly ignored me," Taft writes to his brother of Theodore Roosevelt, neglecting to mention that he also ignored Roosevelt. "His attitude toward me is one that I find difficult to understand and explain."

Sensing political danger, President Taft suddenly switches sides.

As his battle with Roosevelt becomes public, Taft begins attacking large corporations. The Supreme Court in a landmark case finds Standard Oil in violation of the Sherman Anti-Trust Act and orders it broken up geographically. Taft's administration via the Department of Justice succeeds in breaking up the corporation owned by leading "robber baron" John D. Rockefeller. Two weeks later, the Supreme Court approves dissolution of the American Tobacco Company. Taft's administration through the DOJ files suit against U.S. Steel, seeking to break up the nation's largest corporation.

But Teddy Roosevelt is not impressed. On February 22, 1912, the former president announces he is throwing his "hat into the ring," borrowing a boxing term, to show that he wants to launch a presidential campaign.

Instantly, the Republican Party divides in two. Roosevelt is very popular, but not where it counts even in big political machine East Coast states like New York, which he calls home.

This division will forever change the course of the Republican Party. A good many Republicans were progressive. But Taft is now defined as a man who believes in conservative values. Roosevelt is portrayed as a liberal, closer in ideology to the Democrats.

William Howard Taft wins the Republican presidential nomination on the first ballot; it is the fifth day of the Republican National Convention. Roosevelt and many of his supporters walk out. But Roosevelt is not done. A second party gathering, also in Chicago, is held shortly after. Billed as the Progressive National Convention, Theodore Roosevelt is chosen as a third-party candidate for president. Coining the term *Bull Moose Party* for this rogue party, Roosevelt is prepared to go up against Taft and Democrat Woodrow Wilson, governor of New Jersey, in the general election.

The nation has changed remarkably in the past ten years as enormous numbers of immigrants arrive, raising the population from seventy-six to ninety-one million. Many of the new arrivals join the Democratic Party, which heavily recruits them.

Black voters in the rural South are beginning to move to northern cities where factories offer more opportunity. This "Great Migration" will accelerate in the years to come. They tend to support Republicans— though that will change over time.

President Taft's loss is not surprising. As predicted, he and Roosevelt split the Republican vote, allowing Woodrow Wilson to win easily.

William Howard Taft leaves office on March 4, 1913.

On June 30, 1921, after teaching law at Yale, Taft realizes his lifelong ambition of being named chief justice of the Supreme Court. He takes up walking as a form of exercise, shedding one hundred pounds. But his health declines, and by February 1930, Taft is forced to step down from the bench due to poor health. Within a month, he is dead at seventy-two from heart disease and an inflamed liver.*

William Howard Taft is buried in Arlington National Cemetery, the first president to be so honored. His wife, Helen, survives him thirteen

---

* Republican president Warren G. Harding nominated Taft for the Supreme Court. He was easily confirmed.

more years, dying in 1943 at age eighty-one from heart disease. She is buried next to her husband.

Some historians have called the Taft presidency a disaster. This is too harsh. He was a kind man with a thoughtful judicial temperament who had trouble making decisions or articulating a vision for the country. On his watch, little of lasting importance was achieved with the exception of a federal income tax.*

Theodore Roosevelt, who destroyed Taft's second-term bid, summed up his onetime friend succinctly: "Taft, who was such an admirable fellow, has shown himself such an utterly commonplace leader, good-natured, feebly well-meaning, but with plenty of small motive; and totally unable to grasp or put into execution any great policy."

Roosevelt's sour opinion of Taft, however, will be nothing compared to what he thinks of Woodrow Wilson.

---

* The Sixteenth Amendment, ratified into the Constitution on February 3, 1913, formally introduces a federal income tax. A rate of 1 percent of income was the amount levied for those earning the lowest wages. The highest tax bracket was 7 percent for those earning more than $500,000 per year—a figure equal to $15 million today. These rates are not listed in the amendment but are those which Congress originally set.

Chapter Twenty-Eight

AUGUST 6, 1914

WHITE HOUSE

5:00 P.M.

D eath comes to the Executive Mansion.

First Lady Ellen Axson Wilson, the president's spouse of twenty-nine years, passes away from Bright's disease, the same ailment that killed Chester Arthur and Alice Roosevelt. Ellen has suffered from kidney problems since March, when she slipped and fell hard on a White House floor. Over time, she becomes lethargic and unable to leave her bed as renal failure takes over.

Looking out over the South Lawn, a devastated President Wilson says, "Oh, God. What am I to do?"

The summer sun sets over the Potomac. The residence is hushed. Woodrow Wilson and his three daughters grieve. He is wrung out, having sat at his wife's bedside all last night and today. His face is ashen with fatigue and mourning. Congress adjourns as the news spreads throughout the capital. Newsboys hawk "extra" editions telling of the First Lady's passing. Former president Theodore Roosevelt sends his condolences.

"The president," writes the *New-York Tribune*, "is almost prostrated by his bereavement."

The outside world is also intruding.

On August 4, in Europe, the German army invades Belgium. Great Britain comes to her ally's defense, declaring war on Berlin. Other nations throughout the continent now take sides. This conflict is being called the "Great War" for its enormity. The United States is neutral—for now.

Adding to the president's tragedy, a new holiday known as Mother's Day is celebrated for the first time.

The fifty-seven-year-old Wilson has endured his wife's long battles with depression and even a nervous breakdown. She had a soft southern accent and a sweet disposition and was known for her dignity and grace.

Her death is a catastrophe.

"God has stricken me beyond what I can bear," the president writes a friend.[*]

Woodrow Wilson is a man who does not do well alone. He needs female companionship. He has three daughters and no sons. The loneliness of the White House soon overwhelms him. He contemplates suicide, telling his physician he "could not help wishing . . . someone would kill him."

It was 1862 when Thomas Woodrow Wilson first laid eyes on Ellen Axson. He is five years old; she is just a baby. Their fathers are both Presbyterian ministers in Georgia, thus the connection. They will not meet again for twenty years, by which time "Tommy" is a lawyer. The couple get married in 1885.

Wilson's first childhood memory, however, is not of Ellen but of hearing the news that Abraham Lincoln has been elected president. This is not a popular victory in the South—or in the Wilson home. Woodrow's father, Joseph, is a staunch believer in the Confederate cause and serves as a pastor in the rebel army during the Civil War.[†]

Although Wilson's upbringing is religious, it is not charitable. Joseph Wilson is a racist and passes that along to his son. When Woodrow becomes president decades later, those beliefs will still be strong. He will

---

[*] The friend is longtime pen pal Mary Hulbert, whom he met while on vacation in Bermuda and with whom he corresponded with Ellen's blessing. There are rumors the two had an affair. That is still a matter of conjecture. Hulbert burned all of Wilson's letters before her death in 1939.

[†] Woodrow Wilson and John Tyler are the only two presidents to be citizens of the United States and the Confederate States of America.

revive segregation in the federal government after six decades of integration, denying employment to men of color. The president will also screen the racist propaganda film *Birth of a Nation* at the White House in 1915. The movie portrays the Ku Klux Klan as a force for *good* in the South. Wilson will comment that the film is "so terribly true."

In 1870, the family moves from Georgia so Joseph can teach theology at a South Carolina seminary. Woodrow leaves home to attend college at Princeton. He then studies at the University of Virginia Law School. He graduates but finds the law mundane. So, young Wilson moves on to Johns Hopkins University in Baltimore, where he earns a doctorate in history. He is a slow reader, overcoming this difficulty by using focus to memorize almost every word on the page, in this way developing a photographic memory. Wilson also masters the new invention known as the typewriter.

By the time of his graduation in 1886, Woodrow Wilson is already married to Ellen Axson, with baby Margaret on the way. Daughters Jessie and Eleanor follow. The Wilsons soon settle into a lifestyle of academia. Ellen, a talented artist, teaches herself German so she can assist with her husband's research into world politics.

Professor Wilson teaches at Bryn Mawr for two years and then Wesleyan University in Connecticut before finally landing back at Princeton. In 1902, Wilson is named the university's president. He successfully raises educational standards, but tragedies interfere with his work. In 1905, Ellen's brother Eddie, along with his wife and young child, drown in a Georgia river. A distraught Ellen Wilson is consumed by depression.

One year later, it is Woodrow himself who is struck down. He is a cigarette smoker and scotch drinker, both of which combine to cause a stroke brought on by hardened arteries. He loses vision in his left eye. This affliction, combined with Ellen's intense emotional state, brings about changes in Wilson's personality. He becomes critical and aloof.

When his doctor tells Woodrow he needs to stop working and take care of himself, the university president takes his advice.

In a way.

He decides to leave Princeton—and run for president of the United States.

With absolutely no political background whatsoever, Woodrow Wilson tells Democratic Party officials he is interested in a place on the presidential ticket of 1908—adding that he is not talking about the vice presidency. Nothing comes of this whimsical request. But in 1910, New Jersey Democrats have a change of heart. They suggest that Wilson run for governor.

He wins.

Two years later, this leap into politics gets even more improbable as Woodrow Wilson is elected president of the United States, courtesy of the Taft-Roosevelt feud.

★★★

Woodrow Wilson is an intense man but not a hardworking president. He has a second stroke just one month after taking office but refuses to acknowledge it, instead calling the pain on the left side of his body "nephritis." Wilson recovers quickly but, on the doctor's orders, begins taking afternoons off. He spends just four hours a day in the office, sleeps nine hours every night, and puts in as much time as possible on the golf course.

Woodrow Wilson stands five feet eleven and weighs 170 pounds. The president wears his hair in a mild comb-over, parting it on the left to hide his balding pate. When not golfing, he recreates by driving the official White House Pierce-Arrow automobile or cruising the Potomac aboard the presidential yacht, *Mayflower*. He sometimes rides a horse.

On May 7, 1915, President Wilson's days of leisure come to an end. Off the coast of Ireland, in the middle of the afternoon, a German U-boat attacks the English ocean liner *Lusitania*. The ship is among the largest and fastest on earth. She has made the crossing from England to New York 201 times without incident. This time, a German torpedo hits the hull, ripping the vessel in two. The *Lusitania* sinks in just eighteen minutes.

Among the 1,195 killed are 123 Americans.

The war in Europe is now almost a year old. President Wilson's "neutrality policy" is put to its first major test. A sharply worded message is sent to Berlin, condemning the attack. But Wilson's fear of entering the "European War" and the language chosen by his pacifist secretary of state, Williams Jennings Bryan, now embolden the Germans. The kaiser refuses to apologize or pay reparations to the families of the *Lusitania* victims.

The American people are furious. Anti-German sentiment rises. Action is demanded.*

President Wilson sends a second message to Germany, this one using such threatening language that Bryan resigns, believing Wilson is leading America into war.

Not to leave any doubt, President Wilson then issues a third communiqué stating that any further German submarine attacks will lead the US to declare hostilities against Germany.

Publicly, Germany still refuses to back down.

Yet an order is quietly sent to all U-boat commanders for attacks on passenger liners to cease.

On December 8, 1915, just one year after Ellen's death, gossip about a new presidential relationship is proven correct. Woodrow Wilson has been secretly dating widow Edith Bolling Galt for nine months. Forty-three years old to Wilson's fifty-eight, she claims to be a direct descendant of Pocahontas. Rather than marry at the White House, the couple wed in secret at her Washington home, witnessed by forty guests. Advisers attempt to have Wilson hold off on the nuptials, as the next election is less than a year away, fearing voters will not approve of the sudden marriage.

The new First Lady considers herself to be her husband's partner. She is a tall, dark brunette with a striking figure and the confidence that comes from being independently wealthy. Edith dresses in the latest fashion and has a gracious bearing. Soon, America accepts the president's new wife.

Edith sits in on important meetings, offers advice, travels with the president, and is never far from his side. She also seeks to weaken the influence of longtime advisers like diplomat Edward "Colonel" House

---

* The sinking of the *Lusitania* was front-page news and the subject of political cartoons across America for months. The large number of dead, the loss of famous individuals such as millionaire Alfred Vanderbilt, and Germany's defiant response all added to the national outrage. "Remember the *Lusitania*" became a popular rallying cry for Americans who supported entering the war in Europe.

and private secretary Joseph Tumulty, both of whom helped get Wilson elected.

No one must stand between Edith and the president.

Turbulence continues. The Ku Klux Klan experienced a resurgence during the Wilson administration in the state of Georgia. The United States invades Mexico to capture marauding bandit Pancho Villa. However, neutrality in the "Great War" continues.*

On March 24, 1916, Germany sinks another passenger ship, the French *Sussex*.

On June 3, 1916, Congress passes the National Defense Act. The NDA increases the size of the army and National Guard, not the Coast Guard. The president is also given greater authority to federalize the National Guard.

One month later, an ammunition depot explodes in Tom's River, New Jersey. Officials blame Germany for the sabotage.

On November 7, 1916, Woodrow Wilson is reelected president of the United States. His campaign slogan: "He Kept Us Out of War."†

But Woodrow Wilson knows war is coming.

On January 22, 1917, he rises to give a speech in the Senate Chamber. He promotes a "peace without victory" outcome where the fighting would stop in Europe with no repercussions to the belligerents.

Wilson's message is perceived as weakness. Germany responds by resuming unrestricted submarine warfare in the Atlantic.

So it is that, just one month after his second inauguration, President Wilson calls a special session of Congress and asks for a declaration of war. Great Britain's Winston Churchill considers this an act of great

---

*Pancho Villa was a Mexican revolutionary who hoped to goad America into war with Mexico by raiding border towns. Despite a US Army manhunt, he was never captured. The Mexican government offered Villa amnesty if he promised to refrain from politics. He agreed but was assassinated in an ambush in 1923.

†Wilson defeats Republican and former New York governor Charles Evans Hughes, winning the popular vote by the large margin of 49.2 percent to 46.1 percent. The Electoral College is one of the closest votes in US history, 277–254. Hughes also is former associate justice of the Supreme Court.

courage. Without American intervention, the stalemate in Europe would drag on. "It seems no exaggeration to pronounce that the action of the United States depended," Churchill writes, "upon the workings of this man's mind and spirit. . . . He played a part in the fate of nations incomparably more direct and personal than any other man."

Soon, American forces land in France and begin fighting alongside Britain against Germany. The "Great War" means nationwide rationing of gasoline, milk, and wheat to provide more food for the troops. President Wilson draws up a list of "Fourteen Points" to define what peace in Europe should look like. His diplomacy angers some Americans and one powerful man in particular: Theodore Roosevelt.

Writing to a Protestant minister named N. J. M. Bogert, Roosevelt unleashes: "It was I, who for two and a half years, stood for international justice on behalf of Belgium and against the foul inequities of Germany. When Mr. Wilson . . . was deluding the American people, was putting peace above righteousness, and was actually, in his presidential address of 1915, going to the length of saying that he abhorred and condemned Americans who upheld the cause of Belgium and the allies against Germany. And regarded these men as worse than the German murderers and dynamiters."

Wilson ignores Roosevelt's criticism, and Allied forces finally vanquish the Germans, who surrender on November 11, 1918.

The president and First Lady travel to Paris to negotiate the peace treaty.

Then, another blow. On September 25, 1919, Woodrow Wilson suffers his third stroke. A week earlier he told Edith of "unbearable" pain as an arterial blood clot pressed on his brain. Soon, he is incapacitated.

"As I sat there watching," Edith Wilson will recall, "I felt that something had broken inside me; and from that hour on I would wear a mask—not only to the public but to the one I loved best in the world; for he must never know how ill he was, and I must carry on."

One week later, the president falls off the toilet in his White House bathroom. Edith finds him unconscious on the floor, with cuts and bruising on his face. Wilson is immediately placed in bed, where he remains the next four weeks, during which the First Lady pretty much takes over the executive branch.

She is also successful in keeping the news from the public, as little media coverage ensues.

The left side of Wilson's body is paralyzed. He is agitated and irrational. He seems to have no impulse control. Working with Wilson's longtime physician, Dr. Cary T. Grayson, Edith suggests a "stewardship" of the president. The public will not be told of his condition. She will control what he reads and does not read. No outside visitors are allowed. Edith alone approves the president's schedule as he recuperates. "If there were some papers requiring his attention, they would be read to him," chief White House usher Ike Hoover will remember. "But only those that Mrs. Wilson thought should be read to him."

Only reluctantly does Edith Wilson tell Vice President Thomas R. Marshall the truth about the president's condition.*

Edith Wilson's total control extends to medical issues. A urinary blockage and high fever further endanger the president, but she refuses to allow the doctors to perform prostate surgery, believing the blockage will ease itself.

Until his stroke, Woodrow Wilson had been planning to run for a third term. That's over. He spends his last year in office shielded from the world by Edith. His favorite activity is watching newsreels in his office. The president rarely leaves the White House.

On March 4, 1921, the Wilsons depart for good. Republican Warren G. Harding is the new president, easily defeating Democrat James M. Cox, governor of Ohio.

The election of 1920 is not close, with Harding receiving 60 percent of the popular vote. Many Americans are angry with Wilson's plan for a "League of Nations" and want to return to isolationism after the calamity of World War I. Harding labels it "a return to normalcy."

Also, the cost of living in America is rising faster than wages.

After eight years of Woodrow Wilson, it is time for a change.

---

* Thomas Riley Marshall was the governor of Indiana before being selected as Wilson's running mate in 1912. Known for his sense of humor, he served both terms under the president. He survived an assassination attempt in 1915. His office in the Capitol was then bombed in July 1915. Marshall was not at the Capitol at the time. The would-be assassin was a German immigrant professor who opposed US intervention in Europe. Marshall died at age seventy-one in 1925. The cause of death was a heart attack.

President Wilson never recovers from his stroke. The former First Couple move into a small townhouse on S Street in Washington, near Embassy Row, where he dies on February 3, 1924. Wilson is buried in Washington's National Cathedral.

Edith Wilson dies of congestive heart failure on December 28, 1961. She is buried next to her husband.

Despite the hardship of his last months in office, Woodrow Wilson left a legacy of turning the United States from an isolationist nation into a world power. He enacted the regulatory reform of monetary policies through the creation of the Federal Reserve. And he transformed the Democrats from a party mired in Civil War–era southern politics into one bent on progressive reform. Although *not* in terms of civil rights.

★★★

As the nation enters the so-called Roaring Twenties, the new president is a man with no agenda, no plan, and few scruples.

It is Harding time.

Chapter Twenty-Nine

The man with no moral compass is now running the country.

"Forget that I'm president of the United States," says the nation's twenty-ninth chief executive to his fellow poker players. Saturday night. Second-floor residence. Seven powerful guests, known as the "Poker Cabinet," are seated at the table. "Cards and chips ready at hand—a general atmosphere of waistcoat unbuttoned, feet on the desk, and spittoons alongside," one attendee remembers.

Profanity. Whiskey. Tobacco. The evening begins with a stag dinner of knockwurst and sauerkraut. As the night wears on, platters of roast beef sandwiches will fuel the game.

"I'm Warren Harding, playing poker with friends," says the president. "And I intend to beat them."

The game is a "cold hand"—cards dealt face up. The charismatic Harding will play for any stakes, once losing a set of White House china. He stands six feet tall and is fifty-seven years old.

The Ohio-born Warren G. Harding has had a charmed life. Never really distinguishing himself in politics, he secured the Republican nomination in 1920 because of his looks and connections. After two years in office, Americans love Harding—surveys show that he is one of the most popular sitting presidents in history.

This is incredible because Warren Harding has a secret life. He conducts numerous extramarital affairs and three years ago fathered a daughter out of wedlock. The public has no idea.

But the Secret Service does because, at Harding's orders, it sneaks women into the West Wing. Also, the whiskey being consumed in this room tonight is in direct defiance of Prohibition, a new constitutional amendment forbidding alcohol. President Harding calls the trays of liquor "medical supplies." Should there be an issue about legality, Attorney General Harry M. Daugherty is among tonight's players.

The poker game goes well past midnight. Harding's vice president, Calvin Coolidge, and secretary of commerce, Herbert Hoover, are not among those at the table. Both men have disdain for Harding's weekly marathon card sessions, though Hoover realizes they serve a purpose for the president.

"Weekly White House poker parties were his greatest relaxation. The stakes were not large, but the play lasted most of the night," Hoover will write. "I had lived too long on the frontiers of the world to have strong emotions against people playing poker for money if they liked it, but it irked me to see it in the White House."

This is not the case with many other powerful men in the government.

Being beckoned to play poker with President Harding is the best invitation in town.

Warren G. Harding is not a hard worker. Never has been. In fact, he rarely reads briefing papers and depends on his so-called Ohio Gang for advice. This insider group of politicians and industrialists grows to eleven during his administration. Not all are from Ohio, but Harding has cultivated their support. The one thing that binds these men together is their placing personal needs before those of the nation.

Warren Harding was born on November 2, 1865, in a rural section of Blooming Grove, Ohio, where he will live most of his life. He is the oldest of eight children and has the childhood nickname of "Winnie." History does not record why.

His father is a farmer and schoolteacher, while Harding's mother is a midwife. Later, Tryon Harding will purchase a newspaper known as the *Argus*. He teaches young Warren the ways of publishing at a young age, giving the boy skills that will eventually make him a wealthy man.

After graduating from Ohio Central College in 1883, Warren Harding purchases a small local paper called the *Marion Star*. Using his press credentials, he gets his first taste of politics while attending the 1884 Republican National Convention in Chicago. By 1890, the *Star* is Marion's most popular paper. By investing in local business, the twenty-five-year-old acquires enough wealth to enter the world of politics.

But all this upward mobility comes at a cost. Harding is a patient at the Battle Creek Sanitarium five separate times, beginning when he is twenty-three. The causes of his visits are anxiety, severe fatigue, and an enlarged heart.

There is also the matter of a nasty feud. Warren Harding attacks local banker Amos Kling relentlessly in print, offended by his plans for developing the fast-growing town of Marion. Kling responds by spreading rumors that Harding is of African American ancestry and convinces some local businessmen not to advertise in the *Star*.

Enter Florence "Flossie" Kling, the daughter of Amos. She takes up with Warren Harding, and, incredibly, the two get serious. Flossie is five years older than the publisher and doesn't mind that he is an enemy to her father. In 1891, shortly after Harding threatens to "beat the tar" out of Amos if the attacks do not stop, the couple are married. She has a ten-year-old son from a previous marriage. Highly opinionated, good with money, and ambitious, Florence is unintimidated by the feud. Her parents do not go to the wedding, Amos will not speak to her for five years.

The Hardings have no children of their own, and the marriage evolves into an unhappy union. Florence takes over the *Star*'s business affairs as the paper sees a jump in circulation. This allows Warren to enter public life. Politicians throughout Ohio have long been fond of him due to his preference for running positive editorials about them. Harding is elected to the state senate in 1899, and then lieutenant governor, before running for governor in 1910. He loses.

Four years later, just as World War I begins, Warren Harding wins a seat in the US Senate. By now, the new senator is almost ten years into an affair with a woman named Carrie Philips, a former friend of Florence who has deep personal ties to Germany. She threatens to expose her affair with Harding if he votes in favor of war. The senator breaks things off only to begin a new romance with Nan Britton, a woman thirty years his junior. This relationship will continue for the rest of Harding's life and will result in the birth of a baby girl named Elizabeth.

It is 1920. The Republican National Convention in Chicago convenes. Warren Harding is not in the forefront. His time in the Senate has been lackluster, a series of missed votes and general laziness. He has written hundreds of passionate letters to his mistress on Senate stationery.

Yet the Ohio Gang, led by political strategist and wealthy lawyer Harry Daugherty, has a plan. They believe Warren Harding has two strengths: few political enemies and a handsome face. For the first time ever, physical appearance is a factor in electing a president because women have just been given the right to vote.

Daugherty patiently watches the first nine Republican ballots produce no candidate. Harding actually got votes on every ballot, though short of what is needed for the nomination. Then Daugherty suggests Warren Harding. The crowded convention is surprised, but, with nowhere else to turn, Harding is nominated on the tenth ballot. Massachusetts governor Calvin Coolidge is chosen as the vice president, another longshot. Coolidge is chosen because of his tough stance against a police strike in the Bay State.

Almost immediately, things turn dark. Harding is threatened with blackmail by Carrie Philips. He is forced to confess the affair to the Republican Party leadership. Their response is to send the mistress on an all-expenses-paid vacation to Asia, along with awarding her a lifetime stipend to guarantee silence.*

And there's more. Harding's current mistress, twenty-three-year-old

---

* It wasn't until 2014 that Warren Harding's letters to Carrie Philips were released to the public. The correspondence had been the property of the Library of Congress. They were explicit in describing sexual activity.

Nan Britton, is six months pregnant with the candidate's first and only child. She is due to give birth two weeks before Election Day. Harding keeps that situation quiet, and Britton cooperates. Neither the public nor the party knows anything about her.

Election Day is a triumph for Warren G. Harding.

He is elected president in a landslide, seven million votes to three million. Harding wins the popular vote by a margin of seven million votes; the tally is 16,166,126 for Harding to 9,140,256 for Cox. Harding becomes the first candidate to win more than 400 electoral votes, defeating Democrat James M. Cox, governor of Ohio, 404–127.

Even as president, Warren Harding cannot say no. And he seems to be proud of it. The president relates words by his father to him: "It's a good thing you weren't born a gal because you would be in the family way all the time."

Harding and his pals have a good laugh over that.

The corruption begins almost as soon as Harding is inaugurated. Florence brings her chicken pot pie to the White House, teaching the cook how to prepare the midwestern favorite. President Harding brings the Ohio Gang to eat a breakfast of grapefruit, hot cereal, scrambled eggs, and bacon. These men also help themselves to the nation's natural wealth.

Albert Fall is a newcomer to Harding's inner circle, a Kentucky native who moves to the then New Mexico Territory as a young man. After statehood, he serves as a US senator from New Mexico. Fall is chosen by the president to serve as secretary of the interior. He is currently in the habit of allowing private oil companies to drill on public lands, which is illegal. In exchange, Fall receives a secret $385,000 bribe.

Charles Forbes, first director of what is called the Veterans Bureau, is diverting alcohol and pharmaceutical supplies intended for medicinal use to bootleggers and drug dealers.

Attorney General Harry Daugherty, the man who got Harding elected, is involved in a complicated scheme to defraud the government. Daugherty is selling German assets seized in the war and keeping part of the money for himself.

President Harding is complicit, believing the job of president is largely ceremonial. Instead of governance, he spends his days playing golf or having sex with Nan Britton in a secret West Wing location. The Secret Service knows to smuggle her in when Flossie is not watching.

Yet the public knows nothing of all this. What it does hear is the president speaking on the radio. Harding is the first president ever to do so. His warm voice comes right into America's living rooms, calming a nation caught between the end of World War I and the growing abundance of the Roaring Twenties. The president promises a "return to normalcy" but does not state what that means.

America in 1922 is a country besieged by European immigrants who flock to the United States to escape the devastation of World War I. It is also a time when the first mass media outlet, radio, is becoming commonplace. Popular music, news, and comedy entertain the American public. Moving pictures without sound are becoming more popular. But it is the pursuit of alcohol that begins to dominate the culture.

The Eighteenth Amendment, ratified in January 1919, makes the "manufacture, sale, or transportation of intoxicating liquors" a crime. The temperance movement, which pushed forth this legislation, is surprised when the law makes Americans want to drink *more*. Bootlegging, as the illegal sale of liquor is known, rises quickly. Massachusetts businessman Joseph P. Kennedy, the father of a future president, is said to be among those who make fortunes this way. To this day, some dispute that fact.

Clandestine places to drink, known as speakeasies, flourish. These establishments are often run by a new wave of criminals called mobsters. Men like Chicago's Al Capone build empires based on liquor but also provide services such as prostitution, illegal narcotics, gambling, and even murder for hire.

There are some positives during the Harding administration. Alice Robertson of Oklahoma becomes the first woman to preside over the House of Representatives. Former president William Howard Taft is named a Supreme Court chief justice. The president signs a bill mandating federal assistance to mothers and infants by developing prenatal and childcare facilities. Harding also protects free speech by pardoning Eugene

Debs, a socialist who spoke out against World War I and was convicted of sedition.

On April 15, 1922, Harding's administration comes crashing down. Wyoming senator John B. Kendrick calls for investigators to look into an illicit oil deal between Secretary Albert Fall and the Sinclair Oil Corporation.

What they discover is one of the biggest scandals in American history. The Teapot Dome oil field in Wyoming is owned by the federal government, set aside for use by the military in case of a national emergency. But, in 1921, Harding transfers control of the site from the United States Navy to Fall's Department of the Interior. Rather than protect the fuel supply, as intended, the secretary allows Sinclair to drill oil, selling it for profit. The secret payoffs make Fall a wealthy man. Foolishly, the secretary uses the windfall to make lavish changes to his lifestyle. This mistake alerts investigators, who eventually send Fall to prison.

When news of the Teapot Dome scandal breaks, the American public is furious. Then comes more corruption. On May 30, 1923, Ohio Gang member and Assistant Attorney General Jess Smith is shot in his Washington home. The cause of death is ruled a suicide, but Smith is known to consort with members of organized crime.

Sensing he has to do *something*, Harding and Florence take to the road. The strategy is to visit Alaska and the West touting America's good economy. It works. Harding's "Voyage of Understanding" is well received. The Bay Area is the last—and *final*—stop.

August 2, 1923. San Francisco. 7:20 p.m. Presidential Suite, Palace Hotel. Florence Harding reads the *Saturday Evening Post* to the president. He lies on the bed, head propped up by several pillows to make breathing easier, as he is feeling ill.

Warren Harding is exhausted. He has slogged fifteen thousand miles in two weeks. His schedule has overwhelmed him. Now, in San Francisco, he has a fever, shortness of breath, and indigestion. Harding chalks it up to food poisoning.

The article Florence is reading to him is about his presidency.

"That's good. Go on," he tells her after one complimentary passage.

Suddenly, the president convulses.

Then he dies.

Florence Harding races to the door, instructing Secret Service agents to find the president's doctor. Secretary of Commerce Herbert Hoover, staying just down the hall, is also alerted. Hoover is the first government official to arrive at the dead president's bedside.

A call is made to Plymouth Notch, Vermont, where Vice President Coolidge is spending the weekend. At 2:43 a.m. Eastern Time, four hours after President Harding's death, Coolidge is sworn in as America's new president.

★★★

Inexplicably, the First Lady refuses to allow an autopsy on her husband's body, leading some to suspect foul play. The cause of death is officially listed as ptomaine poisoning, but symptoms point to a heart attack. President Harding's body is taken by train to Washington, where he lies in state. His final burial is in Marion, Ohio, where mourners include Chief Justice William Howard Taft, inventor Thomas Edison, and industrialist Henry Ford. One year later, Florence dies. She and her husband are reinterred into Marion's white marble Harding Tomb in 1931.*

★★★

Many historians consider Warren Harding to be one of America's worst presidents. He was overwhelmed by the demands of office, so much so that he placed the good of the nation in the hands of corrupt people while he abdicated the discipline of leadership.

In office two years and 151 days, Warren Harding never publicly acknowledged his illegitimate daughter. As the corrupt administration was exposed after his death, his stock fell quickly with the public.†

Warren Gamaliel Harding constructed no lasting legislation and did not leave a positive legacy.

A cynic might say he dealt from the bottom of the deck in every way.

---

* Florence died of renal failure on November 21, 1924. She was sixty-four years old.

† The mother of Harding's daughter, Elizabeth, sought money after his death. Harding's estate denied her. So, she sold her story to a small private publishing house. Her book, called *The President's Daughter*, came out in 1927.

Chapter Thirty

The man about to become president is groggy.

A kerosene lamp flickers in the family parlor. The home has no electricity. John Calvin Coolidge Sr., a seventy-eight-year-old justice of the peace, stands before his fifty-one-year-old son. Both men share the same name, but the younger Coolidge simply goes by Calvin. He was awakened in the middle of the night and informed that he is due to become president. His wife, Grace, stands at his side. After getting dressed and saying a prayer, Calvin comes downstairs to be sworn in. Placing his left hand on a family Bible and raising his right hand, Calvin Coolidge repeats the oath of office, delivered by his father.

Then the new president of the United States goes back to bed.

So ends the inauguration of Calvin Coolidge.

The *illegal* inauguration.

★★★

Eighteen days later.

Calvin Coolidge's father is not a federal official. There is no precedent for a local justice swearing in a president, so Attorney General Harry M. Daugherty rules that the oath sworn by Coolidge is not binding. Thus, the United States has been without a chief executive for almost three weeks.

The country is reeling from the corruption of the Harding administration. Faith in federal officials is plummeting. Daugherty himself is a member of Harding's corrupt gang. Rather than risk further public doubts about governmental competence, the attorney general arranges a top secret second swearing-in.

So it is that, on August 21, 1923, at the Willard Hotel in Washington, Calvin Coolidge gathers with Judge Adolph A. Hoehling Jr. Placing his hand on a Bible found in the room, the quiet man from Vermont is once again sworn in as America's new president.

Now that his role is official, John Calvin Coolidge Jr. can formally stake a claim to being the only US president born on the Fourth of July. This took place in 1872 in the small town of Plymouth Notch, Vermont. Like his father, Calvin takes his name from an influential sixteenth-century Protestant minister. To avoid confusion, however, the young man is called Calvin instead of John.

Death strikes hard in Coolidge's early years. His mother dies from tuberculosis when he is twelve. His only sibling, Abigail, passes away at fifteen from appendicitis. Shortly afterward, as his father remarries a local schoolteacher, the future president leaves home to attend Amherst College in Massachusetts. Coolidge is shy by nature, prone to silence. But he challenges himself through public debate and by joining a fraternity. He graduates cum laude and then takes up the study of law. Soon, Coolidge settles into the life of a small-town lawyer. He is five feet ten, weighs 148 pounds, has light-red hair, and is extremely close with a dollar. His tight smile, it is said, makes him look like he was "weaned on a pickle."

Coolidge starts his own practice in Northampton, Massachusetts, yet struggles to find clients. So he turns to politics to make connections, elected to the city council at age twenty-five.

It is in Northampton, at the age of thirty, that Calvin Coolidge meets Grace Goodhue, a teacher at the local school for the deaf. She is watering flowers in her garden there one day when, through an open window, she observes a man shaving in a nearby boardinghouse. He wears a hat, which she thinks odd, because it appears he is wearing little else. Grace laughs so loud that he calls out to her. A meeting is arranged. Thus begins their lifelong partnership.

The couple court for two years before marrying in 1905. The union of the taciturn Calvin and the outgoing Grace will lead to the running joke that if she can teach the deaf to speak, why can't she get Calvin to do the same?

It is this blend of opposites that forms the backbone of Coolidge's political career. He is a fine public speaker but cares more about the business of governance than actual people. Grace has a friendliness and charm that make up for Calvin's long silences. She speaks sign language and immerses herself in local social activities, where she shows a flair for remembering names and faces.

Grace Coolidge understands her husband's dry wit, which many people do not. He makes fun of her poor cooking, with Calvin telling Grace that her pie crust should be used by local road crews in place of gravel. When the couple leave for Montreal for a two-week honeymoon, she has no problem cutting it short by one week so he can campaign for the local school board.

Coolidge loses. This is the only time in his career Calvin Coolidge comes out on the wrong end of an election.

Calvin prefers not to purchase a home, thinking it too expensive. So the Coolidges rent a room at a local hotel. When the establishment goes out of business, a thrifty Calvin Coolidge purchases their linen and silverware. For some time after, even upon entering the White House, "Norwood Hotel" is embroidered on the family's sheets and towels.

In 1906, Massachusetts Republicans select Coolidge as a candidate for the Massachusetts House of Representatives. He wins. His oldest son, John, is born the same year. Coolidge writes eloquently of the baby's birth: "The fragrance of the clematis which covered the bay window filled the room like a benediction where the mother lay with her baby. It was all very wonderful to us."

Coolidge is successful as a state legislator, making strong personal connections that guarantee support in future campaigns. Yet when young Calvin comes along two years after John, Coolidge returns home to Northampton to run for mayor, preferring to be with Grace and the boys rather than remain in Boston.

But in 1916, Coolidge returns to state-level politics, running for and winning the job of lieutenant governor. In 1918, he is elected governor of Massachusetts. Then, in September 1919, Coolidge is abruptly elevated into the highest levels of American politics through his deft handling of a strike by Boston policemen.

In 1920, at the Republican National Convention in Chicago, this new fame thrusts him even higher into the national limelight. Party bosses choose Warren G. Harding as president and Senator Irvine Lenroot of Wisconsin as vice president. But those insiders leave the convention too early on the night ballots are being cast, departing after Harding's nomination is assured. In an act of rebellion, rank-and-file party members tired of being told *how* to vote suggest Calvin Coolidge as vice president.

"Silent Cal," as he is soon known, is on his way to Washington.

Calvin Coolidge enjoys a solitary cigar.

The new president's first addition to the White House is a rocking chair, which he places on a private porch so he can smoke in peace. He is proud that no photographer has ever captured him with a cigar in his mouth. As the new president settles in to his job, Coolidge begins a routine that almost never varies: early breakfast, work until noon, a long walk followed by a two-hour nap, back into the Oval Office for a few more hours, and then dinner and a cigar on the porch.

America soon comes to know this quiet man and his belief that "the business of America is business." He reduces the national debt, cuts taxes, and then cuts them again. The economy roars. Though not opposed to the consumption of alcohol, Coolidge believes the Constitution should be obeyed. He is appalled by those intending to subvert Prohibition and the rising crime that follows.

To save time, President Coolidge has the White House barber cut his hair while he breakfasts. He never dines alone. The First Couple entertain more than any other in history. The scene is often similar: the chatty First Lady happily remembering names and faces as she shakes hands while a dour President Coolidge stoically endures the receiving line.

Meals are always called supper, no matter the time of day. Believing that chickens should be as fresh as possible, Coolidge keeps a small flock in a special pen he orders built on the White House grounds. The president snacks constantly, with butlers ordered to bring him nuts, pickles, or slices of roast beef on a moment's notice. The family dinner table is always the State Dining Room, even when there are no visiting dignitaries. Coolidge and Grace dress formally, with the First Lady preferring Asian cuisine while the president likes a special pie of pork and apples.*

President Coolidge believes firmly in a separation between work and family. Grace is not invited to meetings. Her advice is not sought. She is not allowed to give interviews. Yet such is her charisma that she quickly becomes the most popular woman in Washington. She has an eye for expensive clothing, which the president happily indulges. This is his lone extravagance.

The First Lady is also a natural hostess, and invitations to her twice-weekly White House receptions are keenly sought. Visitors who do not know Grace remark that they like her immediately. When one guest confesses that she feels awkward and out of place, the First Lady responds that only makes the guest more interesting.

The president is not as outgoing. Yet when it comes to the American people, he is actually a great communicator. He gives an average of eight press conferences a month, speaks to the nation regularly on the radio, and records one of his speeches for a motion picture. This makes him the first president to appear in a talking movie.

But speaking to humans is different.

"You must talk to me, Mr. Coolidge," one female guest tells him. "I made a bet today that I could get more than two words out of you."

To which Coolidge replies, "You lose."

As with President Franklin Pierce seventy years earlier, the presidency of Calvin Coolidge is marred by the loss of a son.

It is June 1924. The president has been in office ten months. Delegates at the Republican National Convention in Cleveland have just selected him as their candidate for the 1924 election.

Sixteen-year-old Calvin Jr. is playing tennis on the White House courts with his big brother, John, both home for the summer. The teenager is not wearing socks. He develops a blister on the third toe of his right foot. Young Calvin thinks nothing of it but soon develops a fever as

---

* Sons John and Calvin Jr. attend boarding school at Mercerburg Academy in Pennsylvania.

blood poisoning sets in. Physicians attempt to heal the boy, who grows worse with each passing day. But medications to stop the staph infection do not exist. Sepsis soon invades his body.

The president finds the best specialists to treat his son, but young Calvin's condition worsens. He is admitted to Walter Reed Army Medical Center, considered the finest such facility in Washington. Doctors operate but cannot stop the infection.

On July 7, 1924, Calvin Coolidge Jr. dies before his seventeenth birthday.

In New York City, the Democratic Convention at Madison Square Garden halts out of respect for the family.

An entire nation mourns.

Silent Cal, consumed by grief, enters a dark depression.

"The power and the glory of the presidency went with him," Coolidge says of his son's passing.

March 4, 1925. Supreme Court chief justice William Howard Taft becomes the first former president to deliver the oath of office to another president. Calvin Coolidge is fifty-two. In a year, America will celebrate its 150th birthday. The nation has never been more prosperous, partly due to Coolidge's fiscal policies. Credit is easier for most Americans to obtain, so even as the national budget shows a surplus, consumer debt is at an all-time high. So far, there is no sign that this will become a problem.

On this Wednesday afternoon, there is optimism. President Coolidge has banished the corruption of the Harding administration, leading a scandal-free presidency. He wins reelection easily, 382 electoral votes to 136 for Democrat John W. Davis of West Virginia.

However, Prohibition and its effects continue to trouble the nation. Likewise, the Ku Klux Klan has reemerged. In 1923, Oklahoma governor J. C. Walton had even placed portions of his state under martial law to halt Klan terror.

President Coolidge says little about these issues. He prefers to focus on the economy. So it is that, under Coolidge's guidance, the Roaring Twenties keep roaring.

★★★

The Klan demands its day.

August 8, 1925. Tens of thousands of robed Klansmen march down Pennsylvania Avenue. Many do not even wear a mask, as the group is so powerful that anonymity is now unnecessary.

The *New York Herald Tribune* reports that "30,000 men and women, clad in the white robes and conical hoods of the Ku Klux Klan paraded down Pennsylvania Avenue today from the Capitol to the Treasury. It took nearly three and a half hours for the colorful procession to pass."

Klan national membership is now reportedly four million, including many wealthy and powerful white people—some even senators and congressmen. They oppose the flood of immigrants coming from Europe and the large number of black people moving north to find work. The Klan also opposes the country's growing number of Catholics and Jews. They consider themselves "100 percent" American and have traveled to Washington in a long caravan of vehicles. Their goal is to "keep America for Americans."

President Coolidge is wary of the Klan. He does not speak of them by name. Nothing is done to halt their march on Washington. But he welcomes Jews, black people, and Catholics into the White House. Several months after the Klan rally, he will give a speech clarifying what it means to be an American: "Once our feet have touched this soil, when once we have made this land our home, wherever our place of birth, whatever our race, we are all blended in one common country. All artificial distinctions of lineage and rank are cast aside. We all rejoice in the title of Americans."

August 2, 1927. Four years to the day since the death of Warren Harding. President Coolidge is on an extended summer vacation in the Black Hills of South Dakota as the White House undergoes yet another renovation. A press conference is scheduled for 11:30 a.m. Coolidge is a master of these gatherings, bantering with reporters while demonstrating his quick wit and knowledge of subject matter.

As reporters gather, Coolidge hands each one a single strip of paper with a handwritten message: "I do not choose to run for president in 1928."

The media is shocked. Coolidge enjoys enormous popularity. The economy has never been better. "Coolidge prosperity" means the US budget has a $635,809,921 million surplus. America has leapt into the modern age under his leadership, with citizens owning automobiles, homes, and luxury items like washing machines and refrigerators. Only three months ago, in a show of America's ascendance, a brave young pilot from the Midwest named Charles Lindbergh shocked the world by becoming the first man to fly a plane solo across the Atlantic Ocean.

If ever there was a time for a president to capitalize on his achievements, it is now.

The press does not know that President Coolidge made his decision not to run three years ago, after the death of his son. He is exhausted by the office and will not be swayed.

As the press clamors for more information, the president makes a brief statement: "There will be nothing more from this office today."

President Coolidge leaves the White House on March 4, 1929. He and Grace return to Northampton, Massachusetts. He spends the next four years writing his autobiography at The Beeches, his large retirement home. He also writes a syndicated newspaper column. On the afternoon of January 5, 1933, the former president lies down for his daily two-hour nap.

A heart attack fells him in his sleep. He is sixty years old.

Coolidge leaves his entire fortune of $700,000 ($17 million in modern currency) to Grace. She sells The Beeches and moves into a smaller home, then devotes herself to working with the deaf. Grace Coolidge outlives her husband by twenty-four years, passing away from a heart attack on July 9, 1957. The president and First Lady are buried in Plymouth Notch, Vermont.

Coolidge's departure from the White House does not alter the lifestyle of many Americans. They are spending and borrowing money at a record rate. The country seems to be in a prosperous place.

But only for now.

The Great Depression is on the way.

Chapter Thirty-One

OCTOBER 24, 1929

WASHINGTON, DC

EVENING

It is all crashing down on Herbert Hoover.

The president has returned to the West Wing, going over the horrific events taking place today in Manhattan. The New York Stock Exchange has collapsed. Thirteen million shares have been sold as investors dump stocks. J. P. Morgan Jr. and John D. Rockefeller Sr. have been buying heavily, but even the wealthiest people cannot stop the debacle.

In just five hours, the United States loses more money than it spent on World War I. Some devastated financiers leap to their deaths from buildings and bridges: "You had to stand in line to get a window to jump out of, and speculators were selling space for bodies in the East River," Will Rogers will write in his syndicated national column.

British politician Winston Churchill, in New York on business, tells a London newspaper of a crowd gathering to watch a man smoking a pipe patiently waiting his turn to jump off a steel girder over Manhattan. Churchill writes of "the audience waiting in a respectful and prudently withdrawn crescent for the final act."

Confronted with an unprecedented disaster, President Hoover does . . . nothing.

★★★

Herbert Hoover was born into poverty, the middle child in a Quaker Iowa family. The year is 1874. "Bertie," as he is nicknamed, almost doesn't survive his second birthday.

The toddler has croup. He is near death.

A quick-acting uncle resuscitates the boy, and young Herbert revives.

Yet life does not get easier. His father, Jesse, a thirty-four-year-old blacksmith, dies of a heart attack when the boy is six. His mother, Hulda, passes away from typhoid fever four years later, orphaning Herbert and his brother and sister.

The Hoover children are sent to Oregon to live with their uncle John Minthorn, a Quaker physician whom Herbert quickly comes to dislike. The young boy does not want to do household chores and has little interest in school. At thirteen, he drops out to take a job in a local real estate office. There, he educates himself.

By age seventeen, Herbert is accepted into a new California university named Stanford, despite failing every one of the entrance exams. The school is in its first year and desperate for students.

Hoover earns a degree as a mining engineer, destined for a career harvesting gold. He travels to Australia and China, earning a reputation for his uncanny ability to find new gold deposits. He rises to a management position and is a tough boss. Hoover is anti-labor, not believing in a minimum wage, unions, or employee benefits beyond a simple paycheck. He is proud to be a self-made man and disdains those looking for help. Eventually, Hoover starts his own mining business before age thirty—and gets rich quick.

Herbert Hoover marries Lou Henry, a fellow Stanford graduate and Iowa native. She bears two sons, Herbert and Allan. The family travels the world before settling in London in 1902. At this point, nothing in his career path suggests a journey into politics.

His wife, Lou, raises the two boys but is very involved with her husband's business because she also has a degree in geology. An attractive brunette, Lou can hold her own with any man. She hunts, fishes, and is proficient riding a horse. While Herbert is aloof, Lou is friendly—putting people at ease and pretty much running the social schedule for the Hoovers in London. The couple will be married forty-five years with very little strife.

★★★

In 1914, World War I breaks out. More than 120,000 Americans are trapped in Europe. Acting as a private citizen, Herbert Hoover forms a committee to rescue his fellow citizens. The Wilson administration offers its support. "I did not realize it at the moment, but on August 3, 1914, my career was over forever. I was on the slippery road of public life," Hoover will recall. As the war escalates, Hoover's organization aids not just Americans but also provides food and relief for millions of Europeans. He works with German, French, and British officials to ensure civilians on both sides of the conflict do not go hungry. When America enters the war in 1917, President Wilson names Hoover head of the US Food Administration—a role that earns him the nickname "food czar."

After moving back to America, Hoover's public profile continues to rise. He never declares himself a Republican or Democrat, but as the 1920 election looms, his name is mentioned as a possible presidential candidate. In March of that year, he announces that he is a Republican. Once Warren G. Harding is nominated for the presidency, Hoover offers his support. That loyalty earns Hoover a spot in the cabinet as secretary of commerce, a position he continues to hold after Calvin Coolidge becomes president.[*]

★★★

Although holding a powerful cabinet position, Herbert Hoover does not ingratiate himself in Washington. He is six feet tall and weighs 187 pounds. He speaks very little and does not engage strangers. His personal wealth is estimated to be $100 million in modern currency—a colossal fortune at the time.

As the 1928 election looms, Hoover is intent on running. He is well known not just as secretary of commerce but as an able manager who fixes problems in other cabinet departments. However, Herbert Hoover is not a superstar. He is one of many who would like to be president.

Then the levee breaks.

The Great Mississippi Flood of 1927 sees the massive river overflow

---

[*] In a letter dated February 26, 1935, Hoover says, "At the Garfield election in 1880, the town held a Republican torchlight procession of those days. My mother took me to the parade, of which she highly approved."

its banks. Millions of acres of land are underwater. Almost two million people lose their homes. President Coolidge appoints Hoover to fix the problem. He skillfully orders the building of tent camps to provide living space for the displaced. In addition, he raises the modern equivalent of $300 million through public appeals to help the suffering. By the time Coolidge makes the surprise declaration that he is not running for a third term, many Americans consider Herbert Hoover a hero. He easily wins the Republican nomination at the June 1928 convention in Kansas City.

The presidential election is controversial. Religion is the major issue. Herbert Hoover's opponent is Al Smith, the governor of New York and a practicing Roman Catholic. This marks the first time in American history a major party candidate is not a Protestant. Hoover does not participate in anti-Catholic rhetoric. However, he allows it from others in his campaign.

Al Smith is overwhelmed. Hoover and vice presidential candidate Charles Curtis of Kansas, a senator who is three-eighths Native American, have no trouble on Election Day. The final tally is 444 electoral votes for the Republicans to just 87 for Smith.

On March 4, 1929, Herbert Clark Hoover is sworn in as the thirty-first president of the United States. He has long warned President Coolidge that stock speculation and increasing private debt have left America susceptible to financial collapse. During the campaign, he reminds the nation to rein in its free-spending habits. Yet he never suggests regulation of the stock market, believing the government has no place meddling in monetary affairs.*

In the months after his inauguration, President Hoover seems to have nothing to fear. In Hollywood, the success of the movie-making industry is celebrated by the first ever Academy Awards dinner. On the Nevada-Arizona border, a massive dam named in honor of the new president is

---

* Timothy Walch, current director of the Herbert Hoover Presidential Library, and former director Richard Norton Smith make this known on the National Archives website: "As early as 1925, then-Secretary of Commerce Hoover had warned President Coolidge that stock market speculation was getting out of hand. Yet in his final State of the Union address, Coolidge saw no reason for alarm. Hoover, however, remained fearful. Even before his inauguration, he urged the Federal Reserve to halt 'crazy and dangerous' gambling on Wall Street. . . . He asked magazines and newspapers to run stories warning of the dangers of rampant speculation."

about to begin construction. And in New York City, the Empire State Building will rise to become the tallest skyscraper in the world.

Six months later, the Roaring Twenties come to an end.

Hooverville is the sarcastic name given to the hundreds of shack towns and encampments where homeless Americans take refuge. The economy has collapsed. Banks fail. Businesses large and small go under. Millions lose their jobs. Homeowners can no longer pay mortgages, leading to widespread foreclosures. Without homes, the folks have no choice but to live in Hoovervilles.

The population of the United States now numbers 123,202,624. One-fourth of the workforce does not have a job. Some Americans choose to live with relatives, but others "squat," living under bridges or on open public land, building shacks made of plywood and tar paper. Some live in nothing more than a hole in the ground covered by a board. Hooverville occupants do without basic human amenities. No toilets. No running water. These impromptu settlements are everywhere in America. In major cities like New York, Washington, St. Louis, and Seattle, they are home to thousands of suffering people.

A Hoover blanket is the name given for a newspaper used to ward off the cold. A Hoover flag is what happens when pants pockets are pulled inside out to reveal no money. A car pulled by a horse for lack of gas is a Hoover wagon. And cardboard placed inside a shoe whose soles are worn out is known as Hoover leather.*

America's suicide rate is at an all-time high.

But, this time, Herbert Hoover does *not* come to the rescue. He despises government "handouts." Despite his great success feeding the people of Europe during and after World War I, the president believes American "individualism" will defeat the Depression.

He is wrong.

On October 25, 1929, the economy is still in freefall. In front of Congress and on the radio, President Hoover reassures Americans that the economy is on "a sound and prosperous basis."

---

* The term *Hooverville* is coined by newspaper reporter Charles Michelson in 1930. Hoovervilles dot the American landscape almost immediately after the crash and will continue to exist for the next decade.

That is not true.

Within one year, 1,300 financial institutions close, among them New York's Bank of United States. Black residents of northern cities see their jobs disappear as unemployed white residents vie for even the most un-skilled positions. In December 1931, hundreds of "hunger marchers" advance on the White House. They wish to present Herbert Hoover with petitions seeking jobs.

Hoover ignores them.*

Instead, he tells Americans to tighten their belts. To foster a greater sense of patriotism, "The Star-Spangled Banner" is named America's first national anthem. The president asks businesses to allow employees to stay on the payroll, letting private industry absorb the cost of the fi-nancial crisis.

Hoover's strategy is a disaster. The nation places more and more blame for the Great Depression directly on him.

May 1932. Washington. Eleven thousand veterans of World War I and their families descend on the nation's capital. The government has promised them a bonus for their service. Now the soldiers have come to collect. They build encampments and occupy federal properties en masse, refusing to budge until their money is paid.

President Hoover refuses. The bonus is not technically due until 1945. Yet as the Great Depression worsens, the vets will not wait. A stalemate ensues. The District of Columbia police department is unable to dis-lodge the trespassers.

Hoover well knows that America's World War I enemies are in similar straits. Germany is devastated by postwar inflation, with a wheelbarrow of deutsche marks not enough to buy a loaf of bread. So that nation is be-ginning to militarize. A new leader named Adolf Hitler and his National Socialist ("Nazi") Party pledges prosperity through military might.

England, America's primary ally, is also suffering. However, London does not see militarization as the answer. Many Britons swear they will never wage another world war.

---

* Unlike today, in the 1920s, there was no federal backing of banks. When a bank failed, depositors lost their money.

On July 28, President Hoover orders the United States Army to remove the veterans from federal government properties in Washington, DC. Under the command of General Douglas MacArthur, troops use guns, tear gas, and force to destroy encampments and dislodge squatters. Future American generals Dwight Eisenhower and George Patton are among those taking part in the brutal military action.

The veterans are driven out of Washington. Americans are repelled by the images in newspapers of World War I heroes being treated like criminals. But President Hoover is proud of the accomplishment, stating that his administration "knows how to deal with a mob."

Amid the chaos, Herbert Hoover keeps a routine. He begins each morning with a 6:30 a.m. round of exercise using a medicine ball. He breakfasts at 8:00 a.m. with the First Lady, enjoying a light meal of toast, coffee, and fruit that he is known to devour quickly. He rarely sees his sons, both of whom receive graduate degrees in business from Harvard.

President Hoover then begins his *eighteen-hour* workday. This includes calls and meetings with a short break for lunch. Dinner is at 8:00 p.m., followed by an evening spent reading government reports before going to bed after midnight.

As the Great Depression lags on, President Hoover becomes angry. He is curt with the media and his staff. All questions must be submitted in advance. Very often, Hoover ignores the queries, storming out abruptly from press conferences.

Cognizant of public perception, the president and First Lady entertain lavishly but at their own expense. This goodwill goes unnoticed. Hoover continues to be tremendously unpopular with the public.

The inevitable end of Herbert Hoover's time in the White House begins on November 8, 1932. Democrat Franklin D. Roosevelt from New York trounces him in the presidential election, winning 472 electoral votes to Hoover's paltry 59.

On March 4, 1933, Herbert Hoover departs the White House a bitter man. Lou Hoover dies from a heart attack in January 1944. Her husband moves to New York City, where he lives in the Waldorf Astoria hotel the rest of his life. He dies in 1964 from intestinal bleeding, one of only two presidents to reach ninety years of age at that time.[*]

In retirement, Herbert Hoover sees himself as a victim. The American public virtually ignores him. He writes his memoirs. Few care.

In America, it is now time for a "new deal."

And another very wealthy president is about to impose it.

---

[*] John Adams is the other.

Chapter Thirty-Two

Franklin D. Roosevelt declares war on the Great Depression.

The thirty-second president of the United States looks out on a sea of spectators, ready to deliver his first inaugural address. He is dressed in a morning coat, striped pants, and dark tie. Sworn in by white-haired chief justice Charles Evans Hughes, Roosevelt removes his hand from a 250-year-old family Bible written in Dutch. An eagle cartouche is emblazoned on the podium.*

FDR, as he is known, is fifty-one years old, with thinning hair and wire-rimmed glasses. The president is uneasy on his feet, leaning on the podium to support his weak legs. The fifth cousin of Theodore Roosevelt contracted polio at the advanced age of thirty-nine. He spends most days in a wheelchair and "walks" by wearing braces on his legs. His shoulders are broad from hours of swimming as rehabilitation. The public knows little about the atrophy of Roosevelt's legs brought on by his disease.

A glowering Herbert Hoover sits just a few feet away. It is obvious the

---

* Roosevelt will be the last president sworn in on March 4. The passage of the Twentieth Amendment on January 23, 1933, moves the new inauguration date to January 20. Modern transportation is among the reasons for the change, as new presidents no longer need as much time to travel to Washington after being elected.

departing president does not want to be here. However, he and Roosevelt did ride to the inauguration together in an open-air vehicle, blankets covering their legs. Roosevelt is chatty with just about everyone while Hoover remains largely silent.*

The inaugural address is broadcast nationwide on the radio. Roosevelt speaks in a dynamic patrician voice, comparing the fight against the Great Depression with waging war. He rails against the "greed" that brought down the country and requests more power for the executive branch. The new president promises to get Americans working again. Savings will be insured. The old and sick will be cared for by the government. This is what Roosevelt calls his "New Deal."

FDR's confidence is inspiring to many.

He states, "The only thing we have to fear . . . is fear itself."

Chaos ensues.

The White House is the scene of a massive celebration on Inauguration Day. It is reminiscent of Andrew Jackson's raucous 1829 party, with the public filling the Executive Mansion. First Lady Eleanor Roosevelt orders the overwhelmed cooks to feed the masses hot dogs. Chief Usher Ike Hoover, now in his forty-second year at the White House, will note with surprise that no Republicans are present.†

Meanwhile, President Roosevelt is nowhere to be seen. Rather than socializing, he wants to get to work. But the Oval Office is nearly empty. The new president bellows for his staff.

"There he was," one aide will recall, as people came running. "In a big empty room, completely alone; there was nothing to be seen and nothing to be heard."

Within a day, all that changes. The Oval Office begins humming with activity. On March 6, Roosevelt orders a weeklong "bank holiday" to

---

* The tradition of presidents riding to the inauguration together was begun by Andrew Jackson and Martin Van Buren in 1837. An 1889 handbook of presidential etiquette governs a president's exit from Washington: "Departure from the capital is attended with no ceremony, other than the presence of the members of his late Cabinet and a few officials and personal friends. The President leaves the capital as soon as practicable after the inauguration of his successor."

† Franklin Roosevelt will be the last of ten presidents Ike Hoover will serve. The chief usher dies suddenly of a heart attack on September 14, 1933, at age sixty-one. Hoover's death is front-page news in the *Washington Post*.

stop further closures. He then convenes a special session of Congress to push his New Deal agenda.

The president's advantage is that Democrats control the House and Senate, giving him enormous power. He lays out an ambitious vision, asking for fifteen new bills to be passed immediately. An Emergency Banking Act is introduced and approved within an unheard-of four hours. This act reopens failed banks and is meant to restore faith in the financial system.*

In what will become known as his "First Hundred Days," Roosevelt signs bills creating jobs, protecting farmers, and inventing two enormous public works projects—the Tennessee Valley Authority and the Civilian Conservation Corps—designed to put Americans back to work. In all, a record seventy-seven new laws are passed during the president's first three months in office.

Roosevelt dominates the White House—a residence he will call home for the next twelve years. The crux of his daily routine incorporates solitude. FDR sleeps alone, his bedroom simply decorated with an iron-framed cot, a chest of drawers, and a single chair. Medicine bottles, magazines, and official reports line the top of the bureau.

Next door is President Roosevelt's study, decorated in a nautical theme. It is here that he spends the early hours before the rest of the White House wakes up. He reads the papers and pores over his daily schedule. The small room is lined with bookcases, a cheap sofa, and plush chairs. A fireplace remains roaring in winter but is always doused when the president is alone—Roosevelt's withered legs making it impossible to escape in case of fire.

The study is also where Roosevelt takes his breakfast. He favors a strong French roast coffee and warm jelly donuts. His wife, Eleanor, is nowhere in sight.

The president remains in his study throughout the morning, staff coming in and out as he delegates tasks and hears advice on pressing issues. His private secretary and closest confidant, Marguerite "Missy"

---

* The Federal Reserve History website declares the act a success, noting that the public immediately began redepositing their money in banks and that Wall Street "recorded the largest one-day percentage price increase ever."

LeHand, is the gatekeeper—deciding which cabinet officials, members of Congress, and ambassadors get access to the president.

Lunch is cream soup and thin crackers, followed by a long nap. The First Lady's office is right next to the president's bedroom, but she rarely interrupts his day. In the afternoon, FDR takes the elevator downstairs and wheels himself to the Oval Office. He is among the few presidents to not use the Resolute desk, preferring a smaller workspace.

Then there is the "Children's Hour."

Prohibition is repealed on December 5, 1933, allowing the president to openly drink alcohol each evening. He calls this the Children's Hour. Roosevelt is always the mixologist, pulling out his silver cocktail set. He makes martinis for his staff. However, the president's recipe is bizarre. He uses everything from pickle juice to liqueurs, leading many to state that he pours the worst drink in Washington. FDR hears these insults but does not care.

Dinner is typical American fare: creamed chipped beef, cornmeal mush with maple syrup, and bread pudding for dessert. Afterward, the president returns once again to his study, often to work on his stamp collection.*

Franklin Delano Roosevelt has always been wealthy.

The thirty-second president was born on January 30, 1882, in Hyde Park, New York. His father, James, earns a law degree from Harvard but never practices because his own father bequeathed him an enormous inheritance. His mother, Sara, a domineering woman who will live in the Roosevelt White House from time to time, has the maiden name of Delano. Her ancestors came to America in 1621 from England and helped settle the Plymouth Colony in Massachusetts.†

As a boy, Franklin is introduced to President Grover Cleveland by his father. In the short conversation, Cleveland tells the child that he should never seek to be president because of the burden.

---

* President Roosevelt was a philatelist, as stamp enthusiasts are known. He began collecting them as a child. After his death, Roosevelt's stamps were sold at auction, bringing in $80,000—$1.3 million today.

† The Delano family tree includes seven passengers on the *Mayflower*. US presidents Franklin Roosevelt, Calvin Coolidge, and Ulysses S. Grant can all trace their lineage to the Delanos.

Young FDR attends Groton School in Massachusetts. There, he is heavily influenced by the teachings of headmaster Endicott Peabody, who believes that public service and taking care of the less fortunate are incumbent on all Christians. By the time Roosevelt enters Harvard in 1900, he is fluent in French and German from numerous family trips to Europe and a semester of school in Germany. He is an active young man who plays polo, tennis, and golf, as well as being a proficient sailor. At Harvard, Roosevelt is a school cheerleader and president of the *Harvard Crimson* newspaper. He graduates in just three years and then attends Columbia Law School, but he drops out before graduating after passing the New York bar.

This is a seminal time in FDR's life, as his cousin Theodore Roosevelt becomes president in 1901. Franklin idolizes T. R., striving to emulate his bold behavior. It is Teddy who will give away the bride when his niece, Eleanor, marries FDR in 1905. The officiant is Endicott Peabody, an Episcopalian minister and Franklin's Groton headmaster.

Anna Eleanor Roosevelt does not give up her maiden name. She is a Roosevelt by birth, Franklin's distant cousin. Born into great wealth, both her parents are dilettantes. Eleanor is a serious woman who experiences tragedy early. At age two, she is on board the ocean liner SS *Britannic* when it collides with another luxury liner, the SS *Celtic*. Eleanor and her parents are successfully rescued, but she will be afraid of ships and the sea the rest of her life.*

Eleanor is eight when her mother, Anna, dies of diphtheria. Two years later, her father, Elliott, jumps out of a sanitarium window while suffering from delirium tremens. The alcoholic dies—not from the fall, but as a result of a seizure immediately afterward.†

So it is that Eleanor Roosevelt is raised by her maternal grandmother. She is sent to London to attend finishing school, returning home for her debutante "coming out" as a teenager. She first meets Franklin Roosevelt as a child, but their relationship deepens after a random encounter on a train almost two decades later. Franklin is twenty, six feet two, a

---

* The two ships collide in the fog on May 19, 1887, 350 miles east of Sandy Hook, New Jersey. The bow of the *Celtic* slams into the port side of *Britannic*, killing six passengers and opening a hole below the waterline. Lifeboats are lowered and passengers transferred to the *Celtic*, among them Eleanor and her parents. Both ships returned to New York safely for repairs.

† Delirium tremens are fits of shaking and convulsion caused by withdrawal from alcohol.

bon vivant intellectual whom some consider arrogant. Eleanor is five feet eleven, a shy, self-described "ugly duckling" who attends Episcopalian services each week and is prone to fits of depression. They make an unlikely pair. Franklin finds her interesting and intelligent, not unattractive in her fashionable Paris clothes, blond hair cascading down to her waist. Pragmatically, he also sees their relationship as a means of forging a closer bond with his uncle Theodore.

Sara Roosevelt, FDR's mother, does not approve of the union out of jealousy. Yet, she will bequeath the couple the family home in Hyde Park and Campobello, a vacation house in maritime Canada. When Sara later purchases the couple a townhouse in Manhattan, she also buys one next door for herself.

From the beginning, the Roosevelt union is troubled. Eleanor does not enjoy sex with her husband, calling it "an ordeal to be endured." Nevertheless, she gives birth to six children. Their second son, named for his father, dies in infancy.

It is FDR's mother, Sara, now a divisive force in the marriage, who does most of the parenting. She even tells her grandchildren, "I am more your mother than your mother is."

To which Eleanor surprisingly agrees. "It did not come naturally to me," she will state about motherhood, "to understand little children or enjoy them."*

Before the age of thirty, Franklin Roosevelt successfully runs for the New York state senate as a Democrat. He is a vocal supporter of Woodrow Wilson during the 1912 presidential campaign, even though Teddy Roosevelt is running against Wilson.†

President Wilson shows his thanks by naming FDR assistant secretary of the navy. Roosevelt is highly active and influential in this branch of the service throughout World War I, making the acquaintance of British counterpart Winston Churchill, first lord of the Admiralty, during a

---

* Historian Doris Kearns Goodwin quotes the First Lady in her 1994 book, *No Ordinary Time*.

† Throughout his life, Theodore Roosevelt encouraged his cousin to seek elective office and did not try to convince him to be a Republican.

1918 visit to London. The two men instantly dislike each other, with Roosevelt calling Churchill a "stinker" because of his imperious manner.

In that same year, Franklin Roosevelt's affair with Lucy Mercer, Eleanor's social secretary, is discovered. Eleanor offers her husband a divorce. But Sara Roosevelt refuses to let that happen because it will damage her son's political future. She even threatens to disinherit him if he leaves his wife.

So, Eleanor Roosevelt agrees to remain, but on *her* terms. She will stay in the marriage if FDR breaks off the affair and agrees to never again commit adultery.

But the truth is, Franklin and Eleanor lead completely separate lives. FDR soon breaks his promise and begins several affairs. He even secretly takes up with Lucy Mercer again. Eleanor soon finds herself in a relationship of her own—with female journalist Lorena Hickok, who writes for the Associated Press. Apparently, her husband's infidelities have downgraded men in Eleanor's mind.*

Despite the uneasy domestic situation, the couple endure. Franklin's political career continues to rise, while Eleanor indulges in growing public activism for social causes.†

★★★

The New Deal is under fire.

The list of critics is long: Republicans and Democrats, men and women, governors and senators, playwrights and actors. Roosevelt is called a socialist and a communist. He is compared with the Soviet Union's Joseph Stalin, who will soon begin murdering twenty million of his own people through "death by starvation" policies that collectivize farms and deprive landowners of their own crops. The comparison is

---

* Lorena Hickok and Eleanor Roosevelt began a thirty-year friendship in 1932. The couple exchanged four thousand letters in that time, often expressing their love. Eleanor made it a habit to kiss good night a framed photograph of the reporter when the two were separated.

† Eleanor Roosevelt was a committed liberal. Her causes included racial and sexual equality, in addition to assisting the poor and advocating for better wages and conditions for American workers. She resigned from the Daughters of the American Revolution in 1939 to protest its racist policies. Eleanor also delivered a regular press conference from the White House on the condition that the only media allowed to attend were female reporters—causing newspapers to hire more women.

strengthened when FDR opens diplomatic relations with Stalin in late 1933, a first between the US and the USSR.*

In addition to dealing with Stalin, some believe that the president is too tolerant of the new führer in Germany, Adolf Hitler. That tolerance extends to the Italian fascist Benito Mussolini as well. Both dictators seek total control over their countries. Anti-Roosevelt critics claim FDR is trying to do the same thing in America.

Despite a good start to the New Deal, the Depression continues. In some places, lawlessness rules. The 1930s see the rise of a new breed of criminal: Bonnie and Clyde, Baby Face Nelson, Pretty Boy Floyd. These gangsters roam the country robbing banks, and, incredibly, some Americans are sympathetic to them.

To combat this criminality, FDR expands funding for the federal police force known as the Bureau of Investigation. It will soon add "Federal" to its moniker and be nicknamed the FBI. In addition, Roosevelt has to face poverty and deprivation in the nation's Midwest as farmers are devastated by storms and the terrible economy. In Oklahoma, thousands of "Okies" flee this "Dust Bowl" to California for a new life.

On January 4, 1935, Roosevelt delivers a State of the Union address promising more relief. A second stage of the New Deal is coming: Social Security.†

One year later, FDR decides to seek reelection. It is 1936, and hostilities in Europe are building. To bolster his political standing, the president signs the first of four Neutrality Acts. They forbid the shipping of arms and munitions to belligerent nations.

On October 3, 1935, fascist Italy invades the African country of Ethiopia and forces Emperor Haile Selassie into exile. Three months later, at

---

* Union of Soviet Socialist Republics.

† The Social Security Act was signed into law on August 14, 1935. It created a continuing income from the government for retired workers over the age of sixty-five.

the Berlin Olympics, Adolf Hitler brings fascism to the world—taunting democratic nations in a show of Aryan superiority.*

On November 3, President Roosevelt secures an astonishing 523 electoral votes to just 8 for his Republican opponent, Kansas governor Alf Landon. Roosevelt's vice president is John Nance Garner of Texas, formerly Speaker of the House, a known whiskey drinker and poker player who also served as vice president during FDR's first term.†

Roosevelt's victory is all the more shocking because a large percentage of American newspapers back Alf Landon.‡

Three years later, September 1, 1939. Nazi Germany invades Poland, beginning World War II. Anti-war sentiment is high in the United States as industrialist Henry Ford and famous pilot Charles Lindbergh insist the nation stay out of the war. The isolationist Lindbergh believes Roosevelt, Jews, and Britain are trying to force America into "the greatest disaster this country has ever passed through."

However, Franklin Roosevelt understands the dangers posed by the Axis powers. He also realizes that the American public will not back a fight in Europe at this time. So, he waits, quietly planning a third term, which the US Constitution allowed then, in order to eventually confront the totalitarians.

Secretly, Roosevelt moves America into an alliance with Winston Churchill and Great Britain. When Hitler conquers France in June 1940, England stands alone against Nazi Germany. Should that nation fall, Roosevelt believes the Germans will turn their sights to attacking America. Already Nazi submarines prowl the Atlantic Coast, endangering US shipping.

But there is a problem. The American ambassador to Great Britain,

---

* Germany won thirty-three gold medals in the 1936 Olympics. The US won twenty-four. However, Hitler's racial brutality was defeated by American track star Jesse Owens, who won four gold medals.

† Garner is an isolationist. In the ensuing years, he clashes with President Roosevelt over helping Britain fight the Nazis. The two men grow to despise each other.

‡ Publisher William Randolph Hearst likes the Kansan and has ordered his chain of publications to support Landon's conservative policies. Other newspapers follow suit, leading *Time* magazine to declare Landon a "stooge" for Hearst.

Joseph P. Kennedy, is dazzled by Adolf Hitler. He reports back to the White House that he thinks German troops will soon march through Trafalgar Square. Roosevelt does not replace Kennedy, a powerful political force in his own right. However, he isolates the ambassador, refusing to give him any information from the White House.

September 1940. Two months until the election. FDR makes a bold political gamble.

He ignores the Neutrality Acts.

The United States loans Great Britain fifty American vessels to bolster its navy. The aerial fight known as the Battle of Britain soon comes to an end, with the Royal Air Force defeating the German Luftwaffe, temporarily ending threats of invasion.

On November 5, 1940, the American public shows support for FDR. President Roosevelt is reelected to a *third* term in office. His new vice president is Henry A. Wallace from Iowa, the current secretary of agriculture. The two trounce Republican Wendell Wilkie by an electoral margin of 449–82.

On December 29, 1940, during his regular nationwide radio speeches known as fireside chats, President Roosevelt makes it very clear that America will continue to arm Great Britain against Nazi Germany.

"We must be the great arsenal of democracy," he states. His voice is firm and calm, a tone the nation has come to know repeatedly since his first broadcast after taking office eight years ago.

He continues, "No man can tame a tiger into a kitten by stroking it. There can be no appeasement with ruthlessness. There can be no reasoning with an incendiary bomb. We know now that a nation can have peace with the Nazis only at the price of total surrender."

It is December 7, 1941. Sunday. President Roosevelt is just finishing lunch. Harry Hopkins, his chief adviser who lives full-time in the White House, enters from the Lincoln Bedroom. The president lights a Camel cigarette. He plans to spend the afternoon working on his stamp collection.

Broadcast journalist Edward R. Murrow, fresh from reporting on events in London, is coming for dinner.*

The phone rings. A White House operator tells him Secretary of the Navy Frank Knox is calling.

The news is bad. Japan has just attacked the United States at Pearl Harbor, a naval base in Hawaii. The US fleet was bombed relentlessly, sinking nine ships, damaging twenty-six others, and killing 2,403 American sailors, marines, and civilians.

The sneak attack is not really a surprise to President Roosevelt. He has seen intelligence reports stating that the Japanese have been planning a bold move for at least a year. Some will state that Roosevelt allowed the attack to happen, hoping to pull America into war.

There is no evidence that this is true.

What is apparent is that the United States must declare war on Japan.

The following afternoon, the president stands before a joint session of Congress, delivering a sentence for which he will long be remembered:

"Yesterday, December 7, 1941, a date which will live in infamy, the United States of America was suddenly and deliberately attacked by naval and air forces of the Empire of Japan."

But the United States is unprepared for war. Quickly, hundreds of thousands of young Americans are drafted, soon to be turned into fighting men.

On December 11, 1941, Adolf Hitler, an ally of Japan, declares war on the United States. By the time the war ends, more than seventy million people will be killed in all global theaters of the fighting.

President Roosevelt is no longer a young man.

As he settles into the role of wartime president, FDR ages dramati-

---

* Harry Hopkins served as secretary of commerce from 1938 to 1940. During World War II, Hopkins acted as a liaison to world leaders and chief foreign policy adviser. In May 1940, shortly after the death of his second wife, Hopkins moves into the White House with his seven-year-old daughter at the president's request, allowing Hopkins to be close by at all times. The presence of CBS journalist Edward R. Murrow at the White House on December 7, 1941, was a coincidence. Murrow achieved fame for his radio broadcasts from London during the Battle of Britain and just happened to be spending a short vacation at home in America. Roosevelt summoned him to the White House for his impressions on the war in Europe.

cally. Years of smoking clog his arteries, driving up his blood pressure. His face is skeletal and gray.

Yet the president does not slow down. In fact, he increases his workload. Roosevelt undertakes lengthy diplomatic trips to meet with Winston Churchill and Joseph Stalin, fellow world leaders in the fight against the Axis powers. These twelve conferences take the president to the Middle East, Canada, Africa, and Europe. Each involves long voyages by ship and plane.*

In 1941, at fifty-nine years old, Roosevelt is the youngest of the Allied leaders. Churchill is sixty-seven, Stalin sixty-three. But the president looks a decade older than his age.

Franklin Roosevelt is now the most powerful man in the world. Great Britain and the Soviet Union are reliant on American manufacturing to wage war. The US sends ships, clothes, tanks, ammunitions, bombs, and vehicles overseas. The Great Depression is replaced by prosperity as American factories take advantage of the lavish government spending. Employment is at an all-time high.

As the war progresses, the friendship between Franklin Roosevelt and Winston Churchill strengthens. The prime minister comes to America five times during the war and lives in the White House. His late-night hours are a distraction to the staff.

Soon, the friendship changes. FDR foresees a postwar Europe divided between the United States and the Soviet Union. Great Britain, once the world's premier power, is in decline. So, Roosevelt chooses to placate Churchill while at the same time befriending Stalin. This is an enormous mistake.

Roosevelt's wartime routine is intense. He stays up later, often not sleeping until long after midnight. Breakfast is now his only time of solitude. The rest of the day is taken up with meetings about the war with generals, admirals, and politicians from mid-morning until late in the

---

* The Axis powers were Nazi Germany, Japan, and Italy.

evening. The president does not dictate strategy, allowing the military people to do their jobs. But he does make his opinions known.

Increasingly, there is the notation "doctor's office" on FDR's schedule. His secretary, Grace Tully, notes the president often has dark circles under his eyes and his hands shake. Sometimes, he nods off while reading mail. The president's physician, Dr. George Draper, orders Roosevelt to cut his cigarette intake down to six Camels a day and restrict his workload to four hours.

FDR does *not* comply.

On November 7, 1944, Franklin Delano Roosevelt is elected to his *fourth* term in office.*

The fact that Roosevelt remains so popular is a mystery to some. He has made some very controversial decisions, such as allowing Japanese Americans to be sent to "internment camps" out of fear they may be agents for Japan. More than 120,000 men, women, and children will be torn away from their homes and jobs, even though most are American citizens. This is largely supported by the American people—and the Supreme Court.

As early as February 1942, FDR becomes aware of Nazi Germany's death camps. The information that Jews are being exterminated goes public after journalist Edward R. Murrow delivers a December 13, 1942, radio broadcast describing the concentration camps as "a horror beyond what imagination can grasp."

Yet FDR does little to stop these mass murders. His focus is on winning the war. Even when it is presented that Allied bombers might destroy the railway lines into Auschwitz, Roosevelt goes along with military leaders who believe that such an act is a waste of resources that are better used to fight Hitler's army.†

---

* Roosevelt defeats Governor Thomas Dewey of New York in another solid victory, winning the Electoral College 432–99. Vice President Henry A. Wallace, whom Roosevelt believes is too liberal, is dropped from the ticket, replaced by Missouri senator Harry S. Truman. In 1951, the Twenty-Second Amendment was ratified, making it illegal for a president to serve more than two terms in office. Republicans in Congress spearheaded the amendment as a reaction to FDR's four terms.

† On August 14, 1944, John J. McCoy, assistant secretary of war, stated that "such an operation could only be executed by considerable diversion of considerable air support."

By Christmas 1944, it is clear the Third Reich will soon be defeated. Stalin's army has taken Poland in the east. US forces in the west have halted a German offensive known as the Battle of the Bulge and are heading for Berlin.

★★★

In the Pacific, the Japanese are retreating all across Asia. The United States Navy, Marines, and Army Air Corps have vanquished Japan's battleships and shot down most of its planes. It is just a matter of time until Tokyo falls. However, a bloody invasion is foreseen, leaving Roosevelt with no choice but to fund a horrific new weapon—one that will end the war.

★★★

April 12, 1945. Warm Springs, Georgia.

President Roosevelt is exhausted. With Allied forces now in command, he travels to a southern resort for some rest and relaxation. Accompanying him is his mistress, Lucy Mercer. But problems continue. Roosevelt is now regretting his overtures to Stalin because Soviet armies are not liberating countries in Europe, they are occupying them—much as Winston Churchill predicted. FDR believes he was played for a fool and is full of bitter resentment toward Stalin.

The slow train ride on board the *Ferdinand Magellan* from Washington to northern Georgia takes thirty hours. Warm Springs allows a complete break from the stresses of the presidency—or so FDR believes.

★★★

Just after lunch, as Roosevelt takes a break from swimming to sit for his watercolor portrait, painter Elizabeth Shoumatoff notices his hunched posture.

"I have a terrific headache," the president says. Then he falls out of his chair.

Franklin Delano Roosevelt never regains consciousness. He dies from a cerebral hemorrhage. The time is 3:35 p.m.

★★★

In Washington, Eleanor Roosevelt is watching a musical theater show at the Seagrave Club. An attendant whispers that she has a phone call. The First Lady leaves her seat to answer, only to be told that the president "has fainted." She returns to the show and then is summoned a second time. When informed she needs to return to the White House, Eleanor assumes something has happened to one of her sons—all four of whom are serving in the military.

"All of us knew that Franklin was far from well but none of us ever said anything about it," she will later explain.

Upon her return, Eleanor is told that her husband of forty years is gone. She immediately changes into a black dress and sends for the vice president.

Harry Truman is concluding a day presiding over the Senate and is on his way to a libation with his good friend, Speaker of the House Sam Rayburn. The vice president and FDR have barely spoken in the three months since the fourth inauguration. So, Roosevelt is the last thing on Truman's mind. A message soon arrives at Rayburn's office as Truman sips a bourbon. The vice president is told to call the White House immediately.

He does. "Jesus Christ and General Jackson," he exclaims, slamming down the phone. He tells Rayburn about the president's death and instructs him to say nothing.

Ten minutes later, Harry Truman steps into the White House through the Pennsylvania Avenue entrance. The First Lady greets him.

"Is there anything I can do for you?" Truman asks.

"Is there anything we can do for *you*?" Eleanor Roosevelt replies. "You are the one in trouble now."

One hour later, with his wife, Bess, looking on, Harry Truman is sworn in as the thirty-third president of the United States.

In Moscow, Joseph Stalin is stunned after hearing of Roosevelt's death. He orders the Soviet Union to observe a day of mourning for the president.

In London, Winston Churchill stands in the House of Commons to eulogize his friend. The prime minister is eloquent. Churchill concludes his lengthy oratory by reminding England, "For us, it remains only to say that in Franklin Roosevelt there died the greatest American friend we have ever known."

★★★

The presidential railcar, *Ferdinand Magellan*, carries President Roosevelt's body back to Washington. Eleanor has flown down to Georgia by military plane to oversee the formalities. The casket arrives on April 14 and is then carried to the White House by a military procession. A half a million mourners line the route. Roosevelt's body lies in state in the East Room for five hours. A short funeral service is held. Then the casket is transported to the Roosevelt family home, Springwood, in Hyde Park, New York, for burial.

FDR was sixty-three years old.

★★★

Lucy Mercer, who witnesses the president's death, returns home to New York immediately. Her presence at FDR's death will be a closely guarded secret until 1966, when a Roosevelt aide reveals the affair in a book, *The Time between the Wars*. Before that, Eleanor Roosevelt learns the news. She is devastated that her own daughter, Anna, secretly arranged many liaisons between Mercer and FDR. In 1945, upon discovering the unfinished watercolor portrait, Eleanor has it mailed to Lucy Mercer.

★★★

Eleanor carries on her charitable work after FDR's death. In December 1945, President Truman appoints Eleanor Roosevelt to serve as a delegate to the United Nations. In the years that follow, her name is frequently mentioned as a Democratic candidate for office, but she refuses to run. Eleanor becomes a public speaker, in addition to writing her daily newspaper column and appearing on radio and television. In April 1960, she is hit by a car in a minor New York City accident while crossing a street. She tears ligaments in her leg but still manages to give two speeches that day. Soon after, however, the former First Lady is diagnosed with tuberculosis in her bone marrow.

Eleanor Roosevelt dies on November 7, 1962, at age seventy-eight.

President John F. Kennedy orders all United States flags lowered to half-mast in mourning. She is buried at Hyde Park, alongside her husband.

Franklin D. Roosevelt ranks as one of the greatest presidents based on the challenges he faced. While there is debate to this day about some of the actions he undertook, America emerged much stronger due to his leadership.

That opinion is not universal, with some believing FDR damaged his country by creating a colossus in Washington.

However, the safety nets Roosevelt put into place protect vulnerable Americans to this day. And despite his personal failings, FDR won the victories he had to win.

Although not a man of deep introspection, Franklin Roosevelt understood his failings. He enabled Stalin and the Cold War. He did not do enough to protect innocent Jews and other victims of the Holocaust from the Nazi horror. But overall, his presidential tenure would solidify America as the greatest power on earth.

And the extent of that power will dramatically expand under the next president.

Chapter Thirty-Three

AUGUST 6, 1945
USS *AUGUSTA*
10:15 A.M.

President Harry S. Truman has just killed more than seventy thousand human beings.

Sitting in a cluttered state room on board this navy cruiser, the president addresses America on the radio. He is returning from the Potsdam Conference in Germany, where he met with Joseph Stalin, Winston Churchill, and—after Churchill is voted from office halfway through the conference—new British prime minister Clement Atlee. Though he is far out to sea, the president wears a light-gray suit and pocket square. Truman's voice is thin and tired.

He states, "An American airplane dropped one bomb on Hiroshima, an important Japanese Army base. That bomb had more power than 20,000 tons of TNT. It had more than two thousand times the blast power of the British 'Grand Slam,' which is the largest bomb ever yet used in the history of warfare."[*]

It is President Truman alone who makes the decision to drop the atomic bomb on Hiroshima. An American B-29 bomber called *Enola*

---

[*] The Grand Slam was a British bomb used against hardened concrete bunkers by the Royal Air Force in the final months of World War II. It weighed eleven tons. Little Boy, the name given to the bomb dropped on Hiroshima, weighed one ton less, but its nuclear explosive carried enormously greater impact.

Gay completes the mission. This action is the culmination of the Man-hattan Project—supervised by scientist Robert Oppenheimer in New Mexico. The top secret program has developed the most fearsome weapon in the history of mankind.

On the ship, Truman explains his rationale: "The Japanese began the war from the air at Pearl Harbor. They have been repaid many fold. And the end is not yet. With this bomb we have now added a new and revolu-tionary increase in destruction to supplement the growing power of our armed forces. In their present form these bombs are now in production and even more powerful forms are in development."

Three days later, another nuclear weapon is dropped on the city of Nagasaki, killing fifty thousand more human beings.

That is enough for Harry Truman. Another A-bomb is set to fall on Tokyo, but the president orders all further use of nuclear weapons halted.

"The thought of wiping out another 100,000 is too horrible," the pres-ident explains to his cabinet. "I don't like the idea of killing all those kids."*

Harry S. Truman has no middle name.

Born in Missouri in 1884 to livestock dealer John Truman and his wife, Martha, the initial S honors two grandfathers—one named Shipp and the other Solomon. Young Harry is homeschooled until age eight, when his family moves to the Missouri town of Independence. The fu-ture president's childhood is eclectic: Truman is extremely close to his mother, his brother's name is Vivian, he rises before dawn to practice the piano, and at age sixteen he works as a page at the 1900 Democratic Convention in Kansas City.

Truman's family is not wealthy, so he does not travel the Ivy League path of his predecessor. He applies to the US Military Academy at West Point but is turned down for bad eyesight. So, Truman attends a local business school, Spalding's Commercial College, learning typing and ac-counting. He does not graduate, moving on after a year to take a menial

---

* While writing the book *Killing the Rising Sun*, Bill O'Reilly contacted five former presidents about whether President Truman did the right thing using the atomic bomb. Presidents Jimmy Carter, Bush the Elder, and Bush the Younger all said that he did. Presidents Bill Clinton and Barack Obama did not want to comment.

job with the *Kansas City Star* newspaper. He also works as a bank clerk. From there, it is on to working construction on the Atchison, Topeka, and Santa Fe Railway, where the church-raised Truman begins cursing for the first time in his life.

By now, Truman stands five feet ten, with gray eyes and brown hair.

In 1906, at age twenty-two, Harry Truman becomes a farmer. He settles down and then proposes to—and is rejected by—local beauty Bess Wallace. But Truman doesn't give up. In addition to working the farm, he dabbles in financial schemes like land and oil speculation, thinking Bess might change her mind if he makes more money.

Harry Truman also takes on another project outside the farm. Still fascinated by the military, despite his West Point rejection, he enlists in the Missouri National Guard. To ensure he passes the eye exam, he memorizes the chart beforehand. Truman becomes a specialist in field artillery.

Were it not for World War I, Harry S. Truman might never have left farming. But in 1917, his guard unit is called up, going to France. Lieutenant Truman is promoted to captain and soon shows courage under fire. During one particularly horrific night of shelling in the Vosges Mountains, his men turn and flee in terror. But Truman stops them by hurling profanities learned in his railroad days. Stunned to hear their mild-mannered commander speak in such a raw manner, the Missouri soldiers turn back.

Truman sees action through the end of the war, at one time fighting alongside tank commander George S. Patton. He is honorably discharged in 1919, after which he finally weds Bess Wallace in June. They soon have a daughter, Mary Margaret. Truman calls his wife "The Boss," a term he will one day share frequently with the American people on the radio. She is athletic and opinionated, with curly blond hair. Theirs is a private relationship, Bess sharing her strong opinions with Harry away from the public.*

Transformed by the war, Harry Truman is now accustomed to making

---

* Time and persistence change Bess's mind. Harry Truman writes regular letters to her from his farm twenty miles from her home, even after the failed proposal of 1911. He carefully avoids mentioning romance, preferring to keep their correspondence friendly. Finally, in November 1913, sitting on her front porch in Independence, Bess tells Harry that her feelings have changed. They do not announce their engagement and do not get married until his return from the war because he does not want to leave her widowed.

hard decisions. First up, he chooses not to return to the farm. Instead, he opens a haberdashery in downtown Kansas City but quickly tires of selling hats and fabric. So, he runs for public office, seeking election as a local judge despite having no experience in the law and no college degree.

Truman wins.

Thus begins a most unlikely rise to the presidency. Harry Truman is a likeable man, and his friends inside the Democratic Party are many. His father dies in 1914, but Truman remains close with his mother, Martha Ellen, who becomes a fervent supporter of her son's political career.

After serving as a judge for twelve years, Truman is elected a United States senator in 1934. He makes a name for himself investigating corruption and waste in wartime government contracts.

Harry Truman is the compromise candidate at the Democratic National Convention when Franklin Roosevelt asks him to join the 1944 presidential ticket. Henry A. Wallace, vice president during FDR's third term, is considered too liberal for a postwar world. Democratic Party leaders do not want to risk having Wallace assume the presidency should an ailing Roosevelt die in office. Truman is well liked and capable. When top Democrats suggest him as Wallace's replacement, FDR agrees, even though he barely knows the Missouri senator. The truth is, President Roosevelt could not care less who is vice president.

On January 20, 1945, Harry S. Truman is sworn in. He is assigned Secret Service protection as a security precaution, the first vice president to have that. For three months, Truman does little except preside over the Senate and attend ceremonial functions. His lone moment in the spotlight comes when he spontaneously plays the piano for soldiers at a National Press Club event. Suddenly, sultry Hollywood star Lauren Bacall walks over and drapes herself atop the piano—making for a memorable photograph.

Harry Truman's tenure as vice president lasts just three months. Franklin Roosevelt dies on April 12, 1945.

"I felt like the earth, the stars, and all of the planets had fallen on me," Truman will recall of the moment he becomes president.

★★★

President Truman starts each day with a shot of bourbon. Then comes a glass of orange juice. He leaves the White House for a brisk walk, followed by his Secret Service detail and sometimes staff members. His pace is vigorous, 120 steps per minute. The president always walks wearing a business suit and tie.

Then it is back into the White House. He gets a massage followed by breakfast. Usually, the meal is eggs, bacon, cereal, toast, and a large glass of milk. Then, meetings and correspondence. Harry and Bess usually eat lunch together, followed by his taking a short nap and then a swim in the White House pool—the president always wearing his eyeglasses.[*]

An afternoon in the Oval Office is followed by cocktails, dinner, and often a movie. Their daughter, Margaret, attends nearby George Washington University. She is also training to become a singer.

Occasionally, the president leaves the White House to visit friends and play poker. The press and wives are not invited, so Truman can relax and tell dirty jokes. When he takes a vacation, it is often a stag event as well, with he and his friends stealing away to the Little White House in Key West, Florida.[†]

Ending World War II with the atomic bomb is only the beginning of President Truman's foreign policy challenges. Almost immediately, tension mounts with the Soviet Union. When first meeting Joseph Stalin in July 1945, Truman writes home to Bess that "I like Stalin . . . he is straightforward."

To strengthen the cause of world peace, Truman supports the United Nations, allowing countries from around the world to discuss their differences rather than wage war. New York City is chosen as its headquarters.

But there is nothing the UN can do about the Soviet Union's aggressive policies.

By January 1946, Truman changes his mind about Stalin. "I'm tired

---

[*] The first White House swimming pool opened on June 2, 1933, as a way for President Roosevelt to exercise. The rectangular piscine was located between the West Wing and the West Terrace. Richard Nixon ordered the pool turned into a press room, which it remains to this day. President Gerald R. Ford later built an outdoor pool on the lawn.

[†] Truman's Little White House exists to this day. It is a major tourist attraction in Key West.

of babying the Soviets," he states, exhausted by their growing oppression over Eastern Europe and attempts to expand into Greece and Turkey. US, British, French, and Soviet forces occupy Germany, with the capital of Berlin divided among the nations.

Two months later, appearing on a Missouri stage at Westminster College with Winston Churchill, Truman listens as the former British prime minister explains what is happening in the world. The two men have been playing a good deal of poker since Churchill's arrival in the United States, with the shrewd Truman easily taking the prime minister's money.

Winston Churchill is a genius at international relations, not cards. So, Truman focuses as his guest speaks to the audience. Churchill tells of a "special relationship" between the United States and Britain based on their shared history and interests. But in reference to Joseph Stalin and the Soviet Union, Churchill's words are far more chilling: "An 'iron curtain' has descended across the [European] Continent. Behind that line lie all the capitals of the ancient states of Central and Eastern Europe. . . . All are subject in one form or another, not only to Soviet influence but to a very high and, in many cases, increasing measure of control from Moscow."

The Soviets don't just want to occupy more territory, they also want to *force* a communist ideology throughout Europe and the world. Now, Berlin is the center of this controversy. At war's end, the city is divided into four "occupation zones" administered by the victors. But on June 24, 1948, the Soviets make a bold gambit to take the city for themselves. They blockade all rail, road, and water access to the free areas of Berlin. President Truman authorizes an airlift of food and supplies to prevent Stalin from starving the trapped citizens.

The Soviets finally reopen the roads, though it takes a year. By that time, their bid for world dominance is obvious. And it is enhanced by the development of a Soviet nuclear bomb. For the first time in world history, the two most powerful nations on the planet have the ability to destroy each other.

Thus begins the Cold War.

★★★

President Truman enters the 1948 presidential campaign a decided underdog to Thomas Dewey, the Republican governor of New York.

Americans are weary of Democratic leadership. The scales are so tilted in Dewey's favor that the *Chicago Daily Tribune* prints its Election Day headline *before* all the votes are counted. "Dewey Defeats Truman" blares from its front page.

But that is not the case. Harry Truman wins by 303 electoral votes to 189.*

The start of Truman's second term sees not just an escalation of conflict but also a decision to gut the White House before it falls down completely. The floors wobble, rats infest the mansion, and the wooden supports in the walls are disintegrating. Immediately after the election, Harry and Bess move across the street into the Blair House. There they will live for the next four years.†

The Soviet Union is not the only communist nation to challenge the United States. The People's Republic of China, led by dictator Mao Tse-tung, is also fanatically communist. So is its neighbor, North Korea. On June 25, 1950, the North Korean People's Army attacks South Korea, attempting to reunify all of Korea into a single communist nation. China stands ready to offer men and arms to help overwhelm South Korea.

Two days later, President Truman announces that the United States is entering the conflict on the side of South Korea. He believes the Soviet Union is actually pulling the strings. Thinking of Britain's failed attempts to appease Adolf Hitler before World War II, Truman becomes aggressive. World War II hero General Douglas MacArthur will lead the United Nations Command, which is predominantly made up of American troops.

Thus starts the toughest test of President Harry Truman's leadership. Within two months of his decision, American troops are pushed back to the southern tip of the Korean Peninsula. A desperate MacArthur then leads a surprise amphibious invasion to the north at a place called Inchon. It works. American troops quickly push the North Koreans back to the 38th parallel—the dividing line between North and South.

---

* Truman's victory means twenty straight years in which a Democrat occupies the White House.

† Puerto Rican nationalists Oscar Collazo and Griselio Torresola will attempt to assassinate Truman at Blair House on November 1, 1950. Quick-thinking Washington policeman Leslie Coffelt will shoot Torresola dead, saving the president's life.

Truman and the UN authorize MacArthur to attack deeper into North Korea to end the war once and for all.

Then China enters the conflict. Its massive army bolsters North Korean troops. A stalemate ensues. In what will be known as the "Forgotten War," coming so soon after World War II, the Korean conflict results in the deaths of thirty-three thousand Americans.

Things get worse. President Truman fires General MacArthur in 1951 for insubordination, MacArthur among those underestimating Truman's backbone. The general prefers to continue attacking rather than obeying orders to stand down for peace talks.

"I fired him because he didn't respect the authority of the president," Truman will tell a biographer.

Douglas MacArthur returns to the United States a hero, the American public firmly on *his* side. In addition, the Korean War shows no signs of coming to an end. For that, Harry Truman gets the blame.

But when Senate hearings are held soon after, top army general Omar Bradley stands up for President Truman's reluctance to fight China. "In the opinion of the Joint Chiefs of Staff, this strategy would involve us in the wrong war, in the wrong place, at the wrong time, and with the wrong enemy," Bradley states.[*]

With all the turbulence, Harry Truman begins to despise the press.

December 6, 1950. First Daughter Margaret Truman's singing career is receiving mixed reviews. President Truman dotes on his only child and cannot stand any public criticism. When *Washington Post* critic Paul Hume pans her performance at Constitution Hall, stating that "she cannot sing very well, is flat a good deal of the time . . . and still cannot sing with anything approaching professional finish," Truman is furious.

"I've just read your lousy review of Margaret's concert. I've come to the conclusion that you are an 'eight ulcer man on four ulcer pay.'

"It seems to me that you are a frustrated old man who wishes he could have been successful. When you write such poppycock as was in the back section of the paper you work for it shows conclusively that you're off the beam and at least four of your ulcers are at work.

---

[*] The Korean War will not end until July 27, 1953.

"Some day I hope to meet you. When that happens, you'll need a new nose, a lot of beefsteak for black eyes, and perhaps a supporter below!"

April 16, 1951. President Truman shares his ongoing disdain for the press with good friend and personal attorney Rufus Burrus. At question is how the media has treated presidents throughout history.

Truman writes, "Washington was abused in the press. . . . Never was there a more thoroughly misrepresented president than Thomas Jefferson. . . . They almost hounded [Grover] Cleveland to his grave. It is interesting to read the lies they published about him and Mrs. Cleveland. Of course, Lincoln was thoroughly misrepresented, and it took fifty years to get the truth so I don't let these things bother me for the simple reason I am trying to do the right thing and eventually the facts will come out.

"You and I will probably be holding a press conference with St. Peter when that happens, however."

On March 27, 1952, the Trumans move back into the White House. Three months later, the Republican Party nominates General Dwight D. Eisenhower as its choice for president. The Democrats nominate Illinois governor Adlai Stevenson. The terms of the Twenty-Second Amendment state that Truman is "grandfathered in"—meaning he *can* run for a third term if he wishes.

He does not.

On November 4, 1952, Dwight Eisenhower is elected the thirty-fourth president of the United States.[*]

On January 20, 1953, Harry and Bess Truman leave Washington. They return to Missouri, where they spend the rest of their days.

Harry Truman lives to be eighty-eight. He dies of multiple organ failure on December 26, 1972. He is buried in Independence, Missouri, at the Harry S. Truman Presidential Library and Museum.

---

[*] The election of 1952 was never close. Eisenhower was overwhelmingly popular and Stevenson not widely known. Surprisingly, President Truman did not support Stevenson, preferring former commerce secretary and future New York governor Averell Harriman for the nomination.

Bess Truman is buried by his side, having survived her husband by ten years. She dies of cardiovascular disease at age ninety-seven.

President Harry Truman did a good job of keeping the United States relatively stable in the face of the dramatic new communist threat. An honest man who had little patience for ideological politics, Truman led Americans into a new era of prosperity that would continue under his successor.

"Give 'em hell, Harry" wasn't really a hell-raiser, but if you crossed him, there might be hell to pay.

As General MacArthur and others found out.

Chapter Thirty-Four

President Dwight D. Eisenhower doesn't fight.

The most famous military man in the world, now president for five months, has never participated in an actual battle and detests bloody conflict. Tonight, he is making a historic announcement.

"My fellow citizens," President Eisenhower tells America, sitting in a padded chair before a bank of microphones. Dark suit and tie. Makeup on his bald head to keep off the shine from the TV lights. "Tonight, we greet with prayer and thanksgiving the official news that an armistice was signed almost an hour ago in Korea. It will quickly bring an end to the fighting between United Nations forces and the Communist armies."*

Time has passed quickly since Dwight David Eisenhower was sworn in on January 20, 1953. President Harry Truman travels with him to his inaugural, but the two cannot stand each other and do not speak. This

---

* The Korean Armistice Agreement officially ended the war at 10:00 a.m. on July 27, 1953. The document is signed by Lieutenant General William K. Harrison, representing the United Nations, and North Korean general Nam II, representing the Korean People's Army and Chinese People's Volunteers. The two men did not acknowledge each other throughout the ceremony. An estimated three million civilians, one million South Korean troops, one and a half million North Korean troops, four hundred thousand Chinese soldiers, and seventy thousand UN troops were killed in the war. In addition, thirty-three thousand Americans died.

was not always so. After World War II, Eisenhower and Truman were friendly acquaintances. But Truman is so incensed by the conduct of Republican senator Joseph McCarthy that anyone who does not condemn McCarthy is an enemy.

Dwight Eisenhower fits into that category.

After taking office, Ike, as he is called, has had a rough ride. McCarthy is holding hearings with the intent to expose communists infiltrating the US government. There is anti-communist hysteria growing in America, exemplified by the execution of Julius and Ethel Rosenberg last month. The New York couple passed along nuclear secrets to the Soviet Union and faced the electric chair at Sing Sing Prison in upstate New York. Meanwhile, schoolchildren across the country are practicing "duck and cover" exercises by hiding under their desks in case of a Russian nuclear attack.

In addition, Joseph Stalin died four months ago, and chaos now reigns in Moscow.

Today, President Eisenhower assures America that he has communism under control and that the war in Korea was worth fighting.

He states, "With special feelings of sorrow and of solemn gratitude, we think of those that were called upon to lay down their lives in that far-off land to prove that once again, only courage and sacrifice can keep freedom alive."

The president ends his address with a grim look on his face.

Every Eisenhower boy is nicknamed "Ike." There are seven brothers— the offspring of Ida and David. To keep track of the boys, Ida attaches adjectives to the Ikes. Dwight, third born and destined to become the thirty-fourth president of the United States, is Little Ike because of his small stature.

He was born in 1890 in the Texas town of Denison. Soon, the family moves to Abilene, Kansas, where his father works as a mechanic at the new Belle Springs Creamery. Young Dwight enjoys the outdoors, learning to hunt and fish. He also develops a passion for military history, which he studies voraciously during moments when the Eisenhowers are not engaged in their regular family Bible reading. Ida Eisenhower is a devout Mennonite and pacifist.

Dwight plays fullback on his high school football team, growing to a sturdy five feet ten, 160 pounds. The Eisenhowers cannot afford to send their sons to college, so the boy spends the two years after high school working nights at the creamery.

He applies to the Naval Academy in Annapolis, where tuition is free. But Ike is over the age limit. The twenty-year-old Eisenhower then applies to the US Military Academy at West Point, which has a higher age limit. His score on the service academy entrance exam is so high that he is accepted into the class of 1915, which will become known as "the class the stars fell on" because fifty-nine of its members would go on to the rank of general. Ida Eisenhower cries as Little Ike leaves home, not wanting him to become a soldier.*

At West Point, Eisenhower again plays football. His talent as a running back is so great that the *New York Times* labels him "one of the most promising backs in Eastern football."

Then Ike is forced to quit the team after a bad knee injury. A despondent Eisenhower considers dropping out of school altogether. He chooses to remain but becomes a mediocre student with a passion for poker. The young cadet receives demerits for being tardy, smoking in his room, and giving sloppy salutes.

Ike graduates, ranking 64th out of a class of 164. The moment he takes the oath to serve his country changes him forever. "There was no confusion," he will write. "A feeling that the expression 'The United States of America' would now and henceforth mean something different than it ever had before. From here on it would be the nation I was serving, not myself."

After graduation, Second Lieutenant Eisenhower is assigned to his first post at Fort Sam Houston in San Antonio, Texas. There, he meets a young girl named Mamie Doud. Eisenhower is not known for being romantic, but he falls for her right away. He later describes Mamie as "a vivacious and attractive girl, smaller than average, saucy in the look about her face and in her whole attitude."

A wealthy girl from Denver, Mamie stands five feet one, nine inches shorter than Ike. The daughter of a meatpacking executive, she is visiting

* Eisenhower is sponsored by Kansas senator Joseph Bristow. Ike's 87 percent score was the second highest of those in his state taking the West Point entrance exam.

San Antonio for the winter. Mamie has a heart condition due to a case of rheumatic fever as a child, which leads her to avoid strenuous exercise. And though Dwight Eisenhower is instantly attracted to the nineteen-year-old, she has several suitors and turns him down when he asks for a date. After one month, however, she changes her mind, believing the lieutenant looks good in his uniform.

The couple get engaged on Valentine's Day, 1916, marrying four months later. Mamie's father agrees to the union but only under the proviso that Ike does not enter army flight school due to the great danger. Mamie, who grew up in a household full of servants, needs to be taught cooking and simple household chores by her husband. Their first son, Doud, dies of scarlet fever at age four. Their second born, John Eisenhower, will go on to become a military general, an ambassador to Belgium, and a bestselling author. Grandson David will marry Julie Nixon and have the presidential retreat, Camp David, named after him.

It is not Dwight Eisenhower's *fault* that he never fights in combat. His tank unit is due to ship out for France during World War I, but the conflict ends before their departure. Many officers leave the military after the armistice, but Ike remains. He and Mamie move from post to post: the Panama Canal Zone, the Philippines, France, and back to the States, each transfer a climb up the professional ladder. Eisenhower has a flair for organization and is a quick judge of character. Superior officers admire his critical thinking and quick grasp of strategy.

In his spare time, Eisenhower plays bridge and golf, reads western novels by Zane Grey, and smokes Camel cigarettes. He is known to inhale three packs a day.

Mamie Eisenhower travels everywhere with her husband, living the transient life of a military wife. But this changes during World War II. No spouses accompany their husbands into the theater of operations. Eisenhower is transferred to London in June 1942 as a major general with three decades of service under his belt. He is quickly promoted, rising to four stars, along the way acquiring a driver as a perk of his position. General Eisenhower's chauffeur is thirty-five-year-old Captain Kay Summersby from the British Mechanised Transport Corps. An Irish-born woman, she is extremely attractive. The two grow close during their time together, leading one newspaper reporter to comment, "I have never before seen a chauffeur get out of a car and kiss the general good morning when he comes from his office."*

Thousands of miles away, Mamie becomes suspicious—leading Ike to deny the affair in letters home. He writes, "Apparently you don't choose to believe anything I say."

★★★

June 5, 1944. General Dwight Eisenhower, who has risen to supreme Allied commander in the European Theater, gives final approval to the Allied invasion of German-occupied France. In total, 160,000 soldiers, sailors, and airmen will attack the Normandy beaches. The weather has been terrible for days, but there is a small window of clear skies for the morning of June 6, 1944.

"I hope to God I'm right," Ike tells Kay Summersby.

He is.[†]

★★★

D-Day succeeds. General Eisenhower returns to America a hero. Critics like General George S. Patton and British field marshal Bernard Law Montgomery now grudgingly admit that Ike has been an outstanding wartime commander.

Eisenhower now wears the rank of five stars. He is not affiliated with a political party but is so popular that, in a bizarre gesture, President Harry Truman offers to serve as *his* vice presidential second in 1948 if Eisenhower chooses to run for president as a Democrat.

Ike declines. Instead, he writes his memoirs and spends four years serving as president of Columbia University in New York City, still

---

[*] John "Beaver" Thompson of the *Chicago Tribune* made that comment. Summersby will write a book about her relationship with Eisenhower shortly before her death from cancer in 1975. *Past Forgetting* will detail their love affair. According to Truman biographer Merle Miller, Eisenhower asked permission from his superior officer, General George Marshall, to divorce Mamie and marry Kay. This permission was needed because Summersby was enlisted in a foreign army. Marshall denied the request, telling Eisenhower that the scandal would end his career.

[†] The authors write extensively about D-Day in their book *Killing Patton*.

undecided about politics. Ike returns to uniform as Supreme Allied Commander of NATO from December 1950 through May 1952.

Slowly, Eisenhower tilts to the right—believing Truman and Congress are not strong enough to thwart the communist menace.

In 1952, Ike announces that he is a Republican and is "willing" to serve as president.

★★★

The nomination is never in doubt, nor is the election. Eisenhower's main opponent in the primaries is Robert A. Taft, son of former president William Howard Taft. The convention is held in Chicago. General Douglas MacArthur, another retired five-star general who longs to be president, gives the keynote address.

MacArthur's speech, which is highly critical of Truman, is not a success, to say the least, ending any hope he had of being president.

Thus, Dwight Eisenhower wins easily—Robert Taft concedes on the first ballot.

"I never thought the man who is now nominated would ever stoop so low," President Truman says of Ike's refusal to stand up for fellow general George Marshall, who has been falsely accused by Senator Joseph McCarthy of being a communist. The outgoing president accuses Eisenhower of "moral blindness."

Voters, however, do not seem to care. Dwight Eisenhower even campaigns with McCarthy in Wisconsin, later stating that he agrees with the senator's ambitions but disapproves of his methods.

As his vice president, Ike chooses California senator Richard M. Nixon, an up-and-comer. Republicans want Nixon because he is rabidly anti-communist as well as being from a state that is growing in electoral votes. If Eisenhower cannot finish his term, the thirty-nine-year-old Nixon would be one of the youngest presidents in American history.*

The presidential election is a rout. Running with the slogan "I Like Ike," the former general easily destroys Illinois governor Adlai Stevenson. The Electoral College tally is 442–89.

---

*Nixon served on the House Un-American Activities Committee. In 1948, he famously uncovered American diplomat Alger Hiss as a Soviet spy. The statute of limitations on espionage had run out, but Hiss lied about his past while testifying before the committee. Convicted of perjury, Hiss was sentenced to five years in a federal prison.

Even as Eisenhower becomes the first Republican in the White House since Herbert Hoover twenty years ago, the campaign of 1952 also marks a transition. Air travel begins to supplant lengthy railroad rides so the candidates can move quicker. Televisions can now be found in most American homes. That presents a problem to Eisenhower, whose bald head shines so much on camera that it is blinding. In addition, he is not a dynamic speaker, requiring glasses to read the teleprompter. This ages him. So, cue cards with huge letters are substituted.

Richard Nixon also has problems. Quickly, Democrats accuse him of embezzling $18,000 in campaign contributions. This forces Nixon to go on television to defend himself. In what is known as the "Checkers" speech, the Californian declares his innocence. Then, he pivots to his family, saying that there *was* a gift offered and accepted. It was a cocker spaniel named Checkers whom his daughters love very much. Nixon looks into the camera and says that the family will not give Checkers back no matter what the Democrats say.

Nixon's thirty-minute broadcast is a triumph, demonstrating the new power of television in shaping an election.

★★★

President Eisenhower is under duress.

"I have two kinds of problems, the urgent and the important," he states. "The urgent are not important, and the important are never urgent."

The president encourages his staff to offer opinions on issues, allowing dissent. He rises early, does paperwork in the morning, hits golf balls on the South Lawn in the afternoon, and then enjoys a scotch while dining with Mamie at 7:00 p.m. He no longer smokes, having given up cigarettes in 1948 under orders from his doctors. However, he has not given up his sharp temper. To maintain calm, he sometimes retires to a room set aside in the White House for his hobby of painting.

As far as the rest of the residence is concerned, Mamie is in charge. "Ike runs the country, I turn the lamb chops," she explains. She visits the Oval Office just four times during her husband's presidency and rarely speaks to the press. Mamie gets up in the morning when she feels like it. But the First Lady is an extremely busy woman. Working from her pink-and-green bedroom, often wearing a housecoat, she manages the household staff and plans menus and schedules. She is adamant that her husband has sufficient time to relax each day.

The country loves Mamie. Women copy her preference for a certain color that sweeps America. "Mamie pink" clothing quickly goes on sale.

The First Lady has a policy of responding personally to each note sent to her, which always keeps her office staff of fifteen busy. She typically receives seven hundred letters a month. During one of President Eisenhower's health scares, she gets eleven thousand get-well cards.

The First Lady signs every response.

If there is one issue that bothers Mamie Eisenhower deeply, it is the divisive behavior of Senator Joseph McCarthy. She shares this mistrust with her husband.

In time, Ike agrees. The president is irate when the out-of-control senator attacks the army on national television. But once again, Eisenhower refrains from public comment, saying privately to his staff, "I just won't get into a pissing contest with that skunk."

Soon, the skunk is done. By the end of the hearings, the Senate is so embarrassed by McCarthy's behavior that they vote to censure him.[*]

In 1954, a ruling by the Supreme Court known as *Brown vs. Board of Education* ushers in a new era of civil rights. Segregation of American schools is now illegal. In 1955, a woman in Alabama named Rosa Parks takes this one step further, refusing to give up her seat on a bus in favor of a white person. This leads to a thirteen-month boycott of Montgomery buses by African Americans.

In 1957, Ike sends in US Army troops to enforce the desegregation of Central High School in Little Rock, Arkansas.

President Eisenhower supports civil rights, though cautiously. He urges its leaders to proceed slowly. During his only White House meeting with black leadership, Eisenhower grows angry with a young

---

[*] Joseph McCarthy remains in the Senate for two more years after his censure but is shunned by his colleagues. He begins drinking heavily, often showing up drunk to the floor of the Senate. McCarthy also becomes addicted to morphine. He dies on May 2, 1957, at age forty-eight, from cirrhosis of the liver. Robert F. Kennedy attends the funeral representing his family, which had long been close with McCarthy.

minister named Martin Luther King Jr., who demands more federal action against racism.

This is in 1958. Although annoyed, the president will soon accede to King's request.*

★★★

And then there is American culture.

Dwight D. Eisenhower is not with it.

Especially, the music.

The president prefers simple classics: "O Susannah," "Greensleeves," "Stardust."

America's youth, however, are moving quickly away from traditional entertainment. Antiestablishment actors Marlon Brando and James Dean dominate drive-in movie theaters. And an invention known as a transistor radio sends a new kind of music all across the country: rock 'n' roll.

Elvis Presley, a young truck driver from Tupelo, Mississippi, is its star. An appearance on television's *Ed Sullivan Show* introduces the nation to "Elvis the Pelvis," his gyrations scandalizing some conservative Americans.

Jerry Lee Lewis. Chuck Berry. Buddy Holly. These are America's new sensations. The music industry, for the first time in its history, targets young listeners instead of men and women the age of the president and First Lady.

Then there's the television revolution. Shows such as *I Love Lucy* and *The Honeymooners* draw enormous audiences. The Eisenhowers are among those viewers, often eating dinner off TV trays in the residence while watching sitcoms. Typical fare is a steak or beef stew, along with a bowl of vegetable soup. The couple have a policy of not discussing politics while they dine.

Unlike many presidents, Dwight Eisenhower prefers relaxation to work once he leaves the Oval Office each day at 5:00 p.m. When not watching television, he enjoys reading or painting. The Eisenhowers do not entertain often due to the First Lady's lifelong heart condition,

---

* The civil rights leaders in attendance for the meeting are Dr. King, Roy Wilkins, Lester Granger, and A. Philip Randolph. They present nine recommendations to relieve racial tension. They also commend Eisenhower for his role in passing the Civil Rights Act of 1957.

which causes her to suffer from headaches, asthma, and dizziness that affects her gait, with those not knowing of this affliction believing she has been drinking too much.

The First Couple sleep in separate bedrooms, both retiring well before midnight. The president places small pillows beneath his neck to help him sleep better. Mamie, who remains in bed long after her husband rises at dawn, is nicknamed "Sleeping Beauty" by the staff.

Economically, the nation's gross national product is growing quickly—from $200 billion at the end of World War II to $500 billion under Eisenhower. Much of this growth is fueled by government spending on interstate highways, social security, and increased veterans' benefits.

And then there is the "baby boom." Young men and women are getting married in record numbers at a younger age. Families are moving out of the cities into new suburbs. More women are attending college even as many later stay home to raise families, reversing the trend of women in the workforce begun during the war.

Also, America is moving west. California, Arizona, and Nevada are booming as families seek warmer climates and open spaces. Under Eisenhower, two new states are added—Hawaii and Alaska—the first since New Mexico and Arizona in 1912.

President Eisenhower is easily reelected in 1956, once more beating Adlai Stevenson. He again makes use of television. The ad is four minutes long, celebrating Eisenhower's ability to end the war in Korea. "Citizens for Eisenhower-Nixon," it concludes, "dedicated to all thinking voters, regardless of party affiliation."

Ike's second term leans heavily toward foreign policy. Communist oppression is spreading. A revolt in Hungary during his first term is brutally suppressed by the Soviet Union. Cuba becomes a Russian satellite as rebel leader Fidel Castro takes control. Back home, however, things are prosperous. So good that pundits call the era "Happy Days."

Then, disaster. President Eisenhower suffers a stroke during his second term in 1957, brought on by an aneurysm caused by a 1955 heart attack. Mamie Eisenhower, who stayed at her husband's bedside for nineteen days during that earlier crisis, remains with him, monitoring his recovery. She makes sure the public is aware that Ike is still running the country—unlike Edith Wilson's role when President Woodrow Wilson suffered a stroke in 1919.

Despite the health problems, President Eisenhower recovers quickly— although some close to him notice he has lost a step.

It is all over on January 20, 1961. President Eisenhower graciously ushers John F. Kennedy into the White House. Inauguration Day. The two men will ride together to the ceremony wearing top hats on this bitter cold day. All week long, Ike has heard the sound of hammers and nails as the viewing stand is being constructed. Not wanting to hand the presidency over to a man he believes is inexperienced and callow, Eisenhower compares the sounds of the construction to that of a condemned man hearing gallows built.*

President-elect Kennedy arrives early. Eisenhower invites him inside the White House, where they have coffee. In time, Ike will serve as a special adviser helping Kennedy navigate foreign policy. For now, the two men are just getting to know each other.

The inauguration goes very long.

Afterward, Dwight and Mamie Eisenhower attend a farewell reception at the F Street Club. When it is over, they step into their 1955 Chrysler. Chauffeur Leonard Dry drives them all the way to the gates of their farm in Gettysburg, Pennsylvania. The Secret Service follows in a separate vehicle. As the Chrysler pulls into the driveway, an agent honks and makes a U-turn. The job guarding Dwight Eisenhower is over after eight years. In 1965, Congress will authorize Secret Service protection for all former presidents.

Dwight and Mamie Eisenhower retire to their farm in Gettysburg, where they raise Angus cattle. But the former president suffers a series of six more heart attacks. His gallbladder is removed. A tumor is found in his torso.

---

* The National Park Service cites this as a quote to "a friend."

At 12:25 p.m. on March 28, 1969, Eisenhower dies from congestive heart failure at Walter Reed Army Medical Center in Washington, DC. He is seventy-eight years old. Ike is buried at his presidential library in Abilene, Kansas. He is placed in a government-issue coffin wearing his World War II uniform with medals.

Their son Doud Eisenhower, who preceded his father in death in 1921, is buried at his side. Mamie Eisenhower survives her husband by a decade before suffering a stroke. She rests with her husband and son.

History records President Eisenhower presiding over a booming economy and handling the Soviet Union and China effectively—that is, the Cold War did not lead to armed conflict. On the domestic front, Ike was an establishment leader, not a crusader. He avoided the controversy of McCarthyism and did not advance the cause of civil rights for black people until his second term. In 1957, Eisenhower signed the Civil Rights Act empowering federal authorities to prosecute vote deniers. It is watered down but gives federal prosecutors the power to get court injunctions against interference with the right to vote.

Then, in 1960, a second, stronger Civil Rights Act was signed, after which Eisenhower wrote an open letter to the American people: "By authorizing the FBI to investigate the bombings or attempted bombings of schools, churches, and other structures, this act will deter such heinous acts of lawlessness. . . . The new law will play an important role in the days ahead in attaining our goal of equality under the law in all areas of our country for all Americans."

A decent man, President Eisenhower presided effectively over the nation. He valued conformity, modesty, and stability. The next president respected Ike but was his opposite in almost every way.

Welcome to "Camelot."

Chapter Thirty-Five

President John F. Kennedy is in pain.

The presidential yacht *Honey Fitz* glides through Narragansett Bay. She is ninety-two feet long with a wooden hull painted white. JFK, as he is known, wears a leather jacket with the blue presidential seal on the left chest. Ray-Ban sunglasses. There are gray skies and a stiff wind. President Kennedy's reelection campaign starts in just a few weeks, but for now, he is relaxing with his wife, Jackie, and good friends. Everyone on board is wealthy, young, and at ease in opulence. Kennedy likes to be around people such as these.

The media has taken to calling the Kennedy White House "Camelot"— JFK as King Arthur, surrounded by his gracious court. The press does not know about the president's chronic pain and the narcotics he takes to manage it or the intrigues that Kennedy brings upon himself.

Also on board today are *Newsweek* magazine's Washington correspondent Ben Bradlee and his socialite wife, Tony. Kennedy generally does not like the press, but Bradlee is a fellow Harvard graduate and World War II veteran of the United States Navy. The two men are both in their midforties and get along.

Bradlee has to know about Kennedy's appetite for female liaisons. Yet that is *never* written about. The national press has heard the rumors for ten years, beginning when JFK was single and a senator. But no reporter dares investigate.

The ethics of *Newsweek*'s top Washington correspondent openly socializing with the president at government expense are also questionable. JFK's top advisers have long used the media to promote their boss, and major names like syndicated columnist Joseph Alsop and Charles Bartlett of the *Chicago Sun Times* are more than happy to do Kennedy's bidding.

It seems "Camelot" is well protected by the press.

However, Ben Bradlee is a special case. The powerful Graham family owns *Newsweek* and the *Washington Post* and shapes political coverage nationwide. But even as he sails the New England waters, Bradlee is holding a secret.

Six months ago, the president made a failed pass at his wife, friendship with her husband notwithstanding. Tony Bradlee rejected the overture.[*]

But Kennedy has been much more successful with her married sister, Mary Meyer, a Washington artist. Despite those intrusions, Ben Bradlee remains solidly in the Kennedy camp.

The president is a handsome man with a full head of red-brown hair and an easy smile. Jackie Kennedy sits alongside smoking a cigarette, wearing sunglasses, a white sweater, and slacks. She smiles for the camera, despite the recent death of her newborn son, Patrick, from infant respiratory distress. She and President Kennedy celebrated their tenth wedding anniversary on September 12, just three days ago.[†]

Like his wife, JFK has a great deal on his mind. A new war in Vietnam is pulling him into political trouble as sixteen thousand US "military advisers" have been sent to quell the growing conflict in Southeast Asia. In Cuba, the Fidel Castro situation first confronted by President Eisenhower has developed into an adjunct of the Cold War. Even as the president is yachting, the Cuban Missile Crisis of 1962 is still a fresh memory, the Soviet Union having sought to install missiles aimed at the United States, just ninety miles away.

The ship's phone rings.

---

[*] That allegation comes from her *Washington Post* obituary, November 14, 2011: "Mrs. Bradlee told Kennedy biographer Sally Bedell Smith that on a particularly festive 46th birthday party for then-President Kennedy in 1963, he made a pass, which she rebuffed."

[†] Baby Patrick lived thirty-nine hours, dying in a Boston hospital on August 9, 1963.

Kennedy answers. The news is grim. Civil rights is another hard issue facing America. JFK needs white southern votes to win reelection but cannot afford to ignore black voters. This morning in Birmingham, Alabama, four members of the Ku Klux Klan placed nineteen sticks of dynamite under steps leading into the Sixteenth Street Baptist Church.

Four young girls died in the blast.

As the president digests that information, the *Honey Fitz* continues its weekend cruise. Gloomy weather approaches. There are still a few more hours on the water to be enjoyed. Fall is coming, and with it the end of sailing season.

Soon enough, the presidential yacht docks at the Quonset Point National Guard Air Station in Quonset Point, Rhode Island. The president and his guests step off, one by one, not knowing the voyage will be Kennedy's last.

JFK is raised in the Bronx.

He was born in 1917 outside Boston, in the master bedroom of the family home on Brookline's Beals Street. His parents are wealthy financier Joseph P. Kennedy and his wife, Rose. "Jack," as he will be nicknamed, is the second of eight children. His brother Joseph, two years older, is his father's favorite. At the time of his birth, Boston mayor John Fitzgerald predicts that Joe Jr. is "the future president of this nation."*

No such claims are made about the weaker Jack, who becomes so ill from scarlet fever at the age of two he almost dies.

The family moves to New York City when the future president is ten, their Irish Catholic father angered by what he perceives as discrimination in Boston, where signs read, "Irish Need Not Apply."

Growing up, Jack lives in his big brother's shadow, an athlete never as good as Joe. He is a member of Boy Scout Troop 2 in Bronxville, New York. Jack also attends boarding school at Choate, in Connecticut, where he is almost expelled for blowing up a toilet seat with firecrackers.

Health issues are a lifelong plague for the future president, beginning with an appendectomy, then colitis, and, finally, a cancer scare in his youth. JFK's left leg is a quarter inch shorter than his right, leading to

---

* Fitzgerald is Rose Kennedy's father and the source of JFK's middle name.

chronic back pain. He wears a lift in his shoe to compensate, but the imbalance leads to a disintegration of his spinal discs. All his ailments affect John academically as he finishes 64th in his class of 112 at Choate. However, Kennedy's fellow students vote him "Most Likely to Succeed." One instructor speaks of Jack's "flashes of brilliance."

Yet, even when he begins college at Princeton, then transfers to Harvard, the comparisons with big brother Joe never end.

Joe Kennedy plays rugby and football and rows crew for the Crimson.

Jack Kennedy likes to read and write. He pens stories for the student newspaper after a lower back injury ends his football career for good.

In 1938, Jack's father, Joseph Kennedy, is named ambassador to the Court of Saint James's in London. Jack and the family follow along. He travels widely in prewar Europe, spending a great deal of time in Nazi Germany. Like his father and older brother, Jack initially admires Adolf Hitler and believes the German army is unstoppable.

He writes these thoughts in his senior thesis, which is later turned into a book. *Why England Slept* will be published in 1940, selling eighty thousand copies. Ambassador Kennedy's personal and private relationship with British prime minister Winston Churchill has faltered as the elder Kennedy supports Germany. He is accused of being an appeaser—openly against fighting Hitler. His son's book describes the rise of the Third Reich and the apathy of the British government in the face of it.

Now in his twenties, Jack Kennedy suffers from worsening back pain. He self-medicates, taking steroids that will lead to a potentially fatal hormone imbalance. These problems prevent him from securing an army commission as war breaks out in Europe. He tries again, this time with the United States Navy Reserve. His father calls in favors, ensuring that his second son is not just commissioned as an ensign but is assigned to a combat zone.

JFK is sent to the Pacific, assigned to a patrol torpedo (PT) boat, an eighty-foot-long vessel capable of traveling a brisk forty-one knots. JFK plays bridge in his spare time and rarely wears a shirt in the tropical heat. The warm ocean water is good for his back.

On the night of August 1, 1943, having already survived thirty missions in the Solomon Islands, Kennedy's boat encounters the Japanese destroyer *Amagiri* in the dark of night. At more than three hundred feet long, the warship runs right over PT-109, splitting Kennedy's boat in two.

Twelve Americans are scattered into the dark waters. Kennedy re-injures his back but manages to swim five hours to a nearby island, dragging one burned sailor with him. After hiding for seven days, the Americans are rescued. The story is chronicled in *The New Yorker* magazine.

Summer, 1944. John F. Kennedy is now a decorated, well-known war hero. But his brother Joe is *still* the Kennedy destined for the presidency. JFK, it is thought by his father, will go into journalism.

Joe Kennedy Jr. also serves in the navy. The war will be over soon. Ac-cording to the plan laid out by his father, Joe will return home a hero and run for Congress in 1946.

Jack's oldest brother is stationed in England, piloting highly sensitive bombing missions over occupied France. On August 12, 1944, he and copilot Wilford John Willy take off in a plane packed with explosives. The top secret plan is for them to get the aircraft off the ground and then bail out. A controller will take over, using radio signals to guide the now pilotless plane on a crash course to a German target.

But the unstable Torpex high explosive detonates prematurely. Joe and Willy die instantly. Nothing is left of them or their bomber.

A devasted Ambassador Kennedy grieves for a short time. Then he decrees it will be Jack who will run for Congress. The family moves back to Massachusetts so JFK can contest the Eleventh District, which com-prises Boston, Somerville, and Cambridge. The congressman holding that seat, James Michael Curley, conveniently vacates it to run for mayor of Boston.

The campaign is funded by Ambassador Kennedy himself. "With the money I spent, I could have elected my chauffeur," he jokes when Jack wins, capturing 73 percent of the vote.

The next year, 1947, JFK visits London during a break in congres-sional proceedings. Suddenly, he becomes violently ill from a hormone imbalance known as Addison's disease. The situation is so intense that he is given the last rites of the Catholic Church. It seems a second Kennedy son may soon depart the world.*

Despite the chronic back issues, recurring malaria, Addison's disease, and pain so bad he secretly uses crutches, Jack Kennedy forges ahead in the political world. He travels back and forth across Massachusetts to meet the electorate, pushing himself from morning to midnight. His adviser Dave Powers speaks of the thirty-one-year-old JFK "gritting his teeth when he walked . . . but then when he came into the room where the crowd was gathered, he was erect and smiling, looking as fit and healthy as the light-heavyweight champion of the world."

After six years in the House of Representatives, JFK wins a Senate seat. Taking that office in 1953, he serves at the height of Senator Joseph McCarthy's communist attacks. JFK never speaks out against McCarthy's abuse of power. He goes so far as to check himself into a hospital for spinal surgery so he will be unavailable to vote against the Wisconsin zealot in the crucial Senate censure.†

There is a reason for this: patriarch Joseph Kennedy repeatedly invites McCarthy to socialize at the family home in Hyannis Port. The pudgy senator even dates JFK's sisters—first Patricia, Eunice, and then Jean. When Robert "Bobby" Kennedy, Jack's younger brother, needs a job, it is McCarthy who arranges it. McCarthy hires RFK to be a counsel on his committee investigating alleged communists. The bond is so tight the controversial senator even becomes godfather to Bobby's oldest daughter, Kathleen.

By 1953, Jack Kennedy is a married man. He and his wife, Jacqueline "Jackie" Bouvier, are wed at St. Mary's Church in Newport. Boston archbishop Richard Cushing, soon to be a cardinal, officiates. The pope

---

* JFK will be given the last rites five times. A priest was summoned to give the last rites when JFK was two years old and suffering from scarlet fever. The episode in 1947 is number two. Then he suffers a high fever during a trip to Asia in 1951. Three years later, he falls into a coma after a 1954 back surgery. The last time is after his murder in Dallas.

† On December 2, 1954, Senator Joseph McCarthy was censured by a vote of 67–22. Nothing really happened to him other than a public scolding.

sends a marital message from the Vatican to be read to the congregation of eight hundred guests.

However, JFK's new marital status does not change his lifestyle. It is widely known in Washington and Boston that the senator is "available." Senator Lyndon Johnson of Texas refers to him as a playboy.

In 1956, Jack Kennedy publishes another book, *Profiles in Courage*. He tells the story of senators who have changed the course of American history by making tough decisions. The book earns Kennedy a Pulitzer Prize. However, Eleanor Roosevelt is not impressed. Referring to JFK's rumored philandering and friendship with Joe McCarthy, she says of the senator, "I wish that Kennedy had a little less profile and a little more courage."

John Fitzgerald Kennedy runs for the presidency in 1960. Jackie is pregnant with their fourth child, the first two having died at birth. Their daughter, Caroline, is soon to turn three.

Once again, patriarch Joseph Kennedy advises the campaign, though it is brother Bobby who runs the show, serving as Jack's closest confidant. After winning the Democratic nomination in Los Angeles, Kennedy defeats Vice President Richard Nixon in a tight contest. There are accusations of voter fraud, with some accusing Ambassador Kennedy of buying votes. Along with that allegation come sensational charges that Chicago's notorious mayor Richard Daley rigged the Cook County vote in favor of JFK.[*]

Former president Harry Truman, among others, does not support John Kennedy. Like Eleanor Roosevelt, Truman believes JFK is callow and not up to the job. Millions of other Americans do not vote for him because he would be the first Roman Catholic president. Some evangelical preachers suggest that would lead to the Vatican controlling America.

The real reason JFK wins is that his opponent, Richard Nixon, comes across as dour and sour on television during the first televised debate. But even so, the election is one of the closest in history.

---

[*] Pulitzer Prize–winning journalist Seymour Hersh makes this claim in his book *Dark Side of Camelot*. Whether or not Daley did actually rig the election is still unproven.

Kennedy wins by the slim margin of just one hundred thousand votes out of about seventy million cast. The Electoral College is 303–219 in favor of the Massachusetts senator.

The Kennedy inauguration is a huge event, with an estimated one million people attending in person. Kennedy captures the crowd's attention almost immediately.

"Ask not what your country can do for you. Ask what *you* can do for your country," the new president tells America. It is January 20, 1961. The weather is bitter cold, many in the audience wrapped in sleeping bags to stay warm. Washington, DC, is covered with a thick layer of snow. Kennedy does not like wearing hats, and his head is bare, hair parted neatly with spray. Chief Justice Earl Warren swears in the president. Poet Robert Frost writes a poem, but the glare from the bright January sun makes it impossible for him to read his own words. Instead, Frost recites an older poem of his—"The Gift Outright"—from memory.

John and Jackie Kennedy are the youngest couple ever to ascend to the White House. For the next three years, almost everything in American politics will change.

The last inaugural event ends at 3:40 a.m.

Only then do John and Jackie Kennedy step through the front door of the White House.

By 8:52 a.m. the same morning, the new president gets to work. His first visitor: President Harry Truman.

His second: Chicago mayor Richard Daley.

Almost immediately, JFK is inundated. The Cold War is getting hotter. The American economy is in recession for the fourth time since World War II. Unemployment is high, bankruptcies are the worst since the Depression, and incomes are down. There is a recession that begins in 1960 and ends in February 1961, the economy expanding after that recession ends.

But the Soviet Union is most problematic. In addition, a CIA plan to overthrow Fidel Castro's communist government by landing resistance fighters at the Bay of Pigs in Cuba becomes an embarrassing failure, with many fingers of blame pointed at President Kennedy. Two weeks later, on May 12, 1961, racial violence breaks out in the deep South.

Then there is Vietnam.

At the start of JFK's presidency, there are 3,200 American troops in that Asian nation. At its peak, there will be 536,000.

The Vietnam situation is extremely complicated. President Kennedy is actually eager to leave the embattled nation. On October 2, 1963, JFK directs White House press secretary Pierre Salinger to publicly announce that the military is advising him to pull seventeen thousand US troops from Vietnam by the end of 1965. But Kennedy is very cautious about the matter, believing it might impact his reelection campaign.

JFK must appear to support his South Vietnamese allies against the growing communist threat from the North. The Viet Cong are also fighting in the South against the Saigon government. But President Ngo Dinh Diem is a corrupt leader who lacks the support of his people. He not only oppresses communists but also peaceful Buddhist monks—one holy man even sets himself on fire with gasoline in protest. Between August and October of 1963, Kennedy and his advisers discuss a possible coup. "I mean, it's different from a coup in Iraq or a South American country; we are so intimately involved in this," Attorney General Bobby Kennedy tells his brother on October 29.

On November 1, 1963, the Diem problem ceases to exist. JFK is once again meeting with advisers to discuss South Vietnam. A member of the National Security staff walks in, carrying a cable stating that Diem has been arrested, thrown into the back of a truck, and executed at point-blank range.

The United States denies all culpability in the assassination. A later investigation by federal authorities will find no evidence that Kennedy played a role. However, he was routinely briefed by the CIA in the days leading up to Diem's murder. On the morning of the assassination, the

CIA delivered $42,000 to pay the Vietnamese assassins carrying out the hit.*

Throughout his administration, JFK rises early, drinks orange juice, and eats a poached egg on toast while reading six newspapers. Then goes into the Oval Office for meetings and phone calls. Lunch is New England clam chowder and a sandwich, followed by a swim in the heated White House pool. Then a nap before heading back into the office. The president and First Lady have dinner with their two small children before he resumes working until midnight.

Kennedy changes clothes up to four times a day with the help of longtime valet George Thomas, the grandson of slaves, who is on call twenty-four seven. The president carries a black alligator-skin briefcase. He smokes four to five cigars a day, preferring Upmanns or Monticellos. He likes to doodle, jotting notes, geometric figures, and sailboats on paper. He always wears a blue bachelor's button flower in his lapel.

Kennedy is guarded. He trusts few people. His secretary is Evelyn Lincoln, who is the gatekeeper. JFK only confides in his brother Robert and his "Irish Mafia" of advisers from Boston.†

This posture carries over into his marriage. Jackie Kennedy travels the world with her husband. They laugh and smile together, even though she knows of his indiscretions. Jackie throws herself into being First Lady, redecorating the White House in a manner so sensational that CBS television even sends a camera crew to chronicle it.

Eighty million Americans tune in to watch.

Jackie Kennedy is smart, beautiful, and embracing motherhood. She turns the White House sunporch into a preschool for daughter Caroline as well as a dozen children of staff. A tree house is built above the back lawn.

The First Lady likes meat and potatoes. The Kennedys host twenty-six state dinners, with some version of roast lamb, potatoes, and green beans served at many of them.

---

* Proof of payment by the CIA is found in papers at the JFK Presidential Library. The documentation was made by Kennedy intelligence adviser Roger Hilsman. The $42,000 in 1963 currency is now worth more than $400,000.

† Kenneth O'Donnell, Dave Powers, and Larry O'Brien.

Her husband, though he has a sensitive stomach, will eat almost anything.

In the fall of 1963, John Kennedy's approval rating stands well above 50 percent. The media loves him, hiding his "personal" activities. Reelection is thought to be a lock.

★★★

But not everybody loves JFK.

Dallas, Texas. November 22, 1963. A day of sunshine. Crowds line the streets, eager to see Kennedy in person. He rides through the city in an open-air convertible with a smiling Jackie. At a place known as Dealey Plaza, lone gunman Lee Harvey Oswald opens fire with a rifle from a nearby book warehouse. The president is shot in the head as the First Lady reacts in horror. Kennedy is rushed to nearby Parkland Hospital but is pronounced dead shortly after arrival.*

President Kennedy's body is flown back to Washington, where he lies in state. The burial casket is selected at Gawlor's Funeral Parlor, a Marcellus No. 710 of hand-rubbed, five-hundred-year-old African mahogany upholstered in white rayon.

The president is buried in Arlington National Cemetery on November 25. One million citizens line the streets to watch the procession. Dignitaries from all around the world fly in to mourn the slain American leader.

Five years later, Jackie Kennedy will remarry, only the second First Lady to do so. She will die from cancer in New York City on May 19, 1994. She is interred next to President Kennedy, their son Patrick, and their daughter Annabella.†

★★★

It was John Kennedy who promised that America would have a man on the moon by the end of the 1960s, which happened. He founded the Peace Corps and initiated sources of government spending that led

---

* The authors chronicle the entire Kennedy assassination in their book *Killing Kennedy*.

† On July 16, 1999, John F. Kennedy Jr. dies in a plane crash off the Massachusetts coast. His body is recovered, the ashes later scattered at sea.

America out of a recession within a month of taking office. His handling of the Cuban Missile Crisis in 1962, where he forced Soviet dictator Nikita Khrushchev to back down, showed that the inexperienced statesman who blundered at the Bay of Pigs had matured.

It is also known that John F. Kennedy had many progressive social issues he wished to pursue in his second term. He did not believe he would be reelected if he veered left too early. Also, Kennedy planned to pull American troops out of Vietnam.*

President Kennedy's sudden murder leads to governmental chaos. His successor, Vice President Lyndon Johnson, is an old-time politician who is basically ignored by the Kennedys and even, on occasion, an object of their derision.

Johnson endured the slights but was miserable in the Kennedy administration.

That is behind him. Now it is Lyndon Baines Johnson who holds the future of America in his hands.

---

* JFK's social issues earmarked for his second term include decreasing poverty and introducing new government medical programs. As early as April 1963, he was seeking rapprochement with Fidel Castro. JFK's National Security Action Memorandum 263, dated October 11, 1963, details his planned troop pullout from Vietnam.

Chapter Thirty-Six

AUGUST 4, 1964
WHITE HOUSE
EVENING

Lyndon B. Johnson is not backing down.

"My fellow Americans," begins the president. The fifty-five-year-old Texan stands at a lectern, dressed in a dark suit with a thin black tie. Microphones. American flag behind him. Johnson's face is strained and weary. He wears eyeglasses and looks straight into the television camera for this important national address.

"As President and Commander in Chief, it is my duty to the American people to report that renewed hostile actions against United States ships on the high seas in the Gulf of Tonkin have today required me to order the military forces of the United States to take action in reply," he states, slowly rocking from side to side.

Thus, the escalation of the Vietnam War continues. On November 26, 1963, just four days after the murder of President Kennedy, LBJ approves National Security Action Memorandum 273, reversing Kennedy's order to pull troops out of Vietnam. Instead, the new president wants to send *more* troops to Southeast Asia.*

---

* Kennedy appointees National Security Advisor McGeorge Bundy, Secretary of Defense Robert McNamara, and Secretary of State Dean Rusk were pushing Johnson to take a more aggressive approach in Vietnam.

Since then, President Johnson—LBJ—has approved covert operations, air strikes, and greater involvement in South Vietnamese affairs.

Tonight's address also adds something different. American warships off the Vietnamese coast have been attacked. In the morning, Johnson will ask Congress for a resolution supporting further military action.

He states, "This new act of aggression, aimed directly at our own forces, again brings home to all of us in the United States the importance of the struggle for peace and security in Southeast Asia."

The year 1964 has been impactful in America. A young boxer named Cassius Clay, soon to be Muhammad Ali, wins the heavyweight championship of the world. A rock 'n' roll group known as the Beatles arrives from England. In May, Johnson proposes "Great Society" programs aimed at extending entitlements. Two months later, LBJ signs the Civil Rights Act championed by President Kennedy. It outlaws all discrimination based on race or color, sex, religion, or national origin.

But Vietnam overshadows everything.

It is also an election year. If chosen as the Democratic nominee, Johnson will be running against Senator Barry Goldwater of Arizona, a Republican known for his pro-war stance. The president cannot appear weak. Johnson believes he must act aggressively against communism, fearing that appeasement will lead to comparisons with British policies toward Hitler before World War II.

"It is my considered conviction," he tells the American people, "that firmness in the right is indispensable today for peace."

Congress agrees. The Gulf of Tonkin Resolution is approved on August 7, 1964. President Johnson is now authorized to "take all necessary measures to repel any armed attack against the forces of the United States and to prevent further aggression."

There will be no congressional oversight.

Lyndon Baines Johnson now has full authority to do anything he wants in Vietnam.*

★★★

It is a long way from the Texas Hill Country to the presidency. Lyndon Johnson was born in this remote part of southern Texas on August 27, 1908. Stonewall, as the town of two hundred is known, is exceptionally hot and humid in the summer. The soil is not good for farming. The Johnson home has no electricity. Poverty is such a powerful presence in young Lyndon's life that as an adult he will burst into tears while watching the movie *The Grapes of Wrath* because it reminds him of his childhood.

Lyndon is the oldest of five children born to Samuel Johnson and Rebekah Baines. He has one brother and three sisters. He grows to six feet four and graduates from Johnson City High School, where he is a member of the debate and baseball teams. Johnson is loquacious and the youngest in his class. Not wishing to attend college, he moves alone to Southern California in 1924 at the age of sixteen. With no set plan, he soon returns home, finding work as an unskilled laborer.

No president before or since has drifted in this manner. At eighteen, realizing a college education is important to his future, Johnson enrolls in Southwest Texas State Teachers College in San Marcos. He excels in debate and engages in campus politics. On a whim, he accepts a job teaching Mexican American students in a small town south of San Antonio, a decision that will change him forever. Poor as Johnson might be, this is the first time he encounters citizens whose future is limited by race and social class. "I made up my mind that this nation could never rest while the door to knowledge remained closed to any American," he will later state.

Now a college graduate teaching high school public speaking, Johnson gets involved in politics. He works as a volunteer for Welly Hopkins,

---

* Privately, Johnson had doubts about the validity of the "attacks" on US vessels by the North Vietnamese. According to historian Stanley Karnow, Johnson said, "Hell, those dumb stupid sailors were just shooting at flying fish."

who wins a Texas State House seat in 1928, then a state senate seat in 1930. Welkins is so impressed with the twenty-two-year-old that he recommends LBJ for the position of aide to the newly elected US congressman Richard Kleberg.

Lyndon Baines Johnson is on his way to Washington.

LBJ is a hardworking, restless man. He does not tiptoe into the nation's capital, instead aggressively seeking to make his mark. It helps that Congressman Kleberg comes from a wealthy cattle-ranching family and has no interest in the day-to-day chores of his new job. So, Johnson basically runs the office. He becomes one of the top aides in Congress, even making friends with President Franklin Delano Roosevelt and Speaker of the House Sam Rayburn.

But his most important relationship is with Robert Gene "Bobby" Baker, a South Carolinian who rises from Senate page to trusted confidant. The two men first meet in 1948, as LBJ is about to move from the House to the Senate. "Mr. Baker," Senator Johnson tells the precocious twenty-year-old, "they tell me you're the smartest son of a bitch over there. . . . You're the man I want to know."

Baker is a crook. His net worth is $11,000 in 1954, with an annual salary of $12,500. In 1964, Bobby Baker is worth $2.25 million. He makes his fortune through insider stock trading and sweetheart deals arranged through federal grants, the information gleaned from senators and congressmen eager to take advantage of Baker's many "services."

Baker controls a private space at the Carroll Arms Hotel adjacent to the Senate Office Building. The "Quorum Club," as it is known, is reserved only for politicians. There, Baker arranges sexual favors in exchange for congressional votes and government contracts.

For those needing privacy, Baker keeps a private condominium where senators can take their "dates."

Time magazine, quoting a hotel worker, notes, "A lot of people used to come through the back door. That struck us as strange. Most of our guests come through the front door."

Much of the information Baker gathers is passed along to his pal, LBJ. The young pimp is so powerful that his nickname is the "101st Senator." He briefs Johnson before each Senate vote.

"He is the first person I talk to in the morning and the last one at night," LBJ states.[*]

Lyndon Johnson's flamboyant style extends to his own social life. In 1934, he begins dating Claudia Alta Taylor—whose nickname, "Lady Bird," was given to her by a nursemaid. On date number one, he asks Claudia to marry him. She says no. So, he asks her again on every date thereafter until she gives in five months later.

Lady Bird has her own money, coming from wealthy parents. But she dedicates her life to LBJ, learning to cook and clean house. He expects to be served coffee in bed each morning as he reads the newspapers. Once he is elected to the House, the business of Congress keeps him away from home late into the night. Very often, Johnson returns with friends and expects Lady Bird to have dinner waiting no matter what the hour. And LBJ is not always kind. "Can't you serve the Speaker of the House anything better than turkey hash?" he demands when Sam Rayburn arrives for dinner.

Lady Bird is quick to forgive.

"He would run through the door and grab me into his arms," she will remember. "It was the highlight of my day."

However, LBJ is also in love with another woman. In 1937, he begins an affair with a six-foot-tall blonde from Texas named Alice Glass. She actually knew Lady Bird at the University of Texas and is currently the mistress of influential Austin newspaper owner Charles Marsh, who is also a major political backer of LBJ. Lady Bird will always deny knowing of the relationship, but she soon loses weight and begins dressing in clothing accentuating her physical appearance. But no matter what she does, Alice Glass will remain a constant in her marriage for decades to come.[†]

---

[*] Baker is implicated in a 1963 FBI investigation. He resigns on October 7 and later serves a year in prison for income tax evasion. In subsequent Senate hearings, he is accused of bribery and procuring sexual favors in exchange for votes. FBI director J. Edgar Hoover threatens to release embarrassing information about senators involved with Baker. In exchange for Hoover's silence, Attorney General Bobby Kennedy guarantees the FBI chief will keep his job. Kennedy also allows him to continue wiretapping the Reverend Martin Luther King Jr. Hoover, of course, has an extensive file on JFK.

[†] Alice Glass terminates her relationship with LBJ because she disapproves of his handling of the Vietnam War.

By 1942, Lady Bird has had three miscarriages. The couple live in a brick colonial home off Connecticut Avenue just across the street from FBI director J. Edgar Hoover.

This will become important in the future.

Their phone number is listed in the Washington directory because LBJ wants to appear accessible—and there it will remain until he becomes vice president. Finally, Lady Bird gives birth to daughter Lynda Bird in 1944. Her husband is not present, preferring to work. In the hopes of giving Lyndon a boy, Lady Bird gets pregnant again, birthing daughter Luci Baines. Like all aspects of the congressman's life, including dog Little Beagle, the initials L. B. are everywhere.

★★★

Lyndon Johnson is effective in Washington. His ability to work every angle of legislation becomes well known. He is prone to fits of temper and depression. He smokes sixty cigarettes a day but quits immediately after suffering a heart attack in 1955. Through Lady Bird's tight-fisted financial running of their household and shrewd investments in Texas radio and television stations, the Johnsons accumulate millions of dollars.

In 1948, LBJ runs for the Senate. He apparently loses the Texas Democratic primary, but six days *after* the election, a box containing 202 ballots is mysteriously discovered in the South Texas area known as Precinct 13. A total of 200 of these votes were cast for Johnson—awarding him the primary by 87 votes.

LBJ goes on to win the general election, and, in 1948, the United States Supreme Court rejects allegations of ballot fraud. However, in 1977, Associated Press reporter James Mangan breaks a story saying the Precinct 13 votes were indeed phony. So, Johnson won the Senate seat illegally.

But the statute of limitations in Texas is just three years for voter fraud.*

★★★

Lyndon Johnson's power grows. It is in the Senate where he develops the unique method of cajoling known as "The Treatment." Private informa-

---

* Tapes detailing the stolen 1948 election are held at the LBJ Presidential Library in Austin, Texas.

tion gleaned by Bobby Baker is often helpful. To get his way, whether legislative or personal, Johnson corners the individual in question, puts his face very close to theirs, and launches into a verbal harangue that lasts several minutes.

He often ends the treatment by saying, "Come now, let us reason together," from the Book of Isaiah.

Political success almost always leads to an accumulation of enemies. Through his friendship with neighbor J. Edgar Hoover, LBJ gleans knowledge of sexual affairs. Johnson is not shy about insinuating blackmail to an opponent.

One of his targets is a young senator from Massachusetts, John F. Kennedy.

That infuriates JFK's brother Robert Kennedy, and he marks Lyndon Johnson for retribution. However, patriarch Joseph Kennedy is still running JFK's career and sees a better way: make Johnson an ally. Thus, a Kennedy-Johnson ticket in 1960.

Robert Kennedy and much of the family are horrified. However, JFK doesn't really care, even though he sometimes refers to LBJ as "Rufus Cornpone." Lady Bird is called "Mrs. Porkchop" by the Kennedys, who see themselves as far above the country bumpkins.

Lyndon Johnson is aware of all this. However, he also knows, from Hoover, about JFK's perilous health problems. Believing Kennedy might not survive his first term, Johnson makes the calculation to swallow his pride and support JFK.

He does, however, refer privately to Kennedy as a "snot-nosed kid."

The ticket comes together. Joseph Kennedy understands that his son is seen by many in the South as a snooty liberal. So old Joe encourages the LBJ vice presidential play—better to have Johnson on the ticket than Stuart Symington, a senator from Missouri whom JFK prefers.

July 1960. The Democratic Convention in Los Angeles. Lyndon Johnson accepts the nomination for vice president. Four months later, the Kennedy-Johnson ticket wins.

This seminal moment in Johnson's career, coming at the age of fifty-two, should see his power expand. It does not. JFK and his brother Bobby have no use for LBJ.

For almost three years, to the point of severe depression, Johnson is ignored by the Kennedys as he tries to insinuate himself into their official dealings.

Lyndon Johnson encourages the president to travel to Dallas. The trip is undertaken in part to "mend political fences" in a divided Texas Democratic Party. It is seen as a "pre-1964 campaign trip."

Things go horribly wrong. After the president is shot dead in Dallas, the vice president immediately immerses himself in the trappings of the presidency. Even though First Lady Jackie Kennedy is on the plane for the flight back to Washington, LBJ commandeers the president's quarters aboard Air Force One. Among the many conspiracy theories soon floated about the assassination is that the newly inaugurated president knew the shooting was going to take place.*

President Johnson is obsessed. He enforces a schedule unlike few before him. The morning starts with breakfast in bed at dawn. Lady Bird joins him for thick slices of bacon, eggs, toast, and peach preserves. As always, the president reads the papers as he eats. Then he showers, splashes on Old Spice aftershave, and dresses to be in the Oval Office by 7:00 a.m.

Johnson divides the day into two long shifts that tax his staff. The first half lasts until 2:00 p.m. Then, before lunch, he walks, swims, and showers again. The midday meal is usually soup, fish, steak, or Mexican food. Barbecue is a favorite. If guests are present, it is not uncommon for LBJ to eat off their plates if he sees something he likes. Tuesdays are for lunch with General William Westmoreland to discuss the war in Vietnam, should the general be in town.

After lunch, there is a short nap.

"It's like starting a new day," Johnson exclaims as he steps back into the Oval Office to work from 4:00 until 9:00 p.m. Staff are expected to be available at all times. Johnson can be verbally abusive, with a random list of things that annoy him—among them the colors purple and brown.

---

*There has been no credible evidence that Johnson had advance notice of the murder. Subsequently, he was very kind to Jackie Kennedy, allowing her to stay in the White House until December 6, 1963, two weeks after her husband's murder.

The lavish formal dining of the Kennedy administration is no more. LBJ believes it is out of place with America at war. Instead, he spends late nights drinking Cutty Sark scotch and watching John Wayne movies. When his daughter Luci, sixteen years old as her father becomes president, gets a call from a boyfriend, the phone lights up in the president's bedroom. LBJ often monitors these calls or tells Luci to go to sleep if it is too late.

The First Couple have shared a bed since first married, but it is White House custom for them to sleep in different bedrooms. Nonetheless, Johnson likes to brag about their robust sex life to aides. On those occasions when staff accompany them back to the president's ranch in the Texas Hill Country, it is quite common for LBJ and Lady Bird to kiss and flirt suggestively, not caring who might be watching.

The casualties in Vietnam are placing a heavy strain on the Johnson presidency, as well as on the nation. America wages a two-pronged war, with bombers pounding North Vietnam as US infantry fight in the jungles of the South. But anti-war sentiment grows as more Americans die—six thousand in 1966 alone. The average age of a soldier in World War II is twenty-six. In Vietnam, that figure is just nineteen years old. In addition, 25 percent are draftees.*

Protests in cities around the nation clamor for Johnson to end the war. Some Americans even begin to sympathize with the communists and speak out against the US military, claiming that innocent civilians are more often killed than enemy soldiers. Protest music becomes popular, especially with the growing "hippie" movement. The short haircuts and suits of Johnson's generation are replaced by long hair for men and miniskirts for women. Protestors sometimes march around the White House chanting, "Hey, hey, LBJ, how many kids did you kill today?"

By 1967, it is clear that America's superior military might is having little effect against the North Vietnamese. In October, thirty-five thousand demonstrators protest outside the Pentagon. College campuses are in an uproar.

---

* In total, 58,220 Americans died in the Vietnam War, out of 3.4 million deployed to Southeast Asia. An estimated 1.1 million communist combatants were killed.

President Johnson cannot win. Some Americans believe he should bring the troops home. Others state he should intensify the war, leveling the communist capital of Hanoi. This "hawks" versus "doves" argument further divides the nation.

It is the North Vietnamese and the Viet Cong who deliver the deciding blow. On January 30, 1968, they launch simultaneous military attacks on more than one hundred cities and twenty-four military installations during the Lunar New Year. This "Tet Offensive" surprises US and South Vietnamese forces. CBS News anchorman Walter Cronkite openly displays doubt about the war, leading LBJ to say, "If I've lost Cronkite, I've lost Middle America."

The political damage to Lyndon Johnson's 1968 reelection campaign is crippling. In the New Hampshire primary, he defeats the peace candidate, Minnesota senator Eugene McCarthy, by just seven percentage points. The country is shocked.

Soon after, another peace candidate, Robert Kennedy, announces he will also run against Johnson. With 63 percent of Americans now disapproving of the president's performance, LBJ is finished.

On March 31, two months after the Tet Offensive, Lyndon Johnson appears on national television to announce that he is "taking the first step" to de-escalate the war.

He closes the broadcast with these words:

"I shall not seek, and I will not accept the nomination of my party for another term as your president."

President Johnson is sixty when he leaves office on January 21, 1969, returning to Texas. He is replaced by the newly elected Republican, Richard Nixon. The once-powerful leader is devastated by the past six years. Despite the danger to his heart, he begins smoking again, then gains twenty-five pounds. He experiences daily chest pains and develops diverticulitis, yet he continues to smoke.

At 3:39 p.m. on January 22, 1973, Johnson has another heart attack.

This one kills him at the age of sixty-four.

Johnson's death coincides with the second inauguration of President Nixon. LBJ's body is flown to Washington to lie in state. After a funeral service led by Nixon, Johnson's remains are taken back to Texas, where the Reverend Billy Graham eulogizes him. Lyndon Baines Johnson is buried in the family plot near the home in which he was born.

Lady Bird Johnson lives another thirty-four years. In 2007, she dies at age ninety-four and is buried next to her husband.

Had he remained in the Senate, Lyndon Johnson would have been remembered as one of the most powerful politicians in American history. Despite domestic policy accomplishments in civil rights, education, and the war on poverty, his presidency failed because he chose to follow policies designed to "contain" communism.

As a man, Johnson was reckless and inconsistent. According to his black chauffeur, Robert Parker, LBJ often used the N-word. And he actually scolded Parker when he objected.

In addition, LBJ embraced racist politicians like Robert Byrd and Georgia senator Richard Russell. But, on the policy side, he intensely lobbied for a tough federal civil rights law that protected African Americans.*

On May 15, 1964, Johnson writes to Dr. J. W. Storer, a Southern Baptist leader:

"I am deeply concerned over the moral aspects of the Civil Rights proposals. I am confident you would not expect or want me to be deterred from stressing such moral elements by the respect which I entertain for former colleagues in the Congress who might disagree with my conclusions."

That letter was designed to shame religious leaders who objected to the civil rights legislation.

History has not been kind to Lyndon Johnson. The disastrous Vietnam War divided Americans and ushered in a distrust of government that persists to this day.

But Johnson's "Great Society" created Medicare and other federal safety nets that continue to benefit the vast majority of American citizens.

---

* Senator Robert Byrd of West Virginia was once a member of the Ku Klux Klan. Russell and Senator Jesse Helms of North Carolina were longtime segregationists.

In the end, Lyndon Johnson was a larger-than-life figure with a foggy moral compass who hurt the nation more than he helped it.

And his legacy made it possible for another polarizing leader to achieve the pinnacle of power.

Without the presence of Johnson, there would have been no President Richard Nixon.

Chapter Thirty-Seven

NOVEMBER 8, 1972
WASHINGTON, DC
12:15 A.M.

Things are going astoundingly right for Richard Nixon.
Finally.

It is the morning after Election Day. Nixon has achieved a landslide victory over Democrat George McGovern, a senator from South Dakota. McGovern based his entire campaign on leaving Vietnam. American voters do not agree.

Here at the Shoreham Hotel, five thousand guests fill the Regency Ballroom in anticipation of Nixon's victory speech. The president hears the crowd from his seat in the holding room, just off stage. He is accompanied by First Lady Pat Nixon; his daughters, Julie and Tricia; and their husbands, David and Edward, respectively.*

Richard Nixon began his day at the "Western White House" in San Clemente, California. The enormous oceanfront property is an ideal place to conclude the final campaign of his political career. Just before noon, Air Force One takes off from the Marine Corps base at El Toro, flying Nixon and his forty-four-person retinue to Washington—among

---

* Julie Nixon is married to David Eisenhower, the former president's grandson.

the passengers are National Security Advisor Henry Kissinger, Chief of Staff Robert Haldeman, and five reporters.

Nixon's political past has not been so celebratory. His 1960 loss to John F. Kennedy left him bitter and disillusioned. And his 1968 victory over Hubert Humphrey was too close to enjoy until the last ballots were counted.

Once in office, Nixon uses his first term to open relations with communist China, initiate peace talks with the North Vietnamese, and begin trading with the Soviet Union. The new president's strategy with China and the Soviets surprises many Americans, as he is virulently anti-communist. In addition, Nixon shocks the world by visiting China in February 1972, something no American president has ever done.

On the domestic front, the president is having problems with unemployment and inflation. But some of that is offset by a huge public relations victory: on July 20, 1969, astronaut Neil Armstrong walks on the moon.

The world is enthralled.

It is 12:17 a.m. when Nixon is called to the speaker's platform. The enormous crowd erupts in applause. Nixon wears a dark suit and tie. He grins and raises his right arm in jubilation and then wraps his left around Pat, who is dressed in teal. Vice President Spiro Agnew with his wife and four children flank the First Couple.

Completely overlooked is the specter of scandal. Five months ago, on June 17, 1972, burglars broke into the Democratic National Committee headquarters on the sixth floor of the Watergate Office Building in Washington.

No one tonight is even thinking about that.

But they will be.

Richard Milhouse Nixon is the first president born in a Yorba Linda, California, lemon grove. The son of citrus farmer Francis A. Nixon and his wife, Hannah Milhouse, the future president is descended from one of America's first families. His ancestor Thomas Cornell is among Boston's original settlers, and his distant relation Ezra Cornell founded the Ivy League university bearing his last name.*

The second born of five boys, Richard Nixon is named for a medieval British monarch—Richard the Lionheart. The Nixons are Quakers, a religion that forbids drinking, dancing, and swearing. They are also pacificists, meant to abstain from warfare, a tenet the future president will ignore.

The family is poor. Orange County, California, is remote, a land of sunburned hills offering little opportunity. When the lemon ranch fails, Frank Nixon moves the family to Whittier. Richard rides a bus an hour each way to attend high school in Fullerton, where he plays junior varsity football and excels in debate. His is a hardscrabble life that includes rising at 4:00 a.m. to drive to Los Angeles, purchasing vegetables for his father's store.

The young Nixon's grades are so good that he is offered admission to Harvard University. That presents a problem. His family needs help to run the business. So, Nixon enrolls at Whittier College, a Quaker institution. Now approaching age twenty, he stands six feet tall and is solidly built. He is also socially active. In 1933, the future president gets engaged to the daughter of the local police chief. The relationship does not lead to marriage.

Upon graduation, Richard Nixon receives a scholarship to Duke University Law School. This time, his parents step aside. Nixon hopes to join the FBI. But after graduating third in his class, his application to become a federal agent receives no response. So, he returns to Whittier and begins the life of a small-town lawyer.†

In his spare time, Nixon tries his hand at acting, auditioning for a role at a local playhouse. There he meets Thelma Ryan, a thin blonde who goes by "Pat." She is an orphan, as both parents died while she was still a teenager, leaving her to care for her two brothers. Her late father was Irish, and she was born the day before St. Patrick's Day, thus her nickname.

---

* President Jimmy Carter and Microsoft founder Bill Gates can also trace their family trees to Thomas Cornell.

† Richard Nixon later learns that his FBI application was approved but he was not hired due to budget cuts in 1937.

Pat Ryan is industrious, putting herself through the University of Southern California by working in the school cafeteria and as a movie extra.

At their very first meeting, Nixon tells Pat that they are destined to marry. She does not agree. In fact, she wants little to do with the dark-haired attorney who sports a perpetual five o'clock shadow. But the young man persists, first convincing Pat to date him, and then, two years later, she accepts his marriage proposal. The nuptials are held at the Mission Inn, the same Riverside hotel where Ronald Reagan will one day honeymoon with his wife, Nancy.

The Nixons find lodging over a garage in their first year of marriage. Richard works as an attorney while Pat is a teacher. World War II provides a way out for the ambitious future president, who is commissioned in the navy and accepts a series of minor stateside postings. Pat follows him. When Richard Nixon is sent to the South Pacific, she finds work in San Francisco.

Lieutenant Junior Grade Nixon is assigned to an island off New Guinea, where he oversees cargo flights and plays stud poker in his off time. Nixon excels at the game, and his winnings will later finance the early years of his political career.

At the war's end, Richard Nixon enters politics. His rise is meteoric. He wins a congressional seat in his home district of Whittier, which was once solidly Democrat. Taking office in 1947, he works diligently to receive assignments to the most powerful committees.

Meanwhile, Pat gives birth to daughters Tricia and Julie but prefers to stay out of the public eye.

The fight against communism dominates Congress in 1947. Richard Nixon quickly makes a name for himself on the House Un-American Activities Committee. This success leads to a successful run for the Senate in 1950, followed by a surprise elevation to the vice presidency by Dwight Eisenhower in 1952. Pat Nixon is not fond of her husband's new role, later stating, "When he was nominated for vice president, I really hoped he might not accept."

As VP, Nixon does very little. President Eisenhower does not include him in the executive process. Asked about Nixon's contributions, Eisenhower later tells a reporter, "If you give me a week, I might think of one."

Nonetheless, Richard Nixon goes from a political unknown to the second-most-powerful man in America. Despite Ike's comment, Nixon actually does a lot as VP. He is a key political advocate for the administration, travels internationally, speaks widely on issues—and fills in for Ike (without usurping the presidential role) when Ike has a stroke.

It all comes crashing down in 1960. Nixon is defeated by JFK and then returns to California. In 1962, he runs for the governorship against Pat Brown. Again, he loses. "You don't have Nixon to kick around anymore," he tells the press, with whom he has a contentious relationship.

In 1963, the Nixons move to New York City, where the former vice president resumes his legal practice. The money is good. Pat Nixon could not be happier. She revels in being out of the spotlight. *Homemakers Forum* magazine even selects her as the "Nation's Ideal Housewife."

Richard Nixon travels extensively, helping Republican candidates across the country raise money. Pat stays home in New York watching her husband's political involvement warily.

In 1968, Nixon's strategy pays off. In an unlikely return from his self-imposed exile, the "New Nixon" wins the Republican nomination for president, defeating Nelson Rockefeller and fellow Californian Ronald Reagan. Nixon's strategy revolves around capturing the southern states by capitalizing on their aversion to President Johnson's progressive policies.

In a controversial decision, Nixon chooses Maryland governor Spiro T. Agnew as his running mate. He does so because Agnew is a committed conservative who has extensive party connections. Nixon wins the nomination on the first ballot. Agnew is nominated on a separate ballot for vice president.

The presidential election is much closer. Nixon's Democratic opponent is Hubert Humphrey of Minnesota, vice president to Lyndon Johnson. When Robert Kennedy is assassinated after winning the California primary in June 1968, the pro-war Humphrey runs as the Democratic establishment choice.

There is also a third man in the race. Alabama governor George Wallace, a white nationalist, appeals heavily to southern voters, taking support away from both Humphrey and Nixon.

On November 5, 31.7 million Americans vote for Richard Nixon, 31.2 million choose Hubert Humphrey, and almost 10 million vote for the racist Wallace. However, the Electoral College is not as close: Nixon 301, Humphrey 191, Wallace 46.

Two months before the vote, the outcome very much in doubt, the famously reserved Richard Nixon makes an appearance on the irreverent comedy show *Laugh-In*. Nixon's spot is just five seconds. He looks into the camera and utters the catch phrase, "Sock it to me."

Hubert Humphrey, known as the "Happy Warrior" for his optimistic demeanor, is also offered the chance to appear but declines, thinking it unpresidential.

The new president is fifty-six when he takes office. Nixon rises at 7:00 a.m. and has a breakfast of fresh fruit, wheat germ, black coffee, and cottage cheese doused in ketchup. The president enjoys cottage cheese so much that an abundant supply is always kept in the White House kitchen.

Like LBJ, Nixon reads the newspaper as he eats. He then enters the Oval Office at 8:00 a.m., meeting with secretary Rose Mary Woods to plan his day. Chief of Staff Bob Haldeman is usually Nixon's first official appointment of the day—he is the president's chief administrative assistant and gatekeeper. National Security Advisor Henry Kissinger is often next, keeping the president up to date on foreign affairs, especially Vietnam.

Not a man of small talk, Nixon likes his meetings short, five to ten minutes at a time, though some stretch to a half hour. This allows him to fill the morning with dozens of guests.

Lunch is at 1:30 p.m., served unheated: chilled cucumber soup or Mexican gazpacho, then a poached salmon entrée. Cottage cheese with ketchup is common. Another favorite is "spicy pepperoni salad."

There is no exercise or nap built into Richard Nixon's day. He returns to the Oval Office immediately after lunch, working until well past 7:00 p.m., when Rose Mary Woods leaves for the night. Then, the Nixons have dinner in the residence. Their daughter Julie is attending school at Smith, while Tricia just graduated from Boston College.

For formal White House occasions, President Nixon treats himself to expensive Chateau Lafite Rothschild champagne. But it's only for him. To save money, he instructs the servers to pour less expensive sparkling wine for his guests. Nixon actually orders them to wrap a towel around the labels. As with Pat Nixon's chain-smoking, which she will conceal from the public right up until her death, the president keeps this deception a secret.

★★★

The end begins.

On August 29, 1972, President Nixon issues his first denial that the White House played any role in the Watergate break-in. It is just one week since he accepted the Republican nomination in Miami.

That seems to be the end of it. But, of course, it is not. Unbeknownst to him, Nixon is in deep trouble. The *Washington Post*, now led by editor and former John F. Kennedy confidant Ben Bradlee, has unleashed a reporting team to expose the Watergate situation. Details emerge tying the Nixon White House in with the burglars, who called themselves "plumbers" because their task was to identify and plug leaks.

This prompts a Senate investigation.

All hell breaks loose. In 1972, the press becomes relentless covering the Watergate story, finding that Republican campaign contributions funded sabotage and spying against Democratic candidates. The Committee to Reelect the President and many of Nixon's top aides are implicated. Some have already begun to speak openly about the conspiracy.

The big question is—how much did Richard Nixon know?

On April 30, 1973, White House chief of staff Bob Haldeman and domestic affairs adviser John Ehrlichman, two of Nixon's closest political aides, resign. The next night, the president appears on national television accepting blame but saying he had no prior knowledge of the conspiracy.

"There can be no whitewash at the White House," Nixon tells the country, promising "the whole truth."

★★★

The Watergate hearings are televised to the nation. On June 25, 1973, former White House counsel John Dean testifies that Nixon had *full* knowledge of the Watergate operation. Dean had been involved with the cover-up and has been cooperating with the Senate Watergate Committee investigation—this led Nixon to fire him.

The hearings continue throughout the summer of 1973. America is fixated on the constant flow of new information. On October 20, a furious Nixon fires the Justice Department prosecution team in what will become known as the Saturday Night Massacre. To make matters worse, Vice President Spiro Agnew is charged with taking bribes in a separate incident. He is forced to resign on October 10, 1973. His replacement is Republican loyalist Gerald R. Ford, a congressman and House minority leader from Michigan.

The public turns against the president.

"I am not a crook," a combative Nixon tells an Associated Press reporter. But former president Harry Truman disagrees, once stating, "Richard Nixon is a no-good lying bastard. He can lie out of both sides of his mouth. If he ever caught himself telling the truth he'd lie just to keep his hand in."

Finally, on July 24, 1974, White House tapes show that Nixon approved wrongdoing in the Watergate case.*

On August 8, Richard Nixon resigns rather than face a certain impeachment conviction by the House and subsequent conviction by the Senate.

The resignation will take effect at noon on August 9, 1974.

The president and First Lady step one last time from the White House to board Marine One, the presidential helicopter. Nixon turns to the cameras and flashes a broad "V for Victory" salute before stepping on board.

"It's so sad," says Pat Nixon as the helicopter lifts off. Air Force One will fly them to California, there to await criminal prosecution. "It's so sad," she says again.

Gerald R. Ford is now president. But the country continues to be in an uproar. Will Richard Nixon go to prison? Ford is immediately under siege.

---

* There is little evidence that Richard Nixon knew about the Watergate caper in advance. He did, however, approve campaign money to cover it up after the fact.

Richard Nixon lives for twenty more years, at first in California, then New York City, and finally in New Jersey, so he and Pat can be closer to their daughters. He authors several books and speaks often to Henry Kissinger, his former secretary of state.

Pat Nixon dies first on June 22, 1993, of lung cancer. Richard Nixon is devastated. She is buried at the Nixon Library in Yorba Linda, California, with the Reverend Billy Graham presiding.

Richard Nixon dies of a stroke less than one year later, at age eighty-one. He is buried next to his wife. Five United States presidents and several former heads of state attend his funeral. Reverend Graham eulogizes Nixon as "one of the most misunderstood men, and I think he was one of the greatest men of the century."

History has not been kind to Richard Nixon. Even while in the White House, he was an object of media derision. Many Americans believe that Nixon was a cold, heartless man.

As a young researcher just out of Colgate University, Monica Crowley takes a job with Nixon in 1990. She served as his foreign policy assistant and worked closely with him on policy and messaging. Crowley describes the former president as a natural introvert who also enjoyed meaningful social interactions from big political events to one-on-one situations. She also sees his wide intellectual range and sense of humor as well as occasional displays of intense frustration.

However, Crowley respects Nixon as a man. She believes he was entirely devoted to his wife, family, and country. "He did not enjoy power for the sake of having power," says Crowley. "He believed in using power to help the American people."

★★★

Today, Richard Nixon's reputation is almost entirely one of corruption. That may not be fair, but history often isn't.

On May 4, 1977, the former president and British TV personality David Frost present the first of four paid interviews. Nixon receives $600,000 ($2.8 million today) to sit with Frost.

Forty-five million people tune in for the first chat, the most ever for a political interview. That record stands to this day. Eventually, Richard Nixon admits he lied about covering up Watergate. That is the headline on his legacy.

The sagas of Nixon and Spiro Agnew allow Gerald Ford to become the nation's fifth unelected president.*

And while Nixon opens the White House door for Ford, he also closes it.

---

* The other four are John Tyler, Millard Fillmore, Andrew Johnson, and Chester A. Arthur. Ford was the first vice president chosen under the Twenty-Fifth Amendment who had not been part of a presidential ticket.

Chapter Thirty-Eight

Gerald Ford is reaching back to the Enlightenment.

He is channeling British poet Alexander Pope, who wrote, "To err is human, to forgive divine."

The new president may not realize that soon forgiveness will not be granted to him.

Sunday morning is an unusual time for a major presidential announcement. Ford faces a bank of TV cameras in the Oval Office. Down the hall in the press room, assembled members of the media wonder why they've been summoned to the White House on their day off.

Gerald Ford is sixty-one, the same age as Richard Nixon, though the athletic Ford looks much younger. He wears a blue suit and a striped tie in need of straightening. The balding president looks directly into the camera, serious and intense, seemingly unaffected by the enormity of what he is about to say. He knows the *New York Times* is reporting that Richard Nixon is "deeply depressed and . . . the legal troubles he faced were causing him so much agony his health was in jeopardy."

He also knows that his political opponents in Congress will not support any leniency toward the former president. Nevertheless, Ford begins, "I have come to a decision which I felt I should tell you . . . as soon as I was certain in my own mind and in my own conscience that it is the right thing to do."

Since Nixon left office one month ago, the nation has debated whether or not Ford will mitigate his predecessor's behavior or allow him to stand trial in criminal court.

Article II, Section 2, of the Constitution states that a president may pardon anyone he wishes for any reason. For the past ten days, Gerald Ford has had White House counsel researching legal precedents for such an action. In addition, he has consulted with Secretary of State Henry Kissinger and Chief of Staff Alexander Haig about the matter.

There is dissent in the Ford White House. Press Secretary Jerald terHorst has already resigned in protest because of what Ford is about to say.

Ford continues, "I am compelled to conclude that many months and perhaps more years will have to pass before Richard Nixon could obtain a fair trial by jury in any jurisdiction of the United States under governing decisions of the Supreme Court. As a man, my first consideration is to be true to my own convictions and my own conscience."

Presidential pardons can be controversial. George Washington's forgiveness of those involved in the Whiskey Rebellion and Andrew Johnson refusing to prosecute Confederate soldiers for treason were divisive in their day. Richard Nixon attempted to pardon himself before leaving office, but the Justice Department decided that, "under the fundamental rule that no one may be a judge in his own case, the President cannot pardon himself."

Never before has a sitting president faced *criminal* charges, nor has his successor been in the position of being judge and jury for another chief executive.

Ford concludes, "Now, therefore, I, Gerald R. Ford, President of the United States, do grant a full, free, and absolute pardon unto Richard Nixon for all offenses against the United States which he, Richard Nixon, has committed or may have committed or taken part in."

President Ford does not answer questions. He immediately leaves the White House, driving thirty minutes to the Burning Tree Club in Bethesda, Maryland, for a round of golf. He is abundantly aware that what he has just done will not sit well with many Americans.

The furor is immediate. Thousands of telegrams flood the White House, some in protest, others in support. There is talk of a "secret deal" Ford made with Nixon. Many Americans see this as a continuation of the Watergate cover-up. Ford's approval rating immediately drops from 71 percent to 50 percent, from which he will never recover. The pardon will hurt Ford throughout his presidency, leading to one of the lowest job approval rankings since World War II. His later grant of conditional amnesty to those who fled America to avoid the Vietnam War draft further divides the public.

In autumn 1974, Gallup takes a poll showing that 58 percent of the American people oppose Ford's pardon, while 38 percent are in favor.

Republicans are shaken. Donald Rumsfeld, who holds numerous high positions in the Nixon and Ford administrations, says this: "As hard as Ford tried to exorcise the ghost of Watergate, it would continue to linger for the rest of his presidency."

Conservative commentator Pat Buchanan weighs in: "It was one of the worst blows to hit any presidency in my lifetime."

The *Washington Post*, virulently anti-Nixon, editorializes, "The kid-gloves treatment Nixon received created an expectation of criminal impunity for both sitting and former presidents . . . no matter how many laws he might have broken."

The uproar lasts for a few weeks, and Ford takes the hits. He has no other choice.

★★★

Gerald Ford is using an alias.

Born Leslie Lynch King Jr. in Omaha, Nebraska, he is the son of his namesake and Dorothy Ayer Gardner. The year is 1913. The couple have been married less than a year. Leslie Sr. is a violent man, fond of beating his wife. When the baby is a few days old, the alcoholic waves a butcher knife in his wife's face, threatening to kill her and the child. The situation calms, but Dorothy has had enough. She flees with the infant, returning to her parents' home in Grand Rapids, Michigan. After a divorce, she marries a salesman named Gerald Rudolff Ford. He never formally adopts the child, but before young Leslie is two, his name is legally changed to that of his mother's new husband. So it is that America's thirty-eighth president becomes named Gerald Rudolph Ford instead of Leslie King Jr.*

Young Gerald is an easygoing boy who rises to the rank of Eagle Scout. Later, he attends the University of Michigan, where he becomes a star center and linebacker on two national championship teams. Six feet tall and 190 pounds, the future president mulls offers to pursue professional football, but he chooses to take a job as a football coach and boxing coach with Yale. There, he applies to the law school and is eventually accepted. He finishes in the top third of his class and then passes the Michigan bar.

The year is 1941. Japan's attack on Pearl Harbor on December 7 leads a patriotic Ford to join the navy. Commissioned an ensign, he goes on to serve in the Pacific. In one harrowing instance, Ford is almost swept over the side of the USS *Monterrey* when Typhoon Cobra strikes the US Third Fleet under the command of Admiral William Halsey in December 1944. Only a lucky last-minute grab of a ladder rung saves his life.

Ford returns to Grand Rapids after the war a changed man. Having seen the world, he no longer believes the United States can practice isolationist policies. He resumes his legal practice but becomes restless. Ford decides to run for Congress against the sixty-eight-year-old Republican incumbent, Bartel Jonkman, whom many consider unbeatable. The young political newcomer is zealous in his campaigning, going door-to-door to introduce himself as well as greeting workers at the end of their shifts.

Gerald Ford wins by a margin of 2–1.

The new congressman from Michigan is thirty-five and a smart man who makes friends easily. Ford is known for his strong work ethic. He is newly married to Elizabeth Bloomer, a divorcée and ex-dancer. Ford is afraid the public will disapprove of her past.

The couple eventually have four children, sons Michael, Jack, and Steven, as well as daughter Susan. Gerald Ford is a popular congressman, both in his district and in the House. He will remain there for almost a quarter century, rising to minority leader. His weakness is a fondness for

---

* Gerald Ford does not meet his biological father until he is fifteen. Leslie King Sr. comes from a wealthy family but never pays alimony, for which he is arrested in 1930. Leslie King Sr. dies in 1941 at age fifty-six. He has no contact with his son in his later years. Gerald Ford does not attend the funeral.

martinis in the evening and sometimes even a few at lunch. Distracted, the busy congressman does not notice that his wife, "Betty," is developing a substance abuse problem. After she suffers a pinched nerve in the 1960s, she begins taking pain pills. She is also fond of alcohol.

When Spiro Agnew quits in October 1973, Richard Nixon nominates Ford as the new VP under the Twenty-Fifth Amendment. He has to be confirmed by both House and Senate votes and receives unanimous Republican support and overwhelming, if not unanimous, Democratic votes.

Ten months later, Richard Nixon resigns.

On August 9, 1974, Gerald Ford becomes president of the United States.

In the White House, the president is up at 6:00 a.m. He has a quick breakfast of freshly squeezed orange juice, melon, toasted English muffins, and hot tea. Sunday is his "splurge" day, when he enjoys the morning meal with his entire family; they dine on waffles with strawberries and sour cream, as well as a single shared German apple pancake. There is no sugar bowl on the table, the president removing it as a show of support for the public, who are upset about the high prices of this commodity.

Inflation is a major problem for the Ford administration.

The president often works through the day, skipping lunch. Ford has retained much of President Nixon's cabinet, including Secretary of State Kissinger, allowing the same flow from one administration to the other.

Taking some advice, Ford stops the midday martinis. Just before 7:00 p.m., he swims for a very short time, often as little as ten minutes. The former college athlete is still fit. He is the first president to prefer alpine skiing as a form of recreation, taking the entire Ford family on winter vacations to Vail, Colorado.

The Fords usually have dinner at 8:00 p.m., a typically American meal of steak and potatoes. The president's favorite vegetable is cabbage; he also likes strawberries. Ford is in bed by midnight. He and Betty are the first White House couple in history to share the same bedroom.

The press, in general, despises Gerald Ford—particularly after the Nixon pardon. The media attacks relentlessly, calling him "Bozo the Clown"

334 ★ BILL O'REILLY AND MARTIN DUGARD

and, after he trips down the stairs of Air Force One, the "Klutz-in-Chief." When comedian Chevy Chase mocks the president's stumble on the *Saturday Night Live* television show, Ford does not take offense. Later, he appears on an episode himself, uttering the famous show opener, "Live from New York, it's Saturday night."

★★★

Vietnam returns.

It is January 1, 1975, when the communist party in Cambodia, a group known as the Khmer Rouge, attacks the capital city of Phnom Penh. This sets in motion a chain reaction throughout Southeast Asia.

Within a week, North Vietnamese forces are advancing beyond the boundaries agreed upon in the 1973 Paris Peace Accords. It becomes clear the United States will not intervene militarily, so the communists keep right on going. Ford is asked about possible reasons for sending American forces back to Vietnam and quickly says, "I cannot see any at the moment."

By the end of March, South Vietnam is almost overrun. President Ford orders that American aircraft fly orphans away from the danger. Operation Babylift is a disaster. The Air Force C-5 Galaxy transporting the first load of children crashes, killing seventy-eight of them.

The end comes on April 30, 1975. The American embassy in Saigon is surrounded. Panic ensues as civilians desperately try to board US helicopters to get out. Television captures the debacle, which deeply embarrasses the United States.

President Ford issues a comment, saying the conflict is finished as far as America is concerned.

★★★

Death comes close.

On September 22, 1975, an assassin's bullet barely misses Ford after a speech in San Francisco. Sara Jane Moore shoots at the president from forty feet away. She misses.

Moore is immediately taken into custody.[*]

---

[*] Sarah Jane Moore is sentenced to life in prison. She is released in 2007 after thirty-two years, stating, "I am very glad I did not succeed. I know now that I was wrong to try." Moore is ninety-three at the time of this writing. She lives in a secret location.

The reelection campaign of 1976 quickly approaches. Gerald Ford secures the Republican nomination over Californian Ronald Reagan in a hard-fought battle. His opponent is Georgia governor Jimmy Carter, a fifty-two-year-old southern populist. Carter wins the Democratic nomination because his competition is weak: traditional politicians like Senator Birch Bayh from Indiana and Henry M. "Scoop" Jackson from Washington State. Jackson gets his nickname from a comic strip, but America is not laughing. It is looking for new blood.

The first polling has Carter up by thirty-three points over Ford. It is clear the Nixon pardon as well as crushing inflation are hurting the incumbent.

However, the inexperienced Carter soon makes a blunder. Much of the Democratic constituency are religious citizens in the South. Jimmy Carter is a practicing Baptist. Nevertheless, he grants an interview to *Playboy* magazine, which features photographs of naked women. In the Q and A, Carter admits to having "lusted in my heart" at the sight of attractive females.

Jimmy Carter's poll numbers decline.

By Election Day, November 2, 1976, the race seems to be a draw according to most polls.

But after the ballots are cast, Carter comes out on top in a close vote. The Electoral College is 297 for Carter, 240 for Ford.

★★★

The Fords leave the White House with little money. That soon changes. They return to Grand Rapids, where the former president immediately gets into oil investments. In addition, he is appointed to a variety of corporate boards. The cash flows.

Soon, the Fords purchase a lavish home in Palm Springs, California. They also ski often in Colorado.

After defeating breast cancer while in the White House, Betty Ford also kicks her addiction to pills and alcohol, opening up the Betty Ford Center in Southern California to help others.

★★★

Gerald Ford dies on December 30, 2006. The cause of death is acute heart disease. The former president is ninety-three years old. He is buried at the Gerald R. Ford Presidential Library and Museum in Grand Rapids, Michigan.

Betty Ford expires five years later of natural causes. She is also ninety-three. Betty is laid to rest next to her husband.

In 1998, Bill O'Reilly conducted a series of interviews with Gerald Ford for *Parade* magazine. By then, the former president was enjoying his retirement but still angry his presidency was considered a failure. In extensive correspondence with O'Reilly, he cited accomplishments that prevented Cuban intervention in Angola and reduced tension between the United States and the Soviet Union. Ford's proudest moment came when Congress deregulated the nation's airlines, railroads, and trucking industries, an act that he had pushed for, leading to more competition and better prices for consumers.

"Historians generally rank presidents by what they complete while in office," Ford told O'Reilly. "Another way of assessing them is by what they *begin*. Certainly, I'm confident that economic deregulation will stand the test of time."

Gerald Ford served as president for just 895 days. His pardon of Richard Nixon overshadowed everything else. An interesting point is that Edward Kennedy, the powerful senator from Massachusetts, at first harshly criticized the pardon. But years later, in a ceremony honoring Ford, he reversed, saying it was the best thing for the country.

The record shows that Gerald Ford was a kind man and a true believer in American exceptionalism. It is difficult to find any government person who did not like him personally. Many historians, including the authors of this book, believe Ford did the right thing in burying the Watergate controversy. In 1975, America was declining economically. A Nixon show trial of that magnitude would have created tremendous turbulence and weakened the country. It is true, however, that Ford could not overcome his decision.

And a man from Plains, Georgia, took full advantage of that.

Chapter Thirty-Nine

President Jimmy Carter is packing it in.

"The President retired," reads the official White House diary of his activities. The time is fifteen minutes past midnight. But Carter makes several phone calls from the residence afterward—all filled with the worst possible news. Things have gone terribly wrong in a Middle Eastern desert, and American military forces have been killed. The debacle is another in a long line of failures for the besieged president.

At 7:00 a.m., rare for a presidential address, Jimmy Carter goes on national television. Dressed in a dark-blue suit, he looks tense. There is no preamble.

He states, "Late yesterday, I cancelled a carefully planned operation which was underway in Iran to position our rescue team for later withdrawal of American hostages, who have been held captive there since November 4. Equipment failure in the rescue helicopters made it necessary to end the mission.

"As our team was withdrawing, after my order to do so, two of our American aircraft collided on the ground following a refueling operation in a remote desert location in Iran. . . . There was no fighting; there was no combat. But to my deep regret, eight of the crewmen of the two aircraft which collided were killed."*

With that statement, the Carter administration hits a new low. Americans are suffering as oil prices have tripled, and earning power is on the decline. Overseas, the vicious Iranian leader Ayatollah Ruhollah Khomeini has humiliated America by allowing his forces to storm the US embassy and kidnap fifty-two Americans. That was 141 days ago. A ransom of $8 billion is demanded.

Today, as Carter speaks, many are blaming him for all the problems.

The president's approval rating immediately drops to 20 percent—lower than even Richard Nixon's worst numbers during the Watergate crisis.

Like Nixon, Carter will never recover.

James Earl Carter Jr. was born on October 1, 1924, in Plains, Georgia. He becomes the first president in history to be birthed in a hospital, the Wise Sanitarium, where his mother, Lillian, works as a nurse. James Sr. is a state politician who also runs a successful grocery store and peanut farm. Jimmy will one day manage this business, but first he dreams of leaving Plains and seeing the world. He attends the United States Naval Academy in Annapolis, Maryland, but graduates too late to see action in World War II. During a trip home before his last year at the academy, he renews a friendship with seventeen-year-old Rosalynn Smith, whom he also knew as a child. Like Jimmy, she is the oldest of four children.

Carter tells his mother that "she's the girl I want to marry" after their first date. The couple are wed one month after his graduation. They soon have four children.

Then, Jimmy Carter goes to sea. He finds himself at the forefront of the navy's transition to nuclear-powered submarines and is on the fast track to command. But his father's death from pancreatic cancer in 1953 puts an end to that. The future president leaves the navy, returning home to run the family enterprise.

The business thrives under Carter's tight fist. Rosalynn works full-time

---

* Desert storms, especially blowing sand, severely damaged several of the RH-53 helicopters being used in the rescue mission. At a rendezvous point known as Desert One, the decision was made to scrub the mission. During the withdrawal, one helicopter collided with a transport aircraft loaded with men and fuel. The subsequent explosion and loss of life were tremendously embarrassing to American prestige.

with her husband, helping manage accounts. Plains is a town of fewer than six hundred residents, and once again, Jimmy Carter grows restless. In 1962, he enters politics, winning a seat in the state senate. Eight years later, he is elected governor of Georgia. Carter's opposition to segregation and focus on equality for all citizens mark his progressive agenda.

In December 1974, Jimmy Carter announces his candidacy for president of the United States. At the time, it is rare for a campaign to begin so far in advance of the election. Carter believes the Democratic Party establishment is tired and stale. He will provide new energy. Both Jimmy and Rosalynn are skillful speakers, and, despite an initial lack of backing from the party, the unlikely campaign is a success.

At the Democratic Convention in New York City, Carter is nominated on the first ballot. He chooses Senator Walter F. Mondale of Minnesota as his running mate.*

The presidential election against incumbent president Gerald R. Ford makes it clear that Jimmy Carter lacks the political experience of his likeable rival. But the American public wants change from the old politics of Vietnam and Watergate. In the end, the results are close, but Carter wins by fifty-seven electoral votes.

To show his populist roots, Carter steps out of the presidential limousine on Inauguration Day and walks the parade route from the Capitol to the White House, a distance of three miles. This "man of the people" is letting America know they have elected a new breed of president.

Grits are served!

Jimmy Carter's first breakfast in the White House is a southern porridge with cheese on top. At first an oddity, foreign diplomats come to expect the dish when they visit Carter. This is not an affectation. James Earl Carter Jr. was raised on the corn dish.

The president begins each day with a wake-up call from the White House switchboard. The time varies but is never later than 6:30 a.m. He dresses, quaffs a glass of orange juice and a single cup of black coffee,

---

* Jimmy Carter never really has any formidable competition. Congressman Morris Udall from Arizona and Governor Jerry Brown from California come in second, each achieving 10 percent of the delegates. Carter chooses Mondale because he is a northerner with insider political experience in Washington.

and then goes to the Oval Office before 7:00 a.m. After a few hours of work, Carter returns to the residence to dine with the First Lady and their nine-year-old daughter, Amy.

The Carters believe in austerity, and this shows in their White House routine. The presidential yacht is sold. Jimmy and Rosalynn do not use the funds set aside by Congress for redecorating. And Amy carries her lunch to school in a brown paper bag, preferring meat loaf on white bread.

President Carter's Secret Service code name is "Deacon," befitting his Southern Baptist upbringing. He sometimes enjoys a cocktail but in keeping to the tenets of his teetotaler faith, no alcohol is served in the White House. The president is fond of physical fitness, finding time each day for swimming, running, or tennis. He is also a music lover, inviting jazz, classical, country, and rock musicians to the White House. Elvis Presley makes an appearance.

In his off hours, Carter wants to look like a regular guy, so he often wears blue jeans. The president is fluent in Spanish, a language learned in his youth as a Christian missionary. On two occasions, he delivers complete policy speeches in that language, once in Panama, the other in Cuba.

Jimmy Carter is also a micromanager who does not like to delegate. In the midst of his many presidential duties, he finds time to supervise the White House tennis courts, keeping a strict schedule of who can and *cannot* play. When asked about this, Carter originally denies it. But, later, when the press finds proof, he confesses.

President Carter is not a big vacation person. However, on April 20, 1979, he invites photographers along to chronicle a canoe paddling trip in Georgia in order to show his casual side. Suddenly, a rabbit tries to leap on board the boat, and Carter is seen beating the animal with a paddle.

Chaos ensues.

The *Washington Post* puts a picture on page one, calling the incident "Paws" as a spoof of the movie *Jaws*.

Each day, lunch, most often with Rosalynn, is served precisely at noon. The couple speak frequently throughout the day, signaling their mutually dependent relationship. Dinner is shortly after 7:00 p.m. Carter enjoys fried chicken, collard greens, and eggplant sliced thin and then fried in batter.

The president and First Lady are in bed by midnight. Like the Fords, they sleep in the same bed.

★★★

In 1977, the Carter presidency begins with a flashy show of power. He cuts funding for the new B-1 bomber and goes to war with Congress over expenditures he considers unnecessary. This costs him. The Senate and House are both in the hands of his own party, but they are not happy. Gas prices are soaring, stimulating destructive inflation.

Fairly quickly, President Carter's power begins to erode. When he attempts to pass bills for labor reform and consumer protection, they are easily defeated in Congress.

Then there are private problems. Carter's churchgoing image is shaken when his sister, evangelist Ruth Carter Stapleton, is seen holding hands with Larry Flynt, publisher of the pornographic magazine *Hustler*. Worse, the president's younger brother Billy is investigated for influence peddling. He is paid $250,000 ($1.4 million today) by the Libyan government. The First Brother benefits further from his brother's presidency by promoting his own brand of "Billy Beer." Quickly, the rotund Billy becomes a major public relations problem. At one point, he is photographed urinating on an airport runway.*

There are troubles within the Carter White House, as well. The Georgian campaigned on honesty. But his budget director, old friend Bert Lance, is forced to resign when charged with illegal business dealings prior to serving in the administration. Additionally, Carter's chief of staff, Hamilton Jordan, is seen snorting cocaine in a New York disco.†

★★★

The year 1979 is brutal for Jimmy Carter. Not a man who accepts criticism readily, he watches as the Soviet Union taunts him by invading Afghanistan. Some believe this was done because Carter failed to take action against Iran in the hostage debacle.

---

* Billy Carter dies on September 25, 1988, from pancreatic cancer at age fifty-one. Despite a profligate image, he successfully increased profits as a managing partner of the Carter family's peanut business. He was also a former United States Marine and the married father of six children.

† Hamilton Jordan is thirty-four years old when he becomes White House chief of staff in 1979. He is soon accused of doing cocaine and having sex in the famous New York disco, Studio 54. The allegations are never proven, but he resigns after one year on the job. Bert Lance of Carter's budget office is charged with abuse of funds while serving as president of the Calhoun First National Bank before working in the White House. President Carter asks for his resignation.

Now, looking at bad news almost everywhere, Jimmy Carter has few answers, even though the Speaker of the House, Democrat Tip O'Neill, calls him "the smartest public official I have ever known."

Adding to the president's problems is an increasingly hostile media. ABC News broadcaster Ted Koppel nightly reminds Americans exactly how long the hostages have been captive in Iran. Veteran CBS anchor Walter Cronkite does the same. The commentary is devastating.[*]

This is not Carter's first setback. On July 15, 1979, he addresses the nation with his "malaise" speech. At a time when America is searching for hope, President Carter uses that French word in pessimistic fashion. He tells the American people that *they* are undisciplined and need to show more confidence in his leadership.

They do not.

Carter's poll numbers plummet, never to recover.

In California, Ronald Reagan is paying close attention. The Republican candidate for the presidency in 1980 notes Jimmy Carter's pessimism. Reagan vows to run on a platform of optimism, championing the American dream.

The "malaise" speech also inspires Senator Edward Kennedy to challenge the incumbent Carter in the 1980 primaries. The younger brother of JFK and Bobby, "Teddy" Kennedy is forty-eight and a powerful voice in the Senate. As Carter flounders, Kennedy makes his move, despite the fact that he has a closet full of skeletons.

Ten years earlier, after leaving a party on the Massachusetts coastal island of Chappaquiddick, a drunken Kennedy drives his car off a low bridge into a saltwater channel. Also in the vehicle is twenty-eight-year-old Mary Jo Kopechne. Kennedy is able to get free of the car and swim to safety. Mary Jo drowns. It takes the senator *ten* hours to report the accident. Ted Kennedy is charged with leaving the scene of an accident, pleads guilty, and receives a suspended sentence. There was an inquest several months

---

[*] The hostages are held 444 days. They are freed immediately after Ronald Reagan takes office.

later and the judge does not recommend further charges. However, many believe he is directly responsible for the young woman's death.

Once he enters the presidential race, Teddy Kennedy has some explaining to do.

CBS News reporter Roger Mudd is granted a one-hour interview with the senator. Mudd is relentless, zeroing in on Chappaquiddick. In his autobiography, Kennedy remembers the moment: "Roger resumed his questions. The first had to do with Chappaquiddick. Then he asked about my marriage. My discomfort and unhappiness with the line of questioning was more than apparent on my face and in my halting answers."

After the personal grilling, Mudd looks Kennedy in the eye and asks, "Why do you want to be president?"

The senator has no cogent answer.

Jimmy Carter climbs back into the race.

It is a brawl.

Democratic National Convention. New York City. August 1980. Senator Kennedy and President Carter are in a tight contest for the nomination. Kennedy is due to give a speech on the second of the convention's four nights. His goal is to control the party platform.

Carter knows this. On the convention floor, the president's aides are so infuriated with Kennedy's team that profanity flies back and forth between the factions. Fistfights are barely averted.

"I have come here tonight not to argue as a candidate but to affirm a cause," Kennedy says when he finally takes the stage. "Someday, long after this convention, long after the signs come down and the crowds stop cheering, and the bands stop playing, may it be said of our campaign that we kept the faith. May it be said of our party in 1980 that we found our faith again."

This is a direct insult to President Carter.

Nevertheless, the arena erupts in applause, angering Carter even further.

Two nights later, the president speaks on the last night of the convention. He is stiff, monotonous. The crowd is restless. Someone sets off firecrackers during Carter's speech. The band strikes up "Happy Days Are Here Again" as he steps back from the podium. But the celebratory balloons waiting to fall from the ceiling remain stuck in place.

The crowd chants "We want Ted!" but Kennedy has already left the building. A phone call asks him to return. Finally, thirty-six minutes later, with President Carter waiting on stage, Kennedy walks out for the ritual candidate handshake.

However, before Jimmy Carter can lift Kennedy's arm with his own above their heads, the senator yanks his fist away. Jimmy Carter is embarrassed before the entire country.

The president is finished. Despite the convention calamity, Carter secures the nomination. But he is badly damaged. Carter's hold on the Democratic Party is tenuous and a majority of Americans find his one term a shambles. Jimmy Carter will be remembered for the Iran hostage situation, the failed rescue attempt, and soaring gas prices that led to long lines at the pump.

On Election Day, November 4, 1980, Republican candidate Ronald Reagan scores an overwhelming victory: 489 electoral votes to just 49 for Carter.

The landslide for Reagan surprised very few. Jimmy Carter was not prepared for the complexity of a changing world where economic success was partly dictated by oil sheiks in the Middle East.

A stubborn man surrounded by mediocre advisers, Carter failed to adjust to energy problems that spiked inflation and resulted in motorists sometimes waiting for hours to fill up their gas tanks.

President Carter's weakness quickly became apparent—so much so that his own party failed to enthusiastically support him.

The result was failure for the man from Plains.

The Georgian's postpresidential life is more successful. He is awarded the Nobel Peace Prize in 2002 for his charitable contributions. As this book is being written, Jimmy Carter is living in Georgia. He will turn one hundred by the time of its publication.

Rosalynn Carter also enjoys a long life, passing away in 2023 at the age of ninety-six. She is buried beneath a willow tree outside the family home in Plains.

★★★

So, after a short four-year sabbatical, the Republicans are back in power, flush with optimism. But little do they know that Ronald Reagan's "shining city on a hill" will not be an easy climb.*

---

* Ronald Reagan's farewell presidential address to the nation on January 11, 1989, references a quote from the Book of Matthew, comparing America to a "shining city on a hill." The comparison was first made in a sermon by Puritan minister John Winthrop in 1630.

Chapter Forty

JANUARY 20, 1985
WHITE HOUSE
NOON

Ronald Reagan is cool.

Washington is so frigid that the inaugural parade is canceled. The temperature is twenty-five degrees below zero with wind chill. Dozens of high school marching bands who traveled here from all across America are being sent home.[*]

President Reagan and the First Lady begin his second term in office with a swearing-in at the White House Entrance Hall. Nancy Reagan wears a red dress with oversized gold buttons and long false eyelashes. The president, who is already the oldest chief executive in history at seventy-three, is dressed in a dark suit and a striped red-and-blue tie. His face is smiling and lined. Chief Justice Warren Burger delivers the oath in a black robe as television cameras record the moment. More than ninety people fill the small space.

It is four years since Reagan began his presidency by triumphantly declaring the release of American hostages in Iran. The former Democrat has shocked the nation with fiscal policies not seen since Herbert Hoover, cutting government funding for entitlements while lowering

---

[*] Bill O'Reilly covered the inaugural for TV station KATU in Portland, Oregon, where he was the primary anchor.

taxes for the rich. Reagan also increases defense spending, taking a hard line against America's enemies, including the Soviet Union and Iran.

Meanwhile, an assassin nearly takes his life.*

The resilient president recovers from his gunshot wounds and now looks fit as he raises his right hand to take the oath. Nancy holds the family Bible, brown eyes upturned to watch the face of her much taller husband.

The First Lady is one of the few in this room who know the big plans Ronald Reagan has for his second term.

Very big plans.

"I, Ronald Wilson Reagan, do solemnly swear . . ."

1911. Rural Illinois. Ronald Reagan comes into the world in a small second-floor apartment above a tavern in Tampico. His mother is Nelle and his father, Jack, is a salesman. The family is descended from Irish immigrants who shortened their surname from O'Regan upon coming to America.

Jack Reagan is a drinker. The family moves often. By the time "Ronnie" is eleven, the Reagans settle in the small town of Dixon, where he attends high school. An athletic six feet one, the teenager works as a lifeguard at the Rock River Park in the summer, plays football in the fall, and is voted student body president. Ronnie is mediocre in his studies. There is little to suggest that he will one day rise to the presidency.

The first of Reagan's many careers is broadcasting. After graduating from Eureka College, his smooth speaking voice lands him radio work announcing Chicago Cubs games for station WHO in Des Moines, Iowa. The Cubs travel annually to Catalina Island, off the coast of Southern California, for spring training. Accompanying the team, Reagan visits Hollywood. On a whim, he takes a screen test for Warner Brothers. To his great surprise, he is offered a contract. For the next sixteen years, Ronald Reagan works as a movie actor, making fifty-three

---

* On March 30, 1981, John David Hinckley opened fire on Reagan with a revolver outside the Washington Hilton. The president, Secret Service agents Tim McCarthy and Tom Delahanty, and Press Secretary James Brady were all hit. Critically wounded, Brady would live for thirty-three more years but eventually die from his injuries. The authors write extensively about the attempt to assassinate the president in *Killing Reagan*.

motion pictures. He remains in Hollywood during World War II, near-sightedness making him unfit for active duty. Instead, Reagan directs training films.

Eventually, the actor begins dabbling in politics. He is elected president of the Screen Actors Guild in 1947. By this time, Reagan's marriage to famous actress Jane Wyman is coming to an end. The couple have a boy and a girl, but Jane finds her husband's new fixation on politics boring.

Yet Reagan will not quit.

Shifting from movies to television, Ronald Reagan becomes the star of a program called *Death Valley Days*. He is best known for hosting the *General Electric Theater*. Newly divorced, he takes up with young actress Nancy Davis, whom he marries in 1952. The couple have two children, Patti and Ron Jr., both of whom will be rebellious.

The truth is that Ronald Reagan is a distracted father and husband.

"There's a wall around him. He lets me come closer than anyone else, but there are times when even I feel that barrier," admits Nancy.*

Ronald Reagan is a prolabor Democrat, and Franklin Roosevelt is his political hero. But his views shift during the 1950s. In 1962, he formally registers as a Republican and, two years later, campaigns for Arizona senator Barry Goldwater's presidential run. The candidate loses, but Reagan gains important experience.

In 1966, the actor decides to run for higher office. He seeks the California governorship. This is the height of the Vietnam War, and a doctrinaire Republican like Reagan would seem to have little chance in the hippie era. But he portrays himself as a political outsider and blames incumbent opponent Pat Brown for the state's anti-war rioting and budget problems.

Ronald Reagan finds his voters.

He wins with a majority 57 percent to Brown's 42 percent.

Governor Reagan must immediately deal with a budget shortfall. So,

---

* This quote from Nancy Reagan can be found at the University of Virginia's Miller Center website, dedicated to the study of the presidency.

he violates his campaign promise by raising taxes. Most Californians let it go. Cigarettes, gasoline, liquor, and corporate profits are all levied. The deficit soon disappears.

Reagan also signs gun control and proabortion legislation, not exactly conservative positions.

He is easily reelected. Now, the presidency looms. Reagan has tried before. In 1968 and 1976, his campaigns failed. In 1980, his main rival for the nomination is George H. W. Bush, who has little support after being defeated by Jimmy Carter.

It's no contest. Ronald Reagan secures the Republican nomination on the first ballot.

The election campaign centers on the debates.

Just one week before the vote, Carter is accusing Reagan of all kinds of things. The governor just laughs. "There you go again," he states with a smile.

America gets it. Reagan wallops Carter in the popular vote and the Electoral College. He captures support from some Democrats, even winning the South, Carter's stronghold. The president's losing margin is the most by an incumbent since Herbert Hoover fell to Franklin Roosevelt almost half a century ago.

As he enters his second term, Ronald Reagan is feeling his age.

He is a late riser, arriving in the Oval Office around 9:00 a.m. Reagan always wears a coat and tie, the president believing this hallowed setting is no place for informality. He is briefed on various issues, answers letters and phone calls, and very often returns to the residence for a nap. Sometimes the late afternoon involves a scheduled "happy hour" with congressional leaders. The Democrat Speaker of the House, Tip O'Neill, is an enthusiastic attendee of these soirees.

The workday is done by 5:00 p.m., whereupon the president eats dinner in front of the television with the First Lady. Evenings are for reading paperbacks. He is fond of taking Wednesday afternoons off entirely. Friday is also a day of inactivity, with the president often flying by military helicopter to Camp David for a weekend at the Maryland retreat.

Nancy Reagan watches over her husband's schedule closely, making sure he gets rest. She has seen him falter when overworked. The president well knows that appearances matter, so he jokes about his reputation: "It's true hard work never killed anybody, but I figure why take the chance?"

The president is fond of delegating difficult tasks. Many members of his cabinet are longtime friends, such as Attorney General William French Smith and Secretary of Defense Caspar Weinberger.

The 1984 election finds President Reagan at the peak of his popularity. Inflation and taxes are down, unemployment is low, and Americans have taken to chanting "USA, USA" when the president appears in public. National pride has largely returned.

October 7, 1984, is the first presidential debate between Reagan and Democratic opponent Walter Mondale. It is a disaster for the president. He looks confused. The media begins talking openly about his advanced age.

Two weeks later, Reagan takes charge during their second verbal confrontation with a well-prepared one-liner. When asked by Henry Trewhitt of the *Baltimore Sun* if age is an issue, Reagan is ready with a snappy comeback:

"I will not make age an issue of this campaign. . . . I am not going to exploit, for political purposes, my opponent's youth and inexperience."

Reagan's lead in the polls immediately shoots up seventeen points. It never drops.

Election Day results are even more dominating than the landslide four years earlier. Reagan wins 525 to 13 in the Electoral College. He also defeats Walter Mondale in the popular vote by fifty-four million votes to thirty-seven million.

Nothing can stop Ronald Reagan.

Except, it turns out, Ronald Reagan.

★★★

The year is 1985. Year five of the Reagan presidency. The president secretly authorizes the sale of two thousand missiles to Iran in exchange for seven American hostages being held in the Middle East. The profits from the sale are then sent to an anti-communist militia in Nicaragua known as the Contras. This is illegal. Congress is never told.

The story breaks on November 3, 1986, leaked to a Lebanese magazine by a senior official in Iran's Revolutionary Guard Corps. Reagan immediately forms a committee to "investigate," saying he is not at fault.

The so-called Iran-Contra scandal dominates headlines for months. Ronald Reagan is never directly implicated, but his administration is on the defensive. The press senses blood.

It has never been easy between Ronald Reagan and the national media. Many American journalists look upon him as an inferior intellect, and his conservative beliefs have alienated more than a few liberal press people. ABC's Sam Donaldson is openly hostile to the president.

Privately, Reagan vents to his friends about how unfairly the media is treating him. In a private letter to Hollywood producer Douglas Morrow, who won an Academy Award in 1949 for his screenplay for *The Stratton Story*, Reagan excoriates the press.

> Doug, we'd go stir crazy if we couldn't escape the "gilded cage." So, you have to run the South Lawn gauntlet. Yes, a president once smuggled pretty little cocker spaniels in and out of the White House, but believe me, that can only be done as long as he's not with them. Now don't jump to a false conclusion—I'm not engaged in that sport.

> Now, let me show you what we're up against with the press. You saw the coast-to-coast firestorm—Ronald Reagan wants to tax the unemployed. No one called first to ask if it was true. They never do. . . .

> One more sample of what can only be a concerted campaign. A few weeks ago, as you know, the market dived thirty-six points in one day. . . .

> But none of the press pointed out that the thirty-six points were

from a Dow Jones of about 1040. Like Jimmy Durante, I've got a million examples of this press dishonesty.

Even Ronald Reagan's confrontation with the Soviet Union is criticized. However, in June 1987, Reagan delivers a rousing speech in Berlin. Standing outdoors before the Berlin Wall, a symbol of the Cold War
since the Kennedy administration, the president demands that Soviet
ruler Mikhail Gorbachev "tear down this wall."

And so it is that, in November 1989, Moscow unravels, as does communist Eastern Europe. The Berlin Wall is torn down by German citizens. It is a historic victory, directly because of Reagan's policies, which
are carried forth by the new president, George H. W. Bush.

Ronald Reagan leaves office on January 20, 1989. His last trip on Air
Force One is home to California with Nancy. The couple split time between Los Angeles and their longtime ranch on a mountaintop overlooking Santa Barbara, where the president likes to saddle his horse and
ride the many trails.

Reagan receives criticism for accepting a $2 million speaking offer in
Japan but otherwise keeps a low profile. The former president is focused
on overseeing the construction of his presidential library and writing his
memoirs. Life is good for the retired politician, still seen by the public as
a vigorous outdoorsman not yet eighty years old.

Thus, the nation is stunned by Ronald Reagan's November 1994 admission that he is losing his mind. Alzheimer's disease has set in. The
public sees little of him after that.

Ronald Reagan dies on June 5, 2004. His body lies in state in the US
Capitol before being returned to California for burial at his library in
Simi Valley.

Nancy Reagan follows her husband in death twelve years later. She is
buried at his side.

★★★

Ronald Reagan was not popular with every American—no president is.
But his administration was needed after twenty years of Vietnam, Watergate, and the failure of Jimmy Carter. Reagan restored faith in America

despite some dubious moments. The Iran-Contra scandal and questions about his mental acuity marred his second term, and many critics find Reagan's poor record on the environment a blemish on his record. The poor treatment of the mentally ill and homeless will be one of his strongest failures, a legacy affecting America more than ever almost four decades after Reagan left office.

The question of when the president contracted Alzheimer's will long be a subject of debate. Some believe the assassination attempt accelerated his decline while in office. Others state that Reagan did not exhibit symptoms until just before his public announcement, which generated tremendous national sympathy.[*]

Due to President Reagan's popularity, his vice president, George Herbert Walker Bush, is nominated on the first ballot in the summer of 1988. He has little competition.

The general election is similar. Bush easily defeats Massachusetts governor Michael Dukakis. The final tally is 426 electoral votes to 111.

The Republican victory was clearly an homage to President Reagan, who succeeded in reassuring the public of America's nobility and greatness. While not an insightful man, Reagan governed with a strong hand, and economic prosperity resulted. Plus, most voters liked him personally. Reagan rivals Teddy Roosevelt in that category.

As he approaches office, George H. W. Bush is facing changing times.

He is also trying to emerge from his predecessor's shadow.

That will not be an easy thing to do.

---

[*] The authors wrote about President Reagan's dementia in *Killing Reagan*. This was highly controversial. The proof was medical evidence and a White House document stating that the president's staff were prepared to invoke the Twenty-Fifth Amendment, which allows for the removal from office of a president mentally or physically unable to serve. His assassination wounds delivered a huge physical and mental blow to the president. However, this document has now gone missing from the Reagan Library archives. The existence of the memo had already been reported in the *Los Angeles Times*. Both authors stand by their reporting in *Killing Reagan*.

Chapter Forty-One

SEPTEMBER 11, 1990
HOUSE CHAMBER, US CAPITOL
9:09 P.M.

President George H. W. Bush is quickly tested.

The lanky career politician stands before a joint session of Congress. America watches on television. Tonight is the president's address on the Persian Gulf crisis. The topic on everyone's mind is war.

One month ago, Iraqi leader Saddam Hussein invaded the oil-rich nation of Kuwait. A patient Bush did not immediately react, preferring diplomacy. The brutal Saddam is gambling that the American people do not have the stomach for armed conflict and that Bush will do nothing.

The Iraqi despot is wrong.

Looking directly into the television cameras, President Bush threatens Saddam with drastic military action. There are 120,000 Iraqi troops, 850 tanks, and a variety of other weapons already in Kuwait. Bush tells Americans that Saudi Arabia is being threatened.

The president has a sound background in foreign affairs as the former director of the CIA and US ambassador to the United Nations. His administration quickly puts together a coalition to drive Saddam's forces out of Kuwait.

Operation Desert Storm features the United States, Britain, France, Saudi Arabia, Kuwait, and Egypt. In all, forty-one nations will participate. The military buildup will eventually number one million ground troops.

But on this night, Americans do not know exactly *when* the invasion will begin. In fact, it will take five months to launch.

George Herbert Walker Bush is a party man. By the time he is elected president in 1988, the sixty-four-year-old Bush has been a Republican member of Congress, the chairman of the Republican National Committee, and the vice president of the United States. He is a likeable guy, standing six feet two and speaking with a Texas twang earned from years working in the oil business. In fact, he is a native New Englander born in Massachusetts and raised in Greenwich, Connecticut. Father of five children. As he takes office, the president has been married forty-four years to the former Barbara Pierce, a distant cousin of President Franklin Pierce.

The Bush family is a political dynasty equal to that of the Kennedys, but far more low-key. "Poppy," as the president is called, is the patriarch.

The future chief executive comes into the world on June 12, 1924, in Milton, Massachusetts. His family has money. His father, Preston Bush, is a banker who will one day sit in the United States Senate. His paternal grandfather is a wealthy Connecticut industrialist, and his mother's family has accumulated millions of dollars on Wall Street.

Young George follows the path expected of Bush offspring, attending prep school at Phillips Academy Andover. He is a popular young man, elected president of his senior class in addition to serving as captain of the baseball and soccer teams. During a country club Christmas dance, George meets sixteen-year-old Barbara, home for the break from her own boarding school in South Carolina. The band is playing upbeat Glenn Miller dance tunes, but when he asks her to join him on the floor, the music abruptly switches to a slow waltz. Neither one knowing that dance, they choose to talk instead.

The two keep in touch when the night is through. A year and a half later, George Bush and Barbara Pierce are engaged.

By now, however, George Herbert Walker Bush is deviating from the family script. In 1942, he graduates from Andover on his eighteenth birthday. But instead of beginning college studies at Yale, he enlists in the navy. World War II has begun. Bush attends flight school in North Carolina and is commissioned as an aviator—one of the youngest in the navy. He soon sees action in the Pacific as the pilot of a torpedo bomber, launching off the aircraft carrier USS *San Jacinto*.

Bush is determined to be one of the guys. But it is well known by his fellow fliers that the young pilot comes from a prestigious background. Rather than give him a typical one-word flight nickname, the airmen poke fun at his blue-blooded roots, insisting he be addressed as "George Herbert Walker Bush" at all times.

On September 2, 1944, Bush is shot down off Chi Chi Jima, an island five hundred miles south of the Japanese mainland. He bails out of the flaming dive bomber and floats on a small life raft in the Pacific Ocean. A few hours later, he is rescued by the American submarine USS *Finback*. It is not lost on Bush that he is extremely lucky. His radioman is dead, parachute failing to open. Three dive bombers in Bush's attack formation have also been shot down, their crews captured, tortured, and then executed.*

George Bush flies fifty-eight combat missions in the South Pacific before he is reassigned to Norfolk, Virginia, as a training officer. Two weeks after returning to the United States, he and Barbara are married. One year later, they have their first child, also named George.

His wartime service complete, the decorated World War II hero attends Yale—a family tradition. He graduates two years later, deciding to try his luck in the oil business. He drives a Studebaker from New England to Texas. In Abilene, he eats his first chicken-fried steak, not knowing what he is ordering—though it soon becomes his favorite meal. Starting as an equipment salesman, Bush is running his own company within five years. After five years, the family grows. Son George is followed by Robin, Jeb, Neil, Marvin, and Dorothy. Robin is only three when she dies from leukemia.

The Bushes settle in Houston. As the son of a senator and now a wealthy oilman, George H. W. Bush is seen by many as a potential political candidate. He is wooed by the Democrats but chooses to run for a

---

*As a show of gratitude for his rescue, Bush gives his service revolver to an officer on the *Finback*, Lieutenant Albert Brostrom. Sixty years later, the Brostrom family return the handgun to Bush. It now resides at the National Constitution Center in Philadelphia.

Texas senate seat as a Republican. He loses. But, two years later, he wins a US congressional race.

For the next twenty years, as the influence of the Republican Party rises and falls, George Bush never wavers in his loyalty. It is Nixon who selects Bush as the United Nations ambassador and then chairman of the Republican National Committee. After that, President Ford asks Bush to serve as special envoy to China before naming him head of the CIA. In 1980, Ronald Reagan selects him as vice president. Bush is shocked, having mocked Reagan's fiscal policies as "voodoo economics." The two men are not close. But Bush takes the job.

The year 1988 is George Bush's best chance to be president. He easily wins the Republican nomination against Senator Bob Dole of Kansas, then gives a rousing speech at the convention in New Orleans. Often referred to as his "thousand points of light" address, the candidate talks about patriotism. He also makes a promise that brings the audience to their feet:

"The Congress will push me to raise taxes, and I'll say no. And they'll push, and I'll say no. And they'll push again, and all I can say to them is: Read my lips. No new taxes."

It is a statement the future president will regret.

Bush's vice presidential choice is Dan Quayle, a forty-one-year-old senator from Indiana. Quayle's record in the Senate is unremarkable, but Bush chooses him for his youth and his popularity in the Midwest. The two go on to trounce Michael Dukakis and Geraldine Ferraro, the first woman nominated as vice president.*

On June 26, 1990, President Bush shockingly breaks his promise on taxes. The White House releases a statement that levies must be increased. The budget deficit has ballooned due to major military spending by the Reagan administration.

It doesn't take long for the American public to react. President Bush's approval rating drops close to 50 percent, falling even further when Saddam Hussein invades Kuwait on August 2. These are dangerous

---

* President Reagan does not campaign much for Bush, with some believing Nancy Reagan vetoed that. In fact, after George Bush stated that he wants a "kinder, gentler nation," Nancy replies, "Kinder and gentler than who?"

numbers for a man seeking reelection. But that is two years away. There seems to be plenty of time to make the American people forget the broken tax promise.

On February 24, 1991, America goes to war.

Television cameras capture an amazing show of force in the Middle East.

Highway 80, the main road connecting the Iraqi capital of Baghdad to Kuwait, is bombed for ten hours straight as Iraqi soldiers try to flee. Saddam's army is pulverized on the so-called Highway of Death. The killing is so easy that Iraq claims it is a massacre. So, President Bush orders the bombings to cease for humanitarian reasons, allowing the Iraqi army to flee home—ready to fight another day.*

On February 27, 1991, victory is declared.

President George Herbert Walker Bush's approval rating shoots to 89 percent, the highest in the history of the Gallup poll.

The 1992 presidential election is just one year away.†

Life in the George H. W. Bush White House is lively. The president is an active man, sometimes slipping out of the Oval Office for an afternoon jog with reporters. In the summer, he often visits the family compound in Kennebunkport, Maine, where he pilots a speedboat instead of a sailboat, which is much too slow for his liking.

At mealtime, the president does not enjoy health food. When the White House kitchen serves yogurt with breakfast instead of chipped beef on toast, Bush is known to add a candy bar for flavor.

More famously, the president dislikes a certain vegetable: broccoli. "I haven't liked it since I was a little kid and my mother made me eat it and I'm President of the United States and I'm not going to eat any more broccoli," the *Los Angeles Times* reports.

---

* Approximately one hundred thousand Iraqi troops survive—many of them to fight the United States again thirteen years later.

† Bill O'Reilly covered the aftermath of Operation Desert Storm for *Inside Edition*. He was based in Kuwait.

By 1990, the world is experiencing upheaval. President Bush oversees the end of the Cold War, strengthens relations with the Soviet Union, oversees the arrest of Panamanian strongman Manuel Noriega for narcotics trafficking, and oversees the reunification of Germany.

But the economy is challenging. Just months after the Gulf War, America is hit by a sharp recession. Gas prices go up. More than one thousand banks close. It is the most intense financial meltdown since the Great Depression.

That leads to big trouble. A flamboyant Texas billionaire, Ross Perot, launches a third-party challenge, attacking the president's policies.

On the Democratic front, Arkansas governor Bill Clinton is pounding home one simple message: "It's the economy, stupid."

Domestic matters grow worse when four Los Angeles police officers are acquitted of brutally beating a black man named Rodney King after a traffic stop. The nation's second-largest city erupts in racial violence and looting. Television cameras quickly capture the chaos, which is beamed around the world.

As events spiral out of control, Bush's opponents blame him for the racial discord.

The Bush campaign never recovers.

Bill Clinton wins the election with nearly forty-five million popular votes. President Bush receives thirty-nine million, undone by the nineteen million ballots Ross Perot earns.

★★★

George Bush enjoys life after leaving office. He and Barbara revel in their oldest son, George W. Bush, winning the presidency in 2000 and again in 2004. Second son Jeb is elected governor of Florida. Bush the Elder, as the former president becomes known, never loses his adventurous streak. The former pilot skydives in celebration of his seventh-fifth, eightieth, eighty-fifth, and ninetieth birthdays. By the time he dies from Parkinson's disease on November 30, 2018, Bush is ninety-four—at the time the oldest president in American history.

Barbara Bush passes of congestive heart failure and lung issues in April of the same year. The couple are buried at the George H. W. Bush Presidential Library in College Station, Texas. Their daughter Robin lies with her parents.

Many consider George H. W. Bush to be the best one-term president in American history. Those who worked with him speak of Bush as an honorable, hardworking man, without the deviousness of many politicians. He is largely successful during his time in office and beloved by his family and friends. In the end, the economy does him in, leading to Democrats taking the White House for the first time since Jimmy Carter.*

Bush the Elder was defeated by Ross Perot's third-party insurgency and Bill Clinton's charisma. While clearly a patriot, Bush lacked a "common touch"—that is, many Americans did not strongly identify with his presidency as they did with Reagan's. With workers struggling economically, Bush was viewed as dispensable. His achievements in office are largely forgotten.

Thus, the patrician Bush gives way to a youthful southern politician who, on the surface, mirrors Jimmy Carter.

But beneath the veneer, strange things are about to occur.

---

* The authors of this book believe James K. Polk was the most effective one-term president.

Chapter Forty-Two

Bill Clinton is exhausted. The last inaugural ball ended just a few minutes ago, and the gregarious new president stayed until the very end.

It has been an incredible journey for the man born William Jefferson Blythe III. Now, as quiet and darkness envelop the White House, he is surrounded by walls of portraits featuring past presidents and patriots. Looking down on the forty-six-year-old former Arkansas governor is one man with whom he has much in common: President Andrew Johnson.*

Both southerners overcome enormous odds to achieve the pinnacle of power. Their fathers die young, leaving young mothers to support the family. Johnson is actually sold into indentured servitude at age fourteen. Unable to read or write, he trains as a tailor.

Clinton performs well in school but has to deal with domestic chaos as his mother is a fervent gambler and has a number of relationships with men.

Both Clinton and Johnson idolize former presidents. For Johnson, it's Andrew Jackson, while Clinton emulates JFK.

The fact that both these men overcome their backgrounds speaks to the validity of the American dream.

---

* Eliphalet Frazer Andrews painted Johnson's image in 1880. There is a portrait of each president hanging in the White House. It is up to the current president to decide in which room each painting will hang; thus, portraits are moved based on the whim of the current White House resident.

William Jefferson Clinton's first day as president includes the swearing-in, the inaugural parade, and an evening of parties. It's a time of shaking hands with little personal space. Clinton is due in the Oval Office by 9:00 a.m., six hours from now. Yet these first moments in the White House are not to be rushed.

★★★

Bill Clinton's father, William Jefferson Blythe Jr., is a bigamist. The traveling salesman is only twenty-eight but already has had four wives as he marries girlfriend Virginia Dell Cassidy. Blythe's most recent divorce is not finalized, giving him two wives at the same time. But the matter is settled by the time he returns from a stint in the army during World War II. William and Virginia make plans to move to Chicago from their home in Hope, Arkansas. However, she gets pregnant. Three months before she gives birth, William Blythe is killed in a car crash.

His son is born on August 19, 1946.

Three years later, Virginia remarries a man named Roger Clinton, who owns an auto dealership in nearby Hot Springs. Young Bill takes his new father's name. Roger is a gambler and alcoholic who beats his wife. When Bill Clinton is a teenager and reaches his full height of six feet two, he physically confronts his stepfather, stopping the abuse. By then, the teen is planning a career as a saxophone player, intent on devoting his life to music. But he soon realizes his limitations, deciding his gift for public speaking could make him a great politician. The following year, he visits the White House with a youth group known as Boys Nation, and he shakes hands with President John F. Kennedy.

This is not an accident. From the minute his group gets off the bus to hear the president speak, Clinton pushes to the front of the line. He makes sure to be seated in the front row. As soon as JFK finishes, the teenager presses forward, becoming the first to shake the president's hand.

Later, on that same trip to Washington, Clinton lunches with Arkansas senator William Fulbright, an event set up by the group. Fulbright takes to the young man and will be a great help to him in the future.

★★★

When it comes time for college, Bill Clinton is so intent on living in Washington that he applies only to Georgetown University. He is fourth in his high school class, but money is scarce. Fortunately, he is granted several scholarships. In addition, Clinton works part-time in Senator Fulbright's Washington office. He gets to know Capitol Hill, running errands for the senator.

Bill Clinton's outgoing demeanor helps him make friends quickly, and his southern accent sets him apart from the typical Georgetown student. He pledges a fraternity, is elected class president, and spends one summer working on his first political campaign—a good friend's father is running for Arkansas governor. Judge Frank Holt does not win, but Clinton's ability to speak with emotion and articulate issues is noticed. He takes up running to improve his physical appearance. Returning to Washington, he works for the Red Cross, delivering food and other supplies to areas of the city torn by rioting after the assassination of Dr. Martin Luther King Jr.

After graduation, he again works in Senator Fulbright's office. That stint is interrupted when he is chosen to attend Oxford University on a Rhodes scholarship. The year is 1968. Fighting in Vietnam is intensifying. The young student engages in anti-war protests in England. He grows a beard and wears his hair long. Clinton is eligible to be drafted into the US Army. He takes the military physical and is declared fit. On April 30, 1969, while studying at Oxford, Clinton receives news from his Arkansas draft board that he may have to serve. This troubles the future politician. He is protesting against the war but also knows that if he does not honor his service, his future political career might be affected.

So, returning home to Arkansas after his first year at Oxford, Clinton joins the Reserve Officer Training Corps at the University of Arkansas Law School. This is considered an appropriate means to prepare for the military. But as he returns to England for his year as a Rhodes scholar, Clinton continues to protest the war. He then writes home to the ROTC program, stating that he will *not* be joining after all. The Vietnam War ends. Clinton is not drafted.*

For a time, it appears the matter is settled.

---

* The Rhodes scholarship was established in 1902 by British colonialist Cecil Rhodes. Though the award is often given to individuals excelling in academics and athletics, the focus is on "literary and scholastic" achievements. This helped Clinton, who had little interest in sports. Each year, thirty-two such scholarships are awarded in America, providing the winner with two years at Oxford.

364 BILL O'REILLY AND MARTIN DUGARD

However, in 1992, Clinton's letter to the ROTC is leaked to ABC News. The candidate for president will be labeled a "draft dodger" for not serving in Vietnam.

In 1970, Clinton begins at Yale Law School. He does well academically and socially. In an example of the intense focus Bill Clinton applies when pursuing a topic, he completes his classwork before the end of the first semester.

Then there is romance.

"One day in the spring of 1971," Clinton will later tell the story, "I met a girl. The first time I saw her, we were in a class on political and civil rights. She had thick blond hair. Big glasses. Wore no makeup. And she exuded this sense of strength."

Clinton follows her out of the class, hoping to introduce himself. For once, he is tongue-tied. It is not until a week later in the law library that she marches up to him and introduces herself. "If you're going to keep staring at me, we might as well know each other's names," she says.

"I'm Hillary Rodham."

She is his intellectual equal, an outspoken former Republican and daughter of a Chicago businessman. Hillary was a "Goldwater Girl" in 1964, supporting the Republican presidential nominee. But Hillary Rodham is fascinated by Bill Clinton and has no qualms about following him home to Arkansas after they graduate from Yale.

The couple are married in 1975.

Meanwhile, Bill Clinton is planning his political future. With impressive academic credentials, he is elected Arkansas attorney general in 1976. In 1978, he wins the governorship at the age of just thirty-two. Hillary gives birth to a daughter, Chelsea, the following year. The "Young Governor," as Clinton is known, is voted out after a single two-year term. This is because he has developed another nickname: "Slick Willie." In his desire to advance his political career, Clinton too often makes political deals with the wealthy and powerful rather than staying true to his populist agenda.

Bill Clinton learns from this mistake.

He runs again in the following gubernatorial election, winning back his job and spending the next ten years leading Arkansas.

But soon, power and temptation overwhelm Bill Clinton. Rumors of infidelity are emerging. Arkansas state troopers will later testify that Clinton ordered them to find women for him, arrange assignations in hotel rooms, and even keep watch outside as he engaged in sex. But those accusations have not yet been made public when Clinton first runs for president in 1992.

The run-up to the campaign begins in 1985, when Governor Clinton is chosen to give the Democratic response to President Reagan's State of the Union address. In addition, Clinton joins the Democratic Leadership Council, "a politically moderate group which touts a 'Third Way,'" devoting much time to national politics. His party profile grows quickly.

In late 1991, Governor Clinton tells Arkansans he will seek the presidency. He begins traveling the country, raising money and his public profile. But then a roadblock. In 1992, an Arkansas state employee and singer named Gennifer Flowers accuses Clinton of having an affair with her. She has proof in the form of audiotapes. This is a disaster.

The Clinton campaign quickly arranges for Bill and Hillary to appear on *60 Minutes*. They insist that their marriage is strong. The candidate admits he has hurt their union. The episode is aired immediately after the Super Bowl, giving the Clintons an enormous national audience. Rather than condemning Bill Clinton, as the nation did to fellow Democrat Gary Hart four years earlier, some voters feel sympathy for the couple.*

Almost immediately, Clinton slingshots upward in the polls. His rivals, Paul Tsongas of Massachusetts and Iowa senator Tom Harkin, are left behind as Clinton sweeps primary after primary.

At the Democratic Convention in New York City, Clinton gets the

---

* Senator Gary Hart of Colorado withdrew from the 1988 presidential race on May 7 when it was reported that he had extramarital affairs, among them twenty-nine-year-old pharmaceutical representative and beauty pageant winner Donna Rice, with whom he spent time aboard a boat known as *Monkey Business*.

nomination on the first ballot. For his running mate, he chooses a man very much like himself: southern, politically moderate Al Gore, a senator from Tennessee. Gore was born into wealth, the son of a US senator. But their wattage promises a countermeasure to aging Republicans Ronald Reagan and George H. W. Bush.

In the presidential race, Bill Clinton and Al Gore run from the center, appealing to voters who once supported Reagan and Bush. Clinton also speaks out openly against the rise in deaths due to the AIDS virus, an epidemic that many religious Republicans avoid discussing publicly.

Most of all, it is the economy that looms over the election. The incumbent, George Bush, is now suspect because of rising inflation, taxes, and unemployment.

The Clinton-Gore ticket wins easily. Optimism reigns in the Democratic Party as it takes power after twelve years of Republicans in the White House. At age forty-six, the man from Hope, Arkansas, is now in charge.

Bill Clinton is undisciplined.

During the 1992 presidential campaign, America watches the transformation as he gains thirty pounds. The public sees their chubby president-elect's fast-food cravings, dropping in at McDonald's for a spontaneous Egg McMuffin breakfast. He is often photographed eating donuts. Clinton is also known for consuming endless cans of Diet Coke. He openly admits a fondness for enchiladas and jalapeño cheeseburgers.

Now in the White House, the presidential staff see this lack of discipline. The new president often loses his temper and refuses to follow a daily schedule. He arrives in the Oval Office by 9:00 a.m. and then often becomes sidetracked, falling hours behind. Clinton rarely leaves the "Oval" during the workday. When he does finally return to the residence, he reads books and does crossword puzzles. The First Couple share the presidential bedroom, but he often sleeps down the hall due to his fondness for staying up well past midnight.

First Lady Hillary Clinton has a calendar full of speeches, travel, and diplomatic functions. Her schedule is dictated by these events, but on those evenings when she gets to relax in the residence, Hillary's preference is to unwind by watching television. The First Couple are often separated for days at a time, unlike the Carters, Reagans, Bushes, and Fords.

Bill Clinton will admit in his autobiography that he leads parallel lives. The wild Clinton enjoys playing the saxophone and once smoked marijuana (but "did not inhale," as he qualifies the confession). The other is a policy wonk who spends hours reading every page of complicated legislation. Political consultant Dick Morris, who has known the Clintons since the president's time as Arkansas governor, calls these two halves "Saturday Night Bill" and "Sunday Morning Bill."*

President Clinton's first one hundred days in office are troubling. His initial two choices for attorney general have to resign due to hiring undocumented nannies. He attempts to encourage acceptance of homosexuality in the military, but public opposition leads to a watered-down policy known as "don't ask—don't tell."

During the campaign, Bill Clinton promises a middle-class tax cut, but one month after taking office, he announces a *higher* levy to close the budget deficit.

Two months later, Attorney General Janet Reno orders the use of force against a cult in Waco, Texas. The resulting shoot-out leaves seventy-five dead, including twenty-four children.†

The lurid headlines continue. White House counsel Vince Foster, who once worked with Hillary at the Rose Law Firm in Little Rock, is found dead of a self-inflicted gunshot wound.

Another death strikes Hillary even harder. Her father, Hugh Rodham, dies from a stroke.

The First Lady is devastated. Throwing herself into work does not help. Bill Clinton once promised the nation that he and Hillary would work together, the American public getting an offer to "buy one, get one

---

* Bill Clinton hires Morris to help prepare for the 1996 reelection campaign. Morris resigns in 1996 after he admits to allowing a prostitute to listen in on calls from the White House.

† The FBI lay siege to a compound belonging to the Branch Davidian religious cult. Their members were known to be stockpiling arms and ammunition. On April 19, 1993, the fifty-one-day siege comes to an end when federal officials enter the compound and a gun battle ensues, resulting in many deaths.

free." But the First Lady's popularity is in steep decline as many consider her distant and controlling.

So, when Hillary Clinton spearheads the Task Force on National Health Care Reform, the plan gains little traction. America does not want "two presidents."

Six months after taking office, President Clinton's job approval rating is 36 percent.

In July 1994, the White House finally settles down as Clinton hires Leon Panetta to serve as chief of staff. The former congressman enforces discipline on the Oval Office. Achievements in foreign and domestic policy soon give Clinton a new respect among the public. His approval rating rises to 64 percent.*

But there is a specter looming. Even as the president's foreign and domestic policies succeed, a new scandal emerges. An Arkansas state employee named Paula Jones files a sexual harassment lawsuit, claiming that state police officers took her to Clinton's hotel room in 1991, where he initiated unwanted activity.

Clinton denies the accusation.

In addition, evidence points to Vince Foster's involvement in a failed real estate development known as Whitewater. The Clintons are also investors. Shortly after Foster's suicide, documents related to the company are removed from his safe and brought to Hillary Clinton's office with no explanation.

A special investigator named Kenneth Starr is brought in by Attorney General Reno to look into the issue. Starr quickly expands his powers by digging into *all* aspects of the Clintons' lives.†

Starr is a Republican. He was appointed to serve as a federal judge by Ronald Reagan and as solicitor general for George H. W. Bush. As Starr's investigation into Whitewater deepens, he becomes a threat—determined to get to the root of President Clinton's tangled affairs. With Republicans controlling the House and Senate, there is no effort to rein Starr in.

---

* Among Clinton's successes was passing the North American Free Trade Agreement (NAFTA) and brokering peace in Northern Ireland.

† On October 10, 1997, Kenneth Starr released a report concluding that Vince Foster's death was a suicide.

Then comes 1996. There are now three twenty-four-hour cable television networks feeding information to the American people. Special prosecutor Starr is getting massive attention. Despite that, Bill Clinton wins reelection by an Electoral College margin of 379–159 over Republican senator Bob Dole.*

★★★

On January 17, 1998, an internet journalist named Matt Drudge breaks a shocking story. A twenty-two-year-old White House intern named Monica Lewinsky allegedly has engaged in sexual acts with the fifty-one-year-old President Clinton in the Oval Office. "Going to the Diet Coke room" is their euphemism for a tryst.

Almost instantly, the sensational tale becomes a worldwide scandal. On January 26, 1998, President Clinton addresses the nation on television, saying, "I did not have sexual relations with that woman." His acolytes in the media aggressively defend him. The country is in an uproar.

Then comes the evidence. A blue dress worn by Monica Lewinsky is produced by her friend, Linda Tripp. The stains on the dress prove her interactions with President Clinton. Based on this evidence, Kenneth Starr has enough to charge the president with perjury.

Congress almost immediately begins impeachment proceedings against William Jefferson Clinton. On October 8, 1988, the House votes in favor of an impeachment inquiry, 258–176; 31 Democrats desert the president.

On December 19, 1998, two articles of impeachment are approved, the House of Representatives voting 228–206 for one article to impeach Clinton on grounds of perjury to a grand jury. The House also approves by a vote of 221–212 a second article of impeachment of obstruction of justice.

But after a five-week Senate trial, the majority in that body votes to acquit a perjury charge, 55–45. The vote for obstruction of justice is 50–50. Since two-thirds of the Senate is needed to expel a sitting president, Bill Clinton survives.

---

* Clinton's first term ended with a conservative turn. He signed a law mandating work requirements for those seeking welfare. Also, he supported the Defense of Marriage Act, which banned nuptials between homosexuals.

The "Lewinsky affair" looms over the final years of the Clinton admin-istration. Bill and Hillary have difficulty in private, but in public, she stands by her man.

Their daughter, Chelsea, attending Stanford University, is spared much of the chaos that is taking place in the White House. Secret Ser-vice agents protect her at the height of the scandal, most chosen for their youthful appearance so they can blend in on campus.

Things calm. The final phase of Clinton's presidency produces budget surpluses and a vibrant economy.

As the 2000 presidential election emerges, Bill Clinton's approval rating rises to 70 percent. But that doesn't matter to Vice President Al Gore, who wins the Democratic nomination. He does not ask Clinton to campaign on his behalf. The reason: his wife, Tipper Gore, is still furious about the Lewinsky scandal. The Gores' oldest daughter is the same age as the intern. Supporting his spouse, the vice president distances himself from the president.

That proves to be a political mistake. Al Gore loses the election to George W. Bush by the ultraslim margin of 271–266. Florida's twenty-five electoral votes make the difference. The race in that state is so close that a recount is ordered. Before the process is complete, Florida's attorney general rules that Bush is the winner. The Supreme Court upholds the Florida ruling.*

★★★

William Jefferson Clinton leaves the presidency at the age of fifty-four. He has spent his entire adult life in politics. Clinton then devotes himself to writing his memoirs and overseeing the building of his presidential library in Little Rock. He grows his wealth to tens of millions of dollars through corporate speeches, book deals, and business consulting. Clin-ton is never far from the public eye, weighing in on world events ranging from war to climate change.

---

* In his concession speech on December 13, 2000, Al Gore says that, while he disagrees with the Su-preme Court ruling, he will stand aside, "for the sake of unity . . . and the strength of our democracy."

In 2004, the former president undergoes quadruple bypass surgery. One year later, he suffers a collapsed lung. He subsequently undergoes further heart treatment in 2010, leading the former fast-food junkie to adopt a strict vegan diet.

In 2008, Hillary Clinton, then a US senator from New York, campaigns for president against Democratic senator Barack Obama. Bill Clinton gets involved. He raises $10 million for her campaign. She loses. But a short time later, it is Bill Clinton who gives a speech at the Democratic National Convention in praise of Barack Obama.[*]

When Hillary Clinton runs again in 2016, her husband plays a lesser role. In a bitter campaign, she loses to New York businessman Donald J. Trump.

As of this writing, Bill and Hillary Clinton reside in Chappaqua, New York, and Washington, DC. They are often apart.

Bill Clinton's presidency was remarkable in many ways. Unemployment dropped to post–World War II levels, and inflation was the lowest in thirty years.

But impeachment overwhelmed President Clinton. Thus, his accomplishments are shrouded by his dubious personal conduct.

Clinton's successor was also a rambunctious young man. However, by the time George W. Bush takes office, he has learned hard lessons about the importance of appearances.

But that will not matter very much for Bush the Younger. The coming war on terror will totally consume his administration.

---

[*] That surprised many people as Bill Clinton criticized Obama on the campaign trail, saying that his record in the Senate "is the biggest fairy tale I've ever seen."

Chapter Forty-Three

SEPTEMBER 11, 2001
EMMA E. BOOKER ELEMENTARY SCHOOL
SARASOTA, FLORIDA
9:05 A.M.

President George W. Bush is about to be crushed.

He reads a book called *The Pet Goat* to a group of seven-year-old schoolchildren as part of a White House campaign to encourage learning. The president sits on a chair in front of the room, legs crossed. He wears a suit and a red tie. Second-grade teacher Sandra Kay Daniels is next to him.

Without a prompt, White House chief of staff Andrew Card approaches, his face grave. He leans down and whispers that America is under attack. George W. Bush, father of two daughters, makes the instant choice to pretend as if nothing is amiss.

"I made the decision not to jump up immediately and leave the classroom. I didn't want to rattle the kids. I wanted to project a sense of calm," Bush will remember.

In New York City, on a morning with a clear blue sky, terrorists fly two hijacked airliners into the North and South Towers of the World Trade Center buildings. There are other planes missing.

The president quickly wraps up his read and heads to the airport.

★★★

Twenty-three minutes later, another plane explodes upon impacting the Pentagon. Then, a fourth plane, Flight 93, signals distress.

By 9:45, all US airspace is closed, with thousands of planes ordered to land immediately.

At 9:59, the South Tower of the World Trade Center collapses.

At 10:02, Flight 93 crashes into a Pennsylvania field, brought down by passengers fighting back against the hijackers. All aboard are killed.

At 10:28, the North Tower collapses.

Arriving back in Washington, President Bush prepares to address the nation. He does that at 8:05 p.m.

"Today, our fellow citizens, our way of life, our very freedom came under attack in a series of deliberate and deadly terrorist acts. . . . The pictures of airplanes flying into buildings, fires burning, huge structures collapsing, have filled us with disbelief, terrible sadness, and a quiet, unyielding anger. These acts of mass murder were intended to frighten our nation into chaos and retreat. But they have failed.

"Our country is strong."

The murders are the work of a terrorist named Osama bin Laden. At this point, Bush has been president for eight months. Unbeknownst to him, the events of 9/11 will define his entire time in office. One month from now, the hunt for the elusive bin Laden will lead Bush to invade Afghanistan.

This begins a war that will last for twenty years.

As fear mounts, the Bush administration attempts to formulate an effective anti-terror policy. That will prove an extremely difficult task, one that no political figure could have anticipated.

George Walker Bush talks like a Texan. "Georgie" was born on July 6, 1946, coming into the world in New Haven, Connecticut, home to Yale University, where both his father and grandfather graduated.

The Bush family moves to Odessa, Texas, when he is two. All pretense at wealth is suspended as George H. W. Bush forges a career in the oil business. Money is tight because of the Bush mandate that each male in the family must make their own way. The Bushes live in an apartment complex so small they share a communal bathroom with local prostitutes.

Work takes the patriarch, George H. W. Bush, to California, then back to Texas, finally settling in Midland.

There, young George grows up playing Little League and attending Sam Houston Middle School. His sister Robin is born in 1949, but she dies of leukemia in 1953, a loss that forever affects her older brother. Not told of his sister's illness until she is already dead, the devastated seven-year-old becomes extremely protective of his mother.

As expected of young men in the Bush family, George W. attends boarding school at Andover and goes on to Yale. He is popular, fond of history and drinking beer. He plays rugby. For a time, George is engaged to a young woman named Cathryn Wolfman, a junior majoring in economics at Rice University. The *Houston Chronicle*'s society column announces their pending nuptials, but the couple soon break it off.

Later, Cathy Young, her married name, will remember George fondly, discounting stories that he was a hard-living hellion. "If he had wild days, they weren't with me," she will tell reporters.

Graduating Yale in 1968, George W. Bush faces Vietnam. He is likely to be drafted and sent to fight. Given his father's distinguished war record, avoiding the military is out of the question.

So, Bush does as his father did—trains to become a pilot. Later, he will be criticized for joining the Texas Air National Guard because he avoids combat. But Bush fulfills his service, attending flight training at Moody Air Force Base in Georgia and serving out his commitment before going to graduate school. He receives a master's degree in business administration from Harvard University.

From there it is back to Midland, where Bush takes a low-level job in the oil business. It is during this time in the mid-1970s that he meets young librarian Laura Welch. She is a pretty, five-foot-five brunette with a past. Two days after her seventeenth birthday, she runs a stop sign and kills another driver. By great coincidence, the victim is her former boyfriend. Laura is not charged in the incident.

George W. Bush has his own problems behind the wheel. On Labor Day weekend in 1976, one year before meeting Laura, he is arrested for driving under the influence near the family vacation home in Maine.

In addition, Bush faces a disorderly conduct charge at the age of twenty when he stole a Christmas wreath as part of a college prank. That charge is later dropped.

In Maine, his license is temporarily suspended, but the incident will not be made public for twenty-four years.

The first date between George and Laura is miniature golf. He is fond of parties, while she enjoys a good book. The couple make a quick connection. Three months later, they are married at the First United Methodist Church in Midland, with Laura choosing to wear a light-brown dress bought off the rack.

The next year, George W. Bush decides it is time to enter politics. He promises the shy Laura that she will never have to make a campaign speech, a vow he soon breaks. Those who know Bush are surprised he is such a natural candidate. "He loved it, and he was having a great time. My shock was that he was such a good speaker," longtime friend Doug Hannah will state. "I started to notice he sounded just like his father—if you closed your eyes, you heard his father."

In 1978, Bush decides to run for Congress from the Nineteenth District in northwest Texas. His top adviser in that first campaign is a young political strategist named Karl Rove, with whom he begins a lifelong friendship.

Bush loses. He then goes to work on his father's election campaigns. After that, it's back to the private sector, trying to increase his wealth before reentering politics.

Georgie is successful.

Armed with cash, George W. Bush purchases the Texas Rangers baseball team with a group of investors, instantly gaining widespread name recognition in the state. He tells friends that his dream job is to become the commissioner of Major League Baseball.

In 1994, Bush runs for the Texas governorship. Coincidentally, his brother Jeb is campaigning for governor of Florida. He will lose, but then win in 1998—and again in 2002.

However, George W.'s campaign descends into the mud. His advisers imply that opponent and incumbent governor Ann Richards is a lesbian. Bush wins by a 53–46 percentage.

Meanwhile, things change on the home front. He and Laura have twin daughters, Jenna and Barbara, born in 1981 with the help of fertility drugs. The babies keep Laura busy, even as her husband is out politicking and socializing.

That becomes a problem.

The morning after celebrating his fortieth birthday at the Broadmoor Hotel in Colorado Springs, Bush finds himself too ill from a night of drinking to make it through his daily three-mile run.

Laura Bush has had enough: "It's either Jim Beam or me."

George W. Bush quits drinking that day.

The future president also embraces religion. An encounter with the Reverend Billy Graham leads Bush to begin attending Bible studies. "My problem was not only drinking; it was selfishness," he will write. "The booze was leading me to put myself ahead of others, especially my family . . . faith showed me a way out."

After six years of being governor, national politics loom. The Clinton administration alienates many conservatives, including the Bush family. After strategizing with his father, mother, and brother Jeb, George W. decides to emulate John Quincy Adams.

A son following his father into the presidency.

Bush and his top adviser, Karl Rove, believe they can defeat Al Gore. With his extremely high profile, the governor soon finds himself the favorite for the Republican nomination. His main opponent is Senator John McCain of Arizona. The Republican primaries go Bush's way—he wins forty-four contests, cementing the nomination.

Over the objections of Rove, George W. follows his father's advice and selects Dick Cheney as his running mate. A tough former Wyoming congressman, Cheney ran the Ford White House for two years as deputy chief of staff and then chief of staff.

Dick Cheney will soon become a dominant player in the Bush administration.

The campaign of 2000 is close. But then disaster strikes. On November 2, five days before the vote, Fox News breaks the story of Bush's 1976 DUI in Maine. Pandemonium. Rove believes the exposition might cost Bush the election.

It does not.

The governor of Texas defeats the vice president with the help of the Supreme Court.

However, millions of Americans believe Bush the Younger is an "illegitimate" president.

Then comes 9/11.

In war mode, the White House is somber. President Bush keeps an intense schedule. He rises at 5:15 a.m., has coffee with his wife, and is in the "Oval" by 6:45 a.m. There he is briefed by Chief of Staff Andrew Card, as well as intelligence and military officials.

Formal meetings begin at 8:15 a.m. Being late is never acceptable. Bush believes tardiness is a sign of being rude.

Before lunch, there is exercise. The president is an accomplished runner. He expects the White House staff to maintain physical fitness themselves. But that mandate excludes Vice President Cheney, who has heart problems.

For lunch, Bush enjoys a BLT sandwich or peanut butter and honey on white bread. He is sometimes joined by Cheney, Rove, or Treasury secretary Henry M. Paulson.

The afternoon is just as tightly scheduled, though the president may return to the residence for a nap. He is done by 6:00 p.m. With his twin daughters both at college, the president usually dines alone with his wife of twenty-five years.

The public perception of President Bush is that of an easygoing individual. He is not. He is often impatient, eating quickly, preferring Mexican food, chicken pot pie, and biscuits. After dinner, he enjoys watching sports while Laura prefers to read. Even on nights when the White House hosts an official function, the president requests the festivities end early so he can get to bed—9:00 p.m. is preferred. He and the First Lady have had lights installed on either side of their White House bed so they can read as they fall asleep. The president almost always turns off his light first.*

Laura Bush makes fun of her husband's early bedtime. She is the most popular First Lady in modern history, with an approval rating of 85 percent. Americans consider her poised and smart. She has redecorated the White House, shocked by how neglected the mansion had become during the Clinton administration.

In 2005, at the White House Correspondents' Dinner, the First Lady jokes about her husband's schedule:

"Nine o'clock, Mr. Excitement here is sound asleep and I'm watching *Desperate Housewives*. Ladies and gentlemen, I *am* a desperate housewife."

President Bush is taking the war on terror personally. He has despised Saddam Hussein since the Iraqi war criminal ordered his father assassinated. The April 1993 plot failed but left an indelible impression on Bush the Younger, who strongly believes Saddam is a terrorist.

US intelligence quickly locates Osama bin Laden hiding in the mountains of Afghanistan. The Taliban government is protecting him. The United States and Britain attack Afghanistan.

On December 5, 2001, a pro-US government is installed in Kabul, aided by occupying Allied troops.

Osama bin Laden escapes to Pakistan.

The White House anti-terror squad includes VP Cheney, Secretary of State Colin Powell, Secretary of Defense Donald Rumsfeld, and National Security Advisor Condoleezza Rice. They are united in aggressively hunting down jihadists. Four months after the 9/11 attack, the Bush

---

* The White House residence shifts with its occupants. First Ladies Mamie Eisenhower, Jacqueline Kennedy, Lady Bird Johnson, and Pat Nixon slept in Abraham Lincoln's actual bedroom while their spouses had separate quarters. Since Gerald Ford, all the presidential couples, with one exception, slept together. The exception being Donald Trump, whose wife, Melania, occupied a two-room suite on the third floor while he remained in the Presidential Suite one story below.

administration designates the US base in Guantanamo Bay, Cuba, as a terrorist holding facility. A total of 779 terror suspects have been flown there, some of them subjected to "enhanced interrogation."

In September 2002, press and intelligence reports indicate that Iraq is trying to build a nuclear weapon. President Bush steps up scrutiny. Five months later, Colin Powell addresses the United Nations condemning Iraq as a terror haven. The secretary of state uses the phrase *weapons of mass destruction* seventeen times.

Soon after that, the *New York Times* publishes a page-one story saying that Saddam Hussein possesses biological and chemical weapons. That seals the dictator's fate.

The United States and its allies attack Iraq on March 19, 2003. By April 9, Saddam's government is shattered.*

Retribution comes quickly. American forces incarcerate hundreds of Iraqis in Abu Ghraib prison. At least three are subjected to waterboarding, a brutal torture technique. In the meantime, thousands of Islamic fighters flow into Iraq, hoping to kill Americans.

That results in a bloody, drawn-out conflict.†

Time passes.

The invasions of Afghanistan and Iraq become controversial as the 2004 election looms. Critics paint Bush as a weak wartime president who condones "torture." The Democratic candidate is Senator John Kerry of Massachusetts, a decorated Vietnam War hero.

The press is solidly in Kerry's corner. In a 2007 letter to Bill O'Reilly, Bush the Elder writes about the ongoing media bias against his son:

"For the most part, I think there is a clear favoritism for the liberals and Democrats. Some . . . mercilessly hammer the president [his son] all the time, and I don't like it."

---

* The *New York Times* report is proved to be incorrect. No weapons of mass destruction are located. One of the reporters, Judith Miller, is forced to resign over the situation.

† It is estimated that the Bush administration spent $3 trillion on the Iraq War. Some believe that this led to a recession. Out of 466,985 US personnel in the massive operation, 4,400 were killed and 32,000 wounded. It is estimated that 315,000 Iraqis lost their lives.

Two months before the election, CBS News correspondent Dan Rather slams President George W. Bush for his National Guard record. The segment appears on *60 Minutes II*. A subsequent investigation by CBS reveals that some of Rather's information is fraudulent. His career suffers great damage, but that will come later. In the meantime, John Kerry is handed a public relations advantage.

It doesn't help. Kerry has problems of his own. His anti–Vietnam War activism comes back to haunt him. And his vote to support the invasion of Iraq takes away a key campaign issue.

Once again, the election comes down to a few key states. President Bush is behind during early voting but comes back to win by a margin of 286–251 in the Electoral College.

Bush the Younger's second term goes south quickly.

The manhunt for Osama bin Laden has gone cold. American troops are bogged down in Iraq and Afghanistan, with no end in sight. The economy is failing.

In 2005, an enormous hurricane named Katrina becomes the most expensive natural disaster in American history, causing massive flooding and killing 1,836 residents of New Orleans and the surrounding area. Sections of the city with majority black populations are hit hardest. The Bush administration is slow to respond, leading to charges that the president lacks compassion for minorities. His poll numbers drop.

The next year, 2006, Republicans lose control of the House and Senate. Then, in 2008, the economy collapses when major banks fail because of poor lending practices. The economic panic cascades down to regular Americans.

Bush's approval rating sinks to just 25 percent by Election Day 2008—setting up a Democratic Party resurgence.

The presidency of George W. Bush produced notable legislation such as the No Child Left Behind Act, which tried to increase the quality of public schools. The Patriot Act tightened the nation's security as terrorism remained a grave threat. The president's leadership in the days immediately after the 9/11 attacks brought the country together, driving his popularity rating to 90 percent—the highest level in modern history.

But that was short-lived.

The press hammers the president over Iraq and civil liberties. The banking crisis dooms his administration.

It is during the Bush presidency that Americans frequently begin speaking of themselves as living in conservative "red" states or liberal "blue" states. The rising influence of cable television adds to this division. Networks tilt their points of view toward liberal or conservative audiences.

As ideology surges, party politics decline.

"I'm worried," Bush will tell friends, "that I'll be the last Republican president."

George W. Bush is sixty-two years old when he leaves the White House on January 20, 2009. There is no doubt that his legacy is mixed due to the war on terror. But it is also apparent that he conducted himself with dignity. As his successor, Barack Obama, is sworn in, Bush gives him a handwritten letter:

"There will be trying moments. The critics will rage. Your friends will disappoint you. But you will have an Almighty God to comfort you, a family who loves you, and a country that is pulling for you, including me."*

---

* During the Bush administration, Bill O'Reilly reported from both Iraq and Afghanistan. He also visited Guantanamo Bay twice.

Chapter Forty-Four

MARCH 23, 2010
WHITE HOUSE
11:15 A.M.

B arack Obama is aloof.

The question: Is that a problem?

The Roosevelt Room is a scene of happiness. All around the president, staff jubilantly celebrate the passing of the Affordable Care Act— "Obamacare." Hugs, backslapping, broad smiles. The president stands alone in a white dress shirt, slacks, and a red tie, applauding and wearing a solemn expression. Vice President Joe Biden is to Obama's right but knows better than to reach over and shake the president's hand—even at this landmark moment. Biden and the president are not close, Barack only putting him on the ticket to deal with Congress—something the young chief executive has little interest in doing.*

The White House staff are aware that their boss is a serious man with little time for frivolity. First Lady Michelle Obama and senior adviser Valerie Jarrett are his only confidants.

As a senator from Illinois, Barack Hussein Obama was almost invisible on Capitol Hill. He rarely took an advocacy position, voting "present"

---

* The Affordable Care Act has basically provided free or low-cost health insurance to approximately forty million Americans.

an astonishing 129 times on legislation—reluctant to take a stand with a firm "yes" or "no" vote.

But the young senator always had a long-term plan. And it worked. He is the first African American president, an extraordinary achievement in a country that still grapples with racial division.

Two days later, the president is poised to sign his signature legislation. To the applause of an assembled crowd, he walks to the podium in the East Room. Vice President Biden introduces him. As President Obama steps forward to speak, the two men huddle, with Biden privately whispering, "This is a big fuckin' deal."

Microphones capture those words.

The president frowns. Even in this moment of triumph, he knows his vice president is prone to mistakes.*

Like Bill Clinton, the forty-seven-year-old Barack Obama experiences a turbulent upbringing. He was born in Honolulu on August 4, 1961. His Kenyan father is studying economics at the University of Hawaii, leaving behind a wife and child in Africa. Although married, he takes up with Ann Dunham, a fellow student. The African tells Ann that he is divorced. She soon becomes pregnant, and the couple wed just weeks after meeting.†

The union will be rocky. One month after Barack's birth, Ann Dunham Obama takes the baby with her to Seattle, where she will study at the University of Washington. Her husband relocates to Cambridge, Massachusetts, attending graduate school at Harvard University. The couple will divorce in 1964, by which time Ann has moved back to Hawaii with her son. She then remarries and relocates to Indonesia, where Barack is called "Barry" and becomes fluent in Indonesian.

In 1971, Barry leaves his mother in Indonesia, returning to Honolulu.

---

* In 2020, Obama will remark about Biden: "Don't underestimate Joe's ability to fuck things up."

† The future president's birth announcement appears in both the *Honolulu Advertiser* and the *Honolulu Star-Bulletin*. Later, there will be accusations that Barack Obama is actually born in Africa. Bill O'Reilly will demolish those arguments by producing the original newspapers.

There, he lives with his maternal grandparents, attending the exclusive Punahou School on scholarship.

This is also when the ten-year-old sees his father for the last time—a moment young Barack will remember as "transformational."

"He gave me my first basketball and it was shortly thereafter that I became this basketball fanatic. And he took me to my first jazz concert, and it was sort of shortly thereafter that I became really interested in jazz and music. So, what it makes you realize is how much of an impact, even if it's only a month, that [a parent] has on you," the future president will write in his memoirs.

Weeks later, the senior Obama returns to Kenya, taking up with his first wife again and fathering more children. A few years later, he loses both legs in an auto accident. After that, he is killed in another vehicle collision at age forty-eight.

The childhood odyssey continues. A teenage Barack Obama experiments with marijuana, cocaine, and alcohol. He is a good student. After graduating high school, he attends Occidental College in Los Angeles on scholarship. As a junior, he transfers to Columbia University in New York City. His grandparents help with expenses.

After graduating, Barack Obama takes a series of jobs before being accepted to Harvard Law School, where he becomes the first black editor of the *Harvard Law Review*.*

As he enters his thirties, Obama lives in Chicago. He becomes a community activist. On the social front, he proposes marriage to his live-in girlfriend, twenty-three-year-old anthropologist Sheila Myoshi Jager, who rejects his overtures twice.

Soon Obama takes a job at the Sidley & Austin law firm in Chicago, where he meets a local-born attorney three years younger than him.

The outgoing Michelle Robinson is from the South Side and is almost as tall as Barack at six feet two. The couple marry in 1992. Michelle eventually gives birth to daughters Malia and Sasha through in vitro fertilization in 1998 and 2001.

---

* Barack Obama takes out $42,753 in loans to pay for Harvard Law School. In addition, Michelle Obama borrows $40,762 for her own Harvard Law education. They finally pay off these debts in 2004 when Obama signs a $1.4 million book deal.

Barack Obama enters politics in 1996, running for an Illinois state senate seat. He wins. Then he turns his attention to the United States Senate. Along the way he meets forty-seven-year-old New Yorker David Axelrod, who will soon become one of his chief advisers.

Using his considerable political skills, Obama easily wins the Senate seat. The family remains in Chicago. Just two years later, in 2007, Senator Obama announces his candidacy for president of the United States.

He is a man in a hurry.

Over the next year of campaigning, the young senator rises, ultimately overtaking former First Lady Hillary Clinton, now a senator from New York, as the party's top candidate. The two do not care for each other. He disdains Hillary as a "corporate lawyer sitting on the board at Wal-Mart."

She sees him as a shallow striver.

In June 2008, Obama secures enough votes to win the Democratic nomination, but Hillary refuses to quit. It is the Clinton family campaign philosophy to keep fighting "until the last dog dies."

Eventually, Hillary does back out. Barack Obama will later thank her with the job of secretary of state. "It was a total shock," Obama speechwriter Ben Rhodes will state of that decision. "There were some hard, raw feelings in that campaign."

The 2008 presidential race features Barack Obama and Delaware senator Joe Biden against Arizona senator John McCain and Sarah Palin, the governor of Alaska.

In September, just two months before Election Day, the US economy collapses. John McCain suspends his campaign. Obama roasts him. Bush the Younger is distracted and does not help McCain, who is losing ground.

On November 4, Barack Obama wins easily, taking the Electoral College 365–173.

The Obamas move into the White House on January 20, 2009. Their daughters, Malia and Sasha, eight and ten years old, will attend nearby Sidwell Friends School.

The president starts each morning with a workout, running on a treadmill in the White House basement and lifting weights. He is a trim 180 pounds. Obama is not alone in the gym, with Michelle rising at 4:30 a.m. to perform her own exercise routine and get some "me time."

For breakfast, the president likes eggs, potatoes, and wheat toast. He does not drink coffee, preferring orange juice or green tea.

The Oval Office opens for business at 9:00 a.m. Obama is a disciplined man, limiting his meetings to six per day and keeping his circle of trust very small. The first item on his schedule is an intelligence briefing. As Obama takes office the hot spots are Iraq, Afghanistan, and North Korea. Later, the ISIS terrorist group and the Russian invasion of Crimea will become serious problems.

The president works through the day, taking lunch in the Oval Office Private Dining Room. The meal doubles as a meeting, whether with his staff or congressional leaders. The fare is light: fruit, sandwiches, ice water. His private vice is smoking, which Michelle bans inside the White House, so the president often chews Nicorette gum to stem his nicotine cravings. He also snacks on trail mix while sitting at the Resolute desk.

Throughout his eight years in office, Barack Obama will keep a tight lid on his White House agenda. Sometimes, conflict between his staff slips out, such as when economic advisers Christina Romer and Lawrence Summers bicker. Also, there is tension between Defense Secretary Robert Gates and the vice president. In a later memoir, Gates will write of Joe Biden, "I think he has been wrong on nearly every major foreign policy and national security issue over the past four decades."

The president works until 6:30 p.m. before having dinner with Michelle and the girls. His favorite meal is chili and beer. The president enjoys ale so much that he and White House chef Sam Kass brew their own on the premises. What is *not* allowed on the dinner table is mayonnaise, asparagus, or British food, which the president openly derides.

When traveling, however, Obama often puts his healthy diet aside. He is fond of take-out cheeseburgers. He eats almost no sugar, avoiding soft drinks, but is known to enjoy a Seattle-based confectioner named Fran's Chocolates.

★★★

After dinner, the president goes to his private office upstairs in the residence and works a few hours more. At 10:00 p.m., he says good night to Michelle. She is always the first in the family to turn in, even falling asleep before Malia and Sasha. The president sits on the edge of the bed as he and the First Lady talk about the day.

The First Couple are opposites, Barack optimistic about what he hopes to accomplish as president, Michelle more pragmatic and skeptical. Her upbringing in a working-class family—with strict rules, accountability, and consistency—was the opposite of her husband's. Michelle is not the dreamer Barack is, often teasing him about his foggy visions.

The Obama marriage has been tested during the president's political career, with the First Lady admitting there was a ten-year period of tension. She was overwhelmed by parenting the children while he was off campaigning. The White House does not diminish the pressure on the couple, but they have matured with age.

"Ready to be tucked in?" Barack asks when it is time to turn out the light.

"Yes, I am," is Michelle's standard reply.

After good nights to his wife and daughters, the president returns to his office, sometimes sending emails as late as 1:00 a.m. Usually he shuts down at 11:00 p.m., watching Jon Stewart's *The Daily Show* and then reading for a half hour before calling it a night.

But not before selecting his suit and tie for the following day. One less decision he must make in the morning.

President Obama gets hammered in the 2010 midterm elections. Republicans gain an astonishing sixty-three seats in the House, winning the majority. The voter rebellion against Obama's policies focuses on the Affordable Care Act. Some Americans see it as a government takeover of health care and a form of socialism. In fact, 45 percent of all voters say they made their choice based on a dislike for Obamacare.

April 30, 2011. Washington Hilton. Bill O'Reilly and Donald Trump sit together at the White House Correspondents' Dinner, featuring a monologue by President Obama.

There is bad blood here.

Trump, the New York businessman, has been claiming that the president was *not* born in the United States and that his birth certificate is phony.

O'Reilly disagrees, but the real estate baron persists. Barack Obama is not amused.

"Donald Trump is here tonight!" says the president to laughter and applause. "Now, I know that he's taken some flak lately, but no one is happier, no one is prouder to put this birth certificate matter to rest than the Donald. And that's because he can finally get back to focusing on the issues that matter—like, did we fake the moon landing? What really happened in Roswell? And where are Biggie and Tupac?"

Trump is not laughing.

Three days later, a major historical moment.

"Justice has been done," President Obama tells America in a shocking announcement. The president stands at a podium in the East Room, the same location where Joe Biden whispered the F-word one year ago.

He tells America that on this night, almost ten years after the 9/11 attacks, Osama bin Laden has been located and shot dead by United States Navy SEALs. The raid is risky, with United States Special Forces flying into Pakistan by helicopter in the dead of night.*

Throughout the operation, the president sits in a small space off the White House Situation Room with top members of his staff to watch on a secure satellite link. Vice President Biden opposes the raid as "too risky."†

But the president knows this is an excellent chance to find bin Laden. The terrorist has become a phantom, seemingly impossible to locate as he has directed other campaigns against American targets in his decade on the run.

Now, the threat is no more.

---

* Precise details about the Osama bin Laden takedown are chronicled in the authors' book *Killing the Killers*.

† Biden's opposition is confirmed by Barack Obama in his memoir.

It has been a successful first two years in office for Barack Obama. He has received the Nobel Peace Prize for his actions to promote peace in the Middle East, passed the Affordable Care Act, and now presides over the execution of a man Americans despise.

As soon as the president finishes tonight's speech, citizens will flood into the streets, honking horns and shouting "USA! USA!"

But not all is going well.

President Obama has ordered the military to accept homosexual Americans. That leads to controversy. He is also planning to leave Iraq, a decision that will allow the vicious terror group ISIS to gain power. At this moment in history, Barack Obama has become a polarizing president, and the growing national divide over his policies is why Democrats will lose one thousand state legislature seats across America during the next four years.

March 23, 2012. Obama addresses reporters in the Rose Garden. A young black man named Trayvon Martin has been shot dead in Orlando, Florida, by George Zimmerman, a white community college student, who claimed he was acting in self-defense.

The president has learned to be careful about issues of race. In 2009, he verbally attacked the Cambridge, Massachusetts, police after they mistakenly arrested black Harvard professor Henry Louis Gates Jr. Obama said the cops "acted stupidly."

This caused an uproar.

Now, he is under fire from black leaders for *not* commenting on the Trayvon Martin killing, which took place one month ago. He buckles.

In an extremely controversial statement, Barack Obama says, "When I think about this boy, I think about my own kids. . . . If I had a son, he'd look like Trayvon."*

Going into the 2012 reelection cycle, the president's approval rating among white Americans slides to 39 percent.†

---

* George Zimmerman was acquitted of second-degree murder in the case.

† Obama's overall approval rating is 51 percent in 2012.

The Republican presidential nominee is Mitt Romney, the former governor of Massachusetts. He is poised to take advantage of the president's waning popularity.

Romney points to Syrian dictator Bashar al-Assad, who has killed innocent civilians using poison gas. In response to that action, Barack Obama declares that there is a "red line" Assad cannot cross.

But Obama does nothing as Assad continues to wage war against his people.

In addition, Muslim terrorism is on the rise.

Four Americans, including the ambassador to Libya, are murdered by jihadists in Benghazi. Some blame Secretary of State Hillary Clinton for failing to provide adequate security.

Mitt Romney smells blood.

During the second debate, Romney attacks Obama over the Benghazi assault. The president turns to his opponent and replies, "The day after the attack, governor, I stood in the Rose Garden and I told the American people and the world that we were going to find out exactly what happened, that this was an act of terror, and also said that we're going to hunt down those that committed this crime."

Romney tries to call him a liar, stating, "You said in the Rose Garden *the day after the attack* it was an act of terror? I want to make sure we get that for the record because it took the president fourteen days before he called the attack in Benghazi an act of terror."

"Get the transcript," Obama fires back.

When moderator Candy Crowley of CNN confirms Obama's timeline, Romney appears befuddled.

From that moment on, Mitt Romney and his running mate, Paul Ryan of Wisconsin, lose momentum. On November 6, Election Day, Obama captures the popular tally by nearly five million votes and the Electoral College 332–206.

It is April 28, 2016. The annual White House Correspondents' Dinner once again features President Obama. This time, Donald Trump is not present—because he is running for president himself.

The president opens up on Trump.

"You know I've got to talk about Trump! Come on!

"Although I am a little hurt that he's not here tonight. We had so much fun the last time. . . . Is this dinner too tacky for The Donald? What could he possibly be doing instead? Is he at home, eating a Trump Steak . . . tweeting out insults to Angela Merkel?

"The Republican establishment is incredulous that he is their most likely nominee—incredulous, shocking. They say Donald lacks the foreign policy experience to be President. But, in fairness, he has spent years meeting with leaders from around the world: Miss Sweden, Miss Argentina, Miss Azerbaijan.

"And there's one area where Donald's experience could be invaluable— and that's closing Guantanamo. Because Trump knows a thing or two about running waterfront properties into the ground.

"All right, that's probably enough. I mean, I've got more material [but] I don't want to spend too much time on The Donald. Following your lead, I want to show some restraint. Because I think we can all agree that from the start, he's gotten the appropriate amount of coverage, befitting the seriousness of his candidacy."

Six months later, it is Election Day. November 8, 2016. Donald J. Trump is the Republican nominee. Some believe he chose to run because of Obama's jabs. What once seemed like a long-shot candidacy has become very real.

Donald Trump versus Hillary Clinton.

Before the night is through, one of them will be elected president of the United States.

"Dispensing with subtlety," reports the *New York Times*, "Mrs. Clinton's campaign said on Wednesday that it would ring in election night at the Jacob K. Javits Convention Center, the unglamorous glass fortress on Manhattan's West Side. The symbolism seems clear. Mrs. Clinton has referred repeatedly of busting through 'the highest, hardest glass ceiling'—at least figuratively—by installing a woman in the Oval Office. If Election Day breaks her way, she will address the nation beneath a literal one."

But by 2:25 a.m., Hillary Clinton's supporters are filing *out* of the

Javits Center. What began as a night of intended celebration has left many in tears.

Nearby, at the Peninsula Hotel, Hillary picks up the phone and calls Donald Trump. He has just won Wisconsin's 10 electoral votes, putting him over the 270 needed to triumph. Clinton is three million votes ahead in the popular count, but there is no way she can defeat Trump.

The two speak for about a minute, after which Hillary Clinton concedes.

President Barack Obama issues his own statement. "It's no secret the president-elect and I have some pretty significant differences," he says, not using the president-elect's name. "I am looking forward to doing everything that I can to make sure that the next President is successful."*

January 13, 2016. President Obama stands before Congress to deliver his final State of the Union address. He is reflective, stating, "It's one of the few regrets of my presidency—that the rancor and suspicion between the parties has gotten worse instead of better. I have no doubt a president with the gifts of Lincoln or Roosevelt might have better bridged the divide, and I guarantee I'll keep trying to be better so long as I hold this office."

Moving day at the White House. January 20, 2017. The Obamas depart at 11:00 a.m. for the Trump inauguration. As they step out the door for the last time, an army of workers sweeps into the mansion. The Obama furniture goes out. All of it. The Trump furniture is moved in. Carpets are changed. Paint is applied. In just a few short hours, the house will be ready for its new occupants.

But the Obamas aren't leaving Washington. They have purchased an $8 million house in the exclusive Kalorama neighborhood. Their plan is to stay at least until Sasha graduates from high school in two years.

However, President Obama distances himself from national politics. He will give speeches, write his memoirs, and work on his presidential library soon to be built on Chicago's South Side.

---

*The moment-by-moment action on election night can be found in Bill O'Reilly's book *The United States of Trump.*

Michelle Obama will also speak and write books. The couple, still in their early fifties, quickly grow fabulously wealthy.

★★★

History is still evaluating President Obama's eight-year tenure. He governed to the left, but cautiously. His signature achievement, Obamacare, remains controversial but has aided millions of low-income Americans.

There is no question that Barack Obama changed the country dramatically. Not because of what he did with policy but rather because the chain reaction that develops after the nation's first black president takes office spirals in many directions. And one of those destinations is named Donald Trump.

Both Obama and Trump are larger-than-life figures. Both engender loyalty and loathing. But without the administration of Barack Obama, Trump would likely *not* have been president. The backlash against the big government policies Obama embraced directly leads to the success of the populist Trump.

America is a far different country today than it was in 2008. And not for the better. Division and suspicion now rule the United States. Politics has become a bitter enterprise. It is impossible for honest, fair-minded citizens to lay direct blame for that. As the cliché goes, "It's complicated."

But it has happened.

And we are all witness to it.

Afterword

NEW YORK/CALIFORNIA

2024

The legacies of President Trump and President Biden are not complete, so it is impossible for any historian to fairly and fully evaluate their service at this point.

America is bitterly divided over the two, often forming impressions based on distorted data put forth by an ideological media. The authors of this book are not interested in advancing false narratives or promoting fallacious conspiracy theories. We are a fact-based duo that strives for accuracy and insight. Our approach has been successful. We are the best-selling historical authors in the world.

Braggadocio aside, we are also Americans, with an active interest in the welfare of our country. So, we've decided to write separate essays on Presidents Trump and Biden without consultation. We will present our thoughts in this final chapter. An interesting footnote is that Dugard resides in California while O'Reilly lives in New York—two vastly different environments.

One other note. Bill O'Reilly was the solo author of the number-one best seller *The United States of Trump*, a history of the man. He has known the former president for thirty-five years.

Therefore, O'Reilly will kick off the essay exposition. In a fair and balanced way, of course.

DONALD TRUMP BY BILL O'REILLY

He is Dr. Jekyll and Mr. Trump or vice versa. A character so overwhelmingly intense that fiction could not capture him. First off, how can a controversial real estate mogul with a colossally flamboyant personality ever become the president of the United States? Trump had zero government experience and no identifiable ideology. Chutzpah and fame put him into the White House. No person had ever done that before.

Nostradamus could never imagine it. Millard Fillmore would not understand.

Like Bill Clinton, Donald Trump is really two people. A slick deal maker with smarts and vision is the Trump who amassed money and power.

An undisciplined provocateur who seeks constant attention is the public person who has alienated millions.

The early historical record says Trump's four years in office largely benefited the American people. You know the résumé: real wages up, inflation down. Migrant intrusions at the southern border controlled by Trump's "remain in Mexico" policy. Putin relatively contained. ISIS destroyed, Iran punished, its Revolutionary Guard chief assassinated.

Trump put a number of achievements on the scoreboard, and those in denial are not being honest.

Then came his fraudulent election scenario, which resulted in the January 6, 2021, riot at the Capitol. That almost immediately obscured Trump's policy success and gave his enemies enormous ammunition. Historically, the election denial is Trump's "Lewinsky."

The attacks on President Trump rival those against President Lincoln. Nonstop hatred. Lincoln got it worse, of course, but Trump is second in the vilification sweepstakes. When the world's most powerful law enforcement agency, the FBI, sets out to destroy you, little else needs to be said.

Except, maybe, that Trump brought much of the hatred on himself. He often traffics in personal invective. Not a "uniting the country" strategy.

There are two types of Americans when it comes to assessing Donald Trump. The first group doesn't care what he says, they embrace his anti-progressive posture and believe he ran the nation effectively. For them, the "actions speak louder than words" cliché is paramount.

The other crew simply despise everything Trump says and does. He's the devil and belongs in hell, not on the ballot.

The Trump situation will likely never be resolved, as both sides are emotionally committed. The forty-fifth president is a force of nature, to be sure. And the storms that surround him continue. His true legacy will remain undefined for years to come.

From Martin Dugard:

Certainly, you know my coauthor, but you don't know me.

I am the son of a Vietnam B-52 bomber pilot and husband to a social worker, and I have spent each day for the last three decades studying and writing history. I am a man of faith. I grew up on air force bases and believe in a strong military, just as I profess that we need to be more like Jesus—and that means feeding the poor.

I reside in Orange County, a bastion of conservative thinking since John Wayne and Richard Nixon called the O.C. home, though that is now changing.

When the national anthem plays, I stand at attention and place my hand over my heart. When traveling the world, one of my favorite moments of each and every adventure is when I lay eyes on the photograph of the president of the United States hanging above the entrance to US Customs, welcoming me back to the home of the brave.

You might think all this makes me a Republican but I am decidedly liberal. Patriotic American values are not confined to conservatives. I am also a lifelong fan of Bruce Springsteen and know that "Born in the USA" is not a jingoist anthem but an angry song, using our God given right to free speech to call out attitudes and policies that don't mesh with our national ideals. On top of all that, I'm a hardcore historian, making judgments through the greater prism of what has come before.

So, I don't take the presidency lightly. In fact, the very first headline of my career was about the 1976 Republican primary election campaign:

"Reagan Whips Ford in Poll." It ran above a fifty-word piece in the school newspaper at Mitchell Junior High School. I was editor, writer, and poll taker. That interest comes full circle in writing this book.

What have I learned? The White House can be a dump, the balance of power is not written in stone just because the Constitution says so, and presidents are human. Some cheat. Some drink too much. Had it always existed, cable news would have crushed a lot of them.

The one thing each president has in common is leaving. Pack the bags, grab the First Lady, leave the White House front door unlocked. Whether booted by voters or finishing their term, everyone since George Washington has gone home.

This "transition of power" is a bedrock of American democracy. Some presidents don't miss the Oval Office as much as they long for that big show of power known as Air Force One. However, it would seem that a round-the-clock cadre of armed men watching your every movement, as the Secret Service eyes the president, would get old.

As would the grind of having every word you utter parsed.

But most presidents did not want to leave. First Ladies, as well. As Marine One lifted off the South Lawn to carry Richard Nixon into exile, his wife, Pat, exclaimed over and over how sad the moment felt. This from a woman who never was comfortable in the White House.

In evaluating the Trump presidency, I see a man no different than his predecessors. Yes, he broke down the fourth wall of civility by not adhering to presidential decorum. That was his right. Every president gets to riff. And Trump certainly took advantage.

That's politics.

Trump was impeached twice, which is not to be taken lightly. But impeachment has become a highly used political weapon since the days of Watergate—and I suspect it will become even more so in generations to come.

What struck me, as a historian, was how Donald Trump dealt with war criminals like Vladimir Putin. The businessman always believed it was better to have countries *like* the United States, no matter who runs them. This can mean befriending despots like Putin, which makes me uncomfortable. It doesn't make him a horrible president.

Trump claims to be a man of faith, though by the clumsy way he held up that Bible for photographers at St. John's Church in Washington, it's obvious he wasn't all that familiar with the book. Doesn't make him a bad president. America is full of occasional Christians, including many, just like it is alleged of Donald Trump, who think Moses came down off the mountain with ten suggestions instead of ten commandments.

Then there's the "racist" tag, which is harder to overlook. If there's one thing I've learned writing this book, it's that America has *always* had a race problem. It's not just that presidents owned slaves, it's that "We the People" don't always accommodate those who look differently than we do—throwing roadblocks in the path of racial equality and repealing laws ensuring "inalienable rights."

I am a white man who lives in a white neighborhood. I thought John McCain was a badass war hero who deserved to be elected president in 2008. But I was proud when America finally elected a black president.

Not everyone feels the same, as I learned not long after Obama's election. I was in midtown Manhattan. A guy stalked past. Expensive suit, angry stride, cursing about the new president.

And then there's January 6, 2021.

The unthinkable happened that cold morning. President Trump held a large Washington rally claiming he did *not* lose the 2020 election. This was a lie and he knew it. That was enough to send hundreds of furious demonstrators to the US Capitol building. They broke in and tried to stop the Electoral College vote from being certified. I was shocked and revolted. My father did not risk his life in Vietnam for this.

In my view, Donald Trump did nothing to stop this desecration.

The mob failed. Capitol Police escorted them out. Congress certified the election. Yet the world witnessed something that never should have happened.

Because Donald Trump could have immediately stepped up and condemned the Capitol riot, I believe he has fallen to the bottom of the presidential list.*

---

* Here are my bottom five presidents: John Tyler, Franklin Pierce, Andrew Johnson, Herbert Hoover, and Donald Trump.

JOE BIDEN BY BILL O'REILLY

Growing up, the O'Reilly clan was similar to the Biden family. Working-class Irish Catholic, traditional belief system. Joe says he has stayed true to that profile. But he has not.

If you watch or listen to my news analysis programs, you know that I believe Joe Biden is the second-worst-performing president in history, only behind fellow Pennsylvanian James Buchanan.

But that assessment may be flawed because historical facts might surface that could obliterate my theory.

It's possible.

What we do know in 2024 is that most Americans are disenchanted, especially with the immigration chaos and high prices for the essentials of life. President Biden has to live with those things on his résumé just like Jimmy Carter was pilloried for policy failures during his term.

The great mystery is why Joe Biden governs so far to the left. Scranton Joe, traditional guy. On paper, it doesn't make sense. Dwelling in the Senate for an astounding thirty-six years, Joe Biden was a "blue dog" democrat. That is, he championed so-called mainstream positions, some of which were conservative. In 1994, Biden supported the Violent Crime Control and Law Enforcement Act, which promoted harsh penalties for convicted felons.

Joe was against busing to achieve school integration, which Kamala Harris vividly highlighted in the 2020 Democratic presidential primary debate.

In 1996, Senator Biden voted for the Defense of Marriage Act, banning federal recognition of gay nuptials. But, perhaps the most stunning change for a man who attends weekly Catholic Mass is Biden's embrace of abortion with few limitations. He actually *promotes* that policy. No Bill Clinton "abortion should be safe, legal, and rare" for Joe. He's all in with Planned Parenthood.

Tough to figure that out.

Biden always wanted to be president, campaigning in 1988 and 2008. He got nowhere.

Then Barack Obama came along, and Biden signed up for VP. That required a significant adjustment because his boss embraced a variety of progressive positions like fewer criminal prison sentences and the redistribution of wealth.

Joe Biden happily went along.

In 2020, the vice president finally got the big job nod and portrayed himself as "regular Joe," the uniter, not the leftist zealot.

But once elected, his inner Fidel seemed to emerge. We all know what happened because we are living it. President Biden threw open the southern border, brazenly attacked the US fossil fuel industry, and told the nation that equity, the favoring of specific groups over others, should rule the land.

It was a stunning reversal from the person Joe Biden had once been.

Now in the twilight of his life and again facing his nemesis, Donald Trump, President Biden is trying to hold on. He is isolated but remains powerful. He is not backing away from the progressive march.

It is a matter of fact that Joe Biden is the most liberal president in our nation's history, with Barack Obama a distant second.

How Biden's governance will play out in the future is impossible to ascertain. And all you have to do is look at his past to know my statement is true.

Who are you really, Joe?

From Martin Dugard:

For me, President Biden is not an enigma.

I may be prejudiced because Joe Biden is the only president I have ever met. About twenty years ago, I was the guest speaker at a Columbus Day breakfast in Delaware. Biden was still senator. It was an unusual invitation, and I'm not sure how it came about, but I'd written a book about Christopher Columbus, and someone thought to ask if I would fly across the country to say a few words. My wife came along.

The event was in a small hall, a local gathering without fanfare. The senator arrived with son Beau, a handsome, charismatic guy who looked, acted, and spoke like a man who would be president someday. Senator Biden shook my hand and looked me in the eye, as he did with everyone in the room. We went through the buffet and sat together at the head table. When it came time for me to speak, I remember looking down from the stage and seeing Biden whispering a joke in my wife's ear, making her laugh. A nice moment.

This was before Joe Biden became Barack Obama's vice president, tasked with managing White House relations with Congress. Before Beau's untimely death from cancer. Before Biden resurrected a faltering presidential campaign by winning the 2020 South Carolina primary in powerful fashion and then defeating Donald Trump in the most contentious general election in American history.

Back when I gave that speech, Joe Biden was a longtime senator who'd run unsuccessfully for president a couple times. The kind of politician who seemed fated to never attain the White House but whose career was distinguished.

So, when he took office in 2021, my hope was that he would lead the nation back to feeling a little more normal. More regular, if you will. "Business as usual," he called it.

Between the Clinton impeachment, the Iraq War, then Obama followed by Trump, we'd been through twenty-five years of roller-coaster democracy. Add in more than one million coronavirus deaths and America had been the opposite of "as usual" for a long time.

Biden inherited a divided nation, the Afghan War, a porous southern border, and COVID. He also followed a president who did not quietly go away.

In my view, it was America's disunity that challenged President Biden the most. "Leadership" can mean many things, and sometimes the problems can overwhelm even the strongest person. "Unity" means winning over that half of the country who don't believe you actually won the election.

That did not happen.

Shortly after being sworn in, Joe Biden assembled a cabinet of tested experts, surrounding himself with people who could offer sensible advice. The president's approval rating hit 55.2 percent in April 2021, demonstrating that America liked his initial actions.

Then came summer.

It was no secret that America needed to get out of Afghanistan. While researching our book *Killing the Killers*, officials in the Trump administration told me that. But unfortunately, the Biden administration handled the American exit horribly. In the first major test of his foreign policy, television showed frantic images reminiscent of the fall of Saigon. The Afghan government, which America had propped up for twenty years, fell to the Taliban in what seemed like minutes.

Suddenly, President Biden and his advisers looked amateurish.

The president then announced that the pandemic was over. But variant strains brought it roaring back, killing people and making us wear masks all over again. Suddenly, Biden looked too eager to be the bearer of good news. Add in higher gas and food prices and the border crisis. Joe Biden's approval ratings plummeted.

But there were strong things as well. The president succeeded in getting his trillion-dollar infrastructure bill passed. This is a big effing deal, to paraphrase Vice President Biden. The long-overdue legislation to upgrade bridges and roads required bipartisan support, and President Biden got enough Republican votes to make it happen.

The infrastructure bill barely registers with the American public today. This was a major chance for Biden to build unity, showing his doubters that he was working on *their* behalf. But Biden's "Build Back Better" slogan quickly evaporated.

Then things changed.

President Biden did not hold many press conferences, did not do many interviews, and seemed content to stay protected in the White House most of the time. He *did* issue strong statements about Ukraine, Gaza, and China.

To me, the president of the United States is essentially a front man, putting the nation's interests first and encouraging creative problem-solving. I think President Biden tried to do his best in that regard.

However, the Oval Office is not a hiding place. But that's what seems to have happened to Joe Biden. The human connection between America and the president has faltered.

I cannot point to an exact date when President Biden's public profile diminished, just a general sensation that it went away. His speeches became shorter and less frequent. He ceased being spontaneous. The president, never a great orator, began to mumble as he delivered short sound bites that would limit his chances to misspeak or stutter.

Critics began wondering whether Biden is actually in charge or if some nefarious cabal is running the country. It's debatable, but that's what people say when a president goes missing.

Joe Biden is eighty-one. That would not be worth mentioning if his aging wasn't so noticeable. Many people at that point in life aren't allowed to drive a car, let alone run the country. Perhaps because of reluctance to show his age and honestly engage the electorate, he has been a mediocre president. Not great, not awful, but in its own way less impactful than he could have been.

Yet Biden continues to see himself as a two-term president. And like many of us, he believes what he wants to believe. It is possible Joe Biden might reconnect with American voters. In politics, many things are possible. Perhaps a second term is what it will take. I sincerely hope he wins and gets that chance.

But even if you despise Joe Biden, and many Americans do, you have to acknowledge that the man has led an extraordinary life. Forty-eight years of public service. Senator, vice president, president.

Thank you, Joe Biden.

Acknowledgments

Bill O'Reilly would like to thank Makeda Wubneh, Jon Leibner, and George Witte for their support in the writing of this book.

Martin Dugard wishes to thank Eric Simonoff and Calene Dugard.

Index

About the Authors

Bill O'Reilly is a trailblazing TV journalist who has experienced unprecedented success on cable news and in writing eighteen national number-one bestselling nonfiction books. There are more than nineteen million books in the *Killing* series in print. He lives on Long Island.

Martin Dugard is the *New York Times* bestselling author of several books of history, among them the *Killing* series, *Into Africa,* and *Taking Paris.* He and his wife live in Southern California.